THE STORY OF
EDVARD MUNCH

KETIL BJØRNSTAD

THE STORY OF EDVARD MUNCH

Translated from the Norwegian by
Torbjørn Støverud and Hal Sutcliffe

A ARCADIA BOOKS
LONDON

Arcadia Books Ltd
15–16 Nassau Street
London W I W 7 AB

www.arcadiabooks.co.uk

First published in the United Kingdom 2001
Originally published by Gyldendal Norsk Forlag, Oslo
Copyright © Ketil Bjørnstad 1993
English translation copyright © Torbjørn Støverud and Hal Sutcliffe 2001

A catalogue record for this book is available from the British Library.

ISBN 1–900850–44–3

Designed and typeset in Monotype Ehrhardt by Discript, London WC2N 4BN
Printed in the United Kingdom by The Cromwell Press, Trowbridge, Wiltshire

Acknowledgements
Arcadia Books Ltd gratefully acknowledges financial assistance from Norla and
Munin, Oslo, for the translation of this book. We also thank the Norwegian
Embassy, London; Kristin Brudevoll, Norla; Elisabeth Middleton, Munin; and
Eva-Lie Nielsen, Gyldendal Norsk Forlag.

Arcadia Books distributors are as follows:

in the UK and elsewhere in Europe:
Turnaround Publishers Services
Unit 3, Olympia Trading Estate
Coburg Road
London N22 6TZ

in the USA and Canada:
Consortium Book Sales and Distribution, Inc.
1045 Westgate Drive
St Paul, MN 55114–1065

in Australia:
Tower Books
PO Box 213
Brookvale, NSW 2100

in New Zealand:
Addenda
Box 78224
Grey Lynn
Auckland

in South Africa:
Peter Hyde Associates (Pty) Ltd
PO Box 2856
Cape Town 8000

Dedicated to the memory of
Torbjørn Støverud
1918-2000

Yes, this could be good with time.
All it needs is a few small blemishes to be really good.

(EDVARD MUNCH – 1863-1944)

Dear Thiis: It's been five years now. I'm still just as hurt and just as devastated. That creature who hadn't the least desire to remain tied to mama's apron strings, but who, after a fairy tale life full of travel, had *decided* to marry me, propelled me through the very doors of hell. She travelled the length and breadth of Europe and started a string of affairs, blackened my name among all my friends, drove me half-mad with scenes until, in 1902, there I was, a wreck for life. As for her, she calmly and serenely entered into holy matrimony, famous, admired and worshipped, a goddess of art, and far, far away from mama. I am a wreck. I who became entangled with her after she had thrown two uproarious champagne parties. I who did not love her, but who out of sympathy sacrificed everything I had. I am not, like Christian Krohg, obliged to marry a whorehouse or, like him – like the gritty, bloody-horned snail that he is – to carry that whorehouse on my back. I have felt myself compelled to write this on seeing Gunnar Heiberg shed tears from his witty little eyes in *Dagbladet* over that painter who wore himself out and went mad. Is it any wonder that my hackles rise when I see his name? It was not hunger that drove me from Norway but that rotten little bunch of friends who stabbed me in the back. The meanest of all mean tricks: to cry Help! Help! I'm drowning! And then, with a contemptuous snort, to let your rescuer drown.

*

Edvard Munch on the brink of the abyss, just before his breakdown. Wine, brandy and the strongest cigars. Drunken stupor.

All his life he had known of the abyss. In 1908 he plunged into it, was admitted to Doctor Jacobsen's psychiatric clinic in Copenhagen. In 1909 he returned to Norway, after four years' exile.

*

There is a time in everyone's life when everything comes sharply into focus, both what has already been and what the future can reasonably be expected to hold. In Munch's life this moment must have been when, at the age of forty-five, after his breakdown, he arrived in Kragerø, not from the east via Christiania, as I first thought, but from the west, via Kristiansand. Not early in the morning, when the spring sun floods in over the rugged archipelago which in the month of May is no longer pale and battered after the winter, but in the middle of the day, at about twelve o'clock, long after sunrise, in an almost neutral grey revealing light.

The coastal steamer coming from the west did not sail past Jomfruland, as I had thought, but swung into the fjord at Rapen. Munch may nevertheless have seen both Jomfruland lighthouse and two other light buoys on the way in. A boat the size of the coastal steamer could not sail on the landward side of Jomfruland if it came from the west. Nor from the boat could Munch have seen both thrift and blue-bells, as I had thought, because the boat was too far out on account of the skerries, and apart from that because bluebells flower long after thrift does. But at Skrubben, the house in which he was to live while in Kragerø, he would soon see them, as spring turned into summer.

*

Ravensberg! Noble kinsman! Have you not heard the howls from the enemy camp? Have my grenades had any effect? I think that the scoundrels CK, GH and SB have thrown in the sponge at last. It's good to have an outlet for your feelings when you cannot simply beat riff-raff of that ilk to a pulp with your bare hands. You can bet SB heard a few home truths in 10 postcards I sent. I shall tell you later how the Enemy was already at work, poisoning wine in Cologne and stealing the large rolls of paintings. They have spread influenza here and killed my castle guard. I grope my way forward in the narrow passage. My fingers come into contact with a crate. I continue. Cloth. I pause. A terrible stench. I continue. Hair. Nose. A human being. A corpse!

*

It was Munch's cousin, Ludvig Ravensberg, who collected him from the psychiatric clinic. The night before he was admitted he had limped all the way from Klampenborg, his lame leg dragging behind him. His hair unkempt, his clothes in tatters. He was turned away from a restaurant. In the end he had taken a room at a hotel in Copenhagen, convinced he was surrounded by enemies. *Norwegian* enemies. *Two* hotel rooms. One with a window overlooking the courtyard and one with a window onto the road. He had heard voices. They had said his name:
    There he is! Watch him!
    He had dragged himself to the window but had seen nothing. He felt numbness spreading through his body. He had not had a proper night's sleep for many weeks. His wounded hand ached.
    It was Ravensberg who took him away from all the postcards, from the animal drawings, from rages and humiliation, brought him back to the land of his enemies. Why on earth had he come back to Norway, that vipers' nest, to people who had assumed the form of frogs, pigs and poodles? The strangest specimens in the menagerie, which he referred to as this crafty, insolent, decrepit circle, a clique of clapped-out literati, drunken offspring of the rich, whorish women and people who had never had an independent or original thought in their heads, but who spent all

their time, expended all their energy, copying, faking, impoverishing, draining sap from the few sparse trees which managed to gain a foothold and had some life in them, people whose names he still could not mention without getting agitated, feeling dizzy, names that previously he had not been able to hear without feeling physically sick and persecuted.

Up on the deck of the steamer, he must have thought along these lines, must have thought that this journey *might* be a disaster, that Ravensberg had actually misled him, given him to believe that it was a long way from Kragerø to Christiania, even though it was barely two hundred kilometres. And that terrible doubt must have made him waver, not because the sea was rough, because in all probability the weather was good, but because the thought of disintegrating like this induced just as great a fear of death in him as when he had coughed up blood as a child.

*

It was then that he saw in his mind's eye the middle-aged man, racked by many years' hell, destroyed by alcohol, fear and rage, his head so full of pictures from memory, of colours and contrasts, yet all the same back on his feet, shaky but back on his feet, with a vast yearning for control, and at the same time a deep-seated doubt as to whether such control could ever be attained. Yet nevertheless firmly resolved to try, at least so long as Ravensberg cheered him up, patted him on the shoulder or whatever it was he did, while the captain sounded a blast on the hooter, while the crowd of onlookers on the quay scrutinized the queue of passengers waiting to go ashore, while Ravensberg yet again glanced searchingly at his friend, as if to register the minutest change in the closed face which, despite the firm masculine set of the chin, always expressed such boundless vulnerability, and the steamer at last docked at the quay.

The journey by steamer must have done him good after all the weeks in hospital. The smell of mental breakdown had had a stronger effect than the smell of physical ailments and medical preparations. An indeterminate odour of physical decay and desperate thoughts.

Fresh air!

How deeply Munch must have filled his lungs with the sea air, undeterred by the stench of Norway.

*

He was in the process of turning a scandal into a success. He had received the Order of St Olav, which he ventured to construe as a friendly gesture from his own country, even though he declared himself an opponent of decorations and the death penalty.

*

What was it about this country which drew him back? He had used a few square miles of it to create his art. The strip of coast between Borre

3

and Åsgårdstrand, a little town on the western side of the Christiania Fjord. Christiania's main street, Karl Johan. The flaming red sky over Ekeberg. And also the childhood sketches of the church steeple, Telthusbakken, the river Aker. The deserted, almost trancelike atmosphere around Olav Ryes Place, perhaps slightly contributing to the agoraphobia, the dread of open spaces, of which he would later offer such a perfect hysterical example.

But above all it was Åsgårdstrand. That had been the scene of the drama, of the revolver, the Medusa's heads, the broken lover. Perhaps there too the explanation was to be found for all the harrowing events which would subsequently unfold.

In short, the scenes of his past.

He wished to return to his past, to the scenes of everything that mattered to him: his pictures. But he had no desire to relive it! Not *The Frieze of Life* Act II. That was over now. The actors had found their roles. Men and women alike. Now they had acquired their forms, colour and expressions.

*

He sees again all that is Norway, all he has painted time and time again in constantly new versions since the drama played itself out. He has painted white wooden houses, massive trees, a shoreline, some islands, *the sea*. He is coming to Kragerø because he had been looking for a peaceful spot by the open sea. Ravensberg found it. Good news: there is a house by the sea. Bad news: the house is in Norway. Yet it is not so much Norway Munch is against as Christiania. The city he grew up in. The city where he is always judged, weighed and found wanting. The city where the Enemy is.

*

Once blood had dripped from the hand wounded by the shot.

Munch cannot forget.

Cliffs and rocky outcrops tower menacingly before him. Does he still have any feeling in the last joint on the middle finger of his left hand? The one that is no longer there? What has become of it? Is it in a glass jar, has it turned to ashes or to earth while the rest of his body is living tissue and ageing cells?

He gazes expectantly at the onlookers on the quay, perhaps thinking of the old pictures of the enemy. But what drove him out of the country was a woman.

*

He walks down the gangway in Kragerø's harbour. Has chosen to step on Norwegian soil. His soil. But not his town. Not even a typical Norwegian town, but a sort of Italian amphitheatre with narrow streets. It does not have all that many large squares, which he would in any case

4

refuse to cross, but up the steep slope it does have a spacious house with a garden.

Peter Bredsdorf's house. Skrubben, or the bath house. It is empty and to let.

Perhaps he can wash himself clean of the past. Of everything that has happened. Yes, perhaps.

But not of the pictures.

*

They rise up from the bottom of the sea.

The sea bed is like his own memory. He has likened life to a still surface on which one can shift one's gaze from shallow to shallow, from deep to deep. Again and again he has brought up pictures from there himself. He knows the best places to fish. In some places there is always life. In other places there is only death, putrefaction and slime.

Somewhere in there lies Åsgårdstrand.

Somewhere out there the assembly hall sun will soon rise.

It is May 1909 and he will later confide to his friend Schiefler in Germany that his agoraphobia is considerable, very pronounced, perhaps more acute than when he used to drink. The thought of large cities is intolerable now.

Berlin? Paris? Impossible. Even Christiania must seem frightening. Karl Johan. The promenade between Parliament and the Palace. Where he would walk with Hans Jæger and learned how the middle classes can *see*, with just one eye! Oh no, Ravensberg was right. Kragerø is perfect, provided he can avoid the market place.

*

Munch enters a spacious house with linoleum on the floors. It is barren and impersonal, just as he wants it. No furniture, no melancholy air of homeliness which in any case can never be anything but an illusion of happiness in life.

Here is his life, his body. In a large empty house in Kragerø, with council furniture. He will become a night wanderer. A ghost. A button moulder has recast him.

But is there any substance to the material? Is it fit for anything?

He has felt close to death so many times. Weakness of the lungs. Insanity. In Copenhagen he was mad, half-paralysed and shaking with fear. Now it is 'Power' and 'Strength' – his domestic helps Krafft and Stærk – mountains, shandy, nourishing food, which are the order of the day. Farewell to whisky and soda and cigars, to burgundy and vintage champagne. His senses are sharpened. He hears all sounds at double volume. Sense impressions can almost knock him flat with their force. He thinks he can see the flame of combustion around people's silhouettes.

5

This is where he wants to live. This is where he can regain his strength.

Here he remembers everything.

* * *

Munch walks through the city from Grünerløkken.

The commuter ferry or 'papa boat', carrying all the fathers, will steam out along the fjord to all the idyllic little towns and villages, where wives, children and families are waiting.

The air is warm and close down by the jetties.

He boards the little steamer, finds a seat on deck, longs to get out onto the fjord. It is June 1885. Christiania lies there all dust and stench. The sun is baking hot. There is an audible stillness, as though before an explosion, punctuated by hammering from a workshop and the bell of a departing steamer.

Munch sits up on deck sweating. He observes everyone who comes on board. He recognizes a married couple. The Thaulows. Not the painter Frits, who helped him with his scholarship, but his brother and sister-in-law.

Munch has met him before. He is a captain in the naval medical corps, Carl Thaulow, a distant relation. He is a very imposing figure. The lady-killer of Karl Johan they call him. While she is one of those people who are talked about, the daughter of an admiral. Scandalous tales, unfaithful to her husband. Is there any truth in it? Yes, she looks rather self-assured.

The captain has accompanied her to the ferry.

Now she is saying goodbye to him.

The bell rings for the last time.

Then they glide out over the shimmering silver water.

*

She takes a seat opposite him.

She has a lovely neck.

He also notices her shoulders.

The steamer is crowded, ladies in pale blue, pink and white summer dresses, plump wealthy citizens, with port-wine-red faces, weighed down with holdalls and parcels. Students and lieutenants, wholesale merchants puffing and panting in the heat and looking as though they might succumb to apoplexy.

He is sitting directly opposite a married woman with a reputation. Now she greets him. He returns the compliment. Then they sit avoiding each other's eyes. He looks at her in the June sunshine, registers her features. She has large lips. Strange then that everyone should fall in love with her. Odd that she should have tired of the handsome and imposing lady-killer of Karl Johan.

6

Munch waits for something to happen. He is surrounded by love, the scandal with Christian Krohg and fru Engelhart, previously frøken Oda Lasson, the Attorney General's daughter. She has apparently forsaken husband and children for a radical painter. Rumours are rife.

Munch leans back in his chair on deck. They say she's taken another painter as lover recently. Munch knows him. He's not all that much older than himself. Might Munch have a chance? He has been to museums abroad, seen naked women in glistening oils. He draws naked models here in Christiania. As a painter, he is already old in his assessment of women. He is not easily impressed.

Now he looks at fru Thaulow. He sees that her mouth is ugly. Her lips are too large. Her skin is too coarse.

The steamer ploughs its way through the waves.

He engraves her on his mind, etches her firmly into his memory. He surreptitiously adjusts his collar, lights a cigarette, blows the smoke slowly up into the air, knows that his Parisian clothes fit him well.

He wonders whether he should address her by saying: Good day, madam. No, that wouldn't be right. Instead, perhaps: Madam, you probably won't recall? No, that's no good either. He can't pluck up the courage, all he can do is steal furtive glances. Every time she looks at him, he hastily averts his eyes.

Then she takes out a purse, buys some cherries, offers him a handful. Thank you. Thank you so much. Are you going far?

Yes, to Tønsberg.

Well, well, same here!

How nice. Where are you going exactly?

To Borre, near Goplen.

To Borre? Really? Even better, so we live right next to one another!

Munch suddenly finds her very pretty in her thin pale blue costume, thinks she's amusing when the wind blows her thin dress up and she bends forward to cover her legs. She turns to him and smiles. There he sits in his Parisian clothes holding his stick and tries to smile back.

*

In the harbour at Tønsberg stand the military doctor with Aunt Karen, Andreas and his sisters. Munch waves to them. Can they tell from his appearance that he has been abroad? He is a painter now. An artist. Has been in Antwerp and Paris. Has bought new clothes.

Munch walks down the gangway. He loses sight of fru Thaulow in the crowd. His family come towards him. He has come back to what is familiar, to Aunt Karen's gentle solicitude, the military doctor's inquiring look.

They walk along the fjord up towards Åsgårdstrand and Borre.

Munch tells them about all he has seen in the great wide world.

She comes towards him in a coach.

His immediate thought is that he is wearing his worst pair of trousers, the ones he is going to use in the country this summer until they wear out. His tie is crooked.

He freezes. There is nowhere to hide.

Now she is suddenly right in front of him.

The coach has stopped.

Smiling, she leans down towards him, gives him her hand.

There he stands on the country road, between the red and yellow houses with small gardens in front, feels a soft warm female hand. She laughs with white teeth, peering at him:

Your hair's wet. Have you just got up?

He is tongue-tied. The coach she is sitting in is full of flowers. Large yellow flowers.

What a charmer you are, she says.

She picks up a flower and hands it to him.

There you are. It's for you.

He still does not speak. She takes another flower.

And this is for your other hand.

There he stands, a yellow flower in each hand, looking at her.

Will you come and visit me tomorrow? she asks.

Yes, thank you, he replies.

*

He returns home to the family, hides the flowers in a crate in the attic so no one can see them. But his sister Inger has seen him.

Wasn't that fru Thaulow you were talking to?

Yes it was, he replies casually, blushing.

The military doctor glances up from the armchair. Fru Thaulow? She looks so sad these days.

Yes, says Aunt Karen. People say she's not very nice to her husband.

People say all kinds of things.

True.

It is summer. The Munch family are sitting at the dining table. The sound of knives and forks. Aunt Karen coughs. It is a bright evening. The water is light blue and violet. Munch notes the delicate hills and the shimmering air. Deeper and deeper violet. Up there above the tops of the fir trees – the moon small and pale as a silver farthing.

After the meal they walk out into the garden. His father has his pipe in the corner of his mouth. He is sitting on the bench, has put on his dressing gown, peers over the top of his glasses. Laura, wearing a white dress, is tending the flowers. Inger and Aunt Karen are knitting. Andreas is reading a book.

What a lovely moment. How fortunate we are, says the military doctor.

*

The next evening it is raining.

Heavy clouds chase across the sky in huge unbroken masses. The wind is blowing from the sea. The church shines white in the evening light surrounded by the graves.

Munch is approaching the russet-coloured house on the other side of the road.

She is standing on the veranda in a white hat like a jester's cap. She has placed it at such a coquettish angle. It doesn't suit her. He meets her gaze. They go into the house.

The Ihlen family's house. The admiral's home. It is evening. Now she doesn't look so young.

They go into the dark room. Huge heavy banks of cloud outside. She had just been standing on the veranda. Now she is in the house. He is with her. The jester's hat does not suit her. Her fringe tumbles down over her eyes.

She looks like a tart, he thinks.

Shall I show you my precious things, she asks.

*

She shows him the house.

That painting is divine, good colouring. She screws up her eyes and looks at it as painters do. Divine. The view from here is divine too. Look at the sea down there. Just like the first yellow flower she gave him. Divine. Look at the colours above the hills over there. Divine.

I know what I'm talking about, she says, I've spent a lot of time with painters.

Her reputation! Who was it who had whispered to him about that other painter, her lover?

At that moment he happens to glance down at some papers lying on the table. She snatches them away.

A letter, she says. She looks him straight in the eye. Says she is writing to *him*. Says it without batting an eyelid.

Perhaps she's not aware of the rumours.

I've known him since I was a child, she says. I've always been very fond of him. But I so easily tire of people.

Isn't he a bit of a bully, asks Munch cautiously.

She looks out of the window, her stomach pressed against the edge of the table, both hands tucked into the belt around her waist. Her arms are round, half-bare. The red bodice is very décolleté.

Munch observes the full bare throat. Her hair is combed up from the neck. As yellow as ripe corn. Now she is close to him. He is accustomed to observing, doesn't really like her mouth, it is so broad and pouting. Her nose is too large. Cleopatra must have looked like this.

That's a beautiful belt you're wearing, he says.

She stretches the belt down over her stomach and shows him the clasp.

It must be old, he says, stooping to take a closer look.

He feels her arm close to his cheek.

Yes, it is old, she says.

*

She lights the fire. They sit by the hearth. The flames cast their glow into the room. She sits reclining in the chair.

You should be called something else, she says.

D'you think so?

Yes, I do. Something or other. Like in those French novels.

Outside the lamp has been lit, the sea is visible through the door into the garden. The fire crackles. Then he hears footsteps in the corridor. A young woman comes into the room.

*

Supper. Supper with meat. Here's a nice piece. Now there is meat on Munch's plate. Thank you very much. He is not hungry. There is a sort of lump in his throat. Do eat, please. Fru Thaulow and frøken Lytzow. So frøken Lytzow is getting married. When? Tomorrow? Really? My word. Congratulations. Yes, on the contrary, I am very hungry. Meat. It's very good meat.

He feels how hot he is. A heat wave. Must say something, talk, come up with something. The silence makes him much too nervous. Words suddenly come tumbling out of his mouth. False-sounding words. Colliding with the silence in the room. That blue landscape out there is really beautiful, he says. It reminds one of Puvis de Chavannes.

Munch tries to eat the piece of meat, the sweat begins to trickle out of his pores and the food sticks in his gullet. But you're not eating? Yes I am. Are you not particularly hungry? My goodness yes. Very. Munch feels himself blushing. Then he'd gone and mentioned Puvis de Chavannes, thinks Munch, the creator of *Pro Patria Ludus*, four metres high and six-teen-and-a-half metres wide, as it hung at the World Exhibition in Antwerp. Why on earth had he said it? How dreadfully pretentious the words sounded. How boring they must find him. The blue landscape. Chavannes. Perhaps he is pronouncing the name wrong. Perhaps both women speak very good French. Fru Thaulow at any rate. In a few years' time she will be travelling the length and breadth of France singing *chansons*. Dreadfully pretentious. And his mouth is full of meat.

Fru Thaulow glances at her friend. Is that a little smile he catches? My goodness yes. Fru Thaulow is smiling at frøken Lytzow. Now frøken Lytzow is smiling too. So this, says frøken Lytzow, is a tender new shoot you've unearthed?

A budding artist, says Munch.

Good heavens, what was that he said?

It just popped out of him.

Ridiculous.

He is deeply embarrassed. Is it too late to make it seem like a joke? He tries to put on a jokey air. Fru Thaulow's friend then also starts to laugh, either out of duty or to divert attention.

How lovely, she says. Two artistic souls. A meeting of great minds. How very fitting.

Then Munch has to steal a look at fru Thaulow. She looks dreadfully serious. It's quite obvious she's trying not to laugh. She is sitting stock still. Terribly serious. Her face is becoming red with the effort. Dreadfully serious.

*

The laughter explodes. Not ordinary laughter, but a gale of laughter. Laughter which stops suddenly only to start off again, even more uncontrollably. Fru Thaulow has to put down knife and fork. Munch notices that she is hugging her sides with both hands. Now she laughs, her wide mouth open. Munch looks at her face. The lamp and the plates start to spin before him. He feels wretched. Utterly wretched. What can he do? He is sitting at fru Thaulow's table grinning idiotically. Suddenly she can't hold it any longer, gets up abruptly, goes into a corner, crouches down. She laughs so hard she cannot breathe and gasps:

Oh, it's too much, just too much!

He sits at the table looking at her.

Suddenly all grows quiet.

Frøken Lytzow looks at her friend in alarm.

I think you're mad, you've completely taken leave of your senses.

Fru Thaulow slowly gets up, says that she just couldn't help it.

Munch gets up from the table and goes over to the window.

He places his forehead against the window pane to cool down.

*

Later he writes: Kirkegaard lived in Faust's time. Don Juan–Mozart–Don Juan. The man who seduces the innocent girl. I have lived during the transitional period. In the midst of the emancipation of women. Then it is the women who seduce, entice and deceive the men. Carmen's time. During the transition man became the weaker of the two. Don Juan Mozart – Carmen Bizet.

*

He hates her.

A blind, desperate hatred. Red blood courses through his veins.

Steaming human blood. The pulse of life beats in every fibre beneath his skin. Is this life? Is this what it feels like? The enormity of his humiliation.

He had stood at the window. She had come up to him. She had been fanning herself.

How lovely she was.

*

He does not want to see her again. Ever.

He lies in bed. Imagine if he could bend that proud neck out of love for him. He would humiliate her as she has humiliated him.

*

For two days he does not show himself again at Kirkebakken.

Then he meets her again, meets her outside in the garden. I say, wouldn't you like to come in?

No thank you.

Why not?

Thank you all the same, but I was planning to go for a stroll.

She walks along with him.

His head is on fire. He will not forget that laughter. A budding artist. She had sat on the floor writhing like a snake. Abandoning all restraint. To the point where she could contain herself no longer. Now it seems it is forgotten. He hates her. She is a flirt. Her words. Everything is so divine, *too* divine. What does she actually mean? He himself had spoken of colours, been more precise. Mentioned Chavannes. But his words had fallen like lead weights.

He walks at her side. He looks at the beautiful neck. She speaks to him. He looks at her mouth. Her lips part. Then they walk down towards the fjord.

What are you painting? she asks.

I'm painting a mermaid.

*

He asks her to pose so he can see how the light falls.

She removes her hat. The one she has been given by the other painter. Then she starts to untie her hair. Ripe corn. But she cannot untie it. She has to tug at it. Then it cascades down over her beautiful shoulders.

He lets her stand there.

She is standing there for his sake, or for her own. But she is posing as his model. He is not sure what he wants from her. He just leaves her standing there. She has posed for him. That is all she can do. She is waiting for *him* now. She is unmasked, completely laid bare. How pathetic she is. There she stands, motionless, her hair down over her shoulders.

He scrutinizes her. A critical look. He knows that she sees this. A painter's professional eye. No trace of admiration. Lips too large.

You look like a mermaid, he says coldly.

She laughs. Then she starts to talk. Actually, my situation's very good, she says. Married and childless. You're so free when you're married and have no children.

He does not reply.

My husband's so good, she says. But I'm bad. Of course, I'm very sorry about it. But you have to follow your inclination, don't you?

He says nothing.

She falls silent, stands there with her hair down, looking like a mermaid, or a cornfield. He paints her large lips.

Thank you, he says all of a sudden.

Is that it?

Yes, that's it.

*

He accompanies her to the gate.

Would you like to come in?

No thank you.

He goes home. They are sitting there just like before. The military doctor is smoking his pipe. Andreas sits poring over his anatomy books. Munch has already painted him, almost as Hamlet, with a half and a whole skull on the table in front of him. The women are knitting. It is evening.

During the night the dreams come.

*

He dreams of something he once saw: The chair by the white curtains, the window with the view onto the outside world. The sunset filled the clouds with blood. The seamstresses were on their way to and from work. Furtive glances, fearful eyes. An icy blast ran down the street. The spindly trees in the courtyard looked dead and desolate.

He was not yet five years old.

It was dark and grey down the stairs. He held her hand and pulled her. He could not get down fast enough. Then he asked his mother why she was walking so slowly. She paused on almost every step and caught her breath.

Outside he was blinded by the light. His mother stopped for a while. The air was warm, with the odd cold gust. Light green grass was shooting up between the cobblestones. It was spring.

His mother was wearing a mauve hat. The pale pink ribbons fluttered up with every gust of wind, and were blown into her face.

They walked down Slottsgaten to the fortress and looked at the sea.

He dreams of what he saw: The nursery was dark. His brother and sisters and their friends were playing. They marched up and down singing a sad song. Then they disappeared one by one. Finally, there was one girl left. She stood there all alone. No one would have anything to do with her. The boy, a stranger, who had given her the ribbon and the hoop, had also vanished.

Then he had run up to her, taken her hand and comforted her.

On the opposite side of the street lived a man and a woman who were always quarrelling. Once when they were arguing the devil came up behind them and stood there laughing. He had large horns on his forehead, horse's hooves and a tail.

But one of the dreams is stronger and clearer: He sat at the foot of the large double bed with his younger brother. His mother stood tall and dark up against the window. She said she was going to leave them, had to leave them. She asked whether they would be sad when she was gone. They had to promise her they would remain true to Jesus, then they would meet her again in heaven. They did not fully understand this. They thought it was all so dreadfully sad. Then they had both wept. Wept bitterly.

Large snowflakes drifted down from the sky. He could follow one of them with his eyes right down to the ground.

Then he turned and looked at the Christmas tree.

The air was heavy with the smell of candle wax and burnt pine needles. There were no shadows in the room. The light found its way into every nook and cranny.

They had moved her into the living room. She sat in the middle of the sofa wearing her large black silk dress. She was pale and silent. All the children were seated round her. His father paced up and down, then sat down beside her and whispered something. She smiled and tears ran down her cheeks.

Sophie, his eldest sister, sang *Silent night, holy night.*

Then the ceiling opened. You could see right up into heaven.

His mother sat on the sofa, looking at each of them in turn, gently running her hand down their cheeks.

They took her back into the other room. A strange man dressed in black stood at the foot of her bed praying.

It was dark in the room. The air was heavy and grey.

One by one they had to go up to the bed where she lay.

Their mother kissed them carefully.

Then they went out of the room. They were going away. The servant girl took them to some strangers. They were friendly. The children were given all the cakes and toys they wanted.

One night they were woken, all of them. They understood straight away. They got dressed, sleepy-eyed.

Munch lies in bed dreaming of what he saw, all the images he cannot escape.

But fru Thaulow stands on the other side of the dreams and looks straight through them.

* * *

Eve yields to temptation.

A dance at the Grand Hotel, Åsgårdstrand, June 1885. Munch has walked through the forest from Borre. The hotel's large windows look out onto the fjord. He recognizes families from Christiania, actors and painters. There is Hans Heyerdahl and wife. Hello, hello. Heyerdahl takes Munch aside: Shall we look at pictures together? A colleague at last. The hotel has some fine paintings. Heyerdahl is talking. Munch hears fresh voices from the lobby. *Her* voice. So she has come. Absolutely no mistaking it. Heyerdahl points at one of his own paintings.

Very good that, says Munch.

I painted it with turpentine, says Heyerdahl. I think it's come out well, don't you? Turpentine is the only thing, it's wonderful. The old masters also used it, it's so nice to use, I paint with nothing else, I've always done so. Here's another one, which I painted with paraffin, excellent, luscious colour, turpentine and paraffin are good, equally good, give such a delightful surface to scrape in. I always scrape first and paint afterwards. Munch nods. How right you are. Excellent. He listens for her voice. Here she comes now. Lovely turpentine. Juicy paraffin. Munch nods again. Very interesting. She's right behind him now. He turns while talking, trying to make it look natural. Feigning surprise. Hello. Wants his voice to sound rather indifferent. She returns his greeting. Good God, how lovely she is in that light, close-fitting costume and the large summer hat.

Have you no desire to come and visit me any more?

Yes I have, I've been terribly busy. So has your mother arrived?

What difference does that make?

None. Of course not. Then I'll come soon.

*

Heyerdahl asks her for a dance.

Munch sits in a corner and observes his colleague and fru Thaulow on the dance-floor. Suddenly he feels dejected. He leans forward, supporting his head on his hands. What's happening to him? He is no longer thinking of pictures.

Then suddenly she comes up to him.

Are you asleep, Munch?

Asleep? No, far from it. But he isn't fond of dancing, which artist is fond of dancing?

No, she replies. I'm not in the mood either. Not tonight.

*

They go into a side room. Munch feels hot and strange. They lean out through the open window with the upright between them. Munch can think of nothing else to say.

It's divine, she says, look, over there, the water between the trees and the moon behind the clouds.

He nods.

You know, she says, it must be my nature but on evenings like this I could do almost anything. I really feel like doing something frightfully wicked.

*

He sees that the light from the lamp falls yellow on her neck and hair. Outside in the night the moon is pushing through the clouds. She peers towards the dark forest. In this light her lips appear soft. Her throat is pale and bare. Her eyes are in shadow. Now and then he catches a glint of them in the semi-darkness.

*

She speaks to him. He sees her lips drawn up towards one side, the white teeth underneath. He has a feeling that something has to happen.

Then Heyerdahl and his wife come up.

Isn't it rather late? About time to be setting off for home, isn't it?

The road along the shore back to Borre.

They walk out of the hotel, northwards past the small white and yellow houses. Then they join the uneven path, walk through the forest, past cottages surrounded by fruit trees, wooden fences in front. Up the slope there are junipers and small firs.

The Heyerdahls walk ahead.

Munch and fru Thaulow lag behind.

*

Stand up on that mound, he says suddenly.

He wants to look into her eyes.

She does as he bids and stands up on a mound between the trees.

Her eyes are grey and dark beneath the full eyelids.

Stand like that for a moment, he says. Let me look at you. How picturesque you are in this light.

I don't like the light, she says. I like the moon best when it's behind a cloud, like now. Light is so indiscreet.

In the moonlight her pupils become large and her skin pale. He can only just make out her features. Suddenly she smiles. He catches a glint of her white teeth.

What was that?

There are animals in the forest. Beasts of prey, birds, insects, apples. Snakes.

He thinks he sees a head.

No, it's a stone
She goes on smiling.

*

Then suddenly she speaks of things he has never before heard in the mouth of any lady. She mentions Gervex, Henri Gervex that is, the extremely audacious *Rolla* of 1878, the young girl lying naked on the bed after a night of passion. Munch saw the picture in Paris, the draughtsmanship was excellent, but the picture was too glossy.

Then she says: Yes, but young girls *are* like that!

What does she mean? Naked?

She says: Do you remember how brilliantly it was painted? The outstretched leg, the delicate line upwards and the sheet which falls in gentle folds?

Munch follows her with his eyes as she speaks, sees that she is screwing her eyes up, furrowing her brow, making a gesture of the hand as though to underline what she means. In his mind's eye he sees the naked woman lying there, her legs voluptuously positioned. The picture mingles with his own motif, the woman who stands before him talking about a daring picture.

She stands there talking, arms behind her back. She looks straight at him, peers into the forest, her back to the sea. Perhaps there is a boat in the background, perhaps only the still surface of the water, the moon, the silhouettes of the trees.

Sometimes a wave makes its way slow and heavy towards the shore, breaking against the first rocks. Afterwards, a succession of small crashes can be heard all the way along the shore.

The moon is large and yellow. It makes a broad, golden pillar in the violet water.

*

Every now and then a cat flashes past. Munch starts again. What was that? An old woman suddenly stands there stock still in a doorway, staring at them, a cloth in her hand.

They walk on. The rocks tower up from the shallow water. They look like an army of sea people.

She speaks again: Look how like a head that rock is. It's moving!

He does not reply.

She unties her hair and lets it fall down over her shoulders.

Just imagine living there in the forest, she says. Not alone, but as a *couple*.

*

The Heyerdahls have stopped to wait for them.

Who goes there?

Only me.

Oh, *you*.

Yes. I just wanted to hear what you were talking about.

They go into the Ihlen family's house, sit round the fire, drinking coffee as she tells stories from Italy, walks over to the piano, sings the Carilla waltz.

He listens to the seductive voice. Soft, alluring notes. Now teasing, now imploring. She screws up her eyes as she sings, smiles an amorous smile. Then she stops singing, kneels down and blows on the fire. Her shoulder brushes one of Munch's legs. She suddenly leans against him for a moment. When she gets up again he feels her cheek gently graze his hand.

*

The Heyerdahls have gone home.

Munch stands with fru Thaulow outside the house. The landscape lies there vast and empty in the moonlight. The church is cold and white. He feels a sudden timidity, afraid he will again say something stupid. You've no idea how restless I am at night, she says. I have such dreadful dreams. And I walk in my sleep too. What would you say if I were to come to *you*?

* * *

He lies in bed, unable to sleep, thinking of the image of her standing in the light summer night, the pale moon above. He sleeps in close proximity to his father, the military doctor, in close proximity to Aunt Karen and his brother and sisters, cannot tell them what has happened, has been in Antwerp and Paris, but has still never felt a woman's lips, has been to museums, seen young, naked girls who are excellently drawn but too glossily painted.

He thinks of everything that has happened in his life so far. The loss of his mother. His sister Sophie who died when he was barely fourteen. Aunt Karen became the promise of another world, north of the steeple on Old Aker Church, south of the cupola on Holy Trinity Church, perhaps east of Ekeberg, but at any rate west of the blood-red sunsets. He lies in bed thinking of how the military doctor had wanted his son to be an engineer. Instead he had painted Old Aker Church as though it were in Tuscany. He had painted Maridalen valley as though it had been the Loire. He used optical drawing instruments with focusable lenses. *Camera obscura* and *camera lucida*. He read the debate about art in *Aftenposten* and discovered Skredsvig and Heyerdahl. Away from the brown. Brightness, as though through a window. Nordmarka. The forest. The long road up to Maridalen and on through the forest to Hammeren. Then further into the forest to Kamphaug and Hakkloa. He painted pictures which he sent down to the auction room, meanwhile singing in a choir to please his father. His friends teased him because he was always talking about pictures. He could have been an animal painter, a figure painter, a landscape painter. But he became part of the set round Colditz, had to distance himself from nail and twig painters such as Wentzel, felt compelled to paint a study of the head of a red-haired girl, had to paint another girl first thing in the morning, as she rose from her sleep and sat on the edge of the bed, pulling on her stockings. He felt compelled to paint in an unexpected golden light, reflections and shadows which played in tones of grey, the girl bent over forwards in profile. He felt compelled to paint his sister Inger in a dark dress against a smouldering blue-black background, or the military doctor kneeling before God. He had to paint in such a way that Frits Thaulow wrote to the military doctor that everything he had seen of his son's work testified to such an outstanding talent that he was prepared to send him to Paris at his own expense. Christian Krohg had tutored him and he had rented a studio in Pultosten and in Mariboesgate. Manet had said: What is important is to be a child of your time and then to express your own personality in your work, to express your hate and your love. And it is important to live and hate and love.

Now Munch lies in bed thinking about a sleepwalker. He sees her coming in the white nightdress. Barefoot, with closed eyes.

Then he falls asleep.

*

He wakens after a short night, rises early and goes out into the garden, sits on the steps letting the sun's rays caress his face. He feels the cool of the dew on the flowers. The white morning sun shines on the crimson hollyhocks and stocks, the flowers still lie in the long cold blue shadows. The early morning mist flickers over the water.

He is the first up. In all the houses people are still asleep. She is certainly still asleep too. He strains to see the russet-coloured house up by the church, on the other side of the road.

He has not yet experienced love. Has only experienced death. He has strolled with painter friends on the boulevards, drunk whisky and soda, looked at girls, the *cocottes*, and discussed with his painter friends how to reinstate woman as a motif in painting. Now it is 1885. Emile Zola is in France writing *L'Œuvre*, the novel whose hero is a painter, with strong similarities to Zola's close friend Cézanne. He sacrifices everything else in his work to the attempt to create a simple work of art, to strive for perfection, to subordinate everything else in life to art.

Munch peers at a russet-coloured house and knows that ever since he saw, as a child, the procession of blind people walk past in the street, he has been obsessed by the idea of recreating an impression. He ought to have put up his easel and started working by now.

Instead he gazes up towards the house where she sleeps.

If only he gazes long enough, she will waken.

*

One day the summer is over. Munch has to return to Christiania to set up his new studio in Hausmannsgaten. The thought makes him happy. He is going back to town to meet his friends again, to get ready for the Autumn Exhibition, to paint a large portrait of the Bohemian Jensen-Hjell. He will be leaving her behind, but that doesn't really matter. She'll soon be coming back to Christiania herself. Back to her husband, the captain. But he can exchange greetings with her on Karl Johan. He has a large studio. She can come and visit him. Everything is possible.

The Carilla waltz. He's got it on the brain, is singing it incessantly, to Aunt Karen's irritation. Eventually he takes his aunt by the waist and dances across the floor with her. Aunt Karen gets the giggles, Laura and Inger also start to laugh. Even the military doctor chuckles over at his desk, with his back to them. Then he looks up from his papers. Oh do be careful with the old lady, she's fragile!

* * *

Let's walk down the forest track, she says.

It's the last day. They walk into the forest, he has her at his side, feels let down, had been so happy, but she surely thinks him stupid and boring.

Let's sit here among the trees she says.

What are you thinking about?

Oh, all sorts of things.

He is sitting beside her, knows they will perhaps soon be having an affair. One like everybody else talks about. So here he is having an affair with a married woman.

But they have still not kissed.

It is as though she is waiting for something.

He doesn't know what to do.

*

Then she suddenly stands up.

Bewildered, he sees that she is starting to go. He should have kissed her, he thinks. That was the last chance. She must have been waiting for him to make a move. He runs after her, follows her right to her gate. There she turns to face him.

Goodbye, she says coldly.

*

But he does not leave after all. Cannot leave now. Puts it off for a day. He must have one more chance, one more day. A lot can happen.

It has rained. There are puddles along the road. Soon he can see her russet-coloured house. It sits there dismally among the lush green trees.

He knocks at the door. She opens it and asks him if he would like to come in. It is impossible to know what she is thinking.

He goes in to her and her sisters. They are sitting round the fireplace. She sits in the red glow of the fire. He feels excited and warm. His blood pounds against his temples.

But this is not where he wants to be.

She reads his thoughts and suggests going out for a walk. Back into the wet forest again.

He walks beside her, steals glances at her. Her full throat, the thin bodice laced up carelessly in front. He sees her breasts rising and falling. If only he dared. She looks at him with grey-green eyes.

Then he takes her hands.

Let's see who is stronger, he says.

No reply.

He cannot take his eyes off the bare throat. Then suddenly he stoops and gently touches the skin with his lips, then he jerks back his head and looks at her. Is she angry? He is gasping for breath.

I kissed you, he says.

No, she replies gravely.

II

The room is pitch dark. But it vibrates and sparkles. A pale grey strip in the gap between the curtains. (EDVARD MUNCH)

Autumn comes with its cold moonlit nights.

Munch settles into the studio in Hausmannsgate. The summer in Borre has not given him the peace and quiet for work. Now he stands before the easel and tries to gather his thoughts. In front of him is a man. He is 6 feet 3 inches tall. It is the Bohemian Jensen-Hjell. He stands there with a defiant, almost provocative, look in his eyes. Munch is painting a life-size portrait. He is painting the defiance of the Bohemians: There is a small circle of individuals in our society, for the most part the sons of nice decent parents, for whom the empty lacklustre life of modern society holds so little attraction that it is powerless to galvanize their energies.

To paint just what he saw when the motif struck him: for instance when one emerges in the morning from a dark bedroom into the parlour, everything will appear in a blueish cast. Even the deepest shadows will have light air above them. After a while, one will grow accustomed to the light, the shadows will become deeper and everything will come into sharper focus. If the artist is to capture such a mood, peering intently at object after object and painting just what he sees is not the way to go about it. He must paint just what he saw when the motif first struck him. When out on the binge in a group, one sees with a different eye, contours become blurred, everything seems closer to chaos. If one sees double, then paint two noses. And in Jensen-Hjell's case . . .

Munch sees before him the harbour with its red-light district, Karl Johan with its upright citizens, and individuals in this city whom he cannot quite pin down, young students with mysterious looks, people he hears rumours about, a certain type of immorality, sudden suicides out on Tjuvholmen, deep in the woods. The unmistakable feeling of defiance, of pent-up desperation, just as in the dining room back home at Grünerløkken.

More than they can take. The world is harsh and evil.

Suddenly the city's young radicals seem to have absolutely no sense of their own limitations. Contempt for God, for authority and the family are soon to be set down in print. Meanwhile Edvard Munch returns to the bosom of the family and folds his hands in prayer, although even then he must have realized that, as he will later write, he cannot share his father's faith.

Not believe in Christ! After all that suffering! Munch sits there, in the living room with the military doctor, knowing that his father's deep moral scruples have hardly any meaning for him. There's no longer even any reason to let oneself be goaded by the assertion that hell will last a thousand times a thousand years.

The military doctor asks: What tidings shall I bring you? All men are as grass, all their beauty as the flowers of the field. Yea, your sister Sophie is now a flower of the field. The grass shrivels and the flowers wither when the spirit of the Lord blows upon them – yea, verily, men are as grass.

Munch has met Hans Jæger. *Man kann seine Eltern nie schlecht genug behandeln.* There is no limit to how badly one can treat one's parents. The Bohemians' third commandment. Jæger. The sailor returned, fired with all the thoughts that had run through his head between the Bristol Channel and Cardiff port, in gale and driving snow, as a steamboat towed the sailing ship out to sea and as the woman he had clung to but an hour before stood waving to him on the jetty. He was sixteen and just as filled with fear as Munch is now. Ignorance was like a black wall at the end of all thoughts. To do it with a woman, just once?

Jæger on the high seas, on winter nights, beneath the stars. Ship's mate Jæger, who jumped ship in Cardiff and got himself taken on under the alias James Simpson. Sailmaker's apprentice and assistant surveyor.

Out at sea, one's thoughts roamed free, broad horizons, ample vistas. Independent when only fourteen or fifteen years old, and that with an assistant chief constable – later brigade prosecutor – in Bergen, as father. But his father died when Jæger was only ten years old, and his uncle took over. He had been a military doctor and a gold prospector in Australia before ending up as a bookseller and revivalist preacher in Bergen.

But Jæger was in Arendal long before then, living with another uncle who had more literary ambitions. At 13 years of age he stood before the mast, at 15 he was alone with the sea, with big ideas and troubled by urges.

Farewell, respectability! Farewell, knitting womenfolk of Bergen and wizened merchants of Arendal. Farewell, Christian hypocrites and crooked civil servants. Farewell, moral cowards; farewell, lickspittles of the high and mighty, matrimony's obedient servants, sado-masochists behind drawn curtains. Farewell, capitalist exploiters.

Jæger sailed the seven seas. And never let a chance slip past. Every port had its women. He bought what love he could afford and was not very old when he first caught unmentionable diseases.

Then he came home to the district of Nordre Land and to philoso-phizing. He had a view of the river Dokka and the wooded valley floor. At sunset he would lie in a hammock beneath two venerable limes reading

Fichte's philosophy of law, the development of the concept of freedom. How should society be ordered so that freedom became possible? Jæger would feel the book grow heavy in his hands and his thoughts begin to wander. Could men create a society in which nobody curtailed his own freedom more than was absolutely essential to ensure the same freedom for everybody else? An open, free life together among open, free men and women who knew no other law for social life than love, freedom and worldly happiness?

Once more he was back at sea, but on another sea now, the ocean of philosophy and ideas. Here, the storm was well-nigh permanent: My goodness yes! Have men done nought but toil and eat and drink and sleep and act like fools these past hundred years? Did they live in vain, then, those great thinkers? Freedom, equality, brotherhood. Oh yes, he knew all about that revolution. Why hadn't it succeeded? In Jæger's eyes, because it was the rabble who carried the revolution through. The rabble, who had no grasp of the ideas. They had dragged the whole thing down into the gutter. Dragged freedom down to their own level, instead of raising themselves up to it!

Yes, Jæger. Sent by fate to fix Munch with his defiant eye. For the rest of Munch's life Jæger will haunt him. A loser at the table, in love and in politics. Munch meets him before the battle has been fought, while he still seems invincible.

These are the nervous 'eighties. A new age is dawning. The city is split between the old and the new. The age of general education has long been a reality. The major national organizations are setting up their offices and headquarters in the capital. The Missionary Society is building its national chapel in Akersgaten. Temperance societies, farmers' movements, workers' and co-operative societies are springing up.

It is the city of possibilities. Its Norwegian name changes again, from Christiania to Kristiania. As the capital, the city constantly grows in importance, politically and economically, culturally and socially. Civil servants of all kinds are now setting their sights on Christiania. They meet in the theatre, at the Lodge, in the assembly hall at Klingenberg, the gymnasium at Akershus Fort or the concert rooms at the Hals Brothers' pianoforte works. They are the new bourgeoisie in the making. And they support culture both to see and to be seen. They stroll in Kurland, the area between Karl Johan and Stortingsgaten. They are the 'Silhouette Generation'. But they are no longer alone. Newcomers are on their way, flocking in in droves. Rural youth, students from country districts, and seamstresses hoping to find work in the factories.

The city opens onto the fjord. There are regular sailings to Amsterdam, Antwerp, Bordeaux, Bremen, Hamburg, Le Havre, Hull, Copenhagen, Liverpool, London and Stettin. As early as 1861, the

American Ross Browne wrote that the city had become something of a watering hole for tourists en route to the hinterland. British gentlemen with whisky in their hip pockets and dairymaids on their minds.

Hans Jæger makes people sit up and listen. He is strikingly hypersensitive. It gives him a sense of having come into the world too soon, a feeling that his insight cannot yet be shared with everyone. But Munch picks up the signals. Jæger is to be a mighty challenge in Munch's life. For Jæger challenges the military doctor's Christian teaching. As early as May 1881, in the Fram Society, to the accompaniment of toddies, whisky and soda, cigars, short pipes and long pipes, Jæger took part in an attack on Christianity, its monstrous sin against life. In this forum, religion with its doctrine of renunciation was conceived as hostile to life, either stifling the urge in the younger generation towards a freer and richer life than the one that could be lived under the old social forms, or suppressing it. Which therefore meant that, instead of finding expression in efforts to reform society, it took the form of private hedonism, which thus in due course called forth all the social ills which could be grouped together under the umbrella term 'immorality'. Later, the attack turned to marriage as an institution. One February evening in 1882, Jæger had stood up in the Workers' Society in Christiania and started the Bohemian Movement, giving it a name and a face. He had stood there and demonstrated how many women there were who, thanks to the unequal distribution of the proceeds of labour in society, found that their work did not pay them enough to live on. But as long as society could accept such an evil, the pathetic bourgeois lamentations over that impropriety, that immorality, that sordidness or God knows what term they used to characterize prostitution, were no longer appropriate. Jæger had also advocated that it ought to be possible for a man to have relationships with as many as twenty women. Since in marriage you were tied to just one woman, you were therefore cheated of nineteen-twentieths of what life had to offer.

After this meeting and the ensuing press reports, Hans Jæger had become a public scandal, and Munch became his friend. How much was this friendship a gesture of defiance against his father's Christianity? Suddenly, Munch had become one of those young people from strict, middle-class Christian families, with a mother or father who raged at the way their offspring was developing or wept tears of despair over it. It is the coterie surrounding Jæger. Munch meets them at the Grand, at Gravesen's Café, in one of the taprooms in the Cathedral Close. Some of them have already thrown in the sponge. Sluggish, slothful, they sit there with a tired, melancholy cast to their faces, slowly but surely drowning themselves in drink. Or else they stand like Jensen-Hjell right there in front of him, a look of defiance in his eyes.

What keeps you out so late? the military doctor asks one day.

Silence.

You're never at home any more, are you? Just turn up for breakfast.
What would your mother have said!

Whereupon his son explodes: Yes, but what do you all expect?
There's nothing I can talk to any of you about!

Nights in Christiania. Munch perhaps tries to get his sister Inger to
go with him. At any rate, she sits for Munch when he paints a tête-à-
tête: Jensen-Hjell with his pipe in a smoke-filled room. A picture with
clear erotic overtones. A conversation at a table, two glasses of whisky
and soda. The man is trying to win over the woman with words. She sits
there undecided, expectant. It is just before a turning point.

Hans Jæger's presence can be sensed in the picture. Determinism by
lamplight. In this smoke-filled room, preparations are being made for
the assault on the three massive granite pillars supporting the old culture and the old society, maintaining all the shallowness: Christianity,
morality and the old idea of justice. The way things actually are, people
have no choice but to act as they do.

*

Munch's new circle of friends makes the military doctor anxious. But
what can he do? He bottles up his anger until he can stand it no more.
Munch sees home as though through a *camera obscura*. He registers
without taking part. The lunch table. The white plates. The military
doctor eats his soup. The spoon rises and falls, rises and falls. With
every movement, death has edged a fraction closer.

Munch looks at Aunt Karen. He looks at his father. What is it they
are talking about?

How absent-minded you are, Edvard. Do you seriously think it's all
right to go about in that ghastly old dressing gown of your father's?

*

After lunch, he stretches out on the sofa. If only he could sleep till he
sees her again!

The lounge is bathed in sunlight. The gold picture frames and table
legs glint. A little ray of sunshine falls on the scarlet cushion. Father sits
bowed over his desk in a bluish-grey fog, enveloped in tobacco smoke.
Aunt Karen is knitting, Andreas is reading, Inger and Laura are in the
kitchen. Munch lies there trying to doze off.

When he came back from Borre he'd been so optimistic. She had
given him all manner of expectations. They could meet in her apartment. In his studio. Small billets-doux. Glances exchanged in the
street.

He still hasn't seen her.

* * *

It is evening. He stands with the other art students outside the Grand Café. Darkness is falling. The lamps are being lit in the shops. People everywhere. All back again after the summer.

What are you going to exhibit, Strøm?

Oh, I'll put in some landscapes. What about you?

Don't know. Haven't got anything finished yet.

At that moment a lady glides past him. He catches her scent. She grazed him ever so slightly. He turns and recognizes her glance behind the black veil.

Strøm nudges him with his elbow.

She's damned tasty, Munch. Is it *you* who . . .

He doesn't hear. Catches up with her.

Let's walk fast, she says. I know so many people here.

Her words make him happy. They sounded so intimate, like something between just *them* alone. They walk down Karl Johan, past the Cathedral Close towards the railway station. She is a few paces ahead. He follows her down Railway Lane, then turning right under the railway bridges.

Suddenly they are at the river, in the darkness, midway between two gaslamps. Workers glide past, homeward bound from the factory. Unfamiliar faces, uniform, grave. The shadows are long and dark. A train roars over the bridge. The iron pillars boom. He sees the great bloodshot ball of flame in the engine.

Then they are alone. Only the barely perceptible murmur of the river flowing into the fjord. He hears his own voice.

Fru Thaulow, do you love me?

At last, she raises the dark veil to reveal her face.

* * *

He pauses in the hall. Catches her scent. It is mingled with other odours, cigars, mopped floors. Then he slowly mounts the stairs. He has heard about their parties, literati who have been thrown out. Every single step is a bit of her. How many times has she set her foot precisely on that step. He pauses again, listens, glances at his watch, carries on up to her floor, pauses hesitating in front of the glass door, glances one last time at his hands. Impossible to get rid of the paint under his nails. White from Jensen-Hjell's pince-nez. Red from Inger's burning cheeks.

Then he tugs the bell-pull. Is it fru Thaulow or the maid who is coming to the door? It's the maid. He blushes. Does she know who he is? Has her mistress said . . .

I . . . er, have an appointment with . . . fru Thaulow.

Strange to utter her name. He has not done so before, not to anyone. Fru Thaulow. The maid nods and shows him in. She knows all right.

He goes in. So this is what their home is like, hers and the captain's. The smell of a shared life, parties, elegant suppers. Heavy dark curtains. Pictures by her brother-in-law Frits on the walls. No shortage of money here. Large plants in the windows and in the corners. Soft low armchairs. There's what must be the chaise longue she usually reclines on, whiling away the mornings.

Then she comes in carrying cats, a whole armful of cats, large and small, just as when she had come with the yellow flowers. A whole bouquet. Just look at these lovely cats. She strokes and caresses them. He watches her full, voluptuous lips as she speaks. Her bare neck. If only he were a cat! Now he stands there wordlessly observing the affection she lavishes on the creatures. He is lost for words. She tells him what they are called. What they eat. Suddenly he is holding a cat in his arms. He strokes it, feels it begin to purr.

Then she shows him round. She takes him into her husband's study. So this is where he sits, the lady-killer of Karl Johan. The pens are arranged neatly side by side. Account books, writing paper and envelopes. Everything so tidy. There is a little doll on the writing desk.

I made that, she says.

Really? He holds it up, catches her scent. Oh, give it to me! he blurts out. He has nothing else to remind him of her. Just two yellow flowers. Dry and withered.

Oh no, Munch, she says. You've no idea how fond of it he is.

* * *

One day there is a dreadful scene. Munch and the military doctor are standing behind the curtain in the bedroom at home, a corner which serves as his father's office. A mangled picture lies thrown in the corner. The military doctor looks like thunder. His hands are shaking. Both are beside themselves with rage.

So he spends all day lolling about in cafés now, does he? His paintings going from bad to worse?

So cousin Edvard has ratted on him. Splendid wonderful Edvard. Edvard Diriks, the family's successful painter. Now he's gone and blabbed to the military doctor: Watch that son of yours. He hangs about in cafés with louche types such as Jæger and Jensen-Hjell.

The military doctor is purple in the face. He has an excitable temperament.

So you hang about with that degenerate Jæger, do you? Not a penny more for paint and brushes!

Munch rushes out into the street. Aunt Karen cannot stop him. He is on the verge of tears. From bad to worse? Lolling about in cafés? Have they no idea how he stands there hour after hour in his studio grappling with the motif?

He could have come straight out with it, could have said: Had you any idea that I've started an affair with a married woman? Not just anybody, by the way, but fru Thaulow. That's right. Carl Thaulow's wife. And what do we think about *that*?

Heavens. What a coward he is. What a wretched coward. He rushes up to the studio, up to the portrait of Hjell. Why should he work? What's the point of striving so hard to become a great painter? Ludicrous. It's crystal clear. One fine day he'll be flat on his back at death's door. So what in hell's name will it all have been for? Posthumous fame? Too ridiculous for words! He's gone for ever. Become nothing. What a ridiculous illusion all these years. Fancy not having thought of it before. A great painter. What does it mean to be a great painter? Is it any better than being a doctor, for instance? It's nothing compared to being a king of course. But even a king is just one tiny bacterium on earth.

* * *

Then she comes up to see him in his studio, where time has stood still. Suddenly she stands between the picture of Jensen-Hjell and the nudes. She undoes her hair, allowing it to cascade down over her shoulders. He stares at the black dress, overpowered by her perfume. He knew she would come. Knew it. To die now. At this moment. To let oneself be swallowed up *completely*, become one with the earth which, illuminated by the sun's rays, eternally teems with life. To die at this moment, together with her. Things would grow from their rotting corpses. Plants, trees and flowers. The sun would warm them. They would both become another substance. Nothing would be lost. For that was eternity.

* * *

The portrait of Jensen-Hjell hangs in the Autumn Exhibition. Bohemian in a full-length portrait. He looks the bourgeoisie straight in the eye with unconcealed insolence. *Aftenposten* is on the spot, the mysterious signature S.S., which Jens Thiis, Munch's biographer, many years later, reveals is an alias for as many as ten people, including Schibstedt, the editor himself:

> It has not even been properly primed, but roughly daubed on the canvas, and almost looks as though it has been painted with the various lumps of paint remaining on the palette after another picture. A number of these lumps of paint have ended up on the subject's face, including a large white spot in one eye, which the artist, in his impressionistic striving for effect, has omitted so as to give us the white reflection of the glass in the pince-nez instead. This is impressionism in the extreme. A travesty of art. Like a caricature, the picture has made people laugh, and it may of course

be that this was its sole purpose. But it has also awakened indignation, an indignation also directed at the jury which has allowed such a picture to slip through into an exhibition.

*

The members of the jury are Amaldus Nielsen, Frits Thaulow and Erik Werenskiold. And the very same Thaulow offers to buy the painting for two hundred crowns. Munch has to inform him that the picture has alas been sold to the model himself. The payment was a dinner at the Grand for the sum of two crowns.

* * *

It is evening. He stands under the University clock on the lookout for her. A lot of people are taking a stroll in the lovely weather; the street is swarming with people as far as the Palace. They become lighter and bluer the further they are from him. Then he turns. There is the Parliament building in an almost imperceptible haze with deep blue air above it. A pale little moon climbs across the sky. The windows in the Parliament building and down Karl Johan are ablaze with gold.

Then she comes towards him, in her black dress which fits tightly round her neck. She walks with quick, anxious steps. Why does she always take chances? He knows she is afraid of wagging tongues. She is a married woman. There was gossip about her and the previous painter. Try as one might to keep everything secret, people find out all the same. Everybody but everybody knows about Christian Krohg and Oda Engelhart, even though, when she was about to be delivered, they actually went abroad, to a different country.

She glides past him. He sets off, walking beside her as though by chance. Now and then she moves away from him, disappearing suddenly across the street. Then they brush one another again.

Why didn't you come?

What? It's tomorrow, isn't it?

Oh come on, you know very well it was two o'clock this afternoon.

No it wasn't. In any case, I was standing just outside with my mother. Didn't you see me?

What was he supposed to have seen? Such lies aren't even worth answering. So she's lying. She's not telling the truth any more. But he dare not reveal that he knows better. That he is spying on her.

I was only meeting my husband, she says. He'd been at the exhibition.

I see. What did he say? Did he say anything about me?

No, he said that Sinding's picture was neither flesh nor fowl.

Munch listens pensively. He sees him more often now, the lady-killer of Karl Johan. Meets him almost daily, out of the blue, in the strangest places, unexpectedly on a corner, right outside the door to the studio.

I must be off home now, says fru Thaulow. Let me walk alone from here.

* * *

He stands before the mirror for a long time. How thin he's become. How pale. How ill-fitting his clothes are. The shoulders sag on both sides. He straightens up. Rubs his cheeks until they are red. His heart is pounding.

Then he walks down to the Grand and takes a seat in the corner window. There is Jensen-Hjell. There goes Wentzel. And here comes Jæger, mouth crooked, cane under arm. He crosses the pavement at an angle, making straight for the door to the Grand, enters and takes a seat at his table.

Whisky and soda for Jæger.

Well, Munch, how are things? You look awful. Like a skeleton. Eyes dull, not a spark of life. Have a drink, my boy.

Do you think I really look as bad as that? Worse than usual?

Yes. You look like death warmed up. You don't drink enough. You need to knock it back a bit.

Oh, I don't think that's the trouble.

Isn't it? Well, in that case, get yourself a woman. But you don't have one though, do you?

Munch does not reply.

Knock it back and get yourself a woman. You'll see. What shall I have next? Waiter, give me another whisky and soda, will you? One for you too, Munch?

Yes, all right, I'll have one too.

He sits there silent, tongue-tied. Jæger hasn't much to say for himself today either. Munch catches sight of his own reflection in the window-pane. Yes, it's true. He *does* look really awful. Like a skeleton.

Doesn't this tie suit me, Jæger?

No, not particularly. I think you need a different colour to go with that pale skin of yours.

Then suddenly he sees her. She's walking on the other side of the pavement. It's two o'clock. The military band is marching down the hill, on its way to the Palace. Karl Johan is suddenly full of people. He runs out onto the pavement, crosses the street, goes straight towards her. Now she sees him. He gropes for words. Why didn't she come?

But she beats him to it:

Come up to the Drawing School if you want to talk. I'm sitting for a student.

* * *

December 1885. Carnival time in the city. Grand ball at the Lodge. Women in cloaks and veils, harlequins and pierrots. A frisky schoolgirl slaps him on the belly. Hello, Munch. But Munch is lost in his own thoughts. Which disguise will she choose? Queen? Lion? Tiger? Cocotte? Munch comes as himself. Pale monk, the schoolgirl calls him. But he has no wish to seem downcast this evening. He's excited, and has already had a few drinks. There's Kalle Løchen got up as Hamlet. What else! After all, Løchen is both painter and actor. Hamlet is a dream part. The pale face of the knight against the black costume. Very effective. And there is his wife as Ophelia. Hello, Munch. To be or not to be. That's a fair thought, to lie between maids' legs.

Then he sees Jæger.

A whisky and soda, Jæger!

Good evening, Munch.

I've read your book, Jæger.

Oh? And what do you think?

Brilliant. No book has ever made such an impression on me.

Munch hears himself speaking too loudly. His voice is piercing. Whisky and soda for Jæger. Brilliant. Good God, is that all he can find to say?

Where's your girl, Munch?

Yes, where is she? Munch surveys the room. There she is, under the pillar with her husband. He is a prince with helmet and large sword at his side. She is a princess with her page. The lieutenant. Munch knows he has seen him before. A tall page with plumes and a knight's cloak. A new lover? The princess in love with her page? In that case, it's a charming arrangement.

But where has the schoolgirl got to?

Is that your girl, Munch?

Jæger points to a group of young men. In their midst stands the Pistol Queen, frøken Drewsen. Munch knows who she is, having seen her many a time in the street.

How lovely she is, Munch. Just look at her fresh young face. Look at that mouth. Those eyes! How she sways at the hips.

That book of yours, Jæger.

Aren't we on first-name terms, Munch?

The din in his head. He's speaking too loudly. Must make himself heard. Piercing voice. He's only too aware of it. Brief, staccato words.

Here comes frøken Drewsen.

Hello, frøken Drewsen. I know you well. I've seen you many a time in the street.

He offers her his arm. Jæger is right. She really does have a fresh young face.

What an interesting brooch. He reaches for the little pistol on her bosom.

Is it cold?

Shan't we dance?

I don't dance.

Oh yes you do. With *me* you do.

She pulls him towards the ballroom.

Suddenly he feels happy. There sit fru Thaulow and her husband. Now she can see him. He leans towards the girl.

Frøken Drewsen, do you know how happy I am to have met you this evening? I felt so down in the dumps. I've wanted to meet you for such a long time.

He presses her bare arm against him.

Why are you laughing? she asks.

Because I'm so happy, he answers.

He glances at fru Thaulow. Frøken Drewsen follows his eyes.

Isn't Captain Thaulow magnificent, she says. I danced the first waltz with him. He's an excellent dancer. And isn't his wife lovely? He's promised to introduce me to her.

Munch feels elated. He who is usually so tongue-tied. Now words just pour out of him.

Perhaps we should dance after all, he says. But I'm a poor dancer.

It doesn't matter.

They ascend the staircase.

There are the Captain and his wife, says frøken Drewsen.

He pretends not to see, draws her to him, hears the Captain's voice.

May I introduce my wife, frøken Drewsen?

He hears fru Thaulow speak: What a delightful brooch you have.

Munch raises his eyes. There she stands, right in front of him. That strange, sorrowful smile.

Hello, Munch.

Hello.

Then he moves on with frøken Drewsen.

You've stopped talking, Munch.

Let's dance, he says.

He grasps frøken Drewsen at the waist. Throws himself into the dance.

But you're an excellent dancer, Munch.

*

It's well into the small hours. He is standing outside the Lodge with frøken Drewsen. The carnival guests stumble out onto the steps. She presses close to him.

You can have a lift with my cousin and me, Munch.

He sits beside her in the dark carriage. Hears her fresh young voice. She's much more beautiful than fru Thaulow, he muses. I'm tired of *her*. She can keep the lieutenant.

He is suddenly overcome with melancholy.

I'll never forget this evening, Munch. I've never had so much fun.

The carriage makes it way eastwards through the city. Munch sees the workers already on their way to the morning shift. He leans back. Yes, frøken Drewsen *is* much more beautiful. Why isn't he happy?

He lies in bed tossing and turning. Has just had a dream. Is awake. Knows that he'll be awake until morning. He's not going to give her the satisfaction of having destroyed him. Is he destroyed? Far from it. It'll soon pass. Destroyed on account of her? She'll see that he's more cheerful than ever. He will laugh. He will work. Shout for joy. She'll see his name in the papers. His name. The greatest paintings. *He's* the one they'll be talking about.

* * *

Hans Jæger's novel *From the Christiania Bohemians* comes out on 11 December 1885. It is confiscated at lunchtime the same day. The initiative for the confiscation comes from military doctor Augustus Koren, chairman of the Christiania Association for the Promotion of Morality. Some days earlier, he had been approached by a bookbinder who had taken a closer look at Jaeger's novel. Military doctor Koren knows the law as well as the bookbinder. He who scorns or mocks God's holy Word or Sacraments, or otherwise mocks the official State religion, shall be sentenced to imprisonment or to a fine, but if this act occurs in print, he shall be sentenced to the maximum prison term or hard labour in perpetuity.

*

Strindberg's *Married* confiscated in Sweden. *From the Christiania Bohemians* confiscated in Norway. Scandal. The novel about Johan Seckmann Fleischer, a student at the military academy, who on the Wednesday after Easter Monday 1884 the previous year had stood on Tjuvholmen, loaded a revolver, cocked it, felt the touch of cold steel against the roof of his mouth, and stood legs apart to support himself when he pulled the trigger. Fleischer, the suicide candidate, painfully aware of his wasted life, his miserable wasted life, the ability to live withered for want of the right conditions. The hopeless emptiness, instead of a free, open life together among free, open men and women who only recognized one rule for social life, which was love, freedom and worldly happiness. The Bohemians' last commandment: Thou *shalt* take thine own life. A suicide which was virtually ordered and arranged by Jaeger, so that he could later write the book about Fleischer's death. Naïve Fleischer who, after a summer in the mountains, told his mother that the farm girls had let him sleep with them. A young man quite unable to control his own life. But Jaeger took control of it and led him to disaster. At his friend's burial, he had stood there taking down the priest's funeral address in shorthand so as to be able to reproduce it in his book. Now the military doctor reads about the scandalous novel in *Aftenposten*.

Have you seen it, Edvard?

Yes.

And are you still going about with that Jaeger?

He does not answer.

Some hours later, he is sitting at the Grand with Jaeger and Nyhus. So it's a crime to write a novel, is it? Expressing thoughts one is not allowed to think? According to the prosecuting authority, Jaeger has depicted sexual intercourse between men and women. Scenes from brothels and other dens of iniquity. Immoral dreams and ideas. Conversations about sexual matters in a manner which far exceeds the bounds of the permissible.

The whole city regards him with abhorrence. From the street the upright men and women of the bourgeoisie gawp through the café window with cold, glowering looks. Munch looks down.

Have you any cash on you, Munch? Enough for a whisky and soda?

Skint. Not so much as a farthing between them. They all turn their pockets out. Nothing left to pawn. No overcoats or watches left.

Munch is suddenly overcome with rage. He lifts his eyes and stares back. Jaeger is better than all those gawping people put together.

* * *

He notices that her eyes have taken on a certain hardness. Heavens, what had he just said? She unties her hair, allowing it to cascade down her back with a gesture of impatience.

That wasn't fair of me, he adds. I didn't mean to go that far.

Fru Thaulow does not answer.

He puts his arms round her neck. More excuses. He hadn't meant it. What on earth had possessed him to say it?

She meets his gaze. The burning eyes. An explosion of grey and green. He feels mean and wretched. Then she pulls him towards her. She kisses him on the neck, lays her naked white body on top of him.

She mustn't go now. He's aroused as never before. She has never stayed so long with him. He must embrace her once more, kiss her again. The embers are still glowing.

But she gets up from the bed. There she stands between the easel and the mirror putting her hair up. What is it about the way she looks at him? Something hard. He hadn't meant to say it. But why is she taking so long? An unusually lengthy toilet. She is arranging her hair like a queen.

Winter in Christiania. As though the darkness will never end. Fru Thaulow emerges from the darkness and melts back into it. Like all the unknown faces on Karl Johan. Suddenly he sees them, just as he had seen Sophie. All of them bear within them their own moment of death. They go down the street from Parliament on their way towards death. The gaping graves lie there waiting. It could be tomorrow. It could be in a year. In twenty or forty years perhaps. But come it will. They walk down from Parliament. Down towards death.

* * *

Suddenly one day it is spring. The light returns to the sky. Completely different colours. Munch comes back home from Karl Johan. Not a glimpse of her today either.

I think I'm going to have to get a new spring overcoat, mutters Munch.

Yes, let me come with you, says Aunt Karen. We'll go to Sem's. He's so cheap.

He goes with her to the shop. Aunt Karen goes straight to the wall where all the overcoats hang on display.

This one, Edvard. It's hard-wearing and warm. And it's cheap as well. Only twenty crowns.

He tries it on. What would fru Thaulow have said? The broad shoulders. As though he's suspended on a coathanger.

Isn't it a bit too big?

No. You look so well in it.

He doesn't want to disappoint her. She seems so happy. And it's a good many crowns cheaper than the others.

Around lunchtime, he saunters up the street. He looks at his reflection in the large shop windows. Oh no! It *is* too large!

And here she comes! A long way down on the opposite pavement, with her ladyfriends. He stands paralysed beside the shop window. Then she catches sight of him. He tries to blend into the throng of people on the pavement. Too late. There he stands in the gigantic overcoat. A balloon. As though at any moment he might rise up from the pavement. Now they are nodding. Saying hello. He must doff his hat.

Krag, an acquaintance, stops all of a sudden:

It's too big, that overcoat of yours.

Really? D'you think so?

Krag snorts. There he stands with Didriksen, gaping.

So Munch's got a woman, has he? See it in his eyes, don't you know. Bit of a glow in them.

Munch takes his leave and walks quickly east. He crosses the river.

Not quite spring, yet even so. An icy north wind. Dangerous for the lungs.

He draws his coat more tightly around him.

* * *

Then something happens. A clear thought suddenly cuts through the feverishness like an icicle. As though everything has actually led to this moment. It's just that he couldn't see it till now. As though fru Thaulow has made him forget, so that he could one day see with new eyes, see what is most familiar, see the most terrible thing of all. He's in the studio, standing at his easel, when he suddenly remembers a conversation at the hotel in Åsgårdstrand. Heyerdahl was talking. Lovely turpentine, juicy paraffin. Turpentine and paraffin are good, equally good, give such a delightful surface to scrape in. I always scrape first and paint afterwards. But at different times you see with different eyes. In the morning you see differently from in the evening. But he wants to paint just as it looked when the motif first struck him. The naturalist painters said it was dishonest to paint like this. They said that trying to reproduce a mood was painting dishonestly. A chair can be just as interesting as a person. But the chair must be seen by a person! In some way or other it must have moved him and he must make sure the observer is moved in the same way!

Suddenly he knows what it was he saw: He was barely fourteen years old. Suddenly one night the military doctor had stood beside the bed again. A voice in the dark:

You must get up now, boys.

They knew without being told, got up and dressed, silently, without saying a word.

Then they went in to her room.

Sophie lay there in the room which was now a sickroom. At fifteen she was the eldest. She was a grownup girl, used a parasol and had been on a trip to Fredrikstad. She had made sketches, just like her brother. And she was so passionate about everything, the wallpaper, the old furniture, the view from the window. Now her cheeks were hot with fever, her eyes shining. But she didn't want to lie in bed. She wanted to sit in the chair.

They could hear the military doctor's mild, gentle voice:

Do you really want to live, Sophie?

They heard her reply 'yes'.

Then the military doctor cleared his throat and went on: Dearest Sophie, there's something I have to say . . . The Lord will soon be taking you unto Him.

And the Lord heard those words, and took Sophie up to heaven, where her mother already sat waiting for her. She leaned forward, saying she felt tired, wanted to go back to bed. At that moment it was all over.

They carried her from the chair where she died back to the bed. Her limp arms hung down lifeless, her head lolling from side to side.

Munch sees a chair and sees who was sitting in it. He starts to paint *Study. The Sick Child*. Sophie's pale face with the flaming red hair against the white pillow. The translucent skin, as though illuminated by the canvas. The trembling mouth. The limp hands. At last he knows what he wants to paint. *The Sick Child*. The same title as Eugène Carrière's monumental oil painting, with the fat child in the mother's lap, the pet dog and the two sisters.

Betzy Nielsen is sitting for him. The servant girl from home. Now he's making her into his own sister. He wants to find a way to express what moves him. He scrapes with knife or spatula. Gustave Courbet has shown him the way. So has Hans Heyerdahl. Lovely turpentine, juicy paraffin. But impressionism is not expressive enough. He is groping for the term, expressionism, that's it. And he recalls Jæger's words. Youth is modern when *through its own life* it has come to the realization that the circumstances under which it has grown up have hampered and crippled its development, thereby making it a worse youth, in human terms, than it might otherwise have been. Youth which has come to this realization *through its own life* and which therefore seeks a transformation of the circumstances, a transformation which can deliver coming generations from the need to suffer the same fate, *such* youth is modern.

Munch paints the death of his sister. He paints the red hair, the trembling mouth, the thin, bony hands. Countless attempts. It is the moment just before death. What the devil does he care about likeness? It's the tired movement he wants to bring out. The movement, which is not actually there, but which all the same is what the picture is about. Everything that cannot be measured. The almost imperceptible movement of the eyelids, the lips which must look as though they are whispering. Yes, she must look as though she is breathing. Life, that which is alive, the diametrical opposite of Krohg, a picture of nervous construction through and through, a cubistic, colourless picture. What the devil does he care whether the chair is properly painted!

It is a bold experiment. He stands in the studio, painting with a kind of inner rage. He scrapes away with knife or spatula, driven on by the lies. But it's the truth he wants. A picture of life in all its brutality. His sister Sophie sitting in the chair, on the seventh of November 1877, in a draughty apartment on Fossveien. She leans forward, suddenly feeling so tired. Her face flushed with fever. Wide-eyed, her pupils shining. Munch discovers that his own eyelashes influence the way he sees the picture. He intimates them in the form of shadows round the motif, framing it in tears. Wavy lines, peripheries, appear. He paints the subject over and over again. Thinned paint runs down the surface of the painting in dense stripes, in pastose layers of colour. He builds up the picture according to a geometrical plan consisting of a number of squares.

It is autumn 1886. While Munch stands in his studio, Hans Jæger is making his statement in the Supreme Court:

But this naturalistic literature is bound to seem ugly. Ugly and nasty in the eyes of the good folk who take decency, rather than life, to be the yardstick of literature. Such naturalistic writing is penned with steaming human blood. The characters which leap out at you from the pages of these works are alive, alive with the life of reality. Touch them and feel. They are alive beneath your fingertips. They are fashioned from living human flesh. It is the red blood of reality that courses through their veins. Place your hand on them wherever you will and feel: life pulses through every fibre beneath the skin. Listen! You'll hear the beat of their hearts. They are living people. The pulse of warm, living humanity. The pulse of life itself, your honours, which leaps out at you from the pages of these works, which lives beneath your hands. And every time you have finished with one of them, you have lived one human life more than when you began. In just a few short hours you have imbibed all that worldly wisdom which someone else has had to pay for with his life. And reading such literature should be banned, should it? Madness, your honours! It would be read like no literature ever was before. It is penned with steaming human blood!

* * *

My congratulations, Munch. It is your pictures that will create the greatest stir at the Autumn Exhibition this year.

Munch is standing in the street with the chairman of the jury.

Really? And what about *Study*? Does it work?

Heavens, yes. It knocks all the others into a cocked hat. Yes, I think it's magnificent.

Munch thanks him and goes on his way. Then he spies his colleagues.

What did he say, Munch? Have you been accepted?

Yes. He thought it was brilliant.

I think it's way below the mark, Munch. It's rubbish. Not suitable material.

Material? What the devil do I care about material? As I've said, what I'm trying to capture is the tired movement of the eyelids. The lips should look as though they're whispering ...

You'll go mad, Munch, if you carry on like this. All you ever talk about is your paintings; you don't care two hoots about other people.

To hell with you!

And what are all those streaks for? It looks as though it's raining.

Munch turns his back on them, hears their laughter but continues on his way and turns into the Grand.

There he sees Jæger.

Congratulations, Munch. I hear your painting's magnificent.

Bringing any of *your* lot along with you to the opening?

No, I'm not. It would be embarrassing for them. They find the painting frightful.

Jæger laughs.

Shall we walk up there together then?

Yes, let's.

Munch sits drinking with Jæger till midday. Then they walk up to the Museum of Sculpture together.

There is a terrible crush outside the building. Where's Jæger got to? Munch goes in.

Then he sees the painting. It's hanging right in front of him. A splendid position. Perfectly lit. The streaks are very apparent. There's already a crowd in front of the painting. He glances round, strides quickly through the throng of people, straining to catch comments. Who is that laughing? He thinks he clearly heard the word 'terrible'. Yes, there it is again. Unmistakable. Terrible. It rings in his ears. A familiar face. Where's Jæger got to? At any rate, there's Hansen the painter. With a laugh Munch says:

I've just forced my way through the crush. They seem to think it's terrible.

Yes, they think you're mad.

Munch's smile disappears. And what do *you* think?

I think it's poor. I don't understand it.

Munch smiles. Don't you? So Hansen doesn't understand it. He moves on. Where has Jæger got to? At any rate, there's Meyer, the lawyer.

Hello, Meyer. What do you think?

Meyer offers his hand. Munch shakes it.

Congratulations, Munch. The expression in the face. It's so full of life. There's such sorrow in that face.

*

Munch goes outside. There's Wentzel. The naturalist. Cousin Wentzel. What does it matter to Munch that, day after day, he wears himself out on those horrible pictures of his, crude and coarse, like a bear playing the piano with its great big paws? Now the time has come, after all the years of backbiting, gossip, malicious talk. Wentzel stands there with his disciples. Fêted as the popular artist of the day, darling of the museums, at the pinnacle of his career. Here he comes towards Munch now.

Painter? Humbug more like! Wentzel shouts, right into his face.

Munch turns on his heel and walks away. He is stung to the quick. What a damn cheek! And from Wentzel of all people, who can't paint the wood for the trees. But what of the scandal? What will she think? Then he sees Aubert. Who else? Andreas Aubert. He's an old acquaintance, after all. As long ago as 1882 Aubert had shown him his own attempts at painting, a still life and a few landscapes and interiors. Now he's ready to tell the truth about Munch, drawing on all the knowledge and insight which failed to make him a painter, but instead made him a critic on *Morgenbladet*, where he writes:

> For Munch's own sake, therefore, I hoped his sick child would be rejected. Not because it is less indicative of his talent than previous works. But because it reveals such a slapdash approach to his own development as a painter. In its present form, this *Study* is no more than an abandoned, half-scraped-out sketch. He has grown tired of it himself while working on it. It is an abortion, like those so brilliantly depicted by Zola in *L'Œuvre*.

*

Others add their voices to the chorus of derision. An artistic failure. A personal insult to the critics. Trash! It is a scandal that such rubbish should be allowed to hang here! It is tripe served up as art!

*

Here comes Jæger at last. It is the twentieth of October 1886. He is to go to prison the following day. In his commentary on Munch's picture in *Dagen*, he writes:

> Then I moved on but stopped dead in my tracks. It was Munch's *Sick Child,* over to the right of the door leading to the adjoining room. What delicate, muted colours! Hush! Quiet! you feel tempted to whisper to the chattering folk around you, and *Hush!* is what Munch ought to have called his picture. It's a disgrace to exhibit such stuff, I heard someone say beside me as I stood there looking at it. I recognized the voice and looked up. It was an acquaintance of mine, a rather feeble chap who usually has a great deal to say on the subject of art and beauty. Do you really feel nothing when you look at this painting? I asked. No. But don't you see the beauty in the colours either? No. It's a complete disgrace. He glanced round, pointing in another direction. And what are these? These funny stripes here running down Munch's painting? asked the fellow after a while. He too had started to look

at it again. They're pure genius, those broad streaks running down, that's what they are. He gave a snort of contempt. I'll tell you how this painting came into being, I added. First the fellow made a sketch, and in the sketch he showed what it was he was after. In other words, the mood you don't feel at all. The next step was to transform the sketch into a painting. But as he was doing so, the mood evaporated, so Munch put all his energy into painting the whole thing all over again and managed to recapture the mood. Then he wanted to repaint it, but destroyed the whole lot again. And so on and so on about twenty times. In the end, he just had to throw in the sponge and make do with the sketch. True enough, it hasn't managed to achieve form. Great streaks run down the poor failed painting. But what Munch has given us in this sketch is something that cannot be taught. What he did not succeed in doing – that, at least, can be taught.

* * *

Evening in October. There has just been a downpour. The deserted street stretches away into the darkness between shiny wet pavements which reflect the glow of the gaslamps in wavy yellow lines, quivering in black. A cab with raised hood turns into Møllergaten from Grensen and trundles noisily away over the cobbles in the empty street. There in the deep shadow beneath the raised hood sit Krohg and Jæger, each hunched into their own corner, smoking cigars and gazing ahead past the coachman perched up on the driver's seat as gaslamp after gaslamp glides past.

Jæger is on his way to gaol to serve his sixty-day sentence. Munch will visit Jæger often in his cell. For a while, cell No. 1, a small white-washed brick cell with a carpeted floor, immediately beside the guard's cell, serves as the editorial office of the Bohemians' publication *The Impressionist*. Heyerdahl's little black Anna, naked to the waist, also comes here, brought up from Blomqvist's by delivery boy No. 44. It is here that Munch's *Hulda* or *The Morning After* hangs, naked to the waist, reclining on the bed, one hand under her head, her other arm trailing, her black hair tumbling in a dishevelled mass above one shoulder.

Jæger certainly knows how to make himself comfortable. When Munch comes to visit him, cell No. 1 has curtains, assorted paintings, and an antique Black Forest clock with weights and pendulum.

*

It is now that Munch paints *Puberty*. A young girl sits naked and shivering on the edge of the bed with puny little breasts. She clamps her legs tight together concealing her womanhood behind them, showing her vulnerability in the face of everything now about to befall her.

It is that long anguish, that time before life begins in earnest.

* * *

At home the clock ticks.

The military doctor is sitting on the sofa with his bald pate and long pipe reading *Aftenposten*.

That critique of you was nasty, Edvard, says Aunt Karen.

Munch glances at his father, who nods in approval.

Outrageous. You just can't write that sort of thing.

His father glances up from the paper.

Are you still visiting Jæger in prison?

Munch nods. He meets his father's eyes peering at him over his spectacles. That mild face is not made to be angry, it is made for poetry and legend. Munch is aware that he knows all there is to know about diseases, but he's an artist by nature really, with a nervous disposition, and he's also a reputed storyteller. He took part in the 'theatre battle' in Christiania in 1838, on the side of Wellhaven. He was there to hear the supporters of Wergeland cry with one voice: Down with Munch and all he stands for! He is the brother of a celebrated historian who lies buried in Rome. He was working in Løten for the Østerdal Chasseur Corps when he found his beloved Laura Cathrine Bjølstad at Alfheim farm in Elverum and assured her that they would probably get along very well but that the Lord must be their intermediary, must always accompany them into their home. He knew that there was sickness in her family. Both Laura's mother and one of her sisters had died of tuberculosis at a tender age and Christian Munch was himself riddled with anxiety and utterly at sea in all things practical. He couldn't so much as buy a mattress.

Munch suddenly sees that his father looks old. He is burdened by a deep sorrow, atoning for a punishment beyond his understanding, has lost both wife and eldest child. Now he is worried about the massive 'flu epidemics which are claiming so many lives. He sits there on the sofa with his long-stemmed pipe, trying to make it up with his eldest son.

Sixty days was a bit much, Edvard. Tell me, how *is* Jæger, actually?

* * *

The first issue of the Bohemians' journal *The Impressionist* comes out the same day, the twentieth of December 1886, as Christian Krohg's book *Albertine* is confiscated. It is the story of a seamstress driven to prostitution because of a lecherous policeman. The worst thing about the book, in the eyes of the Minister of Justice, is not that it points the finger at the social misery rife among the young girls of Christiania, but its assertion that a police officer could act dishonestly.

No longer are the Bohemians isolated individuals dissatisfied with social conditions, who frequent the Grand or Gravesen's. They are a political movement which, at a given moment, might well have a major impact. Jæger is the logician and Krohg the organizer.

Albertine is a carefully planned provocation. Krohg has painted a series of pictures and written a novel. But who is she? Jæger asks. She is a pale young woman's face glimpsed fleetingly in the gloom then gone forever.

For Jæger is not impressed by his friend's work: Where exactly did you see it, Krohg? You've never actually been down there, have you? What do *you* know about life as it is lived down in the gloomy depths under our very feet, where misery thrives and people live and move, unhappy and yearning upwards towards sun and air, what do *you* know about that? You've never actually been down there. You may now and then have caught the sound of sighs rising up from there. Those deep long sighs, which run like a gentle shudder through the thin crust of the ground we walk on, betraying how wafer thin it is. And perhaps you've ventured as far as the entrance to this nether world just to peep down into it. And you've seen the pale face loom forth from the gloom down there, raise two doomed eyes up to the light of day and then vanish. My God, didn't you realize that it could never work? Aren't you the one, Krohg, who never tires of telling your students that they must paint from nature? Then you go home and paint a studio picture out of your head! And are you not the one who claims to be an impressionist? Then what you give us is *not* the impression you really had, no, but the whole life of a person you've never known and who you could therefore never have had an impression of either! You've painted it so we'll see it. I've seen her sitting at the window, seen Albertine bent over the sewing machine, beneath the pale winter daylight which seeps in, pondering her fate, as the Old Woman prepares the meal over by the stove in the corner and little Edvard, coughing and spluttering, reads *Dagen* at her side. I've lived part of these people's lives, down there in that stuffy room painted blue, where the stink of consumption and poverty and the smell of food mingle to form a heavy, oppressive atmosphere. I have followed Albertine out of the stuffy room into the pastures of life and seen her struggle against her fate, slip, fall and begin the struggle all over again. Until suddenly with a crash the ground is pulled from under her feet. Her female modesty dies. She loses her foothold and tumbles over the precipice down into the mire where we eventually find her. But as a disciple of naturalism, I demand to see something more, and this something more is the essential. I demand that you show me her emerging from the soil where she has her roots. I want to see her grow up among the people she really grew up amongst. See her broken by poverty, ignorance and prejudice. What she feels, what she thinks, what she wants.

We *must* be allowed to see it, in all its loathsomeness, this destructive process that takes place in Albertine, after her female modesty is shamefully killed off and, passive and uncaring, she slides down the slippery slope into the pit where she ends up. I must insist that we see it, this process of destruction, in *all* its loathsome horror.

* * *

Munch is on his way to the studio. Suddenly he catches sight of fru Thaulow in the street. All his anger evaporates. The hatred which had seethed in him. She was supposed to have been at the exhibition, wasn't she? They were supposed to have gone there together. Had she been frightened off by the malicious reviews? Did she hear the laughter even outside, in the street?

I've been ill, she says.

Oh really? And are you better now?

Yes. I'm fine now.

So again he walks by her side. As though there was still hope after all. He knows full well she is lying. She has lied the whole time. She has come to him and he has believed her words, her kisses, believed in the expression on her face when she has looked at him sorrowfully, begging him to believe her.

The galoshes splash in the slush. Drips fall from the roofs. A southwest wind. The smell of damp, steaming clothes.

You didn't come to the exhibition, says Munch.

Oh yes I did. I went with Lieutenant Lund.

So she *had* been with him! And when for so long he had hoped that the rumour might prove false. That his eyes could be mistaken. That what he had seen with his own eyes had not actually happened at all. Several times now he'd seen them together in the street. He'd also seen the Captain. Had gone out under cover of darkness to tail them.

So you didn't have a secret assignation with him that time at the Art Association?

He hears that his voice sounds hard.

Don't be angry, she says, pulling out a handkerchief. I'm so dreadfully unhappy.

They are at the corner of Dronningensgate. Suddenly here comes the Captain. Munch recognizes the pale face of the lady-killer of Karl Johan. Only a shadow of his former self now.

Good day, Captain Thaulow.

Good day, Munch.

Side by side they walk along the pavement. Munch thinks it terrible to be walking there with him, with *her* sandwiched between them.

They pause at the tram stop. She and the Captain are probably going up to Pilestredet to take care of some business matters. The

Captain offers him his hand in farewell. An elegant white hand. Munch shakes it, looks down at his own blue, frozen hand covered in flecks of paint. He notices that he has dirty nails. Then fru Thaulow puts out her hand. A wave of fury sweeps over him.

What about all the others? he says roughly.

She withdraws her hand, taken aback.

Which others?

He's got her now and takes his time over his reply.

Oh, I could name quite a few. Stang, for instance. Hambro, the actor. Then there's Kristoffersen. The literary man.

She says nothing, merely looks down into the slush wearing a fixed expression as she speaks.

He knows he's overstepped the mark.

* * *

He is twenty-three, it's too soon to pack it all in and put a bullet through his head. The calendar says 1887, the year Munch spends the summer at Veierland outside Tønsberg. For Munch, Veierland will become Alpha and Omega's island, the island of the first people, the place where the first woman deceives the first man with lower and yet lower species, a motif. Munch was subsequently to deal with it on many occasions, at the psychiatric clinic too. 1887. The year he paints *Law*, *Holmboe* and *Flowering Meadow*, shows six paintings at the Autumn Exhibition, the year five thousand workers, on Sunday 16th January, gather on Stortorvet beneath the banners of the Workers' Organizations in protest at the confiscation of *Albertine*. This is a massive demonstration of public support, of the sort Jæger never had. All Jæger got was seven hundred unshaven, unkempt students from the country who stood there bawling their opposition to the confiscation in the Student Liberal Organization. But these are five thousand organized workers. As one man they march to Stiftsgården. A deputation to Prime Minister Sverdrup. But according to the newspaper *Verdens Gang*, Sverdrup squanders so much of the Norwegian people's affection and respect that he will not easily be able to win it back. The confiscation and the summons against Krohg are upheld.

*

Some months later, Jæger receives a further summons. In collaboration with the printer Christian Holtermann Knudsen he has tried to distribute his confiscated novel in Sweden under the title *Christmas Stories*. This time the penalty is harsher. On the twentieth of June Jæger is sentenced to a hundred and fifty days' prison and a fine of sixteen hundred crowns. In November, the sentence is upheld by the Supreme Court.

One hundred and fifty days in cell No. 1, with its great black iron grille surrounded by its wooden frame painted in prison yellow and with a small prison yellow table beneath it, the two longer walls with their dismal bare white bricks. Another hundred days? Suddenly, he can't face the thought of it.

In cahoots with Christian Krohg, Jæger flees the country and makes for Paris. He is already deeply emotionally involved with his close friend Krohg's future wife, the painter Ottilia-Oda Engelhart.

This marks the beginning of the end of the Bohemians as a political movement. Is it because she received his first kiss that she steals the sweetness of life from him, is it because she lies and deceives, as he writes, that suddenly one day she tears the scales from his eyes, so that he sees the head of Medusa, the ogress of Greek mythology, a jelly-like polyp shaped like a lampshade or a bell or a freely floating Portuguese man o'war, that he sees life as pure horror, that everything which previously had a rosy hue now looks grey and hollow, that he sees all the people behind their masks, the calm smiling masks, that he sees their naked fear, everywhere sees suffering, a throng of pale corpses, still alive, like a glimmer of light in eternity, as they scurry hither and thither, along a circuitous path, towards their own deaths, towards an open, waiting grave? Is it because he thinks of her day and night, pacing up and down the street, waiting? It is still light, the sun has only just slipped down behind the Palace sharply silhouetted against the limpid air. Spring is just round the corner. Here she is! A wave of desire runs through him, why is he so easily carried away, the air is soft, warm and humid, he feels strangely languid, the head a touch mournful, the bare neck, the pale slightly plump face, terribly pale in the yellow afterglow from the horizon, a touch garish against all the blue. He stops her, tells her that she is the only one for him, that he is mad, idiotic, that he has never deserved any love, that he has had the highest regard for her and that everything is his fault. He tries to hold on to one thought, but his head is just emptiness. Tries to fix his eyes on a window high up. Now I'm going to fall, he thinks. This vertigo. It must not happen. Now he falls, and people stop. More and more people gather round. A great crowd of people.

* * *

It is a cramped, stuffy room. The daylight falls in harshly onto the table, which is oily and sticky from beer and punch. Imagine if his aunt could see him now. Or the military doctor. Or his sister Inger.

Munch is in Jæger's territory, in Jæger's rooms, among Jæger's women. The whores of Vika. A few minutes of bought happiness. He feels disgusted. A cold blue light falls over the bed and the sheets. The woman has plump arms. Her breasts are large and exposed. No sparkle in her eyes, other than what comes from drink.

The brothel.

He wonders whether she is unhappier than he is. Suddenly he asks her whether her father is still alive. Yes, he lives in Sandviken, probably thinks she's in Christiania working as a maid. But she's damned if she's going to work as a servant, not on your nellie.

Her voice is coarse. She dangles a leg over the edge of the feather quilt. Hasn't a trace of modesty. Does Munch know Kran and Lieu-tenant Verner? Nice lads. They'd been to see her yesterday bringing beer and champagne. Kran sang student songs.

Oleane. The finest lass of all. According to Kran, that is.

Good enough to bloody well eat, that lad, and no mistake.

Munch watches her as she speaks.

Don't want to make love then? It'll not take but half an hour. Ha ha ha. Don't you fancy a bit?

She digs him with her bare leg.

More beer. He takes another swig from the glass. Then he pays and takes his hat.

Goodbye, he says, taking her hand.

Come back tonight?

I may well at that.

*

She was repulsive. The image of fru Thaulow hovers before him, more seductive, more tempting than ever. He clenches his teeth, is filled with intense hatred, not so much of her, not really sure of whom. But it's fru Thaulow's lips he sees. He feels that she has done him a terrible wrong.

Destroyed, though? Destroyed because of her? Anything but! No, she's going to see that he looks happier than ever. He's really going to get down to it. She'll see his name in the papers. It will be on every-body's lips. He'll have the last laugh.

* * *

Again he stands by the fence, at the gate.

It's a Sunday morning with brilliant sunshine on the west side of the Oslo Fjord.

Fields and meadows. Brown, red and white houses. Forest running from Borre to Åsgårdstrand. The sea glitters, blue and white.

He's in his own landscape, where it all happened. Once again he has walked over Church Hill, over to the russet-coloured house.

She looks pale, even though it's summer. He leans against the fence beside the gate.

Well, well, Ma'am, and how are *you*?

Very well, thank you, fru Thaulow replies, squinting against the sun.

Munch registers the fact that her skin looks grey and dingy in the bright light.

48

As for himself, he's in a splendid mood. Very happy. Revenge is simmering away within him. It's been a while now. There have been other women. Pretty girls. Far prettier than her.

Still in our morning coat, are we? He looks at her and laughs. He hasn't laughed all that often in her company. She doesn't seem to appreciate his cheerfulness much.

Well, I'd better be on my way. He does his best to look secretive.

Suddenly she stoops and picks a flower from the grass.

Here you are. Would you like it?

Thank you.

He takes it without looking at it. Exactly what she did before. How many yellow flowers has she handed out to her lovers?

Well, goodbye for now, he says, making a deep reverence with his hat. We'll no doubt be seeing one another.

*

Fru M. is also on holiday in these parts. She's a beauty if ever there was one. Munch accompanies her to the bathing hut. As usual, she's wearing her bright summer costume. Then they pass fru Thaulow's house.

Munch catches a glimpse of her. That's a dress he knows only too well. He walks along with fru M. through the forest down to the shore.

All of a sudden a bellow is heard from the priest's bad-tempered bull. Fru M. gives a shriek of fright. Munch takes a step towards the bull, lifts his cane, and at that very moment sees fru Thaulow behind them on the hill, on her way down to the shore for a swim, just like them.

The bull shies away from the thin little cane. Munch knows the animal well from previous encounters. He knows it's not dangerous. After a few moments, it dashes off into the forest uttering tremendous bellows. But he sets off in hot pursuit in order to cut a figure.

When he returns hot and sweating to fru M., fru Thaulow has joined them. All three of them walk down to the shore, Munch chattering away cheerfully to fru M.

The ladies want to change, but the key to the bathing hut is too high up. Fru Thaulow cannot reach it.

Come on, says Munch to fru M. You're the lightest. I'll lift you up so you can reach it.

Fru M. gathers her dress around her.

He puts his arms round her hips.

*

He lies down on the grass a little way off as they undress.

There is movement in the bathing hut. Suddenly the whole window is filled with something light. He sees that it is fru Thaulow. She is naked, standing there still as a statue. Her hair, which she has let down, tumbles over her breasts. He looks down then turns away.

*

Fru Thaulow looks cold after bathing. Munch sees that she looks almost forlorn.

Fru M. has gone on ahead.

For a long time he says nothing.

Well, well, so this is how it all turned out.

She does not reply.

You surely haven't forgotten how close we were during the winter, he says.

No, I haven't, she says softly.

Strange how that love of yours could come to such an abrupt end, he says. When did it end actually? Sometime around Christmas?

She flashes a look of defiance at him.

It lasted much longer than that. That fringe suits you, by the way. You used to wear your hair long.

Did you know who I was before we met?

Yes. I'd noticed you many a time. I thought you looked like Christ.

But that last time, why didn't you come? I'd made the studio look so inviting.

She looks down. Isn't she going to answer?

So who was the unhappy one then? she mutters at last.

*

But when evening comes, he feels the same old unease. He is drawn there. The russet-coloured house stands there dark among the trees.

But the garden now has a gloomy air about it.

There, beneath the tree by the gate, they always used to say farewell.

He stands there for a moment, overwhelmed by memories.

Then the window opens. Bright yellow light floods out into the vast blue darkness.

He sees the shadow of her head.

Don't you recognize me, Munch?

Who is it? Oh yes. Now I see who it is. I was just taking a little evening stroll. Didn't mean to disturb you. Goodnight then, Ma'am.

* * *

Munch is showing six paintings in the Autumn Exhibition. In *Dagbladet* on Sunday 6 November Andreas Aubert is on the job as art critic:

> By accepting such works as Munch's *Genre* and *From Arendal*, the jury displays an insouciance which merely confuses the public's idea of art. They don't know whether to take it seriously or as a jest. True, in the latter of these two travesties you can see a

sensitivity to colour which is characteristic of all that is finest in Munch's talent. Yet there are limits to how much formlessness can be tolerated in a public exhibition. Incidentally, it is strange to observe how the picture has improved of late. It has settled down, become less speckled, and certain fortuitous elements have vanished. This is the Zombie's doing. Munch's better self. He has been there early in the morning making changes.

* * *

He never shies away from any subjects, not the ones he *must* paint. He does not shy away from Laura, his youngest sister but one, when she is struck by the sun's rays, by the sun of Ibsen's Osvald, by her paternal heritage, by a weakness of the nerves.

*

Oh to arrive at Åsgårdstrand on a summer's day!

*

The Munch family has rented a house on the fjord. Laura is sitting outside the house gazing at the sea. Her diary is brimming with Skrefsrud. One day she trailed the missionary from church to church. It was a religious as well as an erotic obsession. But Munch has been in Copenhagen. He has studied Bastien Lepage and closely observed the dry colouring. Now he is painting Laura. She sits dispirited to the left of the picture, beyond reach of her surroundings. Her hands, joined at the palms, are like two clubs. She is sitting outside the house in Åsgårdstrand, has set out on a voyage of the mind, with an air of being far older than her years. She has not absorbed what it was she once saw, has not acquired the necessary distance. She sits there as the daughter of the dead mother, sister of the dead Sophie and of Munch who is painting her.

*

Aftenposten writes: The whole thing is so indescribably dire in every respect that it borders on the comical. For the members of the jury to admit such pictures to the exhibition betrays either a total misconception of their task and their duty or a total lack of artistic understanding, merely serving to lower our art in the public esteem, just as the young artists are confused and led astray by it.

* * *

The group that calls itself the Bohemians, which has issued its own journal since 1886, written books that were confiscated, formulated ten commandments aimed at the children of the future born too soon to profit from them, is to split up.

*

It is the summer of 1888. Jæger has returned to Norway to serve his sentence and to meet Oda. No one had dared predict that Jæger and Krohg, those radical colossi, would this year have to go their separate ways on account of a woman, that suddenly they no longer speak of free love, of naturalism, of lived life and the revolution as a logical extension of insight and experience, but of marriage, civil marriage, of which of them will lose the battle for Oda, of which of them will be the first to blow his brains out with a pistol. They are two utterly paralysed men, with a woman teetering on the edge of a nervous breakdown between them.

Jæger's love for Oda is all or nothing. Logic has given way to blind desire. Marry me, Oda! The scandal could scarcely have been greater. Free love. An idea which has already disintegrated into lies and deception. No longer is Jæger the almost glacial utopian ideologue, who can carry on virtually any debate, with Sverdrup, with Aimar Sørenssen, Minister of Justice, with the Supreme Court, only ultimately, in the hour of defeat, to conclude: faced with the emotional logic which leads you to such a finding, I am completely powerless.

Now Jæger is powerless because of his feelings, while Krohg plays Russian roulette with pistol bullets.

Let me put an end to it all!

No, it is *I* who should die if she doesn't love me.

But it's you she loves, you fool!

Krohg has won that most coveted prize, the Attorney General's daughter, has cuckolded Engelhart, the business magnate, rushed further still along the path to celebrity, to becoming all-powerful, has set his sights on doing away with prostitution, has accused police officials of debauchery, paints glossy pictures, ever on the side of the young, the future. But Oda has suddenly made an old man of him.

Munch listens and learns. The colossus Krohg. In a few years, he will stand in a café, look out over the throng of Oda's lovers and shout in bitter triumph:

Last night I cuckolded *the lot* of you!

It is the husband's sweet revenge over all the lovers. For he is still married to her, is married to her the whole time, regardless of what she gets up to. He makes no demands. Just waits. Patiently. Certain that the tide will come to his rescue. He knows all about ebb and flow. He is sure that she will come back sooner or later. By then Munch has long since lost respect for him. By then Krohg has in Munch's eyes become a snail slithering about with a whorehouse on its back.

* * *

Munch sits with Jæger at the Grand. There is amber-coloured liquid in their glasses. Beer and whisky and soda. Outside the sun is shining. Women and young ladies promenade with their parasols. A lieutenant nods to a veiled woman dressed in black. Merchant Krag raises his hat to a colleague. A delightful slip of a girl giggles as she catches sight of Jæger in the café window.

So Jæger's to be slung into jail again. Has served his sentence twice over. Is to do penance for his refusal to pay the fine. Prison and captivity just for the sake of a few hundred crowns. He sits on the sofa, ill and weak. Oda and Christian are married now. Herr and fru Krohg. They fled to Skagen in Denmark. Jæger set off in pursuit, but they had already left. They had heard rumours that he was on his way and went into hiding for a few days. All of a sudden he had become their worst enemy.

Then Munch *sees* Hans Jæger. He sees the portrait, the painting, sees him there on the sofa. He sees prison and despair. He sees that the fearless old rebel has been deprived of all hope about the future.

Munch sees a bifurcated face. One side belongs to the cold, clear logician. The other side to the despairing, vulnerable, destroyed lover. The crooked half-smile links the two sides together. He is a defeated man. Munch paints him with his own feelings, with his own impotent desperation. Jæger's due back in jail again tomorrow. He sits there shaken, leaning back on the sofa with the glass before him. He has lost her. Now she is fru Krohg. So he has lost everything. Not just the love of his life, but also people's esteem and his own health. There is no strength left in him. Yet he's still going to carry on biting and barking. For one thing, he's going to write hundreds of pages about her. Three large tomes. And he's going to write the anarchists' bible. Hell and damnation. Soon he'll be sitting there in lodgings, head in hands, mumbling hell and damnation. For he is going to carry on talking nonsense, as he puts it, in spite of everything. There are too many thoughts in that head of his which keep him going. Give him a little time. Give him three million francs.

That is all he needs to make a world revolution.

* * *

It's Sunday morning. The sun is shining on the houses across the street, shining in the windows which cast sunbeams back into the dark studio. Munch is making a trip to Hankø with Nils Hansteen, then on to Vrengen to visit Dörnberger. In the autumn he'll call in at Åsgårdstrand then return to Christiania. Soon it'll be winter. But his friends catch up with him:

Vot, oh, vye should we not drink ven you drink yourself under the table every evening? Prosit, Meisse, you are good to me, and prosit, Bolette!

Munch with the Dörnbergers. The painter and dandy is his friend. But Dörnberger also has a mother and a sister. The whole lot of them make up the mad German-Norwegian set. A foretaste of Berlin.

Accompanied by his mother Augusta Mönch and his sister Meisse, Dörnberger visits Munch in his studio. Dörnberger's mother is the first to speak:

Now ve must have a tot of punch, Meisse, not so? Let's sit down and drink a toast with Munch.

The old and the young woman raise their glasses. The mother starts to get carried away:

Meisse, you have been good to me but Palle he has been nasty the whole time. You have brought me girls into das Haus, Palle, and got drunk every evening. All my friends you have driven for me out of das Haus. *Schämst du dich doch nicht?*

Oh vot, don't talk such drunken nonsense, mother.

Munch listens laughing. Then suddenly he is alone with her.

Listen to me, Meisse my dear. Gravely Munch looks into her eyes. Sometimes I'm so afraid. I don't think I can love anyone ever again. I once loved a woman. I don't think one can love more than one woman. I'm not certain though.

*

But Meisse Dörnberger takes the hint:

My dear Edvard! I shall probably be leaving with the steamer on Thursday the 13th. Shall I write to you at the Grand? It's sure to reach you there. Will you be making a trip down here with S. now? Thank you ever so much for the beautiful half-moon. I can't stop peeping at it in the drawer. So long as the beasts don't blab that we've been in Åsgårdstrand, we're home and dry. I'm so happy I had a chance to see you and spend a little time with you. Do please take care of yourself. I'm writing with a pencil because I smoked an opium cigarette Jappe gave me and started making ink blots all over the page. Farewell then for now. I'm just going downstairs to madam. She's in bed today, you see. Because she was so out of sorts yesterday. Your devoted Meisse.

* * *

Munch has painted *Arrival of the Mailboat*, *Evening* (Laura), his sister *Inger in the Sunshine*, *Mending the Nets*. Then suddenly one winter's day he walks from Slagen to Tønsberg after a rough night with Jørgensen and Strøm, at their digs, giving Strøm a black eye. Still drunk, Munch lurches and staggers about with Dörnberger. They are joking and laughing. All of a sudden, his friend shoves him into a large puddle. Munch walks soaked to the skin and frozen stiff for two hours. No Aunt Karen to make sure that the windows don't let in any draught. He feels the cold making his limbs stiff. He knows that he's going to fall ill now, perhaps really ill.

*

He's delirious. Childhood memories mingle with the sound of the people at his sickbed. He cannot distinguish reality from dream. He can see the church steeple and roofs of houses. Grüner's garden, Old Aker Church and Telthus Hill. He sees a group of blind people walking past. They cling on tight to one another, stumbling down the road. He draws them in chalk on the kitchen floor. Spies a medicine bottle and a dessert spoon which suddenly become something to draw. He sees Sophie's bird, the bullfinch, which didn't understand a thing. He sees his own father trudging rather unsteadily down to the emigrant ships, listening to pulses and heartbeats, shining a feeble match flame into pale eyes. Munch's life began with death. Death came with the icy wind as it stole down along the Aker river. It came to seamstresses, weaving girls, privy emptiers, it came to mothers and brothers and sisters. Christiania. The Siberian city. There was tuberculosis in all their eyes, like fear. Suddenly one night he had woken with his mouth full of blood.

Father, the stuff I'm coughing up is so dark!

Is it, my boy?

The military doctor had fetched a candle to take a closer look at what his son had coughed up, held the handkerchief in the light from the candle and scrutinized it, with his back to him.

Father!

Munch had seen that the military doctor was concealing something.

The blood on the sheet.

Goodness, it *is* blood, father!

Thereupon the military doctor fell to his knees, folded his hands and closed his eyes: May the Lord bless you. May the Lord make his face to shine upon you, May the Lord give you peace.

Towards evening, his fever and his cough had worsened. And he brought up another mouthful of blood.

He spat into his handkerchief. It was red and sticky.

Then he screamed: Father, father, I'm dying!

And the military doctor's answer was: In the name of our Lord Jesus. Don't shout, my boy. I shall pray for you.

The haziness of childhood. Those long walks over to Hakkloa and the lake at Bjørnsjøen together with the other art students. A chemical experiment had ended in a terrible explosion. There he had stood at Christiania Technical School holding some test tubes. That was not what he wanted. He wanted to be a painter. There he sat at the supper table at home at Grünerløkken listening to the sound of knives and forks. He heard the echo of grace float out into the silence and knew that he wanted to be a painter. He had made sketches of his brother and sisters, had painted Aunt Karen looking down as was her habit, Helgelandsmoen sick bay. Now everything is merging together. His nerves. His painter friend's searching look. You look so ill, Munch. Oh?

Do I, Colditz? Yes, you look pale to me. Come on, Colditz, out with it! Do you really think I look so poorly? While the military doctor came home tired and weary from work. Haemorrhages, consumption, foetuses stuck in mothers' wombs. They all merge together for Munch, memories and imaginings, his childhood's long journey from one rented home to another, Aunt Karen's encouragement. She who, when the military doctor proposed to her, had turned down the offer of becoming step-mother to the children, but who carried on living with them and looking after them. Aunt Karen with her moss pictures and the Santal Mission, with her solicitude and her feeling for colour. She who had discovered him lying on the floor drawing the passing group of blind people and who, delighted, had exclaimed: Look what Edvard's done! He is dreaming about her now, about that gentle look of hers and her healing hands.

He lies in Dörnberger's bed for a month.

The large room is enveloped in a dark fog, the lamp on the table casts a kind of reddish glow, it is hard to discern the objects in the room.

He has been slipping in and out of sleep for a long time. Again he can see it from the other side, hear the whispering, try to recognize the faces in the diffuse red light. Is it his own blood or the red lamp?

Ach, he is so poorly, doctor, hasn't eaten a bite the whole day.

Munch can study Doctor Didrichson's eyebrows from the bed. They are always knitted together. These eyebrows suddenly get on his nerves, he hates those who are in the room because they sit there so gravely, hates them because they behave as though at a deathbed.

He looks dreadful, doctor.

Munch makes an effort to talk. So they will understand that he is conscious, so they do not start talking about him as though he were already a corpse.

Yes, this is my worst day yet, he says.

He looks really dreadful, don't you think, doctor?

The doctor nods.

His face is all contorted, isn't it?

The doctor nods again.

Really terrible.

Munch wants to say that he has been through worse before, wants to tell them that he is not dying.

Been worse, he says in a curt, staccato voice from the bed.

He'd make such a good subject to paint, says Dörnberger. All the planes on his face.

Dörnberger takes him by the nose and twists his head from side to side.

Munch is too tired to ask him to desist.

His face is utterly contorted.

Have you written home? Ach no, he does not vant zat. You must write immediately. Dörnberger follows the doctor out. Munch hears the murmur of voices in the hall. Now Dörnberger is asking the doctor. Now he's going to learn the truth. Does he have long to live? It's the doctor with the eyebrows who knows. Dörnberger comes back in. What did the doctor say, he asks Dörnberger. But he doesn't catch his reply. Is too tired. The lamp burns with a soporific light beneath the paper shade.

*

But he brightens up after a while. He writes letters to friends and family. And he receives a letter from his father:

Dear Edvard, Thank you for your letter, even though it upset us greatly to learn that you have been seriously ill. However, I hope that, with God's merciful help, you are now well and truly on the mend. Actually, we've been afraid that all was not well with you. Now you absolutely must take care and not travel before you're ready to and see that you don't catch a chill during the journey home. The best and safest course would be to buy a first class ticket, where the compartments are well heated and you would be as right as rain. We are *tremendously grateful* to Dörnberger's family for being so kind to you. Yesterday was Inger's birthday. We were very surprised that you remembered it, especially as you often don't even remember your own birthday. Do bear in mind what I said about the first class railway ticket. I'll take care of it. God be with you. Your devoted Christian Munch.

* * *

Back to Christiania. Away from the Dörnbergers, from Meisse's passionate looks and the drunken brawls. Back to the studio, work, the picture he calls *Spring*. Back to the chair where his mother and Sophie sat, the chair by the white curtains. Where they sat longing for the sun until death claimed them.

But this time it is a more conventionally painted picture. His mother sits with her knitting. The young girl sits debilitated in the chair waiting for the life-giving rays of the spring sunshine. The curtains are buffeted by the wind. One can well imagine that the wind blowing into the room is cold. Great attention is paid to the detail, as though Munch wishes to counter all accusations of artistic sloppiness.

He issues invitations to a one-man show in the Student Society's small gallery in Universitetsgaten from 20 April to 12 May. One hundred and ten paintings. The newspapers call it an insult to the established order. Munch is a young immature artist who has nothing to offer. And then he goes and exhibits everything at once. The portrait of

Jæger, of *Jensen-Hjell*, and *Olaf Ryes Plass*. And an unfinished picture to boot! Why does he call *Spring* in particular an unfinished picture? Everything is unfinished, small and large paintings alike, all hundred and ten of them, or, as *Aftenposten* says: What audacity and lack of self-criticism on the part of a young, immature artist who has obviously nowhere near finished his training and yet carries on like this. The new theories and principles which are currently in vogue have gone to his head and completely befuddled him. Before possessing even the most rudimentary knowledge of painting techniques he has thrown himself into anything and everything that is novel and experimental.

Or Aubert: A pathological sloppiness in self-development, a lamentable devil-may-care attitude towards form and draughtsmanship. If anyone wishes to know the reason for Munch's inharmonious development, it must first be borne in mind how little is done in this country to train artists. Another mitigating factor is Munch's poor health. Yet there is no doubt that, as a student, he must also take some of the blame himself.

* * *

At the same time, he makes the acquaintance of frøken Åse Carlsen, like himself a student of painting. She is twenty years old. She is slim and tall. She has a frank, straightforward look. No full lips here. Something firmer. A core. He can talk to her about pictures, about colour, about possible subjects.

You are so beautiful, frøken Carlsen. You are so much more beautiful than the other one. I cannot speak to anyone else as I can to you. We will certainly not tire of one another. But I don't understand it. For real love is something which I don't think happens more than once in a lifetime.

He has lain awake at night with the certainty that he needs someone to love. He has lain there thinking about what he would like to have said but which he never does say when he is with her. That she is beautiful, that he is fond of her, thinks he is fond of her, longs for her, that he is lonely, that he can't stand it any longer. Yet there is a kind of invisible screen between them when they are together. His arm is paralysed. When the moment to act arrives. When she is warm. When he sees that she wants to. Then he is cold. Hasn't the strength to seize the opportunity.

*

My dear Edvard! It was so good to hear that you've become a regular at the Grand again. You're perfectly well now, it seems, but please do try and take care not to fall ill again. The Newfoundland has been put down. So now I have to console myself with the greyhound. How odd that jury is. Why couldn't your picture just as well have come to Paris as to Copenhagen? They'll obviously see red when you lot have an exhibition of your own. It's so nice that you follow your own bent and don't care a hang about them or compromise with them. I hear there's to be a masked ball in Christiania. Do you think I should go as a nun? I'll bet frøken Carlsen has been dying for you to ask her. I don't suppose you spend much time with her, do you? Now just make sure you look after your health, don't spend too much time at the Grand, don't have too many late nights, don't spend too much time with frøken Carlsen, don't bother your head about all those horrid people who are against you, and spare a thought now and then for your devoted Meisse.

*

He is walking with frøken Carlsen in the streets of Christiania.

These are the same streets he walked with fru Thaulow.

How sad it all is.

All the casual pick-ups. Frøken Drewsen. Girls who without a second thought accompanied him up to the studio. Models who have called in to see him. What was it Meisse had written? I've also heard about that lovely model of yours. They say that half the time you're on your knees before her going into ecstasies about her charms etc. Is it true?

Meisse, whom he is also avoiding, who is down in Tønsberg waiting for him to send a photo of himself.

But frøken Carlsen is a different cup of tea entirely.

So much they can talk about! *She* knows what a motif is. Colour. Form. Rhythm. They are sitting on barrels, each with glass in hand.

But she has suddenly fallen silent. What is she waiting for? Is this the moment? Is she waiting for him to ... But he's far too tired, nervous and dithering. These spring days are always a difficult time for him. The light makes him melancholy. He can see all the others are laughing. But the laughter does not touch him.

They are sitting in Basarhallene, the former market, having a drink.

Now she is waiting for him to say something, do something. He knows that when night comes he will lie there tossing and turning in bed if he does not say something.

Will you hold my hand, frøken Carlsen?

He hears his own expressionless voice.

I'm so lonely, he adds.

No, she replies. Not here.

He sees the young, unblemished face.

How hard she is, he thinks.

It seemed to him such a small thing to ask.

*

They walk up Youngsgaten.

I'm very fond of you, Munch, she says. But I think it's more like friendship.

Friendship is so little, he answers. Life is so short. If we tried to get to know one another better, might love suddenly blossom?

But I feel so young, she replies. My view of life is quite different from yours. I'm an optimist. I don't want to sacrifice myself, Munch. I'm too young and lively for you. You're world-weary and tired of life.

He hears the words, hears the guileless brutality of youth, her voice's light, bright harshness. She's not aware of it herself, doesn't understand it, doesn't realize that she is being cruel, that her words strike him with the same force as those cold phrases of fru Thaulow. Åse Carlsen. She looks round, sees every house, every person. Confidently. As though life is everlasting. As though an eternity of time lies before her.

*

They are standing in front of her gate.

As they were walking Munch observed the two shadows on the ground. When they walked away from the gaslight they suddenly grew, became enormous. Then just as suddenly they shrank and were swallowed up by the darkness.

Like a portent of something.

I won't kiss you, Munch.

He looks at her, hears the echo of her voice, wonders why she said it.

Goodbye, she says quickly and darts in through the gate.

She stands there in the semi-darkness. She smiles at him, awkward all of a sudden.

As though she expects him to follow her?

He feels a sickening paralysis gripping his body. He cannot do it.

Instead he raises his hat.

Goodnight, frøken Carlsen.

*

But he meets her again. In the company of artist friends, in cafés or in their lodgings.

It's dreadful really, Munch. Going on the spree with you like this.

I can't live without you, he says passionately.

No, we're a good match, aren't we? What an odd bird you are, Munch.

Once again he is sitting with Åse Carlsen in Basarhallene. They've been strolling through the streets. Two young painters. They've been discussing Heyerdahl and Krohg, colour, texture and Lepage. She is to become Harriet Backer's pupil. He is soon to study with Bonnat. He sees that she has changed. She sits there smiling with rosy cheeks and sparkling eyes.

He had run into her by chance. She had said that it was nice to see him again, she had been thinking of him, had gazed straight into his eyes, always did so, her fair hair down over her face. He had seen her pale, delicate skin, her white teeth. She wanted to know what he was painting. He had told her about all the pictures he planned to paint. Then they had strolled through the streets. And suddenly here they were.

I'm ruining my reputation, she says.

He cannot answer. He feels a sudden damp chill. It's not the weather. Not the wind. But from within.

* * *

Fru Thaulow steals in between them. As though he can see her quite clearly. She stands there close beside him, with her plump neck and full lips, her eyes with that grey-green glint. He has seen her walking in the streets. He has stood beside a lamppost feeling his heart pound, feeling the dizziness overcome him. The hatred. The overpowering rush of desire.

But Åse Carlsen looks fixedly ahead, her teeth clenched.

I say, Edvard, can I ask you something? If it hadn't been for what happened with the other one, would you, do you think, perhaps have loved *me*?

Yes, I think so.

* * *

One day he meets her up at Ljan.

She has just clasped the photograph he gave her close to her dress. It is brilliant sunshine. The bright blue water stretches away towards Nesoddlandet. Soon the bridegroom will be here to collect her. Harald Nørregaard, Munch's good friend, leapt at the chance. Now he'll be taking her far away, right to Stavanger.

But she's still sitting on the balcony. There is a sudden gust of wind from the south. Munch sees how the wind blows the flaxen hair down over her eyes. Munch sees the tiredness in her features. She's never been more beautiful.

He glances at the clock. Everything has gone wrong for him. Or is it just sweet revenge? He is to meet Meisse Dörnberger at their prearranged rendezvous in an hour.

It's rotten of you to go, says Åse Carlsen. The only time I've ever been at your place. And there I was wanting to spend the whole day here.

He hears how weak and nervous her voice is.

You know how indebted to her I am, he says. You know I can't pull the wool over her eyes.

Let me come with you back to town, she says. Then at least we can be together as long as possible.

*

Bekkelaget Station. The little green café. They sit close together, as usual.

The owner thinks we're married, she says laughing. So we'd better be on first-name terms.

She beckons to him. Orders for both of them. Could we have some beer?

They sit there both with their glass of beer and are lost for words.

Their hands touch suddenly. He feels her burning skin. Her smooth palm. It's just before the wedding. My God, what on earth has he done?

*

Then he gets up and goes in search of a cab. They've been sitting too long. He sees the look of tiredness come back into her face. He walks down the hill to get a horse and cab. She stands by the fence, back to him, head bowed. Motionless. He walks up and stands beside her. Speaks to her.

She turns towards him with tears in her eyes.

A look of hopelessness. Pale and sad.

They look at one another wordlessly. He senses that, at this very moment, the greatest joy of his life is slipping through his fingers.

She turns away.

Come, he says, with trembling voice. The horse is waiting.

Frøken Carlsen, he says. Some future occasion perhaps? Perhaps we can meet *then*?

It doesn't do to be frivolous, she replies. If I marry, my first duty will be to my husband.

They sit in the cab on their way to town.

Then she takes out a little gold crucifix.

I've worn it since I was small, Munch. Would you like to have it?

* * *

He stands in the church with Stang and sees the sun slice obliquely in through a window high up. There is a bluish-white swathe of dust. Åse Carlsen walks slowly up the aisle. Her final minutes as frøken Carlsen. Her eyes half-closed. Like a sleepwalker. Her face is almost white.

He stands behind a pillar in a corner by the door and watches the marriage ceremony. Why the devil did she have to marry? He had stood there in the church waiting for the carriages, heard them arriving, one after the other, heard the horses champing at the bit and whinnying, the rocking sound of wheels on springs. Why in hell's name? There she was. The congregation followed her lead in the singing. He had heard the priest's accompanying voice at the altar. Together with Stang he tiptoed, hat in hand, into the dark corner, watched her float across the church floor like a spirit.

Now she is kneeling before the altar in the black dress he knows so well. A ray of sunlight falls on her blonde hair. Almost inaudibly she replies 'I do' to the priest. Will she love Harald Nørregaard? She replies

'I will'. Why in hell's name? He thinks of all they have spoken about. That time in the wine bar. Frøken Carlsen, will you hold my hand? She had said no then.

* * *

Åsgårdstrand. The garden which the old woman has looked after, planting beds of stock and asters and decorating it with seashells. Munch is there with Inger and Laura and a kitten. He goes sailing on the fjord, paints, draws, eats fish stew and flounder prepared by his sisters.

Here there are old acquaintances from Christiania. Ludvig Meyer and his wife. Bødtker, Michelsen and Dedichen. Munch takes walks in the forest with frøken Drewsen.

Will you sit for me, frøken Drewsen?

No.

Please will you sit for me, frøken Drewsen?

All right then, I will.

1889. A decisive year, when Jæger is already a broken man, when Oda and Christian Krohg get their second child, but no longer need to make a secret of it, are able to have it baptized in Borre church with Edvard Munch as godfather, even though he is not entered in the church register.

The remaining Bohemians carry the new-born Per Krohg to the font. Oda and Christian Krohg are among the few survivors after the emotional battle. As are Gunnar Heiberg, Lyder Brun, Emilie and Bokken Lasson. There they stand in the ancient medieval church, witnesses to free love in Jesus' name. 1889. The year of Van Gogh's self-portrait with severed ear, Skredsvig's *Willow Flute*, Gauguin's *Yellow Christ*, Toulouse Lautrec's *Dance at the Moulin de la Galette*, the year Anna Ancher becomes a pupil of Puvis de Chavannes, the year of the Exposition Universelle in Paris and when Jæger schemes about winning a flying competition around the Eiffel Tower, the year the first issue of *La Plume* comes out.

During the summer Munch is in Åsgårdstrand, has perhaps been on a short trip to Paris and bought a hat for his sister Inger, at any rate has painted her on the shore, has painted *Military Band on Karl Johan*, the counterpart to the later *Scream*, and for once an experience not rooted in melancholy or sorrow, but in registering the throng flocking down Karl Johan on a sunny day, the white houses against the blue spring air, the band playing a march as it makes its way down the hill. All at once Munch sees the colours differently. The cream-coloured facades shimmer, the colours dance in the river of people, in scarlet and white parasols. Yellow and light blue spring costumes against the navy blue winter ones. The golden trumpets shimmer, everything sparkles in the sun, blue and red seem to quiver. It's the band approaching. It makes him see differently. The music separates the colours, filling him with sudden elation.

* * *

Dear Åse. You haven't said a blessed word about how things are going in Stavanger. That's not very nice of you. Will you please tell me in words of one syllable how you're getting on? What your sitting-room looks like, how you spend the day. All that kind of thing. Monsieur Stang and I watched your wedding. We were in a corner by the door and crept away on tiptoe when it was all over. You both looked very pious. As for me, I'm working hard on a painting of frøken Drewsen in a forest. Even though the forest is so pleasant and the waves plosh against the shore close by, it hardly looks as though I'm going to fall head over heels. Your devoted Edvard Munch.

*

Dear Munch: You're a queer fish, Munch, wanting me to give you an exact description of what it's like to be married. There's damn all to say about marriage, you see. Either you feel dashed good or dashed awful, luckily only dashed good in my case so far. Yet I've only been married two months. And what about yourself, Munch, how are things with you? Aren't you soon going to tie the knot with frøken Dörnberger? I think you jolly well ought to, Munch, it's very healthy to be married, you see. One leads a more regular existence and I think that would be a good thing for you. Or perhaps it isn't frøken Dörnberger any more? Sigurd Høst wrote something about your being quite taken with frøken Drewsen. But that is something I don't think you should do, Munch. In that case, I think the former is better. Your devoted Åse Nørregaard.

* * *

New pictures. Work. No one woman is going to gain total power over him, no one event, sentence or newspaper review is going to put him off his work. Munch is painting *Inger on the Shore*, inspired by Puvis de Chavannes, the Nordic twilight and Manet's strong colours, the picture which will attract such a hail of criticism that Munch's father resolves to cancel his subscription to *Aftenposten* after the drubbing at the Autumn Exhibition. *Inger on the Shore*, his own daughter, is condemned as rubbish, dilettantism, a mockery of the public, should not have been accepted. The reviewer considers that the stones on the shore are nothing but soft, shapeless lumps of matter, just as the blue area in the background has little to do with water. The woman herself is portrayed as a physical creature without a hint of life or expression, equally false in both form and colour. All things considered, the picture seems to possess so little artistic merit that its presence in the exhibition is well-nigh indefensible.

64

What does it matter? Munch is leaving now anyway, turning his back on the forlorn streets and the icy wind, the endless lampposts with their dreary flicker of gas, where he has so often stood waiting. The depressing rooms, where death has dwelt or where he has managed to snatch a little fleeting tenderness. Dismal lobbies where he has glimpsed sea captains' shadows. He's leaving it all behind now. Going abroad. Away. Away from Aubert and his hatchet jobs concealed in tones of false bonhomie. Away from the Bohemians' remorseless self-destruction. He has been granted a national scholarship of fifteen hundred crowns, thanks to a recommendation from Hans Heyerdahl, Christian Krohg, Amaldus Nielsen, Frederik Borgen, Theodor Kittelsen and Christian Skredsvig. He is going to Paris.

*

Yes, he is leaving now, leaving it all behind, sitting at the table at home in Schous Plass, hearing the clatter of knives and forks. His aunt is subjecting him to her critical gaze, as though to convince herself that he really is fit to be sent out into the wide world. After all, even the papers have written about his poor health.

Have you packed enough socks, Edvard? Don't you think you ought to wear two shirts on the boat? The wind can be nasty, you know.

The military doctor clears his throat.

For goodness' sake, be careful in Paris, won't you?

His father sits hunched over his plate, back to the window. The lights floods in onto the bare head and the almost white hair.

It's damp in that part of the world, you know. A tricky climate so close to the Channel. You can easily get rheumatism.

Munch nods.

You must write often.

He nods again.

Farewell. Fifteen hundred crowns. Going to Paris. He sits there thinking of all the times he has crossed swords with his father. Thoughts which never should have been thought, words which never should have been spoken. For how many years is the sinner in hell, father? A thousand? No, a thousand times a thousand years! All those conversations which ended in temper, rage and fury. Father and son. The military doctor will not allow him to paint naked women. Yet in Paris models willing to take off their clothes are ten a penny.

They eat on in silence.

The military doctor clears his throat again.

Take camphor drops when you have a cold. I've packed them in little cartons for you. How long is it again you're going to be abroad? Eight months? That's a long time, Edvard.

Munch nods yet again.

From now on nothing can ever be the same again.

*

Munch shakes hands with each of them in turn. He feels embarrassed, doesn't want to show too much emotion. Farewell to his brother and sisters. Farewell to Aunt Karen. The military doctor stands waiting out in the passage.

Goodbye, Edvard. Do take care.

He turns on his heel and begins to descend the stairs. The military doctor calls out once again. Do take care!

Then he remembers that he has forgotten a rug.

He runs up the stairs and back into the apartment. He clasps his father's hand one more time. Aunt Karen stands there watching. He knows that she has wanted this. He registers her calm understanding look. He knows that part of her is leaving with him.

Then at last he is on his way from Schous Plass down to the harbour.

*

There lies the ship. Kalle Løchen is already on board.

It's delayed, Munch. The boat's not leaving for another three hours.

Three hours?

Munch strolls up Karl Johan with Kalle Løchen. Shall we find a bar? Then they run into Drewsen and his wife. Won't Munch and Løchen come home with them for coffee while they're waiting?

But Munch feels there is something drawing him back to Schous Plass, to yet another farewell. For eight months suddenly seems such a long time, for him *too*.

No, thank you, says Munch. I think I'd better go home to the family. What a good chap am I, don't you think?

He laughs.

So many years away. Now he is walking right across town just for the sake of half an hour. What will they think? Will they be touched that he walked all that way just for this?

On the stairs the feeling of embarrassment returns.

So many times he's been here. 1 Schous Plass, has climbed these stairs since 1885, come staggering back late at night, stealing in on tiptoe in the early morning, dashed down these stairs crimson with fury, lugged canvases and frames up and down them, sometimes faint from the scent of woman on his coat collar.

Now he is coming here for the last time. As he opens the door, the military doctor is at his desk writing. Half turning his head, he peers at him over his glasses. Munch had thought he would be pleased, but he remains at his desk and carries on writing as though nothing has happened. Then luckily Aunt Karen comes in. She looks at him inquiringly.

The boat's delayed, he explains. I hadn't anywhere to go.

Go on, stay at home, says the military doctor. I've heard the weather's turning nasty.

Cancel his study trip just because of the weather? Can he be serious? Absolutely no question of it. Not one day longer in this town.

He hears the defiance in his own voice. Like an echo of previous spats, everything that has been bottled up, the scorn of his friends, reviews that have been read out aloud in drawing rooms, cafés and studios, an echo of stifled rage, everything he could not say, even though he still said too much. Everything he has put up with. His hurt pride.

Aunt Karen digs out yet more things her nephew ought to take abroad with him. A scarf, underclothes, some extra socks.

Goodbye, father. I'd better be off again now. He offers his father his hand once more.

Goodbye, goodbye. We should have come to see you off. But I haven't got time. The silence between the military doctor and his son echoes long in the room.

*

He admits to himself that he would have liked his father to accompany him down to the ship, would have liked to see his father standing there on the quay as the vessel cast off, would have liked to hear him wish him all the best.

Instead, he walks alone down to the quayside again. His departure for Paris with Valentin Kjelland and Kalle Løchen. Young Løchen, Krohg's favourite pupil – not like Munch brimming with sarcastic remarks – walks about the deck smiling on this early October day in 1889. A painter as well as an actor, who has played Hamlet in Bergen with his wife as Ophelia and Gunnar Heiberg as director, has played the lover in Zola's *Thérèse Raquin*. Now he strolls about on deck, repeating over and over again the same trivial phrase: By the way, we're going to Paris.

A whole crowd of friends have come to see them off. They are drinking from hip flasks and are already well away. Joking and laughter. By the way, did you know we're off to Paris? Some of them want to stay on board as far as Kristiansand. There's going to be one hell of a shindig before Skagerak and the onset of seasickness.

There's your father, says Stang suddenly.

Munch looks up from his place on deck. My goodness, yes, there he is. There's the military doctor. He's squeezing his way through some stacked pallets. Munch can see that he's put on his Sunday best and is wearing his smartest overcoat. Now he is straining to pick out his son up on deck.

Munch waves to him, suddenly feeling strangely moved by the sight of him down there. He gets up and goes back down again onto the quayside.

The military doctor comes over to him, now almost elated.

My, what a fine ship she is, Edvard.

Yes, isn't she?

So you're not leaving yet? Come back home with me, then.

Oh no I can't, father. Not now. My pals have come on board to see me off.

Oh, I see.

Goodbye then, father.

Goodbye, Edvard.

* * *

Hôtel de Champagne, 62, rue de la Condamine.

Munch arrives in the metropolis one day in October, at about the same time as the opening of the Moulin Rouge, sees Gauguin and the Groupe impressionniste et synthéiste at Café Volpini, perhaps also sees the fifth exhibition of the Independents, including Van Gogh's *Les Iris* and *La Nuit étoilée*, perhaps also Luce's *Vue du Pont-Neuf*.

He is a pupil at Léon Bonnat's painting school, working in the studio in the mornings, extending his arm and with a pencil measuring the proportions of the body of the naked model standing there in the middle of the studio. How many times does the head go into the body, how wide is the trunk in proportion to the length of the body? It bores and tires him, dulls his senses.

Dear Aunt, I feel extraordinarily well here; it's like September, a vast amount of traffic in the streets, it drives one quite mad. Soon I'm going to visit famous sites of the Revolution.

*

Dear Edvard, Thank you for writing so often; it's good that you got there safe and sound. Today we received your most recent postcard. The reviews from *Aftenposten* and *Dagbladet* are being sent to you. Our subscription to *Aftenposten* has been cancelled on account of all this. Salicyl is being sent to you instead of the *Aftenposten* review expressly at your father's wish. If you notice any rheumatism, you must take the Salicyl in water. It was very quiet after you had left. Do write when you need the money sending. Your devoted Karen Bjølstad.

*

Munch practices nude drawing under Léon Bonnat. Male models. He goes to the Exposition Universelle on the Champ de Mars and sees his own five-year-old picture *Morning* hanging there among the other famous painters. The Norwegian jury would not let him exhibit anything more radical.

Dear Aunt, We've more or less settled in now. At eight in the morning, we eat baguettes and drink chocolate. Then we go to Bonnat's. Then we eat lunch – a couple of hot dishes. Then we go to the Exposition or somewhere else and eat supper at about six-thirty. It's really not all that expensive here. You can get an excellent lunch for one crown, but the distances are so enormous that you either have to take a cab or take a rest in a café, so you do have to spend money all the same. Do please send that terrible review from *Aftenposten* and others as well.

Dear Father. I've moved. My address is Neuilly, Rue de Chartres 37, Paris. I still haven't had time to visit the historical sights as I have to seize every opportunity to see the Exposition. On Sunday I went to Bilbao Bill. Bilbao Bill is America's most celebrated fur trapper. He's come here with a whole gang of Indians and fur trappers and has built an entire Indian village outside Paris. Bilbao Bill has been involved in loads of Indian wars, particularly in a great battle against a well-known Indian chief. It was a duel between the two of them. Bill killed the Indian chief with a knife and took his scalp. The knife and the scalp are displayed in his tent.

*

The military doctor has moved house with his family to Hauketo outside Christiania. The air is first-rate. To his son he writes:

Dear Edvard. Do make a real effort to look after yourself. You forgot the Salicyl powder but three packets have been sent to you and I may send another three. Unfortunately I forgot to give you your hymn book as you were leaving, but I'll get Wang to take it with him. One can't be completely without the word of the Lord. It must have been fun seeing the Indians, but I doubt whether Bill really is an old fur trapper. As soon as I can, I shall go down to Grøn's with your painting, which has been beautifully framed now and looks extremely well, he'll certainly be pleased with it. It's a pleasure for me to be able to hand him this gift. Farewell and God be with you.

*

Bonnat's painting school. It is after morning chocolate but before lunch. Hertzberg takes him by the arm.

Munch, old chap?

Yes?

Hertzberg goes out into the passage and beckons to Munch to follow him. He is holding a paper in his hand. Munch realizes it must be something important.

What is it? A letter?

There's something I need to talk to you about.

Hertzberg's voice is strangely quiet.

I've heard ... he says, glancing down at the letter. Something's happened.

Munch at Bonnat's. The panic cancels out the distance, all those miles away from home. Separation is not a ship crossing the sea, separation is something in his head that can never happen. Something is amiss. Something has happened to someone at home. Munch stands in the studio and opens the letter, his hands shaking, staring eyes wide as though through a haze, then finally he finds out what is in the letter:

Dear Edvard, You'll be able to change the money from Dewold at your banker's to whom the money order is made out. We've been expecting to hear from you each day, but did not want to put off writing any longer, as you might be running short of money. Here at Hauketo life is very quiet and peaceful for us, Inger has started having piano lessons with frøken Goplen once a fortnight. Andreas walks into town every morning as usual and three times a week takes the route over Ekeberg. But father is a stay-at-home, pacing up and down on the veranda for exercise. He's well, as are the little girls. At this precise moment, all of them are reading, father and Inger are sitting in the large lounge which looks old-fashioned. We have a new chandelier and tablecloth . . .

Edvard reads. Something's happened. To someone at home. But nothing's wrong, is it? Just the letter from his aunt. So he's managed to borrow the money from Dewold. His father, aunt and sisters, nothing has happened to them. He feels a surge of joy. He strides quickly across the floor and hears Hertzberg say: Yes, well . . .

There is a sudden silence.

How strange. Why is Hertzberg so solemn, why had he thought something was wrong, what on earth had put that into his head? Munch glances at Hertzberg once more. He is still wearing the same expression.

Then he understands that something terrible has happened.

Now he can see it quite plainly in Hertzberg's face. He knows something. Something he hasn't told him.

I think something's wrong at home, Munch.

The words come out cold and lifeless. Without any feeling. Munch suddenly feels hatred. There's a ringing in his ears. His heart begins to pound. Is it his sisters? His aunt? His father?

My father? he says.

Hertzberg nods.

Your father's dead.

Dead? He's *dead*? You've read it in *Morgenbladet*? Does it say military doctor? But is it spelled with a 'ch'? Are you sure? Does it say Ljan? Does it say Hauketo? It must be him then.

The letter to Kjelland! The letter with his brother's handwriting! The letter he has been carrying in his pocket since the previous day, which he has not managed to deliver because of moving house. Munch takes it out. Yes, it is his brother's handwriting: Dear Kjelland, Since I know you share lodgings with my brother Edvard Munch, I am taking the liberty of asking whether you would do me the great service of informing my brother that our father . . .

The incomprehensible words. The letter from Andreas to Munch's friend Kjelland. And with an accompanying note from Aunt Karen: Dear Kjelland, May we ask you, *if Edvard is not ill* – to give him the enclosed letter, which alas is to inform him of his father's death. Will you do what you can for him at this time, he needs support. Would you send us just a few words about how he is and about how he takes this news? Could you address the letter to Andreas Munch, Ljan, Christiania?

Munch leaves.

Tidies up his things and leaves. Walks in the din from the boulevards, without registering a single face. He finds a restaurant, reads the letter over and over again: God give you strength and comfort at this time, you know he was a pious Christian, and has therefore entered blessed eternity, so we must not despair, we must just seek strength where father sought it. He had a sudden stroke, was paralysed so he couldn't speak and was apparently unconscious until the end, though we think he recognized us at certain moments, smiled at us, pressed our hands. Father deeply regretted not having given you your bible. Buy a copy and read a little every day so you can find something good in it to comfort you. Our thoughts are with you so far away. Do take care of yourself. There was something quite special about father.

*

The restaurant is large and dreary. Nobody else there but a couple of waiters. A vast billiard table stands there gaping. Munch pulls his hat down over his eyes. Has to get out. Decides to walk down to the Café Régence and find the obituary notice in *Morgenbladet*. Walks down St Honoré. At the Madeleine it is swarming with people, a constant procession of carriages driving past, how soundlessly the wheels roll, all that is audible being the rhythmic clip–clop of hooves against the tarmacadam. He threads his way carefully across the street to avoid being run over, it is teeming with people, all of them looking so contented, yet death must be a reality for some of them too, he walks down the boulevard, huge shop windows, looks at a few ties, stares unseeing, pauses in front of a newspaper kiosk, looks at the cartoons in *Le Courrier*, sees an old man a good way off. Munch starts, the man looks like the military doctor, slightly stooping, all old people look like him, one hand resting on their paunch. Avenue de l'Opéra, in Café de la Régence, *Morgenbladet*, he stares at these lines, Ljan, Hauketo, Munch with 'ch', it looks so curiously simple and natural, the funeral is on Thursday, the military doctor at his writing desk, pipe in the corner of his mouth, grey and round-shouldered, with such a pleasant smile when you spoke to him. It is the fourth of December 1889, it is really true that father is reunited with mother and Sophie in heaven and really does see our deep sorrow, Inger promised him on behalf of all of us that we would trust in the Lord.

*

Then suddenly they are closer to Munch than they have ever been before, closer than when he sat at the supper table observing them, closer than when the military doctor became soft and he became hard and Jesus Christ was between them, closer than when Jæger, than when fru Thaulow, than when he painted *The Sick Child*. Closer than when Sophie fell ill and the military doctor folded his hands in prayer. Closer, because he is dead. Now it is irreversible. Now the military doctor has become part of memory, a place on the sea bed with all the other things to which he can dive down whenever he chooses. Part of the landscape. Beneath the still surface which mirrors air, light and colours. Which conceals the deep with its slime, its maggots.

Death!

Munch came to Paris in order to break free, to assert his independence. Now he sits in his room again, by the stove, warming himself.

It is the fourth of December. It's getting dark. The stove casts a red glow.

It has snowed in Paris. A thin layer of snow reminding Munch of his own childhood in Christiania. The period in Slottsgaten. The first years. Christmas. The military doctor wore black. The tree had to be decorated. A festive atmosphere. Munch sits in his room. Snow over Paris. Europe in the grip of the cold weather.

Munch knows that he is the family's breadwinner now. Knows that there is no money. All he has is paintings which are stigmatized and which only the best painters are willing to buy. Not so many good painters. Werenskiold, Heyerdahl and Krohg, and they're not always so good either.

Hertzberg knocks at the door, wanting Munch's company for a meal.

They sit down at their usual places. The same people as yesterday are sitting there. The waiter Jean with his plates. Just as before, yet quite different. The elderly gentleman over there in the corner, the one who always folds up his napkin so painstakingly. There he goes again, wiping glass, knife and fork, looking down at his handiwork, cocking his head on one side like a hen. Now it's doggie's turn to eat. The elderly gentleman starts cutting up some meat. Why are animals always present when Munch is teetering on the edge of the abyss? Aunt Karen has written to him about the cat which is playing with the dummy mouse they've made and which regularly turns up with real mice. Inger will write about the military doctor, crouching on his haunches playing with the cat, for supper he ate three helpings of broth and belly pork, for Sunday lunch they had a roast of lamb, he ate a whole cup of fatty gravy and two huge portions of stewed fruit. Inger writes that he had recovered somewhat from his religious brooding, they had walked to Munkerud chapel, they felt warm and snug in the large sitting-room, the military doctor was completely taken with it, saying he thought it was reminiscent of the sitting-room in Asbjørnson's well-known description of an old-fashioned Christmas Eve, on Sunday evening had stood out in the yard admiring the house, both verandas beautifully lit from within, he said he was looking forward to summer, wanted to go exploring in the locality, had bought a chandelier, a new tablecloth, the military doctor was so fond of the apartment, afraid that someone would come and offer more so they would be given their notice. Munch sits in the restaurant looking at the elderly gentleman with the large monocle, it's too comical, Munch gets a terrible fit of the giggles. I can't help it, he says, everything seems so comical. Waiter, more wine, please! He drinks the wine, feels more and more flushed, the colonel with the monocle, the jovial painter with the good eyes, the thin beardless sculptor with a face like a coconut, all the heads pointing at the cocotte, all in the same direction, now one of the elderly gentleman's eyes falls out, Munch gets another fit of the giggles, hears his laughter echo loud and long afterwards. Another glass, Jean! Jean does not hear, all his attention focused on the cocotte. She's not bad, actually, Hertzberg, she has lovely bright eyes, and she looks so jolly, I say, Hertzberg, I've suddenly got such an urge to get drunk and take her home with me, it's so dismal being alone. Well, why don't you then, says Hertzberg. No, says Munch. Leans back against the wall, feels the pressure against his eyes, gazes vacantly ahead. How do you get on with your father, Hertzberg? What wouldn't I give to be able to put my arms around his head and tell him how fond of him I was, there was always this embarrassment, not all the sorrow I have caused him, but the smaller things, the fact that I was hard when he was soft.

*

Dear Laura and Inger: I think such a lot about what a terrible time this has been for all of you. The pain I felt on receiving the news of father's death makes me realize that it must have been even worse for all of you. I hope father didn't suffer during his last illness and that, even if he had many a struggle in his life, he was granted a peaceful death. Perhaps it was for the best, for he was somehow unfit for life. It's hard for me to imagine the furniture and the sitting-room without him. I should so much have liked to be with you all now, terribly sad though it would have been.

Munch at Bonnat's. He is drawing standing male nudes and standing male nudes holding a staff, attending lectures on perspective and geometry, but is constantly drawn back to his own past and unable to concentrate.

Dear Edvard: it's the 12th of December today, I don't know whether you've remembered it yourself. It's your birthday. Many happy returns.

Another letter from Aunt Karen. She tells him that father had decided to give him ten crowns. And besides this there is other news about the military doctor's final days, his boundless contentment with the house, the sun which shone so gloriously in through the veranda. He wouldn't hear it said that the sitting-room was dark. Munch sits in Paris reading about the pickled cabbage for Christmas and the lamp which had been lit, the Christmas tree that Eriksen had felled, coffee and Christmas cake, Karen had been baking and made a whole supply of sausages and buns, the larder is full. As Munch makes preparations for Christmas at the home of the writer Jonas Lie, the only one of the 'greats' to show any understanding of Jæger.

Munch at Bonnat's. He is not thinking of large canvases and new subjects for pictures, but of his father's death and the 'flu epidemic raging in France. It strikes him on Christmas Eve. The mortality rate is as high as in a major cholera epidemic. He regularly meets three or four funeral processions in the streets. The undertakers have so much to do that they have to work at night as well.

He flees to St Cloud.

The Seine flows past his windows. On the horizon he sees the silhouette of Paris, higher up is the park with the ruins of the old castle. He takes the steamboat in to the studio. C. Simon's Hotel Belvédère, *Café et bières, friture et matelote, prix modérés, confort moderne*, telephone number 60. In the restaurant, he can order eel with wine and onion sauce, speak French with the patron, sit in the light from the fire as twilight falls and watch the steamboats with their red and green lanterns glide past the window.

Dear Aunt, I only wish you were here and could see what a lovely room I have.

Munch is sharing lodgings with the Danish poet Emanuel Goldstein and the Norwegian officer and politician Georg Stang. He comes under the influence of such fellow artists as Monet, Sisley, Whistler, Seurat, van Gogh and Raffaëlli. For a time he must have thought he had broken away, that he could make his first free choice, artistically speaking. But his father's death throws him back to the past. Diary and easel assume equal status, the memories demand his concentration. Processing. During these days, weeks, months, he is adrift, rubbing shoulders with Frits Thaulow, Thorolf Holmboe, Jørgen Sørensen and Jonas Lie. Later, hardly anyone will remember him. Munch in Paris? No memories, episodes, anecdotes. No-one who will later record his name, what he said or did on various occasions.

Munch sits at the window in St Cloud and is on the verge of the most important artistic choice of his life. But before that moment arrives, he is restless, sits alone, cannot bear it. He leaves his room to meet friends, but they cannot give him what he needs. He hears the laughter. It jars his ears and he takes flight. Sits at the window. *Night in St Cloud*. Night by the Seine. He is digesting the shock of his father's death, thinking of women he has known, not just one, fru Thaulow, whom he remembers in his diary, but also fru Åse Nørregaard, formerly frøken Carlsen:

How many evenings have I sat alone at the window bitterly regretting that you were not there so we could marvel together at the scene outside in the moonlight, with all the lights on the other side and the gas lamps outside in the street, and all the steamers with green, red and yellow lanterns? And then that strange half-light inside the room, with the bright bluish square cast on the floor by the moon.

*

Night in St Cloud. Munch at the parting of the ways. He knows what economic fate will now befall the family. His father leaves no money and no pension. Munch has now become head of the family, and doesn't even know what paintings he's going to paint. He sits at the window, sees the night outside and the boats gliding along the Seine, sits alone with millions of memories, millions of daggers in his heart, the wounds are open. It is a city, the city of the dead, side-streets and boulevards. The graves lie side by side, towers and palaces. Silent people live there, the dead. A populous city, with many streets, housing a host of people, whole families down the centuries, bones crumble and make way for new ones. The omnibus into Paris is a seething mass of human maggots.

*

He finds the slightest sound a torment, watches Goldstein making overtures to a girl, hears the boisterous *joie de vivre*, tells him to shut up, you must excuse me, but you've no idea how painful it is. He lives in fear of sudden noise, fear of a chair, fear of he knows not what. He is his father's son, has inherited the family nervous weakness, stares at people whose language he doesn't understand, registers the fact that they stare at him puzzled, intrigued by his peculiar habits, his fastidiousness with food, his way of suddenly getting up and leaving a restaurant.

A host of small things comes to the surface now, events that have preyed on his mind, words which have been hurtful. He was as cold as ice when the military doctor wanted a reconciliation. He had seen him sit grey and tired on the sofa, seen that nice pale old head begin to nod, seeking rest. But Munch was as cold and hard as ice. The tears well up in his eyes. He stuffs the sheet into his mouth. He never explained the business with fru Thaulow to his father. Why didn't he make a clean breast of it? Tell him why he was so nervous, always flying off the handle, so hard and cold, why he didn't stay at home when his father asked him to, why he so often came home in the middle of the night? He simply had to go out! Out to drive the thoughts away, out to forget her and also to seek her out, all the places she had been.

*

Night in St Cloud. Munch at the window. What he learns at Bonnat's in the mornings is less important than what he thinks during the afternoons, evenings and nights. The light fades so quickly. Everything gradually becomes silhouetted against the window. Chimneys and roofs. There is a thin layer of snow. The stove gives out a fitful red glow. Somewhere in the room Jæger sits looking at him. Jæger at the Grand, Jæger in Christiania. Now Munch almost feels hatred for him, cause of the military doctor's greatest sorrow. All the little things, when his father came home from Helgelandsmoen military camp, having been away for a long time. He took out a bottle of wine. Here you are, it's for you, we'll drink it together! It was cheap champagne. Munch remembers his lukewarm answer: I'm not sure I like it. The disappointment in his father's face comes back to him. Why hadn't he embraced him, as he sat there in the corner of the sofa beside the window in a bluish cloud of tobacco smoke, with the sun shining on his silver-grey hair? When he glanced up, when he spoke to him? That gentle, questioning, nervous look.

*

It's light out there. You would think it was day. Munch lies there with the curtains drawn back. It is the moon shining over the Seine. It shines into his room through the windows, and casts a bluish square of light on the floor. A train crossing the nearest bridge. Suddenly the white sun-light, the bridges with their many arches, the mansions in Ancers, the cranes and factories. Bewildered by the shifts of his darting mind, he presses his face into the pillow. Suddenly it strikes him how lovely life is after all.

* * *

He takes care to ensure that his top hat always sits firmly on his head, yet doesn't know why this should be. There is no-one here he cares to impress.

To begin with the waitress came to see him in his room, offering to teach him French, so he would have to spend a lot of time in her company. *Toujours ensemble*, she said, gesturing at the great wide bed. Munch deflected her hint with a joke. The presence of girls, not the right girls, always the wrong ones, the ones who came to the studio and sat there for ever, the horrible ones, with red bodices. There is a waitress in his room now. He hears her chatter, finds it unbearable, so in the end he says he needs peace and quiet. But she comes back, tells him one day that he has only to cross the passage, the door is open at night, it's warm inside. He doesn't reply. Then she gets angry, starts to make fun of Munch's habits, the fact that he drinks *eau de vie*. Munch stands there in his room, staring at her, but can't get a word out. He takes his gradually shorter walks round the castle, but is drawn to the fireplace when dusk falls over the room, when the glowing coke starts to come to life, with movements, small creatures, faces.

He puts his face close up to the fire.

Suddenly he sees his own huge shadow covering half the wall, right up to the ceiling.

Life beckons to him, summer days with sunshine, in two months perhaps he'll return to Åsgårdstrand. His sorrow turns into self-loathing. A sudden urge sometimes wells up in him: kill yourself, then it'll all be over. What's the point of living? It's cowardly to live such a life!

But how is it cowardly? In painting terms, he is feeling his way. He paints *In The Bar*, various versions of *The Seine*, experiments with impressionism and neo-impressionism.

Pissarro is holding an exhibition in February, Munch goes to see it, absorbs, learns, will try out the technique of pointillism on monochrome surfaces, will try to acquire the impressionists' softness, counteract his own sloppiness, drawing inspiration from Monet, as he moves towards the picture *Night*, his own existential situation, is drawn back to Jæger's imperative, write and paint your own life, but has not yet reached that point, has not yet consciously formulated it. The depressive passages in the literary jottings indicate that the St Cloud manifesto, the artistic programme which will give him something to live for, is not yet written. For the time being, he toys with the thought of taking his own life, why drag oneself through the world with this miserable body, with this filth, with medicine, sees himself as a corpse, yet cannot stand the thought of death, the thought that his own flesh will stink, that his own fingers will become blue and rigid. He sees his past and his possibilities, always carefully taking note, sees his own ghostly face, lives with the dead, his mother, his sister, his grandfather and now his father too, above all with him. All the memories. The smallest things surface.

* * *

Goldstein is standing in the doorway.

Stock still. My God. Is he mad?

Then Munch hears a strange sound.

The front door down below. Regular rhythmic slams. On and on.

Goldstein doesn't say a word. Stands there rooted to the spot looking at Munch.

The sound of the railway.

Eerie.

They both say it at once.

Goldstein is suddenly standing down on the stairs.

The whole day's been eerie, says Munch. You won't be alone tonight, I'll bet.

Goldstein is on top of him in two bounds. His hands round Munch's throat. Pulling him against him.

At last, he lets go.

Munch registers that his friend looks quite deranged.

*

Munch meets Goldstein the following day.

I say, old chap. What came over you yesterday evening?

I wanted to kill you, says Goldstein. I thought it was so deliberately nasty of you when you said: You won't be alone, I'll bet. That was what it was. It was so mysterious, so eerie.

You're mad, says Munch.

Yes, Goldstein nods. There's madness in the family.

*

Then he starts to think of fru T. again, thinks of the dust in the streets, the throng on the pavement, Christiania, the places where he waited and hoped, where despite everything he has lived and loved, Åsgårdstrand, thinks of the sun falling in through the window, a white layer of dust slicing diagonally onto the ochre-coloured floor, snagging a little bluish-white patch on the edge of the sofa, thinks of her! He writes: what a deep imprint she has made on my mind. No other image can completely erase it.

He lies with the curtains drawn back. The moon shines over the Seine and casts a bluish square on the floor.

* * *

Danseuse espagnole. One franc. Let's give it a try.

Munch is standing outside the Montagnes Russes at 28 Boulevard des Capucines, *Tous les soirees*, looking into a long hall with galleries on either side, with chairs and tables, beneath the galleries and in the centre stand young dandified Frenchmen with shining top hats. At the far end, a woman clad in a mauve leotard is walking a tightrope above all the black top hats. Munch is expecting a girl with a beautiful face, but all he sees is a mask with a fixed expression gazing vacantly ahead. It is the moment before a new landscape opens up. He is a student of the patriarchal Academician Bonnat. In painting Munch has sought something to give purpose to his life. When, in a fevered, agitated state or in euphoric mood, he has come across landscapes he would have liked to paint, he has fetched his easel, put it up and painted the picture naturalistically. Has later written that it was a good picture, but not the picture he wanted to paint, not the one he saw in the fevered or euphoric mood when the picture was first conceived as an idea. He would then sift his memory for the first picture, that very first impression. Now he goes into the Montagnes Russes. A woman in a mauve leotard is walking the tightrope above a sea of top hats. Munch has searched, fumbled, heard Jæger whisper in a dream, has seen Puvis de Chavannes' *Doux Pays* on the staircase at Bonnat's. He is conversant with the theories, knows that Gauguin has returned from Pont-Aven and served as inspiration to the Nabis, the name derived from the Old Testament prophet, now a group of artists seeking a synthesis of line and form, who cultivate planes, surfaces and the decorative. He is torn between Jæger's logical materialism and a pantheistic materialism which, for the time being, he has only vaguely formulated in writing, but which, forty years later, as an old man at Ekely outside Oslo, he will greatly amplify. Previously, he had been hostile to his father folding his hands in prayer, but now the military doctor is dead and Christianity is no longer a threat. He cannot espouse Jæger's violent criticism of that bigoted, hypocritical Christianity which made Christiania so impossible to live in. He feels nothing but self-loathing for his own lack of generosity, the little things, the bottle of champagne he wouldn't drink, his father's outstretched hand he would not shake. Now he goes into the Montagnes Russes, after all the philosophical discussions with Emanuel Goldstein, after all the walks around the castle, all the hours alone with the glow from the fireplace and his own shadow, after seeing all the boats pass by 12 Quai de St Cloud, Seine-et-Oise, after hearing the latest news from Hauketo about his aunt, the little girls, Andreas and the little kitten, about the birds on the veranda which make the cat, miaowing mournfully, water at the mouth, he goes in and is met by the warmth inside, suddenly hears some Romanian singers playing their national folk music. Munch feels that the pain and yearning of love are one with the music, are one with the surrounding colours. So far he has felt his way forward, stumbled, tried anew, been driven back by the criticism, at night has carried on painting pictures already hanging as exhibits. He has listened to Jæger, to Krohg, to Heyerdahl, to Bonnat. He has travelled to Paris to learn, to get away from Christiania's swaddling clothes, the straitjacket of his own life, the problematic relationship with his family, an overwhelming love affair which nevertheless did not prevent him from being fascinated by other women. Duplicity, lies, sadness. It is 1890. The year Van Gogh dies. Monet will paint haystacks and poplars, Whistler will paint *Nocturne in Blue and Silver*, Munch will paint his related picture *Night* at a time when he had no inkling of Whistler's picture, Harriet Backer will paint *By Lamplight*. Munch stands in a music hall on Boulevard des Capucines, observes the Romanians in dazzling white and red, just like in the paintbox he received as a child, as the flats represent palms and water in green and yellow, as the tobacco smoke floats in great bluish-green clouds enveloping everything behind it in a haze. Munch stands in this common dive and knows that it is impossible for him to break free, that the past, that his own life, has caught up with him, that his father's death brings him back to the point of departure, to the vulnerable little family in Christiania, the neurotic military doctor who was not even up to buying mattresses, his mother who had to go to meet her maker, his sister who so dearly wanted to live, who sat in the chair, her face burning with fever, leaned forwards and died before she could get back into bed, the fear of illness which constantly drove him on through life, gave him the feeling that life was not really for him, that it was something he could observe, something he did not dare venture into, not even when he was twenty-two, when he could not summon up the courage to kiss a woman, when he did it all the same and she said that he hadn't. He stands in the middle of a smoke-filled music hall listening to some Romanians sing about love. It is then that it happens, that he suddenly thinks: I ought to do something, begin something, something which should strike others as forcibly as it now strikes me. But is this new? Isn't it just the same old story he's been boring his friends to death with for years, from Colditz to Goldstein? Isn't it just his Jæger-inspired thoughts about the magic of the passing moment which he has taken over as his own? He says: I ought to do something, begin something. It sounds like the same words, yet suddenly he *sees* the motifs, not a landscape in the morning light, not just any chance event, not the vintner in St Cloud, not the bar, not random people he comes across on the road, who in any case mean nothing to him. He thinks of two people, a man and a woman, at the most sacred moment in their lives. A sturdy bare arm, a strong tanned neck, a young woman lays her head against the arched chest. She closes her eyes and listens with quivering, open mouth to the words he whispers into her long flowing hair. He stands in the Montagnes Russes and knows what the motif means, knows what he saw, knows that he is going to paint it in a blue haze. He sees *Summer Night/ The Voice*, *To the Forest* and *Eye to Eye*, he sees *Kiss* and *Vampire*. He stands there in the smoke-filled music hall and feels that it is going to be so easy, is going to take shape beneath his hands as though by magic. The woman closes her eyes and listens with open, quivering mouth. At that moment, the man and woman are not themselves, but are just one link among the thousands connecting one generation to another. He stands there and thinks that people should understand how sacred and majestic what is happening between the man and the woman on the canvas is, they should remove their hats as though in church. Not just *one*, but a whole series of such pictures. The flesh will take on form, the colours take on life. The man and the woman breathe and feel, suffer and love. No more interiors, people reading and women knitting. Munch stands in the Montagnes Russes and sees *The Frieze of Life* take shape, the stages in the lives of people, his own history, love, anguish, death. He sees the sickroom at Fossveien, the russet-coloured house in Borre, the summer night at Åsgårdstrand. He is an orphaned lad in St Cloud. He has sat night after night at a window watching the boats glide past. Now violins are being tuned, now he hears notes he recognizes: the Carilla Waltz, the one she sang at the piano, captivating with her sweetest, most charming voice, now cajoling, now beseeching. He is ensnared. She is laughing, joyful, mocking, pushes him away then takes pity on him. Now he is no longer hers. She is his. He can use her however he likes, because here he stands in the Montagnes Russes and sees all the unpainted pictures in front of him. He is going to paint his life. His *own* life. A sturdy bare arm. A strong tanned neck. The forest. The sea. A blue haze. And he remembers everything that happened as though it were yesterday.

III

A German said to me: You can get rid of many of your torments, you know. And I replied: They belong to me and to my art . . . I want to keep these sufferings.   (EDVARD MUNCH)

Munch lies red and burning hot in bed.

He felt the fever even when he was on board ship. The captain advised him to have himself admitted to hospital in Le Havre. Great waves of dizziness, his heart racing. The unmistakable sweating.

He writes reassuring letters to his family at home: Am drinking Bordeaux and eating grapes all day.

But he is in hospital, receives Aunt Karen's reproaches from Christiania: You should have travelled in a first class compartment. I don't need to remind you that you must travel in the best class when you are going to Paris!

*

The first years of *The Frieze of Life*.

Munch has been back home in Norway, looked searchingly at his aunt and his brothers and sisters, heard the whole story of the military doctor's death over again. No letters or diaries he left behind shed any light on what actually happened. But Munch was once again among scenes of the past which he has defined for himself.

Borre, Åsgårdstrand, Christiania.

The scenes of his love.

The Frieze of Life is still growing within him, in diaries, in pictures which are not yet painted.

*

He is faithful to his memories, protects them, focuses on his inner self, makes what happened sharp and overwhelming, or almost formless, blurred, as though in a haze. But it is his own choice. He owns these events now. It is his artistic treasure chest. The only thing he has.

A time for reflection. The first summer without the military doctor. Munch is twenty-six years old and head of the family. It's up to him to earn the money. But there isn't any as yet. His aunt and brother and sisters will have to live on the breadline for many years.

He emerges from the forest. His own forest.

He comes out onto the shore. The light summer night sinks over him. The sea with its golden horizon. The moon is shining, casting streams of gold towards land.

It was just here that he once stood and looked at her.

He saw that there was a yellow glow to her face, a yellow shimmer over her white dress. That there was yellow in her eyes too, where she stood gazing at the horizon.

It must overwhelm him afresh, all that happened five years earlier. Now is the summer of reflection. Both his childhood and youth sink into the sea. In another country Freud analyses betrayal. How clear and self-aware is Munch's own view of woman. The sense of loss drives him on. His mother's death, his sister's death, fru Thaulow's lies.

Åse Carlsen's will.

It's all lost to him now.

All the same, he is going to reach out towards them, in picture after picture, reach out to the moments when he still had them, to the seconds before he lost them.

In St Cloud he felt only contempt for himself because he was always just an observer. Now he becomes the observer of his own volition, because it is his own memories he is observing. The life he has lived. The brief moments which nevertheless contain all dimensions. Powerful moments, as he writes.

Love, angst and death.

The content of *The Frieze of Life*.

*

Morgenbladet 16 October 1890:

> Edvard Munch too exhibited a few interiors with figures, but of quite a different kind from previous ones. One of them, which he calls *Night*, makes such unacceptable demands on people's powers of divination that only a handful can be bothered to pursue the matter any further. We can say that patient study will be rewarded with the discovery that the picture is supposed to represent a room or a corridor in which a man wearing a tall top hat is seated looking out over the water, where a steamer with its lanterns is passing by. However, the passing mood is so unclearly expressed that it slips away before one can grasp it. Munch's pictures at the annual autumn exhibition are the fruit of a stay in Paris which would not, however, appear to have added clarity to his artistic production.

*

Munch at the Autumn Exhibition. It is Monet, Degas and Pissarro, also showing pictures, who are the inspiration. Munch as the unruly pupil. Bizzarro then. As for Seurat, the Christiania critics don't know him at this point. So they cannot draw any conclusions about his possible influence on Munch.

But Aubert is on the job. On 5 November, this time as critic for *Dagbladet*, he writes:

> If I have called Wentzel's talent healthy, muscular, able-bodied,

I would call Munch's taut, hedonistic to the verge of morbidity, of an extraordinarily noble pedigree. Of all our artists, Munch has the most neurotic temperament. He belongs to that breed with delicate, unhealthy, sensitive nerves, which one encounters more and more often in more recent art and who not infrequently derive a certain satisfaction from calling themselves Decadents, the children of an over-refined, over-civilized age. An age whose salient characteristics point in this direction is an age I do not salute. I *want* the healthy. And for ourselves, I hope we shall have a *healthy* culture and a healthy art. We have the Bohemians, but we also have the outdoor life, walking and skiing.

*

Munch nevertheless receives a new State scholarship. Fifteen hundred crowns. He sells *Night* to Doctor Arents for one hundred crowns, a third of the catalogue price. Besides this, before the exhibition opened, he has also sold *The Absinthe Drinkers* for five hundred crowns to the American Richard A. McCurdy, who in the purchase contract demands that the picture be called *Une confession* instead. Munch knows that he has to sell pictures now.

And to think of money too.

* * *

Dear Munch: Thank you very much for your letter. It was so nice to receive it, even if you were a bit tipsy. Oh, yes, it's good to have the bottle to turn to for comfort when life is hard. Well, you must have got to Paris ages ago, after you had taken leave of the one with only one tooth and the one with the pretty face. You're a funny chap, you know, Munch. They say it's damned cold down there at the moment. Feeling the cold as you do you're probably quite miserable now. But mind you don't fall ill again. I think it's mostly your own fault when you do. You've probably become thin, skinny and down in the dumps again by now. And when I saw you last, you'd made such a good recovery. It would be so lovely if you could come to Stavanger sometime, Munch. Our home is so nice, outside as well as inside. We've covered the sitting-room walls with lovely hand-woven tapestries and paintings and outside we have all the beautiful mountains, now completely covered in snow. Yes, life is wonderful. I've never wished I hadn't been born. There are so many beautiful things in the world that I could easily live twice and still give heaven a try as well. P.S. Today I received a long, anonymous note from a member of the public who threatens me with the most terrible things if ever I dare to exhibit my daubings again. The author concludes by saying that, if I will not listen to other people's advice, then at least listen to Frits Thaulow, who said of me that I had not a jot of talent, but was just one of the multitude of Norwegians churning out dirt cheap pictures to hang on farmers' walls. Your devoted Åse Nørregaard.

* * *

Yet when he again sets sail for Paris, the fever returns, the November wind over the North Sea, ice needles in his chest, rheumatic fever yet again. As he lies in the hospital in Le Havre there is a fire at the Christiania Gilders' Workshop and quite a number of his paintings are lost, including the first version of *The Morning After*. But it is money that is on his mind. The pictures are heavily insured, valued at seven hundred crowns. Apart from this, he intends to do as Krohg does, make literary sketches, write illustrated letters, get them published in the newspapers back home.

*

Munch in hospital. For two months he is among the dying in the public ward. Outside it is brilliant sunshine. The sea and the air blend into a shimmering sea of light. The birds sing, a train whistles, in every sound there is joy.

* * *

The dying man presses his face into the pillow, squeezes it with his bony fingers, starts suddenly, then glances anxiously around him.

The nurse over by the window gets up, large and brimming with health, comes over to the patient, hips swaying.

I don't want to die! Not now!

The dying person grasps her by the shoulders. The bony fingers dig into the flesh like steel springs.

In the evening, the nurse pulls the sheet up to the deceased's chin. She takes hold of the wrists and bends them slightly.

Then she crosses the man's arms upon the sheet.

*

Munch sits in the armchair, seeing all that goes on.

Around him there are women. Pale nurses. They bring medicine. Then they disappear again with empty glasses and bottles.

The smell of medicine. Of female skin.

He hears the young nurse's swaying step in the next room. He pictures her round hips and her sensual mouth. The brown eyes.

Was she as he imagined her? Was he a fool? Never the seducer, but the observer. Safely ensconced in the armchair.

He glances round him. Sick patients. Pretty nurses. He does not seize the opportunity, but holds it up for scrutiny. Perhaps the impression can be utilized in some way.

Stolen embraces. He has long since seen through sister Amalie and the young medical student from Paris.

It is the year of sorrow, of impotence and of realization. The year when for the first time he sees his future as a painter. He sees all the pictures he has to paint. But there is no coherence in his life, no obvious straight line leading from one point to the next. He returned to France to work, conquer, realize himself. And here he sits exhausted in a chair in hospital.

He sees the rain, the fog, the wind driving in from the Channel.

The sheets are cold.

A compatriot of yours has been admitted, says Jean.

Munch starts, glances suspiciously around. A Norwegian?

Yes. He's very hard on the wine. He's already drunk the bottle which was to last him the whole day, and he's eaten the bread intended for lunch. He's thrown the empty bottle on the floor. Now he's lying there calling out: Bread! Wine!

*

Christmas in Le Havre, Munch hears the cries of the dying, the whistle of trains, fantasizes about stinking bodies and funeral processions.

Munch, come on, let's have a bit of a chat!

Beer! Munch, do you know Halvor Mührer from Myra? What a devil! Stricter cap'n there never was, cracked the whip at home and everywhere else. Came from the little cottage across the sound, he did. Poor as a church mouse. Got on though. More bread! Wine! Hell of a pirate! Pinched the fishermen's fish and nets. Real devil. Took the stick to his kids. Beat 'em over the shoulders. Ingeborg was his first missus. Strong as a rock she was for 'im, brought the 'ole damn family up. Steva, Lars's missus, she drank, a real cow she were. She were the only one could handle 'im. Scared stiff of her he were. Pricked 'is bloody conscience. So crude she were that, in broad daylight, she pulled up her dress and showed off her bare belly and the whole shooting match for all to see, more embarrassed 'e could never be.

* * *

Dark, dreary streets.

The horse is a lifeless machine enveloped in a cloth. The coachman perches high up on the seat.

Munch in Paris. Should have stayed here. This was where he'd wanted to come to. Now he's just passing through. He sits in a gloomy horse-drawn carriage, shouts to the coachman:

To the Gare du Nord.

Past the gaslamps, clattering along, passing black top hats and elegant ladies. Gare Saint Lazare, Place de l'Opéra.

The start of a new year. 1891. The year of *Spring Day on Karl Johan*, *Evening*, *Rue Lafayette* and *Night in Nice*. The year of Seurat's *Circus*, of Seurat's death, Anna Ancher's funeral, Zola's *L'Argent*,

Vuillard's *In Bed*, Bonnard's *Women in the Garden* and Gauguin's *La Perte du pucelage*.

Munch on his way south. He can still feel the rheumatic fever in his body. Impossible to remain in this damp, ice-cold city. Interlude in Paris. Horribly cold. Dear Aunt, you have no idea how cold it was!

For three days he lay frozen stiff in a miserable room. The last day, he had an attack. Frightfully nervous. Racing heart.

South! To the Mediterranean with its balmy breezes.

There are blizzards in Algeria and Italy, children freeze to death on the streets of Toulouse and Marseilles. Yet Munch wants to go to the Mediterranean. To Nice.

*

Gare du Nord. He finds the train and immediately sets about looking for a seat. He has heeded Aunt Karen's words and bought a first-class ticket.

Then he discovers the enormous sleeping cars. They have seats which can be folded back to make them almost like beds. He climbs aboard with all his things, his huge feather quilt strapped tight together. It is always ready for use, in case he is too cold.

Munch opens a door. To his delight, he sees that the compartment is empty. He goes in, closes the door behind him with a feeling of well-being, unrolls the feather quilt and lays it on the couch, stretches out full-length to see whether it's long enough. He'll be able to sleep perfectly here. He takes four eggs out of his pocket, uncorks a bottle of wine and has also brought a little bread with him.

Suddenly there is an uproar out in the corridor. He hears the voices of a man and a woman in heated dispute about the compartment. They are right outside the door, arguing. Then they open the door and see Munch.

I beg your pardon!

Munch stands up: Isn't this my seat?

Your seat? Did you say *seat*? Let me see your number!

My number? I don't have a number, do I?

Let me see your number, I said!

A conductor comes along, starts to wave his arms about like one possessed.

Out, out, out, I said!

He is completely beside himself.

Munch reaches for his belongings, is pushed out into the corridor and down onto the platform, his belongings follow him. The feather quilt, a spare collar, the bottle, the eggs and the winter overcoat.

He stands crimson with rage outside the compartment window. A man pokes his hand out and places Munch's hat on his head.

Munch sits frozen stiff in another compartment, his jacket collar turned up over his ears.

Two Frenchmen, an English couple and a sick German from the hospital in Le Havre. Frozen to the marrow. Poison thoughts. The German is also bound for the warmth and the sun.

The train clatters through the night. Munch dozes, feels his nerves gradually getting the better of him. Sudden palpitations. Cold sweats. The compartment is dark and gloomy. The other passengers are transformed into shadows. Suddenly, it is as though all of them are sitting in the antechamber of death.

In Marseilles the train swings east. The sun streams in, the ice on the windows begins to melt. Munch wipes away the condensation from the windowpane.

Then suddenly he sees the Mediterranean. A small bay opens up with a white villa on the headland. Long green waves break on the shore.

Open the windows! Back to life again! The sick German leans back in his seat, surrendering himself to the beams of sunshine which flood into the compartment. He smiles wanly. Another year. Sun. Warmth. Perhaps he is saved after all.

The Englishman sits there motionless, but the Frenchmen jump for joy.

Let me tell you, Sir, I've been so very ill. Two months of it.

Oui, oui, Monsieur.

Then comes Cannes. The coastline. The green trees.

At last he sees Nice. He sees the gardens and the villas, he sees the deep blue sea. He sees the orange trees.

* * *

Dear Aunt: In a warmer climate I can paint something I'll be able to sell later. The doctor said I should take a sulphur bath. The trees are in leaf. There are roses in the gardens. I realize I must look after my health.

Munch feels he has been set back by the fever. Now he is writing occasional travel articles. He sends an almost ecstatic letter to *Verdens Gang*. Nice, Queen of the Mediterranean. Munch writes a piece about façades, enthusiastically describes the rows of large hotels, red and white parasols, pale demoiselles, stylish Parisiennes, dandies from the boulevard with bell-bottomed trousers, hollow-chested consumptives wrapped in shawls. The flowers in the market square. Soon it will be carnival time.

By the end of January the illness has finally released its grip. He travelled to Nice with twenty crowns in his pocket. When his aunt sends the longed-for sixty crowns, he can leave his disgusting hotel and eat his fill for the first time in a fortnight.

Oysters and wine. He'd even had to pawn his watch for three francs. But now the restaurant doors are open and there is music outside. It is January. Munch notes that the weather is as glorious as it is in June at home in Norway.

*

He has always been afraid of dying, though he has never shown his horror of it. At the Dörnbergers in Tønsberg he was the calmest person in the room. In hospital in Le Havre he wrote reassuring letters home to his family. He is not yet thirty, but has been at death's door several times. He has coughed up blood, developed fever that no doctor could check. He is neurotic and unbalanced. He can fly off the handle for a bagatelle. He grieves for the loss of his mother, his sister and his father. He has a broken heart as a result of what he himself regards as fru Thaulow's betrayal.

But in Nice the public is not his enemy. One year older now, he has the courage not to be put off when confronted by incomprehension. Deep down, he knows that the most important people, Krohg, Heyerdahl and Thaulow, are with him in spirit. The enemy is a more practical one. The military doctor is dead. The family needs money. He needs money. As Aunt Karen hints: the fire in the Christiania Gilders' Workshop was quite opportune. He checks out of a disgusting hotel and rents a reasonably-priced room in the city's gloomy criminal quarter. He wants to be fully cured. Now he carries his sketchbook with him everywhere he goes, starts to write new literary notes, his *Violet Book*, is unable to concentrate on a single painting, instead spilling ink on a feather quilt, a great big blot, like a huge map of Russia. He fears reprisals from the proprietor. Everything he saw so clearly before him at the Montagnes Russes is now overshadowed by impressions of Nice. As is the thought of quickly earning some money. He wants to please them at home. Aunt Karen is selling moss pictures and his sister Inger is giving music lessons for fifteen crowns a month.

He is sensitive to the situation at home. Letters take a long time from Christiania to southern France, up to a fortnight. Also snow and winter storms now stand between Munch and his family. If there is a letter he has not received, he notes down all the dates of the last letters in order to make sure that the apparently missing letter is not actually missing at all. He knows how his aunt, sisters and brother save. They are still a small family. Andreas is completing his medical studies, travelling in three times a week from Nordstrand, the family's new home, taking the first train in the morning. The money is disappearing, Munch has credit in a restaurant, is waiting for the insurance money and the scholarship to come, sharing accommodation with what he terms dandies and ragged down-and-outs, as well as an Arab. A raincoat which was his pride and joy has been stolen by someone. He doesn't want to go on living there. People who smell, stink of onions and cooking oil, speak Piedmontese. He gets a new address, 53 rue de France, Villa Cille-Boni just behind the Promenade des Anglais, which looks like a splendid palace, but is actually quite cheap. Twenty-five francs a month. He is waiting for money, is unable to focus on anything but walking. All the practical things. Dear Aunt: Still nothing? Incomprehensible why the scholarship money hasn't been sent to me yet.

Munch tries to write like Krohg. He gets the seaman, his compatriot from the hospital in Le Havre, down on paper, tries to catch the jargon, the pithy expressions. He knows that this is the sort of thing Krohg has earned money by. Drawing or writing, the newspaper will pay.

He sits in Nice writing. It is the city of pleasure and flowers. And everyone here is writing travel articles, selling occasional impressions. Boulevard des Anglais is dazzling in the sunshine. Munch writes about the waves surging towards him. He tries to portray the gentle melancholy, the vast loneliness. But the words bring him no peace.

* * *

What a nasty squall.

A little nervous, he loosens the main halyard around the mast. The sail flaps and strikes him in the face.

It was old Bjølstad who taught him to sail. Now he lets out the jib and secures the sheets.

He has loosened the backstay. The mainsail flaps noisily.

He hesitates a little now, his hand on the forestay. Then he clenches his teeth. The cowardice. Will he never be rid of it?

A squall fills the sails. He puts out to sea.

He feels his heart pounding as he sits there, hand on the tiller.

The cowardice. He must drive it out of every sinew. Knows this is highly dangerous. But he must try and rid himself of it.

What if he capsized now? The death struggle would be brief. His lungs would fill with water. He has seen people who have drowned. He has seen the foam round their mouths. The wild gaping eyes. It is not death he is afraid of. It is the death throes. The moment it happens.

Must drive out the cowardice. Become another person now. Not one who stands waiting by gaslamps. Not one who wastes his time spying on women who are carrying on with other men.

What if a wave were suddenly to seize the boat? Oh, he would struggle, scream, perhaps even pray to God. But nobody would hear anything. Just a few minutes. Then everything would be over. Life. The cowardice too.

He is shaken out of his reverie. The boat luffs up into the wind, levelling off. Here comes a little wave. He looks out over the water. It is as black as night over there. It is getting nearer and nearer. Like a small tornado.

Suddenly the boat picks up speed and heels over.

He tries to luff and level the boat. To no avail.

The gunwale is completely submerged. Water pours in.

Then he lets go of the sheet.

The boat rights itself again. The sail flaps noisily in the wind. The boat shoots away. Foam at the bows.

What became of his cowardice? Another sailing boat swishes past just at that moment. He greets the occupant who stands there watching him.

Blasted squalls! he shouts.

The stranger nods. Lousy wind, he agrees.

Then they are far past one another.

Now he runs before the wind, back to land.

Now there is nothing he is afraid of.

* * *

Dear Munch, I was so glad to hear that you've got to Nice. I only hope it'll do you some good. Here it's still very wintry. There are a good few inches of snow outside, and it's cold, horrible and nasty. But it can't be long till spring comes. I long for it so terribly. The blackbirds, the larks and the lapwings got here ages ago. Now all we need is a bit of sunshine and everything will be fine. Thanks ever so much for your letter. You suggest we should drink to being on first-name terms next time we meet. Yes, I'd really like that. It's not a bad idea. At least, we can see how it works out. It'll probably be a bit tricky to start with. In any case, we'll make sure we really have fun when next we meet. Harald and I were talking about it only the other evening. There we sat so warm and snug in the cottage, getting a little tipsy, and thinking how absolutely wonderful it would have been if you and some other nice people could have been here with us. I must say we really miss some nice people here. That's quite a lot of 'nices', but it's so nice to have a nice time, I think. Don't you think so too? Your devoted Åse Nørregaard.

* * *

He thinks of pictures, of unwritten laws he will break in the attempt to create a sense of shimmering on the canvas. Then he writes: It might have been fun to treat all those people who for so many years now have looked at our paintings and either laughed or shaken their heads in dismay to a little lecture. They simply can't comprehend that there could be just a trace of sense in these snapshots, these impressions of the passing moment, that a tree can be red or blue, that a face can be blue or green. They know that it's wrong. From when they were small they have always known that leaves and grass are green, that skin is a delicate shade of pink. They simply cannot comprehend that the intention is serious. For them it can only be a hoax, cobbled together any old how, or the work of a lunatic. Preferably the latter.

* * *

One day he meets Mr Moen from Bergen.

Have you been to the casino, Munch?

No, not yet.

Would you like to come with me to Monaco, then?

Munch is following in Dostoyevsky's footsteps. He boards the train, sees dazzling white villas, mountains which strike him as profoundly naïve, sees how the smoke from the train settles white and shining amongst the orange trees and the palms. He is travelling with some acquaintances. A Dane and a man he calls herr Horneman. Nice, Villefranche, Beaulieu, Monte Carlo. The obvious route for a penniless artist. He sees the prince's palace before entering the huge rooms, observes the sombre elegance. The ceiling is lofty and there are large mirrors. The air is stifling and his feet slip on the polished floor. Little knots of people have gathered round the tables. In the inner sanctum there sits a pale plump little man holding a black rake. A fat, shiny yellow snake lies beside him. He scoops the gold towards him. Hundred franc pieces. Munch notes the silence in the room. Women and men stand there concentrating and following the game, women mostly, their faces strangely flushed right up to the temples, like heavy makeup. The men are pale, with small, nervous flourishes of the hands. Munch is in Dostoyevsky country. The celebrated writer was obliged to send novels back home to Russia in instalments to keep himself afloat financially. Munch is in the very same spot, knows that he could win a vast amount of money in seconds. On a bench lies a man staring vacantly in front of him. His face is crimson. He is smiling, his lips are moving, he looks like a madman. A moment later, he sees a fat person with a red sash throwing his hat into the air and laughing.

Horneman is in difficulty. He is drawn irresistibly to the gaming table. Munch notes that he is pale, with beads of sweat on his nose.

Don't you want to have a go, Munch?

No, I don't think so.

Just stake five francs.

No. I don't know how to play.

You stand beside the roulette wheel. It makes a little clicking sound. I've lost, as you see. Five hundred francs.

Don't tell me. I want to go now.

Really?

Yes, I think so.

Well, I'll leave too, then.

Munch and Horneman go out into the lobby.

Pull your tie down, Horneman. It's right up round your neck.

But Horneman doesn't hear. He smiles vacantly. Won almost a thousand. Then lost fifteen hundred. Then won a hundred back again.

Munch is distracted by the visual impressions, the human fates which are suddenly revealed to him. The lady over there, for instance. And lovely to look at she is too. Munch sits at the station waiting for the train. The lady comes up to him, rigid, pale, looks right at him – no, she is staring fixedly ahead. Her pale lips are moving. Munch can hear her counting, reckoning up. Un, deux, trois. The language of roulette. But Munch is outside it all, sees potential paintings instead of untold riches. He sees the dreary Monte Carlo hills rising against the evening air.

* * *

On 10th March at long last the scholarship money arrives. At a stroke Munch ceases to be preoccupied. Now he need no longer think of transfers, all the short, anxious letters home to the family, the uncertainty as to whether he can afford to eat. He has lived very frugally, sat at the window in the little side street hearing the din from the carnival, heard familiar tunes, seen one or two masks, felt the humiliation of asking Moen for money, which he lent him with great reluctance. Now he has the money, now he can stretch the canvas once again. He paints with light, sparingly applied brush strokes. For once he basks in the sunshine, luxuriates in the warmth, the palms, paints a neo-impressionist portrait of a couple of buskers using pointilliste technique, portraying the spring green palm leaves in light blue. He paints the joy, of the kind he felt in the revelation on Karl Johan, paints the Promenade des Anglais with people who symbolize nothing but carefree everyday life. The woman with the flower basket, the man with the stick, a cocky fisherboy with a cap.

From his room or from the roof of the Villa Cille-Boni he sees Nice by night. He paints *Night in Nice*, which the National Gallery will buy later that year, when it is displayed at the Autumn Exhibition. Another blue painting. The moon is reflected in the facades of the houses, it shines in pink, blue and mauve. From the window a reddish-gold gleam is thrown out into the night. As in Seurat's *Banlieue*, Munch builds up the picture's rhythm and architecture. A firm touch. But the brush strokes are still like dots.

* * *

Dear Edvard: Aunt Karen has come down with a serious bout of pneumonia. A week last Tuesday, she sat down and wrote to you. When she had finished, she suddenly started to feel cold and to shiver violently. During the night, she became feverish, had a pain in her side. Her condition gradually deteriorated. She grew delirious and her mind was wandering. Andreas and I were with her and expected her to pass away at any moment. She was thinking about you so much. You were constantly in her thoughts.

*

Dear Inger, You must write to me each day and let me know how Aunt is. I wish I'd been at home, it's not very pleasant being so far away. It's simply beyond belief how things go wrong. My hopes are pinned on Aunt's strong constitution. When the wine arrives from Gløersen, you must all have some. If things take a turn for the worse, I'd like you to telegraph me. If possible, I would come home.

*

Dear Edvard: Isn't Aunt remarkable, managing to get over such a serious dose of pneumonia? If you could paint a nice little picture of Nice for Dr Lindboe, we'll make sure it's beautifully framed. He's very fond of simple, straightforward pictures. I haven't slept for seven nights. Isn't it nice that I'll be getting the post of organist in due course? Aunt sends you many greetings.

*

Dear Aunt: This was so out of the blue. From your last letter, I had the impression that all was going well. The weather has been treacherous this winter but I don't think you've been very careful either. Overexerted yourself perhaps. It's a good sign that your pulse is normal, as Inger tells me in her letter, but you could have a relapse. I've written to Gløersen to ask him to send you some of his finest wine. You must drink generous amounts of it when your fever has subsided.

*

Dear Edvard: Just this minute three bottles of wine have arrived from Gløersen. I realize this is your work. Thank you. It will certainly build me up. I've already drunk a glass of the most delicious port.

* * *

In late April 1891, Munch arrives in Paris by train, third class. He takes up residence at 49 rue Lafayette, must have seen Gustave Caillebotte's Boulevard Haussmann picture before himself painting *Rue Lafayette*. But Munch's perspective is more angst-ridden and extreme, like the first signs of agoraphobia. In the vast light spaces of the boulevard the human figures are mere dots. He makes the rounds of the exhibitions, trying to make up for what he has missed, wishes to remember for ever how he too, in his time, had the courage to formulate his first timorous admiration of Monet and Gauguin and was accused of being influenced by the loathsome, hypocritical Wentzel, the twig painter. Now he probably sees Gauguin again. He will later place Gauguin above Van Gogh, will be attracted by the great raw energy in both of them, the vast contribution they made in the transition from realism to synthetism and symbolism. At the end of May, Munch is standing in the lobby of the Théâtre de Vaudeville and is once again infused with the power of the Montagnes Russes. He feels the power of the writer Maurice Maeterlinck who succeeds in getting *L'Intruse* staged to raise money for the ailing, penniless Verlaine. Synthetism and symbolism. A foretaste of the coming summer. All that is already complete. Dismal living life.

* * *

From Antwerp Munch returns to Norway with Håkon Jarl. He stands on deck looking healthier than ever before, has noticed that other people think he looks well, the sunshine in Nice, the walks, he has borrowed sixty crowns from Aunt Karen, put off his return home in order to see the Gauguin exhibition. On the boat, he reflects on future subjects for paintings, is drawing closer to his old haunts, Borre, Åsgårdstrand and then Christiania, is getting close to resuming work on his *Violet Book*, closer to painting new pictures based on memories, the same streets, the same forest and the same coastline as before, but now with different actors. Soon he'll be back in Åsgårdstrand. The thought of seeing Norway again makes him nervous.

* * *

Munch is sitting on the steamer from Christiania to Åsgårdstrand.

Hello, says Doctor Graff. You recognize me, don't you?

From Tivoli?

Yes, that's right. I say, Munch old fellow, you seem so down in the dumps today. What can we do to cheer you up?

I'm no more down in the dumps than usual, Munch replies. But I do have a touch of rheumatism and slight palpitations. Can you suggest something to take? Incidentally, what excellent clothes you're wearing. Elegant and practical. Where did you buy them?

You're so melancholy though, Munch. Please don't give me that melancholy smile!

Oh that, says Munch. I'll never be happy.

*

Jappe Nilssen joins the boat at Horten.

Munch notices that his friend must have drunk a lot. He looks tired, ravaged, has become Oda's new lover. Once again, Krohg the husband is a mere spectator.

How are things with you, Jappe?

I had a slight attack of nerves in the night, Munch. But it's passed now. Couldn't sleep. I came to Horten to buy some chloral. Peculiar visions, as though I was delirious. But it was only nerves.

Munch nods, listening. Jappe Nilssen reminds him of himself six years earlier. But Jappe is not as helpless as Munch himself was. Jappe carries a pistol around with him.

Oda Krohg is no fru Thaulow either.

Two strong wills have clashed. Oda and Jappe. Munch is coming to Åsgårdstrand to paint with fru Krohg this summer. They are hoping to exhibit their pictures together at the Autumn Exhibition.

But now she has Jappe in tow.

*

There they all sit in the hotel, the atmosphere is unbearable. Jappe suddenly starts laughing. Then come the tears. Suddenly he throws himself down, drags himself across the floor. Then fru Krohg starts to weep too. She tries to talk to him to calm him down. He has not slept for several days.

Tight-lipped, Krohg looks at his wife.

What a face, says Oda. Looks as though he's just read *Monte Christo*. Shall we be friends then, Christian?

Never.

So this is the end, is it?

Yes.

Oh dear. That's terrible. We're not good friends any more, then?

I'm not like Jappe, Krohg says stiffly. I'm not just a yes-man.

Oh dear. Someone who never says anything but yes and amen, you mean? Eh? D'you think Christian's a nice chap, Jappe dear?

No.

See, Christian? Jappe can say no after all.

What a wet rag! says Krohg haughtily. When I'm painting and need a rag, I'll think of Jappe. That's the kind of wet rag he is.

Don't you think I'm pretty, Christian? You've said I'm so pretty. Said I'm the fairest of them all, didn't you?

Jappe sits nervously on his chair without uttering a word. He stares at the floor. It's as though he likes having her there beside him, regardless of what she says.

*

Munch notices that Oda has a bruise from a blow above the eye. He proposes they go down to look at his pictures. They're supposed to be painting together, after all. She thinks it's an excellent suggestion, but cannot concentrate. Instead, they remain in the hotel lounge waiting for the steamer. Munch notices that she is extremely nervous. She says hardly a word, constantly flits out onto the veranda to get a better view of the channel through which the boat passes. Munch knows that she is expecting her two children from her marriage with Engelhart. But it is Jappe who is the reason.

A duel with pistols, she says suddenly. Imagine if it comes to a duel. Jappe's as mad as a hatter, you know.

She is on the lookout for the boat. There it comes at last. She's straining to see the children.

Would you like to come home with me for supper? Munch asks.

No thanks. I'll drop in later.

He eats alone. Then he goes up to his hotel room to bed. He removes his coat and waistcoat. Then he hears footsteps. There is a knock at the door. Oda's voice.

Are you just going to bed, Munch? I've only come to return the one-crown piece you lent me. Why don't you open the door?

Munch opens it.

I was half-undressed, fru Krohg.

Bah, that doesn't matter.

She stands there in the half-light in her pale grey cloak.

He is embarrassed, clears the clothes from a chair.

Won't you sit down? Or shall we order some wine? We can go down to the lounge, or to your house?

They step out into the corridor. Munch sees that the two children are sitting on the stairs.

* * *

It is evening.

Munch walks beside the sea, along the edge of the forest between Åsgårdstrand and Borre. The moon pushes its way through the clouds. The large round stones stick up out of the water, suddenly looking like sea people.

He recalls that she who once walked here at his side looked like a mermaid. She had shining eyes and flowing hair. Jappe Nilssen's unhappy love life is conjuring up memories. Munch hears the water lapping and gurgling between the stones. He sees the grey clouds along the horizon. A man and a woman strolling out along the jetty towards the yellow boat.

Then he writes: It's her, her gait, her movements, as if she were standing hands on hips. But I know she's miles away from here. Oh God, God in heaven, Munch writes, have mercy on me, let it be her, I beseech you, just this once! He writes almost the same words as Jæger does in *Sick Love*, doomed and yet moving towards a painting, with Max Klinger's etching *Evening* of two years before as inspiration. Now it is the turn of Munch's *Evening*, later known as *Melancholy*, with Jappe Nilssen as model, a picture which Christian Krohg, the model's rival, will eventually find himself praising to the skies: A violet charm with two venomous green flecks in it, flecks you can lose yourself in and become a better person for seeing, it moves you like a story of young love, reminding you of something fine and gentle in your life, heralding, almost with a hint of menace, a new sombre, serious note in art.

Munch's *Evening*, painted at Åsgårdstrand in the company of the heroine of the drama. Oda Krohg does not try to dupe him with yellow flowers. That is why he lets her into the room, in the half-light where she stands in her pale grey cloak. They paint together and are going to be in a special category of their own at the Autumn Exhibition.

She paints *Sunspots*. He paints the unhappy *Jappe on the Shore*.

* * *

Christiania. Warm, dusty August. Munch goes into the Grand where he sees Christian Krohg sitting with Jappe. They've probably been sitting there all morning drinking together. At present all Krohg can offer is friendship. He carries a brothel on his back and Jappe knocks at the door. United by a shared loss.

Munch feels weak, knows what lies ahead of him now. He calls in at the picture framer's and inspects his pictures, feels that he is distancing himself more and more from public taste, knows that he is going to cause people even greater offence. Is this why he writes that he is tired, dragging himself through the streets, going to bed at eight o'clock of an evening and awakening at eleven o'clock the following day, just as tired, suddenly writes that painting as such is unimportant, writes on Saturday 31st August that he is sitting at the Grand, so weak that he can scarcely hold his head up. Oda and Jappe cross the street, she in a black dress, younger and prettier than ever, gliding over the ground, fresh and smiling, whereas the men lie dying in the morass. Krohg is the wiliest, the most patient, wants to save his wife from downfall, perhaps already knows that, if he waits long enough, he will get her back. Munch sits at the Grand listening to Jæger talk about the woman who almost cost him his life, sits at the Grand and sees that the playwright Henrik Ibsen is sitting on his right, as remote as ever, hears fru Holmboe assert that Munch's voice is so cold that he'll probably never fall in love with anyone, not with that voice anyway. But he himself was once like Jappe is now, like Jæger was three years ago. There is something comical about love. Oda and Jappe drive out of town along Drammensveien. Munch suddenly feels a pang of jealousy.

* * *

Drink up, Munch!

No, I'm not interested in drinking any more, I just get listless when I'm drunk. I'll probably soon get used to not drinking.

Really?

I think you'll end up dancing the cancan on the graves of all your friends. The ones who've drunk themselves to death. The ones you've driven to drinking themselves to death.

Jæger laughs.

*

Munch drinks all the same. He has his memories which he can't get out of his head. They are driving him towards lethargy, exhaustion. The memories of fru Thaulow are still painful. The days and nights become blurred, indistinguishable. Suddenly he is sitting at the Grand with Jappe and Bokken, Oda's sister. A private room just for the three of them. Two bottles of champagne and some fruit. Munch sits there feeling the effect of the alcohol, while Bokken sings French chansons. Is this the sort of song fru T. sings now?

He has reserved a room in the hotel for himself and Jappe. Jappe cannot be left alone in such a state.

Bokken and Jappe are going up to Oda's.

Munch walks to the hotel.

He lies in bed. Tries to sleep. An hour passes.

Then Jappe arrives.

Want a beer, Munch?

No thanks.

Rubbish. You're jolly well going to have a drink too.

Jappe sits beside the bed, but forgets the beer. He sits quietly on the edge of the bed and stares straight ahead.

I think I'm going mad, Munch.

Has she been beastly to you?

She's vile, Munch. Utterly vile. I'm so fond of you, d'you know that? You're the only person I really like. I love Oda most. Like you best.

Jappe falls to his knees beside Munch's bed, buries his head in the feather quilt.

Have you any idea how much I love her?

* * *

Milly. Who's that saying Milly's name? Suddenly he hears fru Thaulow's name.

They're talking about her!

But she's not called fru Thaulow now. She's called fru Bergh. Wife of Ludvig Bergh, the actor.

Oh my God. Not the other one surely. Not the lieutenant.

Fru Milly Ihlen Bergh. Previously the captain's wife. Now a chansonnette singer.

Munch is sitting at the Grand with the Krohgs, Michelsen and some other people.

Milly is ill, says Michelsen all of a sudden. She's had an operation on her mouth. Her jaw. They think it's brittleness of the bone. Bergh himself looks ghastly. They say he hasn't slept for a fortnight.

Love, in other words, says Christian Krohg dryly.

Is she any better? asks Oda, with more feeling.

Munch listens to the voices, the trivial replies, all the things they are ignorant of. Feels as though he could have shouted it in their faces. His own life.

It'll recur, Michelsen goes on. She may have to have another operation.

And she was so beautiful, says Krohg, taking a sip of his whisky and soda. Is she ugly now?

No idea, Michelsen replies.

Silent, Munch sits there listening. In his mind's eye he sees the soft lips, the irresistible neck, her eyes which could suddenly flash green. Every word is like a heavy blow. Milly. She who for six years – my God, can it really be six years ago? Oh my God. He would never have imagined that Ludvig Bergh, a common actor – it's beyond belief. Munch sits there at the coffee table and feels his heart pounding. Rapid, heavy beats. The whole world must be able to hear it.

* * *

Dear Munch. First I wrote you a long letter. It ended up in the waste paper basket. I've now rewritten the beginning three times, and it's ended up in the same place. I think it's because when we've been together recently you've shown such contempt for me and all women that, where you're concerned, I've lost my cheery self-confidence. All I can see is your cold, contemptuous face, and it destroys me. True, I'm nothing but a poor woman, but I take it to heart when you are like that. I've been on the verge of tears a few times recently, when I've met you, and I don't think this was your intention. Yours, Åse Ng.

*

Yes, there is a harder look in his face now.

Fru Bergh. He can't credit it. So she did leave the captain after all. Precisely what she said she could never bring herself to do. Flew straight into the arms of an actor.

Munch is at the circus. He is spying on her now. Sure enough, here she comes now with her mother in that white dress with the black hem. Her husband is on stage. How charming!

She's more beautiful than ever.

Then she catches sight of him. He feels her eyes on him. It's as though she were looking straight through him, as though he is simply not there.

Executed! Dispatched with a single blow!

She's won now, won hands down, what a humiliation.

He can't stand any more looks of that kind. Shaking, he gets up from his chair and walks – creeps – towards the nearest exit.

* * *

He paints Jappe's desperation in several versions. Yet it is himself he is painting. Himself out there on the greyish-white shore at Åsgårdstrand, where he got to know the new world. The world of love. How young and inexperienced he had been! He'd come straight from the monastic

family home at Grünerløkken. Unlike his friends, he had no idea whatever of the world of women. Was almost twenty-two years of age, but
had never known the intoxicating power, the first kiss, the joy. She was
two years older than he, was an experienced salon lady from Christiania.
A seductress with eyes larger than celestial orbs. Yellow hair, tentacle
hair, snake hair. The deadly serpents on the Gorgon's head, which insinuated their way into his blood, coiled tight round his heart. He hates
her, feeling as he does that he will never be free of her, that the echo of
her laughter will ring in his ears for the rest of his life. That terrifying,
wonderful laughter.

*

It is over for good. No more false hopes. For six years he's behaved
like an idiot. He hurls himself into his work. In the midst of the drama
between Jappe, Oda and Christian Krohg, Munch sits trying to talk
about painting, impressionism, symbolism and colour with Oda, sitting
beside her, leafing through a few magazines, paints the Caillebotte-
inspired portrait of her sister Alexandra, paints the woman in a trance-
like light, perhaps influenced by the atmosphere of hysteria around him.
Christiania is buzzing with rumours. One night Oda was about to jump
out of the window in her nightgown and run off. But Krohg restrained
her, went to fetch some water, came back and saw her sitting weeping on
the fence, calling for Jappe. The threshold to madness, paranoia. The
rumours. Have you heard? Fru Krohg won't drink any water now
because she's afraid it may be poisoned.

*

Winter is in the air, autumn in Christiania, Munch has lost his equilibrium, is confronted by dark powers, not just in his own mind. First all
the business with Jappe Nilssen and fru Krohg, then seeing fru
Thaulow again at the Circus Theatre. At the autumn exhibition, he
observes Albert Besnard's etchings. With his *La Femme*, Besnard
comes close to Munch's own intentions with *The Frieze of Life*, portraying people at a moment in their lives when all inessentials are stripped away. Besnard's *Suicide* shows a woman in the act of throwing
herself from a bridge.
  Munch observes, yet cannot maintain the observer's distance from
what he sees. Ever since childhood, he has been receptive to the powerful melancholy and existential impulse of Nordic nature. The flaming
red sunsets. Perhaps it was as early as the autumn of 1885, after the summer with fru Thaulow, that he went up to the vantage point at Ekeberg
and experienced the attack of angst which he was later to capture in
Despair and *The Scream*. In any case, it is likely that he revisited it in
autumn 1891. He walks along the road with two friends as the sun sets.
He feels a kind of breath of sadness as the sky suddenly turns blood red.

Then he stops, leans against the fence, feels deathly tired. He sees the blazing clouds, like swords dripping with blood, above the indigo fjord and the city.

Munch at Ekeberg. Since puberty, his sister Laura has battled with insanity, has had shorter or longer bouts of it. Right beside the vantage point stands Oslo Hospital, the women's asylum, ringed by slaughterhouses. Is this where his sister Laura will end up? His sister who is capable of disappearing into herself completely, only to re-emerge suddenly from the darkest despair. Munch hears the cries of mental patients and of dying animals. He stands on the edge of the abyss and is overcome with angst. Yet this too is one of those sacred moments of the sort he experienced at the Montagnes Russes, those moments which will be transformed into paintings. His friend Vilhelm Krag tries to put into words what happens in Munch's mind:

How dark it fell in the blink of an eye. How ominously black the sky now grew! Infinite deathly hearkening hush. Close, close by yet far, far off. Not clouds near sunset's glow, not a reflection of the day now done. But flickering fire and pouring blood, flaming swords and molten streams, doomsday's dread and pangs of death, a blazing text in the hall of night, all life's unfathomable horror.

* * *

Tiredness, angst, palpitations, dizziness.

Always the same symptoms. A sensation of not being able to avoid falling.

The picture of Jappe is hanging in the exhibition. *Evening.* Later the picture is called *Melancholy.*

The public stand before the picture and laugh. Then Krohg writes in *Dagbladet*:

A young man sits in the foreground, head in hand, gazing out across the calm water. The public jostle one another in front of it. Yes! It's quite true, any fool can see that the man looks as though he has toothache, and that he has no nose, ears or mouth. But what on earth has that to do with the mood in this picture?

Mark my words, though. It is not without reason that Munch's pictures are so much discussed. You will not believe this, but a time will come when you will ridicule anybody who says what you are saying now. Like every fickle public, you will, of course, forget this and deny that you ever said anything of the kind.

* * *

Munch meets the Skredvigs at Christiania East Station. The night train south leaves at 11.15. Back to Nice.

A terrible wrench leaving Bekkelaget, says Munch. It was so lovely today.

But you're ill, Munch, aren't you? Surely it must be nice to get away?

Christian Skredsvig notices that Munch looks even thinner and more poorly in his grandfather's old-fashioned overcoat. He arrives at the station with his painting chest, campstool and umbrellas. Is the long painter's umbrella stick with the shiny steel point also meant to come along? Of course! Then his portmanteau, full to bursting, gapes open to reveal an undigested primus stove. Perhaps he also has petroleum in his luggage. As the wheels begin to turn, he unwraps a roasted capercaillie.

Such a wrench to leave Bekkelaget. Aunt Karen never complains, but Munch knows that she is worried about an uncertain economic future. Besides this, Laura has disappeared without trace.

First Munch stops off in Copenhagen, sees Paul Gauguin's *Aux roches noires*, or *Life and Death*, two naked women, one of them with her hands over her ears and gaping mouth, just as Munch will later paint the protagonist in *The Scream*. Inspiration, reminders, revulsion. He stands in Hamburg's Kunsthalle and sees what he calls loathsome German art, languishing women, pictures of massacres with rearing horses, shiny canon balls, you find it repellent, disgusting, until, that is, you stand in front of a picture by Böcklin, *The Sacred Fire*: dusk settles over the grove, the huge massive forms of the trees stand against the air, but between the stems there is still light, the dwindling daylight, which streams in from outside.

Then he continues his train journey south.

Munch lies, sits and stands his way through the journey, in fourth class, on a train which stops at every station. At night the cold seeps in through the walls. Munch gets into arguments with what Skredsvig calls growling grey workers. They are arguing about the seats.

Skredsvig is sore and stiff from sitting and also irritable. Why couldn't they have travelled third class?

Munch's reply is to curse the government for giving such stingy scholarships. He has received a national scholarship for the third time running. But only one thousand crowns.

Still, he is used to humiliations on train journeys, knows what it means to travel without any luxury to speak of, is bound for Nice, that Nice he is already fond of, the city of hope and light, makes a quick sortie into Paris, 7 Avenue de la Grande Armée, visits Visdal and Hjerlow in a repulsive room in Rue Condamine, a room where there is a regular hurricane from draughts through the windows. He asks Aunt Karen to send fifty or sixty crowns to Jonas Lie, PS if she hasn't enough money, twenty crowns will do. The waves rush in towards the shore. Wave upon wave. Wave upon wave. The sea opens its mysterious bluish-green maw, as though to show what actually dwells down there in the depths.

He sees that the waves fall breaking towards the shore, tumbling over the sand like shining, molten silver, sparkling in the sun with the sheen of mother-of-pearl. Before them they cast their shining foam, white as snow, splashing his face with salty spray.

What is that out there behind the azure line, behind the shining clouds?

Munch goes from one end of the spectrum to the other in his innermost self, reflects on the beginning of life, the seed of life, launches into a monologue with himself on the theme of immortality, refuses to deny the existence of the soul, writes that it can justifiably be asserted that the seed of life, the breath of life, must exist after the death of the physical body. The property of holding a body together, getting all the constituent parts to develop, makes him think that nothing is lost, indeed there is no example of it in nature. The body which dies does not disappear, the parts disperse, are transformed, but the breath of life, what actually becomes of it, is something no one can tell. To claim that it continues to exist after the death of the body is certainly just as foolish as trying to say how or *where* it will exist. Fanatical belief, such as Christianity, prompted scepticism. Foolish, Munch writes, to make any assertions whatever about what comes after death. And what of realism? The tidal wave which suddenly swept the world. What one learned was that nothing existed unless proven. Yet the mystical will always exist. The more discoveries are made, the more things there will be that cannot be explained, for instance, everything that is so fine and delicate that it exists only in vague notions, experimental thoughts, inexplicable things, in new thoughts as yet without form.

*

In Nice, you can walk about without a coat in early December.

It's as warm as July. There are hyacinths and roses, blackcurrants and figs.

Dear Aunt: Skredsvig lives a little further out of town. They are nice but terribly careful about their money.

Munch in France, the land of Meissonnier, the interpreter of the pleasures of the bourgeoisie. Contemporary art, Munch notes, is the art of the large salons, of the academies, of medals. Yet naturalism, impressionism and symbolism have become means of expressing just one thing, that which is human. Munch feels the irresistible draw of Åsgårdstrand, sees Oda Krohg and Jappe Nilssen in a passionate embrace, remembers the execution at the Circus Theatre.

Then he begins to paint.

Our forefathers were right when they said that love was a flame, for just like a flame it leaves behind nothing but a heap of ashes. A snake is burrowing deep within his heart. But he paints.

* * *

In *Dagbladet* on 16 December 1891 Bjørnstjerne Bjørnson writes:

> Artists' scholarships thrown away! We recently read that the painter Munch has travelled to Nice together with his colleague Skredsvig and wife. We also read that Skredsvig and wife were apparently to continue their journey. Presumably this means that Munch is to remain in Nice, in other words, that he is in poor health and will be staying in the spa. When he recently received the scholarship for the third time, it was rumoured that this was because he had been in poor health and still was. However, our scarce and extremely modest artists' scholarships are not some kind of sickness benefit scheme. Private funds should be used to provide for a sick man. The scholarship should be given to someone who can derive full benefit from it for his art.

*

Ørebladet the following day:

> The way the Government has allocated the national artists' scholarships this year has attracted a certain amount of attention. In particular, a number of people visiting the exhibition have been not a little surprised that Edvard Munch has now been awarded a scholarship for the third year running. The many people who cannot understand what is so special about the pictures Munch has exhibited this year, and who are none the wiser after Christian Krohg's explanation and defence, have in all humility and simplicity commented that they think it rather strange that this man is to receive yet another scholarship. In *Dagbladet* yesterday, B.B. informs us that Munch is ill and that, for the sake of his health, he is to stay in the spa town of Nice. If this is so, we can only agree with Bjørnson that Munch should not have been awarded a scholarship. As B.B. says, the few scholarships we have are not some kind of sickness benefit scheme.

*

Frits Thaulow in *Dagbladet* the same day:

> Reply to B.B. Your protest against Munch's scholarship stems from ignorance of the factual circumstances and lack of understanding of his art. It is easy to be hostile to what one does not

understand. So he is ill, is he? No, far from it. Munch is in excellent health, thank goodness, he is not taking the baths or any other cure; he is simply painting. Just let Munch carry on painting in Nice and we will never ask for a scholarship to be put to better use. Look at the lovely little picture just bought by the National Gallery. You should have heard him at my home just a few days before his departure: The pale green tints and the blue! The dry, brown power of the cliffs. The vast lines, against an infinite Mediterranean. There are things in Munch's pictures which, with his exaggeration bordering on caricature, have spoilt them for me, but there are also things in his works which unquestionably place him in the front rank of the young painters. He is bound to become the vanguard of the rising generation. He should have an artists' scholarship for as long as he lives.

*

Bjørnstjerne Bjørnson in *Dagbladet* five days later:

It is rather nice to see a painter acting decently. Something of a rarity these days. But not even my friend Frits Thaulow can pull off the feat of writing like other ordinary mortals where art is concerned. I offer you the amusing detail that I, who have seen far too little of Munch's paintings and therefore did not express any opinion of them, am now said to have expressed a clear, definite opinion which can be read between the lines. In several columns he takes issue with this clear, definite opinion expressed between the lines. I thought hr. Munch was ill. If that is not the case, my first criticism falls by the wayside. But my second criticism holds good. If Munch is to continue to receive help, then hr. Frits Thaulow must help him himself and also enlist the help of others. The national scholarship cannot permanently be associated with one man except at the expense of others.

*

On 4 January 1892 Edvard Munch writes in *Dagbladet*:

To Bjørnstjerne Bjørnson. Not until just the other day did I see your quite extraordinary comments about the artists' scholarships. I have therefore been unable to refute them before now. You complain that I have received a scholarship three times running, and that our artists' scholarships are not a sickness benefit scheme. You say it was rumoured I had received a scholarship this time too because I had been ill and still was so. Do not believe rumours, Mr Bjørnson! I was struck down by an acute illness the last time I was abroad, so that I did not derive full benefit from my stay, which was one reason why I received the scholarship again, not because I was still in poor health. Incidentally, it is not all that uncommon for painters to receive the scholarship for three years. You say that Munch is remaining in Nice while Skredsvig is travelling south. So Munch is ill, is he? Why don't you check your facts, Bjørnson. Let me reassure you, Skredsvig is living just round the corner, has no thought of travelling and, like me, is very absorbed in painting. Let me further reassure you that I feel extremely well, that I have still not yet taken any cure at the spa and would also inform you that Nice is in any case not a spa, but a rather large town on the Mediterranean, a town which is much frequented by painters because of its natural beauty. If you would like further details, I shall be only too happy to oblige.

* * *

Winter in Nice. Christmas with the Skredsvigs, who chop down a large cactus for the occasion and use it as a Christmas tree. The garden is full of roses and orange trees. The Skredsvigs are in a miserable state, down with influenza. But Munch is only affected for one day. He feels above it all, has probably already begun painting *Despair*, the first version of the attack of angst at Ekeberg.

1892. Munch will paint new versions of *Puberty* and *The Morning After*. *The Mystery of the Shore*, *Inger*, *August Strindberg*, *Despair*, *Death in the Sickroom* and *Evening on Karl Johan*.

News reaches him that his sister Laura has been admitted to Gaustad Hospital on the twenty-ninth of February, at twenty-five years of age. His sister Laura, who was always so ambitious. Laura, with her first-rate memory, who read vast quantities of books, who could not tolerate being corrected by anyone. Now she is being admitted to the hospital, is convinced she has bungled her exam. A strong, nervous agitation. Her father's sudden death. At an early age she had to try and fend for herself. Started work as a teacher, but was too nervous. Set off to see a Swedish layer-on of hands, wanted to go to China. Came back to Christiania and for a time lived at the women's hostel, in the chapel, in the railway station. Seven øre a day. Later, a year living with relatives. Now she is being admitted to Gaustad, her mood vacillating wildly, one minute elated, the next sombre and taciturn. What is that under her bed? And why does one of the doctors have three red feathers in his hat, she cannot imagine anything worse than red, cannot stand red, is it just to annoy her? She refuses to take chloral, stuffs snow down between her breasts in the hope of catching pneumonia, an involuntary nervous shaking, convinced that both she and her family are complete wrecks. Is transferred to room C.

*

Munch is at the other end of Europe.

Then it insinuates itself back into him.

The slender threads. The tentacles. Snakes.

He sits by the fireside, ill and weak.

Not influenza, some other type of illness. A feeling that his very thoughts are on fire. He has not worked recently, only his brain has been working, it works the whole time, the memories come seeping back ineluctably, like a rising tide.

Spring is always worst. The light returns. Everyone else is smiling. He feels the pain in his chest, deep inside, can point to the exact spot which is the focus of each painful memory. Memories of the dead. Everything he did, everything he neglected to do. Never to be able to remedy it.

He sits by the fireside and is overcome with a ridiculous feeling of gratitude to certain individuals who at one time or another were nice to him, an old captain who once smiled at him. Munch sits by the fireside almost in tears. The ever-present fireside, the fireside of childhood, the fireside at St Cloud, now the fireside in Nice. He sees it crackling and burning, thinks melancholy thoughts about his father, at the same time reflecting on the Inquisition and all the ill religion has done. He has seen fru Bergh's name in the newspaper. It strikes him as terribly upsetting. She had been holding a concert somewhere. It is enough to kindle his thoughts. Yet again he must ask himself: Did she ever love him?

He describes himself as a lanky, split wreck.

Does he mean divided? And what does lanky mean anyway? At all events, he lets the woman bear responsibility for his pain, his angst, his fatigue and his melancholy.

She chains him to the fireplace, to the memory, to the lethargy. He is not yet able to reach right back to the summer six years ago, to paint her as he saw her then, eye to eye, mouth to mouth, on the shore and in the forest. The lethargy, the breakdown came *later*, but he gropes his way back, gets closer to her, memories of a lost existence: Let's hurry, she said. There are so many people I know. They walked down the hill leading up to the church. Hurrying. We'll go down to the railway, she said. Happy, he walked along at her side. There was something between them. She and he – something between them alone. They turned down beside the railway, walked along Railway Lane to the bridge. She led the way, he followed, they turned right, under the railway arches, here they walked to and fro along the river, looked down whenever they came to a gaslamp, withdrawing their arms, walked down the other side of the river, where it was completely dark. How could she forget?

* * *

The lovers stand in a room embracing. It could be an apartment, or a house. First the man and the woman stand to the left, then to the right of the window, like a shadow on the wall, offset by the chair on the other side. Munch paints three versions of it.

With each version the street outside becomes clearer. The world. People. Who cannot reach the lovers inside. They are wrapped in each other's embrace, lost in one another. Outside life goes on at its usual hectic pace in stark contrast to the silence within. The silence of *The Kiss*.

The cypress sets a serious note. The proximity of death. The tree's silent mystery.

In the first version the light is unsettling. Nothing can be relied on. The exterior can fall to pieces. The walls are cardboard, the light too harsh, a quivering unease, anything can happen. A scene from the past! A blood-red sunset and a mysteriously lit room.

Already when going about with Colditz, Munch had begun to speak of love as an autopsy. Corpse, blood and entrails, scalpels and instruments. The lovers' blood, the blood of the sky, the particular congealed blood of angst! The consequence of the kiss.

*

He writes: When you are in a state of great agitation, the clouds in a sunset strike you as reminiscent of a layer of blood, so it is surely pointless to paint ordinary clouds. You take the direct route and paint the immediate impression, the picture. You paint the blood of the clouds.

* * *

At the beginning of March Munch moves in with Skredsvig at the Villa Bottazini, Saint-Jean-Cap-Ferrat, perhaps mainly because this will save him more than thirty crowns a month in rent. He never forgets that it is *his* duty to provide for the family.

Andreas has passed his medical degree with honours, Inger is teaching, but Aunt Karen will never earn much from her moss pictures. Munch also knows that he is controversial, that the paintings he intends to paint are not necessarily all that marketable.

*

Then he discovers that roulette is a capricious creature with a will of its own.

Valets open silent velvet doors. Munch feels he is beholding a mythical monster. He is surrounded by Hungarian counts, Russian princes, gloved stewards, who gravely place the stakes after instructions communicated with the utmost discretion. Old Parisian dragons, beaming happy ladies of the demi-monde in the latest elegant fashions from Worth smiling throw their golden louis on several tables at once. With a questioning look, the croupier clinks his rake on a little pile of gold.

Mon Dieu! Gagné!

Munch loses. Skredsvig wins. He invites Munch to the Café de Paris. Louis Roederer in cold silver buckets. Munch drinks from large crystal wine glasses.

*

Days spent gambling in Monte Carlo.

Could it be possible, though? A millionaire for five crowns?

Munch gets himself some bread and a bottle of cheap red wine. In Monte Carlo everything is expensive. When overcome by hunger and thirst, he finds a seat in the gardens.

A gendarme claps a hand on his shoulder: Not here.

All right then. Munch stands up and walks further along with the bread and wine. There, a bench. And he is completely alone. Can eat and drink and look at the sea.

Two stern looking detectives dart out from behind the myrtle hedge at his back:

Circulez! S'il vous plaît!

*

Then he wins thirty francs at roulette.

Suddenly it begins to switch from red to black several times, once red, once black. Munch feels a strong impulse: act upon it! It's going to continue like this! But he does not yield to it, not until red comes up twice. Now it'll be black, he thinks, and bets on black. Munch with Skredsvig in Monte Carlo, has been to a concert and heard Svendsen's symphony, black comes up for the fourth time, he wins sixty francs, hears the whirr of the wheel, works out a method, lies awake at night, sees the little strip between the curtains, it gets lighter bit by bit, he lies hot in his bed, tosses and turns, notes it down on paper, has a method, works out a system, needs money for his work, needs money for Aunt Karen, for his sister Inger, for his brother Andreas, for his sister Laura.

*

Suddenly he wins a hundred and fifty francs in five-franc pieces.

During the night he returns to Nice and builds a kind of altar of the coins on the bedside table, with two large candles on either side.

The glitter of mammon.

In the morning the altar has disappeared.

During the night he has knocked the coins onto the floor.

He soon loses the money in a little casino for *petits chevaux*.

Afterwards, he stares at the golden wine in the glass.

How much better and nobler one becomes by eating one's fill, by sitting in well-lit dining rooms seeing beautiful, rich, unworried people around you. But there is just one thing which counts, just one thing beneath the loss, the sickness and the merciless criticism: Never to forget *why* he is a painter.

This is why he paints pictures from the gaming table in Monte Carlo.

* * *

In late March he leaves Nice. He has enough pictures for a large exhibition, knows that Christiania is once again where he must be, there are wolves and vultures aplenty in those windswept streets. Back to the critics, not just the ones who write under their own names, but to the ten contributors to *Aftenposten* who over the years have hidden their identities behind one signature.

It is September 1892. Fifty pictures are hanging in the premises of Tostrup the jeweller, right opposite Parliament, right opposite the building where, ten years earlier, Munch had shared a studio with six colleagues and received tuition from Christian Krohg. The exhibition includes *Inger in Black* and *Evening*. It includes the beaten yet defiant *Hans Jæger*. It includes *Night in St Cloud*, *Kiss*, *Jealousy*, *Despair* and *Man and Woman on the Shore*, as well as the pictures of Paris and a portrait of Gunnar Heiberg, who was later to become so loathsome to him.

Munch has been in Åsgårdstrand during the summer. May already have painted the two Juell sisters from Kongsvinger. But has definitely painted *The Lonely Ones*, penetrated even further into his vision at the Montagnes Russes, depicted two people with their backs turned, she in light-coloured clothes and with golden, flowing hair, he dark and gloomy, transfixed in a tentative movement, torn between action and paralysis. It is a decisive moment in the lives of both of them. One can imagine that suddenly these are the only two people on earth, at the moment they emerge from the forest onto the shore and see the light summer night settle over the sea. Munch has carried this painting within him for seven years. Now he paints the inexpressible loneliness in a corner of nature.

Munch in the gallery at Tostrupgården. Some of the paintings have been given new titles. *Portrait of Inger* is now called *Harmony in Black and Mauve*, *The Lonely Ones* is called *Colour Mood in Blue and White*, and *Despair* is called *Mood at Sunset*. At the same time, the Dane Jens Ferdinand Willumsen exhibits his synthetically inspired paintings in Abel's Art Salon a stone's throw away. A secessionist exhibition in the middle of Christiania. The strongly Gauguin-influenced Willumsen and the – in the titles at least – Whistler-inspired Munch.

14 September 1892, a repetition of previous clashes, smugness, petty bourgeoisism and malice: Is Munch making a mockery of the public? The shore looks as though it is strewn with huge chunks of whale meat and old saddles. Delirium and fevered hallucinations. Yet some critics

also write of a sensitive observation of nature which makes him almost, but only almost, into a classicist. Willumsen has drawn the fire away from Munch: Whereas Munch only gives vague hints of the sense impressions the objects have made on his nervous mind, Willumsen's hand is as strong as a blacksmith's, nervous people should keep away, his pictures can induce acute insanity.

Verdens Gang acknowledges Munch's courageous independence and total refusal to allow himself to be influenced by attacks so totally bereft of understanding. For Munch the exhibition is mainly a fresh statement of his aloofness, of his defiance, a warning that under no circumstances will he be stopped, not even with the newspapers, not even with Bjørnstjerne Bjørnson, as his enemies.

And he has sold three pictures.

*

Then another painter comes into the gallery.

Munch's compatriot Adelsteen Normann, a member of the Düsseldorf group who, with his pastose virtuoso technique, considers it his life's mission to recreate Norwegian fjord landscapes. He comes into the exhibition and sees paintings that both aesthetically and in their form of expression are as far removed from his own art as can possibly be imagined. But he does not turn on his heel at the door, does not shout 'Painter? Humbug, more like!'. He stops before every single picture. There is something about these pictures which strikes him, a violent force, a vital nerve. The Norwegian is a member of the Verein Berliner Künstler, a traditional painter in the land of Wilhelm II. He stands now in Tostrupgården in Christiania and it occurs to him that it is precisely Edvard Munch who should exhibit in Berlin, among Prussian Schlacht und Stiefel painters, in a society whose very chairman, Anton von Werner, is the official battle artist of the Academy and of the Empire.

On the fourth of October, Edvard Munch receives an official invitation to hold the first separate exhibition in the Verein Berliner Künstler, the first exhibition in the newly opened circular gallery in the Architektenhaus, and there is nothing in Munch's character or temperament that would make it natural for him to decline such an offer.

He has nothing to lose.

* * *

He arrives in Berlin, the imperial capital with its monuments, palaces, parks and museums. By this time, there are well over a million inhabitants. Berlin has become a city that artists in other countries have started to talk about. Strindberg's *Father* was staged two years ago and promptly banned. *Miss Julie* was put on only seven months ago. Owing to strong reactions from the female element in the audience, the play was taken off after only one performance. The Freie Bühne has become renowned for its controversial stagings of Dostoyevsky, Ibsen, Zola and Tolstoy.

Wusts Hotel zur Stadt Köln, Mittelstrasse 47.

Dear Aunt: To be on the safe side, I am going to repeat what I asked before. Do you think you could possibly send me the drawings which are in the portfolio as well as any other drawings you have there? Then there are all the reviews by art critics in my chest of drawers. It's probably best to send them by steamship. And then there's evening clothes. Those items of clothing are extremely important down here, so I think you'd better send them as well, by the cheapest method; it's more than likely that I shall have a good many social engagements once my exhibition is in full swing.

*

The exhibition opens on the fifth of November 1892. Munch has been advised against being present in person in the circular gallery lit by sky-lights, for it is feared that some of the older painters may kick up a fuss.

Yet there is nothing to suggest that Munch has come to Germany in order to shock. He has expanded the exhibition with a few paintings from the 'eighties, including *Spring*, in other words revealing a desire to be liked for paintings which at this stage no one can possibly find provo-cative any more. He has come to Berlin with enormous ambitions, dreaming like any artist on the threshold of a major venture that he will earn understanding and recognition. Hitherto he must have thought that Berlin could give him both. He cannot be so self-assured that what the public thinks of his pictures has become a matter of indifference to him. He has revisited galleries at night, re-working pictures which have just been panned by the critics. He has displayed an almost over-sensitive receptivity to criticism, a form of vulnerability which is a fur-ther sign of a longing for acceptance. It is therefore most likely an elated almost frenzied young painter who hangs his paintings for the exhibition.

He listens to the warnings of his friends and colleagues, has a beer, shrugs his shoulders, awaits his sentence.

On the stroke of ten o'clock the doors are thrown open.

The German public marches in, connoisseurs of the naturalistic pic-tures of Max Liebermann and von Uhde, experts on battle scenes and brown paintings. They are coming to see what a young whippersnapper of a Norwegian thinks he is doing in Berlin. They arrive, their senses long since deadened by knowledge, opinions and prejudices. They decide to honour this particular exhibition with their presence because they are so utterly certain what a painting should look like, indeed they know it down to the last detail, know that art is based on laws, a corpus of laws which, as far as they are concerned, is already written, a hefty tome replete with prejudices and paragraphs on aesthetics. What confronts them is a world they do not know, a world of youth, passion, fear and desire.

They file into the elegant, circular gallery lit by skylights. At the sight of all the pictures on the walls they cannot believe their own eyes. Their thoughts suddenly become audible, a wave of indignation, of almost embarrassed but at any rate bewildered outbursts of laughter, of exclamations of surprise, and even cries of anger. These are the pictures from Tostrupgården, the pictures depicting the key scenes from Munch's past, two people on the shore, the blood-red sky, the kiss, night, the same pictures but with new critics: *National-Zeitung, Kunst-Chronik, Frankfurter Zeitung* and *Berliner Tageblatt* instead of *Aftenposten, Morgenbladet, Dagbladet* and *Verdens Gang.*

*

Art in jeopardy! All true aesthetes should mourn this day! Good Lord deliver us!

*

Even Anton von Werner, like George the dragon slayer, joins in the fray against the Nordic daubings, the polluter of art Edvard Munch, or E. Blunch, as the *National-Zeitung* calls him, who has subscribed to the laws of French impressionism to the letter and who, like all his compatriots, strives, if at all possible, to outdo his Parisian models in throwing off the shackles of all the laws which applied to earlier art.

The exhibition must be closed straight away! Such excesses of naturalism have never been shown in Berlin before. The Norwegian's achievements as regards formlessness, brutality in painting, crudity and baseness of feeling, completely eclipse the sins of the French and Scottish impressionists, not to mention the naturalists in Munich. It is pointless to waste any words on Munch's pictures, for they have nothing whatever to do with art. An impressionist, and a deranged one at that, has thrust his way into our flock of fine, reliable bourgeois artists. A complete maniac.

*

Dear Aunt: I've received your letter and parcel, thank you. Sell the evening things as soon as you can, as I need money more than clothes. Yes, the exhibition has opened now, and is creating enormous indignation, since there are a lot of terrible old painters here who are beside themselves about the new trend. The newspapers are complaining bitterly, though I have been highly praised in a couple of them. All the young artists on the other hand are very keen on my pictures. Unfortunate that *Night* was already sold as I immediately received an offer for it. Lots of people are coming to see the exhibition, a major art dealer here has suggested I should show my pictures in Cologne and Düsseldorf. Of course the only reviews you will see will be bad ones, the right-wing press will no doubt take care of that. So I'd better send you the good ones I have. Money is in short supply for the moment. I've written to Hjelm and a few others. Couldn't you drop Hjelm a few lines, he owes me twenty-three crowns.

*

It is November 1892. Kaiser Wilhelm II convenes the members of the Verein Berliner Künstler to find out exactly what this business with the Munch exhibition is.

The general plan is that the imperial capital Berlin will lay the foundations for a Germanic golden age in art, express pure ideals which will promote and unite the German State. In this context French influence is undesirable. After the discussion with the Emperor, the governing body of the Verein Berliner Künstler calls an extraordinary general meeting.

Only three days after the opening of Munch's exhibition, Professor Hermann Eschke has collected twenty-three signatures of painters and sculptors who have called for the exhibition to be closed out of respect for art and honest artistic endeavour. The chairman, von Werner, supports the request but despite all efforts cannot get the exhibition closed without a formal decision. Four days later, two hundred and fifty members sit locked in heated debate.

The *Berliner Tageblatt* has come out in *support* of Munch. The subsequently famous editor Theodor Wolff admits that he went to the exhibition for a really good laugh. Instead he writes: Let it be said by all that is holy that I did not laugh at these fine, hypersensitive mood paintings of dark, moonlit rooms, of lonely country roads on still Norwegian summer nights. My ears could catch the breath of strange melancholy individuals who wordlessly concealed their torment against the backdrop of the desolate boulders on the shore.

Professor Köpping, A. V. Heyden and Ludwig Knaus have also appointed themselves Munch's sword bearers, but Professor Eschke's proposal that the exhibition be closed is nevertheless adopted by one hundred and twenty votes to a hundred and five. With Professor Köpping in the lead, a hundred and five people rise and walk out. Such is the beginning of the German secessionist movement and of Munch's international fame.

The pictures are taken down from the walls. The exhibition is closed.

*

In its report on the stormy meeting *Berliner Tageblatt* makes it clear that the decision to walk out must not be interpreted as meaning that those who voted against the closure of the Munch exhibition were thereby paying tribute to the artistic trend it represents. The number of

Munch's friends is negligible in this circle, even among the younger element. The main issue was the question of principle. The basis of the opposition's standpoint was simply the demand that, in art, everyone should be given his say.

*

Dear Aunt: This is the best thing that could have happened to me. A better advertisement I couldn't have wished for. The art dealer Schultze has offered me either 200 marks in cash or one-third of the admission fees. What do the Norwegian papers say?

He wishes to be aloof, thick-skinned, above it all. His face displays no outward signs of being hurt, shocked or bewildered. The first reviews must have stung him to the quick, he cannot have read them without becoming flushed, not with shame, but with anger, perhaps horror too. As if he were in a court of law. Not a critique but a sentence, something intended as a punishment, some crime he has committed, for which he is supposed to feel guilty.

A complete maniac.

He *knows* he is not as bad as that!

Then his indignation is aroused. Trying to put him in his place, are they? That's one satisfaction he is not going to give them.

*

Dear Aunt: Isn't it incredible that something as innocent as painting could create such a to-do; I've never enjoyed myself so much as during the last few days; you ask whether I'm nervous. I've put on 6 pounds and have never felt better. Well, I see you are all very upset about my fiasco. Yes, *Aftenposten* doesn't change, does it? It reprints an excellent review from a German newspaper here but edits out all the favourable comments about me and doesn't mention my name.

*

Perhaps they expected him to take to his heels. But he decides to remain in Berlin. He wants to rent rooms and a studio. He wants to take the city on.

*

His pictures transfer to other galleries in Düsseldorf and Cologne which, after all the ink expended on him in the papers, catch the scent of financial gain.

When the pictures return to Berlin, Munch mounts an exhibition in the Equitable Palast at his own expense.

Suddenly he has money, eighteen hundred marks, the equivalent of a modest annual income for a middle class family.

On the twelfth of December it is his twenty-ninth birthday. For some time now, he has shaken off his anxiety, has forged ahead with an artistic vision, does not take any time off to celebrate his birthday, does not even take the time to stretch the canvases properly on the frame, hammers cheap frames round the pictures, hangs them higgledy-piggledy on the wall.

* * *

Then he meets Strindberg. Suddenly there Munch is in Berlin painting a portrait of the man they had sat discussing at the Grand back in Christiania. The poet, painter, photographer, chemist. The man they have read with mingled horror and fascination, the Strindberg scandal, the sex-fixated Strindberg who, as early as 1888, wrote: Friedrich Nietzsche has shot such a monstrous load of semen into my spiritual life that I feel I have the belly of a whore. Nietzsche is my spouse! Strindberg who, during his life, has had such a disastrous desire for suicide, who has already written: Get thee behind me, evil woman, then I shall again be good to all people, also to you. Strindberg, who after his initial infatuation with Germany, has become more critical, who arrived in Berlin a month before Munch, followed the laws of the market place and opted for emigration, turned his back on Stockholm for the simple reason that his plays were no longer being performed in Sweden, settled in Friedrichshagen, which he refers to as Friedrichsruhe, Friedrichshölle and Friedrichshald as the spirit moves him. Now he is a painter, producing pictures which he sells for a song, would have committed suicide had it not been for the children, is on his way to yet another marriage, this time with Frida Uhl, in November moves to the centre of Berlin, makes preparations for the staging of *The Creditors* at the Residenztheater, the story of a divorcé who wears down his former wife and kills her new husband with no visible weapon. Strindberg, the scandalous author who in a short while will present himself as Munch's pupil. Strindberg the neurotic, who has pointed the way and who will soon stroll in the streets of Berlin and, as a joke, trip Munch up so that he falls full-length on the pavement.

*

Strindberg shows him the way to the place E. T. A. Hoffmann, Schumann and Heine also used to frequent, the bar on the corner of Neue Wilhelmstrasse and Unter den Linden, Türkes Weinhandlung und Probierstube, a wine merchants' where you can not only eat and drink, but where you can carry on your life, have your own table, where you can choose from over nine hundred different brands of alcohol, where you can send telegrams and receive postcards, where you can sit and write poems and novels, make sketches for new paintings. The Turk's wine bar, with three stuffed Armenian wine bags suspended from rusty iron chains serving as a sign and making such a racket in the wind that on one occasion Strindberg says: The pig is grunting its welcome to us!

From then on, it is called Zum schwarzen Ferkel. At the Black Piglet.

*

Dear Inger: We Scandinavians, Strindberg, Gunnar Heiberg, Drachmann, myself and a chap called Paul, are virtually always together and meet in a little wine bar. I probably won't come home now until well into spring, by which time you'll all probably have moved somewhere else. Have you found somewhere to live yet? How is Laura? Send her my greetings.

* * *

It is 1893. Munch has taken up residence in the Hotel Hippodrom, Hardenbergstrasse, Charlottenburg. In April, he gets a studio at 11 Mittelstrasse. But it is still winter, the winter when, at a literary reception, the forty-four-year-old Strindberg meets the twenty-two-year-old cultural journalist Maria Friedrike Cornelia Uhl, educated at convent schools in France, England and Austria, and who has all the qualities Strindberg condemns in a woman: she is emancipated, impetuous, independent. The winter when the twenty-five-year-old music student Dagny Juel, née Juell, from Kongsvinger, comes to the German capital to study piano at Holländer's Conservatory. The winter when Munch will embark upon an intense friendship with both her and her future husband, the twenty-four-year-old Polish cultural rebel Stanislaw Przybyszewski, who had come to Berlin four years earlier to study neurology, mysticism and Satanism, who has already published his three psycho-physiological studies on Nietzsche, Chopin and the Swedish poet Ola Hansson, and who later that year will make his debut as a novelist with *Totenmesse*.

It is the year of the myth, the year when a little wine bar in Berlin almost attains the status of cultural centre of non-Latin Europe. It is the year Munch paints *The Storm, Vampire, Madonna, Moonlight, Death and the Maiden, Starry Night, Dagny Przybyszewska, The Voice, Sunrise at Åsgårdstrand, Evening (Melancholy)*. It is the year he paints *The Scream*.

More strongly than ever before Munch is drawn towards painting, work, towards the realization of the vision from Montagnes Russes. He has only just begun to speak of the series of pictures he will paint. The series which will become *The Frieze of Life*.

He is excited by the pictures he visualizes, by the company of Strindberg, by the various Scandinavian painters who pass through the city and are game for an evening of boozing.

* * *

It is then that he becomes aware of her, Dagny, or Ducha – the Polish word for soul – the name she is called by her future husband,

Przybyszewski, who later that spring writes: What difference does it make to me that the picture I love previously hung in a sleazy wine bar? People have maligned her most dreadfully, though much of it is true, and I know all about her previous affairs, but what difference does it make to me? Dagny or Ducha, who eight years later, on the fifth of June 1901, will be shot by her lover Vladislav Emeryk in Tbilisi, Georgia or, as Munch on that occasion says to *Kristiania Dagsavis*: butchered like an animal. Because she is a woman, because her lover has such definite ideas about what a woman is and therefore writes, before also shooting himself, that he is killing her for her own sake, kills her when she is least expecting it, kills her as she is smiling, kills her because she is not of this world, because she is so ethereal that her true essence is unfathomable, kills her because she seems like an embodiment of the absolute, writes that she is God.

Munch introduces her into his circle. Perhaps he knows her from before. She comes from a place by a river, among the trees, a place called *Tranquillity*. She looks like a sacred goat, like a kind of Titania or siren, like a wood nymph. There is no shortage of descriptions. For Munch she is perhaps above all a music student from Norway, and not the clinging type he has lately started to become aware of. Jappe Nilssen will later note her completely white hands. She soon becomes the focal point of the circle. Is this because she has gone to school with boys and learned to think of men as friends, is it because she takes men familiarly by the arm, tells them risqué stories, changes wet stockings in their presence and has a friendly drink with them, no strings attached?

She cannot fail to awaken memories in Munch, and longing too perhaps. But he knows how to keep his distance now, does not go so far as to let her spoil his working time.

One day she strides into the Ferkel with Munch at her side, blonde, slim, elegant and dressed with a sophistication which no doubt enhances her supple body yet without over-emphasizing her contours, thus dressed and swaying her hips she moves among the self-appointed geniuses.

It is the ninth of March 1893. Dagny Juel comes into the Ferkel, where Strindberg notices her, is already sure then that Munch and Dagny have had an affair, cannot comprehend that this is not the only possible relationship between man and woman, so long as she goes about with Munch in this fashion, walks proud and free in their midst, encouraging and sometimes reassuring, as only a woman knows how, her whole appearance at once calming and inspiring.

What this means for Munch is that her presence gives him fresh inspiration, new ideas, awakens his creative urge. But for Strindberg she becomes far too great a challenge: He is not a strident self-confessed cliché of a misogynist, but, as the French poet and psychiatrist Marcel Réja points out, a shy and extraordinarily introverted person, a man who does not choose but lets himself be chosen, a man who for all his preciosity, his Swedish haughtiness, is extremely vulnerable, completely unable to control his strong sexual urges, a man who cannot help compromising himself over and over again because he feels unsure of himself, inferior. Strindberg who, like Munch, lost his mother at an early age. Dagny Juel is an overtly sexual creature, but is quite able to lay down her own terms, is the opposite extreme of the virginal, motherly creature Strindberg has dreamed of. She comes as Munch's friend, and it is from within a great mist-filled grotto that Strindberg sees her. He is an antiquated badger who dreams of new worlds. But she is a sacred goat. Which animal is Munch in this scenario? *She* at any rate is The Lady, *die Dame*. Quite soon the stories, the anecdotes, the poetry begin to flow, their tone midway between adoration and revulsion. With a few exceptions, this is a bunch of people in their twenties, the twenty-five-year-old Dagny Juel, the twenty-nine-year-old Edvard Munch, the twenty-four-year-old Stanislaw Przybyszewski. Dagny creates utter confusion in the anthill, so that suddenly it is all Dagny's parties, Dagny's suppers, she gives rise to myths about female excesses, breaks down the limitations of time and space, becomes the source of fantasies about new, eternally changing life forms, the same fantasies as those already generated by Oda Krohg. She becomes a queen, a sacrifice, an angel, a demon, a fallen woman. A myth, an unfortunate word whose meaning lies somewhere between rejection and embrace, between apocrypha and dogma, simultaneously inspiring confidence and doubt, longer-lasting than what we call lies and truth. Ultimately the myth becomes its own truth, a concentration of the essence of a culture or a milieu, a projection of culture's dreams and nightmares.

Munch's myth is fru Thaulow, Munch's friend is Dagny, soon to be Ducha, the soul in Stanislaw Przybyszewski's life, though Stach is her husband after just a few months. They will live at 6 Louisenstrasse, where there are a table and chairs in the middle of the room, above the table a paraffin lamp with a red shade suspended from a wire, two beds only partly hidden behind a folding screen, a piano equipped with a muffler so they can play all night without disturbing the rest of the house.

She wants to play Grieg, he wants to play Chopin.

*

Stach. Twenty-four years of age, passionate eyes in a pale face, brimming with *joie de vivre* and belief in the future, a notorious liar and alcoholic, who considers extramarital relations as a right, nervous and sensitive, according to Munch elated one minute and depressed the next, before suddenly leaping up in ecstasy, and rushing over to the piano at full tilt, as though summoned by an inner voice. Then dead silence, then Chopin, Stach deeply moved by his own playing, and also able to move his listeners.

* * *

The Krohgs have arrived. Heiberg is also there. Strindberg looks up from the table wondering what the impact of Hans Jæger's novel *Sick Love* has been on this marriage. The book is a ruthless unmasking of them all, of Jæger's own perversions, of Krohg's generous stupidity, of Oda's doubts and passion.

The Black Piglet. Alcohol enough to ensure that ailing nerves deteriorate still further. Rumours enough to ensure the break-up of marriages.

Munch glances coldly around him.

Wherever Gunnar Heiberg is there is trouble.

There they all sit now, egging one another on.

Drachmann rises, wishes to drain a glass for Strindberg whose misogyny rivals his own, is forced to his knees for Aspasia, for woman, that masterpiece of creation. Drachmann characterizes those present by emphasizing how different he is from them: Nor am I like Munch, who came here to Berlin and had a *succès de scandale*, and who is now so full of it that being happy is beneath his dignity.

*

What happened?

Munch lies in bed trying to recall. He had stood up, had shouted something to Drachmann. Krohg had intervened. The atmosphere became unbearable. He had allegedly called Krohg a pretentious windbag. The words had just tumbled out. Bottled up contempt.

Afterwards, he had taken his hat and left, as Strindberg had shouted to him: Quite right too, Munch. If you hadn't said it, I would have!

*

Keep his distance.

What really happened between him and Dagny? In any case, they are now the best of friends. Przybyszewski got her. Przybyszewski, already teetering on the edge of the abyss. Przybyszewski who will later write: I have tried to portray a person's life as it is, warts and all, with his fall from grace, when he tumbles headlong down into the abyss, with all his longing: *n'importe où! n'importe où hors de ce monde*, to quote Baudelaire, in all his grandeur and his ridiculousness. That man, Przybyszewski continues, whom one has hitherto admired in novels as hero or despised as villain, has always been a pure fiction. His thoughts, his actions were a series of *conscious*, intentional actions. He assumed responsibility for his own actions, and was held responsible by others. Yet *true* life is an endless series of *unconsciously* ripened acts of will which will one day be realized, without consciousness being able to prevent it.

It is the surfacing of dark desires. Desires which destroy all moral considerations. It is a never-ending series of volcanic eruptions, Jacob's eternal battle with the angel, it is a constant revolt of the fiery core, which wishes to burst open the thin crust of learned convention, of the infinite variations of the phrase 'to be or not to be'.

*

Przybyszewski's novel *Overboard*. The painter Mikita's monologue:

> Yes, yes, it is strange how such a feeling can churn one up. What was bottom-most comes to the surface, as though unsuspected depths open up. A dozen worlds emerge. Then there are all the strange, unknown things which begin to stir, feelings so fleeting that they barely flit into the mind for a thousandth of a second. And yet one is influenced by such things for the entire day. And how nature reveals herself to one! You know, at the start, when she rejected my advances, I lay like a dog at her door. In the midst of winter, in the most terrible cold, I slept outside her room, and forced her to consent. But have I suffered! Have you ever seen a sky scream? No! Well I have, let me tell you! It was as though the heavens opened to reveal a thousand gaping maws and screamed out colour into the world. The whole sky: an endless series of stripes, deep red, then over into dark, pouring blood ... no! a pool, in which the sunset was reflected, and then a dirty yellow. Horrible, frightful, but grandiose ... Great Heavens! And then such happiness! I reached out and reached out. I could light my cigarette by the sun!
>
> ... but you see, love of a woman, that's something quite different, isn't it? You expect something in return after all. But friendship, well, you know, it's something that can't be pinned down, something delicate, something which slips through the fingers. And then, when you've been with a woman for three months without let-up ...

*

Munch heeds Przybyszewski's advice.

No to women. Yes to the easel.

Munch among gallery owners, collectors and businessmen, people who press coins into his hand: *Ich möchte Sie gern unterstützen.* There he stands, in the studio, in spring or autumn 1893, trying to find his way back to the scene of his original inspiration, another studio, autumn 1885, Christiania, Hausmannsgate, afternoon: in the room the furniture has the appearance of dark shapes, he sits slumped in the middle of the sofa, tired and lonely, has wandered up and down the streets, feels the urge to lay his tired head against a woman's breast, breathe in the perfume, hear her heart beat, feel her breasts against his cheek. It is just seconds before she will arrive, the studio in Hausmannsgate, she arrives tall, dark and clad in black, passionately he asks her to come to him, she steps calmly towards him, he opens his arms to embrace her, pulls her down beside him, unbuttons her coat, pulls aside her veil, throws his arms around her before she has removed her coat, buries his head in her, lies like this at length.

Munch in Mittelstrasse with a female model in his rooms, not Dagny Juel, but another woman with flaming red hair. It flows down over her naked shoulders. Like blood.

Is it mere coincidence that it should be Adolf Paul who turns up? The Finnish author whom all of them despise, who will later write his Strindberg book, lay bare Strindberg's persecution mania, his headlong flight from the ogress Dagny Juel.

Adolf Paul stands in Munch's rooms in Mittelstrasse. He is asked to place his head in the model's lap. She bends over him, presses her lips against his neck.

*

A woman's rapacious teeth. The bite of the vampire. Munch paints a bent, broken man. The woman has lain on top of him and forced him to his knees. The background is a strange blend of blue, green and yellow spots of colour. Przybyszewski sees the picture and finds it frighteningly calm and dispassionate, a resigned fatalism so deep it cannot be measured, the man rolls over and over in the depths of the abyss, lethargic, listless, delighted that he can roll just like a stone with no will of his own, yet still cannot escape the clutches of the vampire, nor can he rid himself of the pain.

The woman will always sit there and for eternity bite with a thousand snake's tongues. With a thousand venomous teeth.

* * *

In June, Munch shows his paintings together with Strindberg at the Freie Vereinigung Berliner Künstler. The works they exhibit are what the German critics call incredible daubings, what they mistakenly call the Norwegian Strindberg's pictures, and which are even less appreciated than Munch's blobs of colour, which herr Strindberg appears to have learned from.

But Munch and Strindberg become closer and closer friends, drawn together by their discussion about Eros and Psyche, drawn together by conversations about French symbolist literature, about Schopenhauer and Nietzsche, about psychology, alchemy and spiritualism.

Munch paints *Vampire*. Strindberg paints spontaneous Courbet-inspired tachiste seascapes, the like of which no one has ever seen before.

During the summer Munch does not go to Åsgårdstrand. Instead, he remains in Germany, paints landscapes with deeply atmospheric, smouldering colour, paints *Starry Night*, *Moonlight* and *The Storm*. Holds an exhibition in Dresden.

Dear Aunt: I'm now living just outside Dresden beside the Elbe. It's a beautiful spot. On the whole, I could manage very well here in Germany if I could make the necessary practical arrangements. I have a lot of wealthy friends down here, you see. I sold the little picture which, you will remember, was lying on the floor, for 100 marks.

He returns to Berlin, then on to Munich, lives by the Starnbergsee. Has little or no contact with German painters, is a lonely individualist, talks with Strindberg about the random element in artistic creation, proves to himself the value of spontaneous expression, of the chance discoveries which arise as he develops the painting, he is perhaps the very first painter to squirt the colours from the tube direct onto the canvas and let them run. Munch back in Berlin, unlike Gauguin he has no need to travel to Tahiti, has Tahiti inside him, paints *The Dead Mother*, paints *With Death at the Helm*, paints *Death in the Sickroom*. That at least is no chance discovery.

* * *

Autumn comes. Munch takes coffee and brandy in cafés, visits Ducha and Stach who are living from hand to mouth, pawning their clothes, selling furniture, playing Grieg and Chopin, writing poetry and prose: I hear the call of a beloved voice, seest thou the firmament of stars which fall upon my life? *De la musique avant toute chose*, music before everything.

The destructive urge in Dagny Juel, the destructive urge in her alcoholic husband. Munch follows their life together at close hand, sees how that strong and highly talented woman, the sacred goat, remarkably enough becomes submissive, he observes her somnambulistic psyche when Stach maintains that there is room for only one artist here.

When Munch paints the Juell sisters – it is Dagny who calls herself Juel – Ducha sits with her back turned, will not let herself be captured. Perhaps it is this remoteness which unhinges Strindberg, who calls her Aspasia, lover of Pericles, friend of Socrates, renowned for her intellect, her sensuality, her ability to influence powerful men. Strindberg, who claims to have had a three-week affair with her as early as March, in other words, immediately after her arrival in Berlin, while Frida Uhl, to whom at the time he was secretly engaged, was out of town.

The net effect on Munch of this chaotic environment must be titillating, exciting, a sort of counterpart to his own inner rhythm. He paints *Scream* in a burst of frenzy. He has seen the Medusa's head of life at an early age, but the Medusa's head has serpents for hair. The screaming individual painted by Munch is hairless. Is it because Munch wants to paint the absolute counterpart or is it the terrible fright, the thought of Laura's fate, the feeling that the hair is falling out, the paralysis of the muscles of the speech organs makes it difficult or even impossible to get the words out, the voice becomes hoarse and disjointed, one is struck dumb with horror, the tongue becomes rigid, the face slack, the bottom jaw hangs so the mouth gapes. The eyes are large because the closing mechanism has seized up, leaving them wide open, locked, staring. A person struck with horror can fall stupefied to the ground. What characterizes fear as opposed to sorrow is that the paralysis of the voluntary muscles is often heralded by a momentary convulsive spasm taking the form of a sudden shudder, a scream at the initial onset of the horror. Munch at Ekeberg again, overpowered by the colours, the blood-red sunset over Christiania, he paints the boats, paints the contours of a church, the small and perhaps trivial things which catch the eye, as in Dostoyevsky's *Crime and Punishment*, the particular little things, completely insignificant details, he paints *Scream*.

* * *

He comes home to his family at Nordstrand outside Christiania in September. Again he takes walks round Ekeberg, passes the women's hospital and all the slaughterhouses. Laura is appreciably worse, severely deranged. Neurosis. Her heritage from the military doctor. The past is catching up with him.

It is now that he paints *Death in the Sickroom*, paints Sophie's death in a completely different version, like an orchestrated, theatrical tableau. She is sitting in the apartment in Fossveien, but the room has become a stage room, a theatre set. Sophie is a blurred, indistinct figure in a chair. It is the family members who are clear. Her father, aunt, brother and sisters. Himself. Death dwells in this room. The dying Sophie is merely a symbol of something all these individuals will experience one day.

* * *

He returns to Berlin via Copenhagen. For two hundred crowns he sells four pictures for reproduction, hangs paintings in a couple of rooms on the first floor of 19 Unter den Linden, one of the most elegant buildings in the best part of town, carpets and sofas, the same evening as, a stone's throw away at the Lessing Theater, Strindberg's one-act *Playing with Fire*, a play about an erotic triangle, is premiered. Munch charges an entrance fee of one mark, a shocking price, arranges things so that the first painting people see as they enter is *Death in the Sickroom*, the work which most directly links him to synthetism and symbolism, to the symbolist poet Maurice Maeterlinck, perhaps also to the perpetual inspiration of Søren Kirkegaard, and his analysis, in *The Concept of Dread*, of the conscious dimension, in which the passing moment and eternity meet. On later occasions, Munch will call the painting *The Moment of Death*.

Further into the rooms hang the six paintings which Munch is showing as a study for the series *Love: Summer Night/The Voice*, *The Kiss*, *Vampire* (*Liebe und Schmerz*), *Madonna* (*Das Madonna-Gesicht*), *Jealousy* and *The Scream* (*Verzweiflung*). It is the germ of *The Frieze of Life*, the first series, yet including only some of the death motifs.

*

He paints *Madonna*, a subject which later, in the form of a drypoint etching, he will mount in a broad, flat frame thus giving himself an opportunity to decorate it with sperms and foetuses. Female lover, surrounded by snakes.

Munch is moving towards occultism and reads *Spiritismus und Animismus* by Alexander Aksakov, a gift from Przybyszewski, in a single night. He paints *Madonna in the Graveyard*, a woman in a Protestant cemetery with scattered gravestones, perhaps inspired by Krist cemetery in Christiania, where his own mother is buried. Madonna is a not-unambiguous image. Her lips are like snakes, fleshy, carmine-red, like rotting meat or fruit. Voluptuous lips. They part in pleasure or in pain. They open, as though in ecstasy, as though on a corpse.

Such is woman's earthly beauty.

It is death reaching out to life, the moment when a thousand generations of the dead become visible, together with the thousand generations to come, through one single face.

It is December 1893. Edvard Munch's thirtieth birthday.

* * *

Munch removes to 23 Englische Strasse, Charlottenburg, in February. The year is 1894. The year the tension mounts between Norway and Sweden. The year Laura is eventually diagnosed a schizophrenic. The fear of madness pursues him, yet Munch still feels strong. He works every day, has no need of all the nine hundred varieties of alcoholic drink available at the Ferkel. It is the year of *Fear*, *Evening Star*, *Ashes*, *Three Stages of Woman*, a new version of *Madonna*, as well as *Rose and Amelie*, the fat whores about whom Munch uses the word revulsion but who nevertheless look so amiable. It is the year of the first etchings: *Death and the Maiden*, *Vampire*, *Sick Child*.

Together with Servaes, Pastor and Meier-Graefe, Przybyszewski works on *Das Werk des Edvard Munch*, whose subtitle is *18 Pictures from the Contemporary Life of the Soul*, the first monograph devoted to the Norwegian painter.

Ducha has written her first novel, *Rediviva*, in which she anticipates what will happen in 1896, that Stach's mistress Marta Foerder will commit suicide. Marta Foerder, by whom Stach already has two children, by whom he will have more children, in addition to the children Ducha will give him. Ducha says to Munch that she does not have literary ambitions. At the same time, she admits that, having first started to write, it is impossible to stop.

Munch is a family friend, perhaps understands what might be termed Dagny Juel's search for her lost self, in music, in plays, in poems. She is like a ship in full sail, searching for her soul in an ill-fated lover who eventually shoots her and then himself, leaving behind a letter to Stach in which he writes that Dagny Juel has never loved anyone but Stach. Is this why she accepts her fate, falls down, down, together with the unhappy, destructive Pole who ultimately, according to close friends, quite consciously wishes to do her harm?

For the time being this is not yet realized. For the time being they are living in Berlin and have nothing but scorn for order. Any thought of the morrow is both ridiculous and unnecessary.

* * *

Just as Leonardo da Vinci studied the insides of human bodies and dissected corpses, Munch endeavours to dissect souls. He has perhaps started the year with another version of *Puberty*.

Dear Aunt: I have so many letters to write over the next few days that I'm just sending you a few lines for now. In March I have an exhibition in Frankfurt, one in Hamburg in April and one in Leipzig in May. Greetings to all.

*

August Strindberg leaves Berlin, on the way to his inferno. The Ferkel now becomes the focus of boozing on a grand scale in the circle surrounding the Przybyszewskis. But Munch has had enough. He moves to Café Bauer, coffee and brandy, has no desire to be at the root of fresh scandals. Der Fall Munch, the Munch case, is now an artist who sells precious little, who no longer shocks. The result is that demand also evaporates, and the influential art dealers in Jewish circles lose interest in him. He is more or less a spent force in Germany, and it is only in his hotel room and, for certain periods, his studio that he can continue to pursue his artistic vision.

The Munch case. He is invited by Count Julius Meier-Graefe to submit pictures for the journal *Pan*, its name decided upon by Ducha, and to which she will also devote a great deal of energy.

The Count is captivated by Munch's philosophical reflections as they are expressed in pictures. He wants what he refers to as *The Hair Picture* for the journal; this must be the first version of *Separation*, a new variant of the Medusa's head.

The picture shows a man standing with his back turned. He is completely at his wits' end. It is clear that the woman will now go her own way. The man is humiliated. He stands there only seconds after the execution, the execution of his emotions. His heart has literally become an open wound. But the woman has already stood up, moved away from him. She is going down to the sea. But her hair flows down behind her, entwining the betrayed man. He feels the pain. His heart bleeds. For it is not *his* separation.

* * *

In May Munch receives a letter from his brother Andreas:

Dear Edvard. Here too it will soon be summer. It's been a strange spring. As early as mid-March spirea and honeysuckle had started to flower and I regularly saw larks and butterflies. Ever since then I've been able to work with the windows open in the middle of the day. Yesterday, the first leaves on the chestnuts were out and one cherry tree is a mass of blossom. Apart from this, the trees are bare, but with buds ready to come out. The lawns are green. At midday it was as high as 16 degrees in the shade. Karl Johan is lovely in the daytime. When the orchestra plays there are masses of brightly-coloured clothes and gaudy parasols. Up at the exhibition your friends are obviously still in evidence. And your influence can easily be seen in most young painters. In a couple of weeks my time at the National Hospital here in Christiania will be over. I'll most likely be going to Lillehammer as locum, and after that I'm going to settle near Kristiansund, unless I get a position up in Nordland or Finnmark. My planned trip to the tropics has been postponed for a couple of years. I may make a trip to the Arctic Ocean to visit the Norwegian whale and seal hunting grounds. Your devoted Andreas Munch.

* * *

In the autumn Munch travels to Stockholm. He shows sixty-nine paintings and various drawings, including the series *Love*. He is very pleased with the spacious premises and with the hanging of the pictures. He notes almost without emotion that the paintings are greeted with revulsion in the newspapers. In all other respects the Swedes are extremely nice, provided he doesn't broach the subject of politics.

Munch is living at the home of Professor Helge Bäckström, meets the model for Ibsen's Rosmer, Count Snoilsky. He also meets Gejerstam, the theatre director Poë, as well as the influential Count Prozor, who promises to help Munch arrange an exhibition in Paris.

He has grown very close to Dagny and Stach. He receives letters from both of them when they are on their travels. Ducha writes like a close and trusted friend. Whereas Stach writes highly emotional letters, saying he would like to spend as much time as possible with Munch, always beginning his letters with *Mein teuerster Bruder*, *Mein teurer*, *lieber Freund* or *Lieber, teurer Edzin*.

Munch helps him out with money. But also has to think of his own family. From Stockholm he writes to his brother Andreas at Hadsel in Vesterålen.

Dear Andreas: How are things with you on that island all the way up there? It must be strange. Perhaps I'll come up this summer. Do describe the place for me and also tell me when you're thinking of getting married. Then we must come to some mutual agreement about how we're going to help Inger and Aunt Karen with Laura. Obviously we must take responsibility for Laura. We must plan on giving 30 or 40 crowns between us per month. So we each owe about 100 crowns now. We must also look after Aunt Karen. That will mean each contributing about 20 crowns per month. If you don't have any money at the moment, I can pay your share. Your devoted Edv. Munch.

*

It is in Stockholm that Munch first shows *Three Stages of Woman*, possibly inspired by Jan Toroop's *De tre bruder* or Max Klinger's *Die blaue Stunde*, which depicts three nymphs on the shore. For the time being Munch calls the picture *Sphinx*, in other words further inspiration from Greek mythology: the sphinx, part beast, part woman, who guards the harbour of Thebes. In order to get past the sphinx, the man must solve a riddle if he is to escape with his life. Oedipus' answer refers to the three stages of human life: beginning, middle and end. This will also be the form of Munch's *Frieze of Life*. *Love, Angst, Death*. Three stages. Munch may also have read about the psychiatrist Jean Martin Charcot's experiments with hypnotism. Young women are hypnotized, so that the hypnotist can take them to three different stages. The first of these, the cataleptic stage, shows woman motionless, frozen like a statue, with fixed, staring eyes. The second stage is lethargic. The young woman is now relaxed, dreaming and at the same time extremely sensitive. The third stage is somnambulistic. The young woman is completely under the influence of her senses. Now she looks common, repulsive, vulgar.

* * *

Dear Aunt: I've now got a much more practical menage and live in a pension, so things are more orderly. There are two Japanese, two people from California, so it's a completely cosmopolitan pension. Recently I've been spending all my time on visits, now know a lot of people here, yet still have the feeling that I'll soon have had enough of Berlin, so I'll either move to Paris or come back to Norway. It's going to be some time before Berlin is a city of art. Has the parcel arrived with my personal effects from Filtvedt? Unfortunately, I left out two or three pairs of boots. Can you ask Inger whether she could run up to Marten Hotel when she has time, as I've also forgotten a pair of boots there which are probably quite good ones? P.S. Hope to be able to send you a bit of cash soon.

*

Third winter in Berlin. Munch has been in Hamburg and completed a portrait commission for two hundred marks. Things are looking up as regards earnings. The Stockholm exhibition was very crowded during the last few days. Munch has started etching and will later issue a portfolio containing eight items.

At Café Bauer he glances through the Norwegian newspapers, reads *Politiken*, savours his coffee and brandy, is distracted by Thiis and the other Norwegians.

Now then, Munch, how are you these days, what are you up to?

Munch looks up from the newspaper. According to Thiis, he is incapable of starting and finishing a single sentence. He sometimes starts in the middle of a thought and then elaborates at great length. He jumps from one thing to another, one idea tumbling over the next in rapid succession, commenting on his own work, in other words what he is working on in his studio, indeed, can go on at length about this, before launching out on a fresh tack.

The Finnish painter Gallén comes to Berlin and is surprised at what he terms Munch's sickly appearance, his egocentricity, his poverty. Gallén is toying with the idea that the two of them should hold a joint exhibition.

*

Berlin without Strindberg. Gustav Vigeland and Sigbjørn Obstfelder are staying at the Hotel Janson. Come on, Munch, come with us, you can't just sit there, we're going to see Richard Demel at Villa Pankow, Künstlerabend at the Wilder Mann. There stands the anxious, neurotic Sigbjørn Obstfelder reading poems which are interpreted into German by Dagny Juel. Obstfelder is making his way on foot through Europe with rucksack and violin. He is at Villa Pankow on the evening Thiis will later describe as wonderful, in other words, a booze-up, perhaps the last one before everything falls apart, before the group disperses, before they follow Strindberg's example. There sits the man Strindberg dubs that bloody Pole playing Schumann and Chopin, there stands his wife interpreting poems, there sit an unknown number of people downing one glass after another as Vigeland passes round the photographs for his *Hell*, the first passionate love ensemble. Does Munch already know His Glutinousness, the copycat Vigeland, his perpetual rival, who steals first from Rodin, then from Maillol and now from Munch? Does he already know the Vigeland who, many years later, will be given a whole park to play with, thanks to the desire of the citizens of Christiania to spend money at cinemas, an entire park, right outside Munch's windows at Ekely, where Vigeland can put up his own Frieze of Life, his gigantic stone phallus? Vigeland is in Berlin with *Hell*, in a short time will hurl a sculpture, a bust of Munch probably, and later also a bust of Dagny

Juel, out of his studio window, a murder attempt on the model herself walking in the street below. Even then Vigeland must have been unbearable, highly dangerous, in Munch's eyes a sponger, menacing, unoriginal, shockingly facile. Munch who day after day stands in front of a copper plate producing a mirror image of a ten-year-old motif.

The party moves on to the Przybyszewskis'. The host, Stach, is sitting out in the woodshed, naked as the day he was born, perched high up on a pile of birch logs, believes he is Satan, and perhaps with very good reason. It is 1895, the year Munch once again paints *Death in the Sickroom*, as well as *Death Agony*, *Jealousy*, *Self-Portrait with Cigarette*, the year he creates mirror images of *The Morning After*, *Madonna*, *The Voice*, *The Lonely Ones*, *Kiss*, *Vampire*, *Scream* by using copper plates. Etchings and lithographs. The year which will end in death, unexpected death. The death Munch could least of all have anticipated.

* * *

Obstfelder comes up to the studio. Knocks gently at the door.

Are you there, Munch?

Yes, I am.

May I sit with you, Munch? I won't say anything. Not a word. Just sit for a little while. I can't stand being with the others.

* * *

Munch holds a joint exhibition with Gallén in Ugo Baroccio's gallery on Unter den Linden from the sixteenth to the twenty-fourth of March. Gallén's romantic idealism has no chance. Munch himself has absolutely no commercial strategy, is exclusively concerned with consequences, with the vision from the Montagnes Russes, the portrayal of life's sacred moments, the deepest insight, his own lived life, pain, love, angst, death. He has experienced it, has no need of anything else, with twenty-eight paintings and seventeen etchings completely overshadows Gallén. The Finn has no chance with his Nordic heroes.

Berlin has grown accustomed to the Munch scandal. They are almost starting to like him.

Munch realizes it is time to leave.

* * *

Visits from women. Women he visits. He paints them naked, fully clothed, with back turned, has painted *Young Man and Whore* many times, has painted himself between the breasts of very fat women, almost with an air of resignation, acknowledging his sexual urges, or else the exact opposite: he portrays the male model defeated, but protesting, drowning in red hair.

Have a bit of skirt, Munch. Get yourself a lady friend.

A lady?

He knows of only *one* real lady, and she is a sacred goat. She teaches him what it would mean to tie himself down, to yield to his feelings, disaster. She who has drunk at love's deep well now feels that the water is like poison in her veins, sees a gallows in the moonlight, sees that the water she thought was clear is cloudy.

During these years Munch will observe from a distance what happens to Ducha and Stach, will perhaps for the first time be able to identify with the fate of a woman, the unfathomable doctor's daughter from Kongsvinger. After all, he's a doctor's son himself. But at the point where he himself had to draw back from love, Dagny Juel lingers, married to a notorious liar with nerves in tatters, remains with him, even when he strips naked in the woodshed and believes he is Satan, remains with him, cooks for him, retypes his manuscripts for him, writes to his publisher, writing her own poetry and plays almost covertly, giving piano lessons, begging money from friends and gambling on the lottery.

Munch sees that the inconceivable happens, that this woman whom men fall for in droves allows herself to be used up, degraded, of her own free will, by a man incapable of looking after himself, a man who begs, steals, borrows, lies, who uses Munch as model for the Russian painter Mikita in the novel *Overboard*, yet denies it, denies that a painter who talks about blood-red clouds in a setting which has every appearance of being a carbon copy of Zum schwarzen Ferkel has no connection whatever with Munch. And who is supported by Ducha, who does not protest when Stach uses their last few coins in a café, who on the contrary says that her husband needs these hours of happy relaxation. An almost manic loyalty, or is it pride? It is her defiance which makes her choose *not* to show their friends and acquaintances that she made a bad choice, that she chose ruin, but that at least it was her *own* choice, and that she chooses to remain loyal to her actual choice itself. For financial reasons she soon has no option but to return to *Tranquillity*, her childhood home at Kongsvinger, and Stach is forced to return to Marta Foerder.

*

Dear Munch. What you write about a book by Stach upsetting you is quite incredible. In *Overboard* there may well be a man who is a painter. But the painter in question is as different from you as two people can be, created as they both are in God's image, after all. There really is no limit to the malice in this world. I don't understand how for a second you could believe that Stach could write anything to upset you. I don't know anyone he is fonder of. Regards, Dagny P.

* * *

In 1895, the Przybyszewskis have also left Berlin. Only the hangers-on remain. The ones who have begged the most money, had the most grandiose visions, drunk the most alcohol, who will later write the most anecdotes and biographies.

Munch leaves the city almost unremarked, wants to return to Norway straight away, but probably has money problems, is also suffering from influenza, in Braunschweig visits his friend Arthur von Franquet, a wealthy and avid collector of Munch's work, and then travels to Christiania via Amsterdam. He has laid down the foundations now, created the core, found his way back to the vision from the Montagnes Russes, six years of his life, six years with nothing but loneliness, easel, copper plate and trance for company. He has captured the woman, captured the moments, captured what he defines as his past, what at thirty-one years of age he defines as his life, as though there were not going to be any more life, leaves Berlin, the laughter, the drink, the emptiness, leaves the stories which the hangers-on at Zum schwarzen Ferkel still sit there repeating as the hollow laughter echoes from the cellar walls.

* * *

Skjeggedal Peaks. Back to long-legged Norway!

Up in the north lives his brother Andreas. Hadsel in Vesterålen.

Dear Edvard: My life up here is scarcely anything to write home about. I live in total isolation, have not even paid any social visits to the cultured families on the island. My practice was going well until February, but then fell rather quiet owing to the fishing season in Lofoten.

Andreas, who in April that year got married in Lillehammer, who at barely thirty years of age writes that he will never be satisfied until he has set eyes on the Tropics and lived there for some time. He is now on an island in North Norway making plans, writing repeated letters to his brother without receiving any reply. Andreas is following in the military doctor's footsteps, making up medicines while it is the herring season up in Eidsfjord. The patients earn enough money to visit the doctor, but the doctor is already tired, ensnared in the daily grind, dreaming of travelling to South America in a year or two, when he has paid off the bulk of his loan for furniture, instruments and so on, for all that a home needs when a wife joins the household. He writes to his aunt that the picture of Vrengen now hangs above the sofa, and that he is going to have the painting of the military doctor and the portrait of his brother Edvard framed. For the picture of Edvard, a wide, black frame with a matte silver edge on the inner rim would perhaps be the most suitable, that is what he thinks rhymes best with the idea behind the picture, for it is a strangely profound psychological portrait.

His brother Andreas, who has the medicines ready when his sister Laura visits him, who is looking forward to the next year, when he is to be visited by his relative Karl, when he is to make a trip to the Sulitjelma iron works and the thickly forested valleys of inner Norrland.

The weather in August has been so warm that he has been bathing every day. Dear Edvard: I'm sure it was I who wrote last, but as that was already three and a half months ago and I haven't heard from you, I'm going to write again. I hope you're still well.

* * *

When Munch returns to the scenes of the past, Åsgårdstrand and Christiania, he paints *Ashes* and *Jealousy*. Yes, love is a flame, but like a flame all it leaves behind is a heap of ashes.

Decay, destruction, the final truth, the recognition, after the jealousy, hatred, love. Munch perhaps chooses Stanislaw Przybyszewski's face to represent the losing party, the man who is deceived, the naked woman in the background, with another man, not unlike Munch, the picture which will fuel the myth that there *was* an affair between Dagny Juel and Edvard Munch. There is nothing in the letters between Edvard Munch and Dagny Juel to warrant the supposition that *Jealousy* is such a documentary picture. Does he perhaps see himself in Stach? The ambition, the talent, the submission, and then the drink, the madness, the degradation?

At all events he sees the hysteria, whereas in Dagny Juel he sees a trance-like calm. He paints *Jealousy* when he has probably read the first volume of Jæger's trilogy about his affair with Oda Krohg. Harrowing prose, neurotic and paranoid, full of pathos, here and there bombastic, man as a weak and helpless creature, Jæger the analytical leader of the Bohemians, a logician of world stature, turned to jelly, to ashes, to inconsistency.

The logical conclusion of love!

Precisely what he is trying to escape from.

He has learned enough, suffered enough.

Women, Munch?

No thanks.

* * *

He comes to Christiania, has brought his pictures with him, the pictures from Berlin, shows the Madonna pictures as a single group with the title *Loving Women*, portrays Dagny Juel Przybyszewska in blue tones, exhibits the portrait of her sister Ragnhild.

The women's father, the district medical officer, writes from his home *Tranquillity* in Kongsvinger on the tenth of October 1985 that he has been to see Munch's exhibition at Blomqvist's Gallery on Karl Johan with great interest but mixed feelings. He has visited it, swarming with people, seen many of the pictures on show, cannot imagine how it could ever have occurred to Munch to exhibit the series *Loving Women* publicly in Christiania, where of course the police will be summoned and there will be calls for the exhibition to be closed and for the pictures to be confiscated and so on. Or was Munch's idea behind these pictures of women surrounded by foetuses something quite different? He asks Munch to forgive him, a total stranger, for expressing his opinion on his works; he also asks Munch, in the name of the friendship he knows exists between Munch and two of his daughters, to do him the great service of removing the portrait of his daughter Ragnhild, or *our* Ragnhild, as he writes with evident proprietorial feelings, from the exhibition. The district medical officer is well aware that Munch and perhaps a good many other people construe the picture quite differently, but for the district medical officer it is deeply embarrassing to see his daughter's face portrayed like this, this much at least he feels bound to say, having asked such a service of a total stranger. The district medical officer also asks Munch not to be offended by this appeal, and remains respectfully Munch's H. Juell.

*

Munch immediately withdraws the picture from the exhibition, lifts it down from the wall, obediently lifts it down for Dagny's sake, for Ragnhild's sake, will soon be thirty-two years of age and is once again the centre of a storm. In artistic terms, he strikes people as someone suffering from hallucinations, or as a prankster who looks upon the public as fools and who makes a mockery of art and of people's lives. If only these travesties had at least been funny, but the worst thing is that utterly contemptible pranks are played which cause a commotion and mean that the police have to be summoned. *Aftenposten*'s review is not the only one; a *Morgenbladet* leader calls for a boycott, and during a debate in the Student Society, Johan Scharffenberg, subsequently to become a psychiatrist and senior consultant, casts doubt on Munch's mental state, asserting that his art is abnormal:

It's quite simple. The man is insane!

Then the pale, anxious Obstfelder enters the arena. He states that, a few years before, he had been admitted to an asylum and says that insanity and avant-garde art are related concepts but in a *positive* sense.

Back in Christiania. Munch hears it said that he cannot tell the difference between a lily and a turd. It is to no avail that the National Gallery purchases *Self-Portrait with Cigarette*, the picture Scharffenberg considers to be particularly abnormal. He is the centre of a scandal again, someone who attracts attention when walking in the street, when sitting at the Grand.

*

But there sits Ibsen too.

Is that you, herr Munch?

Yes, indeed it is.

I'd like to see your exhibition, Munch.

It is a sensation that Ibsen should speak to anyone at all when he sits at the Grand. Munch accompanies the writer to Blomqvist's. Ibsen goes into the exhibition, has a quick look round. Then he begins to scrutinize every single painting in detail, pays particularly close attention to *Sphinx. The Three Stages*, seen through three women.

First the young woman, the woman of light. She strides out towards the sea, towards eternity, towards what she takes to be her own shining future. Then there is the naked woman. The woman who has learned from experience and understood, who offers herself, with a grotesque grimace. Lastly, the dark woman, framed by the trunks of the trees. The nun, a sort of shadow of living woman. She stands for sorrow and death.

The man can be glimpsed to the far left, between the trunks of the trees.

He has lost his reason.

Only the pain remains.

Munch explains. Ibsen observes. They walk round the exhibition at Blomqvist's Gallery. It may well be that Ibsen gains inspiration here for his forthcoming play *When We Dead Awaken*. The Three Women. Irene, dressed in white, yearning towards life. Maja, full of *joie de vivre*. While the naked one, the woman of sorrow, with the staring pale head framed by the trunks of the trees, symbolizes Irene's fate as a nurse in Ibsen's play.

Ibsen has finished looking at the paintings.

Now he looks at Munch, recognizes the man who sits hunched and bent on the shore, the origin of all the pictures. Then he says:

It's the same for you as it is for me. The more enemies you make, the more friends too.

* * *

Munch rents a studio at 22 Universitetsgaten together with the painter Alfred Hauge. He tries to plan his future.

Then he receives the news of his brother Andreas. The newly-married but already tired doctor. Thirty years old, his wife expecting a baby. It all happened so quickly. More earnestly than ever before he was planning his journey to the Tropics, to South America. He lay there with red cheeks and shining eyes, delirious, went to Verdens ende – world's end – as their sister Sophie had also done once, needed the medicine *himself*, his pneumonia making him gasp for breath, raised himself from the pillow, journeyed literally to the place where life ended, where death was all that awaited him.

IV Then she left and I began work on *The Dance of Life*. In the evening I dreamt I was kissing a corpse and gave a sudden start of fear. I had kissed a corpse's pale smiling lips – a cold, clammy kiss.   (EDVARD MUNCH)

Ljan, Sunday. Dear Munch: I hope I can avoid coming to town until sometime in March. But you must come here and let my 25 or 30 teachers get a look at you. I am living at frøken Hammer's, that'll do for the address. But if you're used to drinking, you must bring it along with you as we simply don't have any here. Come and cheer me up, will you, as I'm pushing myself so hard I'm horribly bad tempered. But I do have some cigars, which Maurer kindly sent me. I'm dashed fond of Maurer. Yours, Knut Hamsun.

By the way: when do you leave? It's obvious that I'll have to come into town again before very long. Let me know how much time you can spare me. Use the telephone. Instructions: Ring Bekkelaget. Then frøken Hammer's pension. Then me.

*

The first weeks of a new year. The Munch family in Christiania. Without Andreas. Munch is planning an etching of Knut Hamsun. Then he goes to Paris. Enticed there by Meier-Graefe. Enticed by the thought of conquering the world.

*

Dear Aunt: I hope Inger hasn't suffered any harm from the influenza. Tell her that I have a large white cat, as big as Lucie but completely snow-white, actually, it's semi-wild and I don't know whether it'll ever be house-trained. All day it lies behind some picture or other, only emerging when there's something to eat. At night it makes a terrible din. Buy some good wine for 10 crowns. You can expect to receive more money from me.

32 rue de la Santé; proprietor: Hyacinthe Bidart, a medium-sized door resembling a carriage entrance, in the courtyard to the right a square two-storey dwelling house, to the left of the courtyard, on a rise, a two-storey building containing artists' studios. On the ground floor lives Alexandre Toupey, a graphic artist, a member of Artistes Français, a regular exhibitor at the Salon. Immediately next door is La Cité fleurie, city of flowers, with twenty-nine studios.

Munch in Paris, 1896. The year Verlaine dies, the year Egedius paints *Dance to the Fiddle*. Munch will paint his *Seated Nude* and a new version of *The Sick Child*, the latter also as a lithograph, besides *Room of Death*, *Attraction*, *Death Agony*, *Separation*, *Heiberg*, *Obstfelder*, *Strindberg*, *Jæger*, *Mallarmé*, *Hamsun*, *Moonlight* and *Fear*.

Back among the cloisonnistes, Bernard, Lautrec and the Nabis.

Gauguin is in Tahiti, but Strindberg is here, as are Frederic Delius, Oscar Wilde, Molard Vercingetorix. It is also the home of *Mercure de France*. According to the art critic Rambosson, Munch is a tall, fanciful fellow who strolls up and down Boulevard St Michel, is an habitué of La Closerie des Lilas and Bullier on the opposite side of Boulevard Montparnasse, where before very long Oda Krohg's son will dance the tango with a close-cropped French working girl.

Munch in Paris, countless versions of *Separation*, as though to emphasize that he is ensnared. He submerges himself in fresh pictures of whores, young man with whore, revulsion, the experience of lying in ooze among maggots and slime, of yearning to float up to the surface, lift his head above water, catch sight of the swan, its brilliant whiteness, the pure lines he yearns for. He reaches out towards the swan, which comes nearer but not right up to him. Then he sees his own reflection in the water. Oh, how pallid he is, his eyes and hair smeared with ooze, understands why the swan was frightened off, the swan which knows what lies under the shining surface, can never be united with one who lives among illusions.

Munch starts to write again, meets the twenty-five-year-old painting student Tupsy Jebe, an officer's daughter from Trondheim, who later that year will make her debut at the Autumn Exhibition in Christiania. Her brother Halvdan is a violinist and a close friend of Delius. He plays the violin in a Parisian orchestra every Sunday at the Châtelet Theatre.

Strindberg comes to Munch's studio to have his portrait painted bringing a pistol with him. Paris is not what it was. Munch receives the gift of a white cat from a friend. It is brought to rue de la Santé in a basket. At first it is shy, hides behind the paintings, takes fright at the slightest sound, but calms down after a while, lies in a sunbeam and purrs.

The next day, Munch writes, it had done its business on the floor.

Then he seizes the cat, rubs its nose in its own dirt as is the custom. The white cat shoots away in terror, becomes even shyer, so Munch has to place sand and a bowl in a corner, wait to see what happens, talk to the cat at a reassuring distance, emphasize that they will soon be friends.

The next day, Munch writes, the cat has again done its business on the floor.

He grabs hold of it once again. Listen, cat, we can't have this! And when we could have been such good friends too! He seizes the cat, rubs its nose in its own dirt, the cat scoots off into a corner and does not reappear for the rest of the day.

Sharing his life with the little white creature overwhelms him, the spring overwhelms him, spring in Paris, the chestnuts with their erect candles rising up from the palm-like leaves, which spread their fans over

138

the damp, steaming boulevard, over men and woman walking arm in arm. Everything is in love. Birds, chestnut trees, flowers and animals. The great game of life.

The following day the cat has again done its business on the floor.

Munch hears it whining pitifully behind a canvas. So it knows what it has done. He thinks – shall he keep it, punish it, kill it, he decides to punish it, smacks it hard. It lets out a pathetic miaow and leaps away frightened out of its wits.

One evening he has invited some guests. Ladies and gentlemen are lolling about on carpets and divans in the studio. All of a sudden a white cloud flashes over their heads. The ladies shriek. The white cat whizzes through the air.

It disappears until the following day.

Two men are working on the glass roof. The cat emerges, slowly, glances up at the roof, with an anxious, testing look. Munch sees that there is something familiar about that look, not the eyes of a cat, but the look of a human being, the look of a creature with a soul, which can express fear, pain, horror, joy, the look of the white cat, a look which makes him feel uneasy.

Another day he has a naked female model in his studio, a little Parisienne, lithe and supple in every limb. Munch sees the cat steal up to the white body, sees how the model suddenly looks like an animal, a cat and a white cat. Two cats. One morning the cat has done its business on one of the paintings.

He speaks to the cat: We two could have got on so well together, cat. If you'd had ears like humans, you could have understood everything. Now I'm going to have to kill you instead.

The most horrible thing he can think of is dead cats, you see them everywhere, like half-rotten berries, stinking of putrefaction, on the beach where you're about to bathe, beneath wooden fences and in the street.

He does not kill the white cat. He puts it out in the garden.

When he comes home one evening, the doorstep is fouled with cat mess. Then he stops feeding the cat, tries to put it out in the street. But it howls so pathetically that he takes it back into the garden again. Heart-piercing cries. The neighbours think he is a monster. You'll just have to die, cat, he says. He gives it to a boy he meets in the street: Take the beast way, please.

The following day he is eating saddle of hare in a nearby restaurant.

It tastes good.

Then he sees the boy who was given the white cat. He is standing outside the restaurant window staring with a look of anticipation. Why is he looking at him like this while he is eating?

Just at that moment, he hears the scream. His own scream. What is it he is eating?

The cat!

*

Transformation of matter, change, fear of death. The cat's real or symbolical death is his responsibility. He will remember the look of the cat when, three years later, he looks into Tulla Larsen's eyes. He recalls that he could peer into the animal's very soul, which is deeper than a woman's.

Munch is back in Paris. Writing prose again, a sure sign that something is happening. The short time he shared his life with the white cat makes him long for a human being, makes him feel that there must, after all, be more to life.

He works. *Le mort joyeux*. Death desired is cheering. Death laughs, with dark hideous eyes. The antithesis between life and death is *une charogne*. Matter which is born as it is consumed. Matter which is born as it is produced. The human body which fertilizes the earth as it decays, providing nourishment for new life.

Instead of a face: a corpse.

Munch writes about Monsieur Piat, the man with the cheerful, slightly lacklustre eyes. Monsieur Piat died a week ago. But in the dream it is not Piat who is dead but Munch:

Tell me, Munch, says Monsieur Piat, what is death like, what did you think when the doctor said that you were passing over?

Munch feels the pressure against his eyes. What is the man asking him? He isn't dead, is he?

But Monsieur Piat will not be put off. Tell me, Munch, did you believe in God? Is there a God?

I haven't much time, says Munch. I really have to go now.

But Munch! Was death terrible? When you knew you had a quarter of an hour left ... A quarter of an hour is a long time. But when you had five minutes left? Just tell me, before you go, is there a God, is there a hell? Is there really? Go on, tell me, Munch. Is there a God?

*

He sees all people behind their masks, sees familiar faces turned into corpses, already yielding to decay. Now he is living, instead of Andreas, instead of Sophie, is living in Paris, in Montparnasse. Ironically, Jæger is living on the opposite side of the city, rather modestly it seems, in Montmartre.

It is copper, stone and wood that bring Munch to Paris, it is the first-class printers Lemercier and Auguste Clot. Meier-Graefe is trying to make him into a household name in France. All signs point to Paris, to the city where the plays of Strindberg, Bjørnson and Ibsen have been staged in the small experimental theatres of Paul Fort and André Antoine.

The sound from the boulevards. All the impressions. He breathes more freely here than in Berlin.

Strindberg is far ahead of him in the race. Things have already come to grief with Frida Uhl. In autumn 1894 Strindberg is divorced for the second time. He calls himself poet-chemist. Penniless, despairing and embittered. He has ensconced himself in his *pension de famille* in Montparnasse, writes chemical sonnets, is completely obsessed with that damned Pole, that damned whore Aspasia, the people who have destroyed everything for him, who are persecuting him from a distance.

Now he carries a pistol, as Stach and Ducha are reunited in Copenhagen, as Marta Foerder commits suicide in Berlin and Stach writes desperate letters. *Mein teurer Edvard. Ich habe so lange nichts von dir gehört. Wie geht es dir, mir geht es sehr schlecht. Wir sitzen hier in Kopenhagen und wissen nicht was wir anfangen sollen.* It does not pacify Strindberg. Inferno in Paris. The period of the Ferkel was only playing with fire. Now the flames have set light to his mind. He writes an *Introduction to a Unitary Chemistry* the same month as Louis Pasteur dies. He is an antiquated badger who dreams of new worlds. His close relationship with Munch is destroyed by his suspicious nature, his profound conviction that Munch himself has had an affair with her, Aspasia, the worst of the lot, a female threat of the most dangerous kind.

Mère Charlotte's Crèmerie, rue de la Grande Chaumière, on the other side of the road from where Strindberg lives at number 12, the place where artists can get a meal for one franc, as well as unlimited credit.

The highly suspicious Strindberg feels like a poor beggar, convinced that Munch has come to poison him. With Frederick Delius he takes walks in the city, but cannot go where he pleases, not necessarily up to the left, no, absolutely not on that side of the pavement. He moves to Hotel Orfila in rue d'Arras, forty francs a month, where he mixes evil-smelling liquids. Strindberg the alchemist, convinced he can make gold from sulphur.

Shaking, Munch comes bearing the news. Przybyszewski's erstwhile lover has gassed herself in Berlin. Despite the fact that Stach is now married and has children by Dagny, Marta Foerder was also mother to another child.

The following day Munch receives a postcard from Strindberg:

Your attempt to poison me by the Müller-Schmidt method has failed. Better luck next time!

What a slap in the face for Ducha! What contempt! Strindberg is convinced that the woman's death is not suicide, but the fault of that bloody

Pole. Gassing. Munch has already tried to kill him. Now Dagny Juel, that damned whore Aspasia, is certainly on her way to Paris to do exactly the same. Pettenkofer's experiment. A gas ring. Blow a candle through a wall.

Dear Munch, the last time I saw you, you had the look of a murderer.

*

It is Strindberg's turn.

A journey with heart and mind, nervous crisis in Paris. Munch, in a campaign to support a kindred spirit, has learned from Hamsun's failure, what Strindberg called a disgusting begging campaign: Keep the thirty silver coins and let's have nothing further to do with one another for the rest of our lives! Hamsun could not bear to look on as Strindberg wore a light-grey summer suit all winter in Paris. He could not bear to see that his colleague had just a tiny bed-sitter and owed money everywhere. Couldn't accept that Strindberg did not want to enter a restaurant with him because it was too well-lit and looked too expensive. So Hamsun organized a collection. Contributions were to be sent to the editors of *Verdens Gang*.

*

The fund-raising campaign is a complete failure.

While another kindred spirit, Hans Jæger, is up at Sacré Cœur in the same city pondering how he can blow to smithereens the capitalistic hell he considers Paris to be, throw bombs, inspired by Ravachol, become a gambler at the racetrack, a gambler who can crack the code, win three million crowns to finance the world revolution, waits for a letter from his friend Schjander who is seeking a possible location for a free State in South America, a free State in Patagonia for animals, Manzanero Indians and Scandinavian failures.

Munch is working with copper, stone and wood, his mind on etchings, lithographs, woodcuts. He notes that Strindberg looks old and ill, boils sulphur in his room, is afraid of being considered mad, has become a beggar covered in burns, cannot report various attempted murders, most certainly using gas, cannot go to the police without proof, how can he prove that Munch is a murderer, Przybyszewski's lackey, Aspasia's envoy, how can he prove it, gas is invisible, gas seeps in through the walls, is inaudible, envelops people, who only notice the smell when it is too late. What is that smell at the Hotel Orfila, in Strindberg's room, a quite special smell, the special smell of gas? Help! Murder! Quite definitely gas, seeping in through the walls, a little hole in the wall, gas through the wall, poison gas, certainly deadly, just as in Pettenkofer's famous experiment. Who is in the next room, Munch? Aspasia?

Stach has to go to prison for some months, is suspected of complicity in the suicide, Strindberg's mind is in ferment, someone is coming, someone is standing outside the door, but if he mixes sulphur, saltpetre, liquid nickel, if only he doesn't walk on the left-hand side of the pavement, in other words not into rue Delambre but keeps to Boulevard Montparnasse, if he doesn't go down to reception but waits just two minutes, who is it who lives on the floor above, what is that smell, the unmistakable smell of poison gas, that is until the painter Paul Hermann finds a stinking red rat at the foot of his bed, doesn't want to report the murder attempt, cannot report Munch, hasn't enough evidence, the police wouldn't believe it, but Strindberg knows.

*

Strindberg hears that an uncomfortable silence has developed round his chemical experiments. To re-invent himself he wants to produce gold. Why does iron sulphate in a solution of a gold salt produce metallic gold? Because iron and sulphur are part of the composition of gold! The proof: all naturally occurring sulphur and iron compounds contain smaller or larger amounts of gold.

Strindberg works on this with solutions of iron sulphate.

In the fireplace he burns the type of coal called monks' pates because of their smooth, round shape.

One day when the fire goes out in the grate before the coal has completely burned up, he plucks out a piece of coal, now a fantastic figure, a hen's head with a splendid comb. The following day he picks up two brownies the worse for wear, two sprites locked in an embrace and decked in flowing garments, a masterpiece of primitive sculpture. The third day, it is a Madonna and Child in Byzantine style.

Strindberg writes that a painter friend comes to visit him, sees the three sculptures lying on the table:

Who made these? he asks, interested.

Vigeland, says Strindberg in reply, or at least says a name, is trying to test the painter.

Oh, I can well believe it, replies the painter, but I'd have guessed Kittelsen.

Strindberg enrols in the faculty of natural sciences at the Sorbonne founded by Saint Louis, thus gaining entitlement to carry out analyses in the laboratory, dreams that Jonas Lie is working on a wall clock in gold bronze, hears Schumann's *Aufschwung* ringing out over the tops of the trees, cannot pluck up courage to go into a café, does so all the same, the following day, the Lilas, finds his usual corner free, the absinthe is served, he is well into his cigarette. *Le Temps* has big news. But what's happening? A chimney fire breaks out above the poet's head. The café is cleared, Strindberg remains sitting there, sees the soot fall from the ceiling, two large lumps of it straight into his glass, is it a sign, an omen, is there an evil spell on him? A young gentleman places a sou on

Strindberg's table with a gesture the poet does not understand. As a foreigner and alone in a crowd of people he lacks the courage to do anything, but a dagger pierces his breast: Beggar! The young gentleman is giving me a sou as he would to a beggar! He orders another absinthe, a horrible stench of ammonium sulphide seems to be choking him. Woe to him who is lonely! A sparrow on the roof! Never in his life has he felt so miserable. He weeps like a child, is afraid to sit down for fear of attempts on his life, goes to bed but dare not fall asleep, on the wall opposite the window he sees the silhouette of a human form, is uncertain whether it is a woman or a man, but from experience presumes it is a woman.

*

Munch sees his friend in rapid mental decline, his reason clouding over; Strindberg now claims the earth is flat, no, not just that the earth is flat, but that all the stars in the firmament are holes in a wall, Strindberg knows, knows something nobody else knows, knows about countless murder attempts, about holes in the firmament, what it looks like on the very edge of the pancake, where the earth ends, where you can fall off if you go too far towards the edge. He knows something extraordinary, how you make gold for instance, if you mix, oh no, not he! He is not so foolish as to broadcast the fact, that damned Pole is eavesdropping on the other side of the wall!

Munch in Paris. He came here among other things to meet Strindberg. Now he is losing Strindberg with every day that passes, losing him bit by bit, the disintegration of a mind, until the charitable Frits Thaulow invites him to his villa in Normandy, in Dieppe, shows him the sea, lets him feel the wind, see that the horizon is curved.

* * *

Munch remains at Mère Charlotte's Crèmerie, at the Lilas, at Bullier, at Café de la Régence.

Paris without Gauguin. And Jæger on the other side of the city. Jæger writes somewhere that he has been alone for so long, so utterly alone, that he no longer knows whether he is connected to his surroundings. He has written about the mad weeks with Oda Krohg, but has no money to publish the next two volumes of the trilogy, nor has he enough money to make the world revolution.

Munch meets Delius again, the composer who goes hiking in Jotunheimen, writes sweet, passionate music, the swansong of Romanticism. Delius is also a friend of Milly Bergh. All the old things return. Munch feels uneasy.

* * *

Dear Edvard: It's rather late, but I still want to write a few lines. Inger, Laura and I were reading the papers, scaring the wits out of one another. It was about that tornado that had been in the news, but surrounded by millions of people as you are, it would be extraordinary if something had happened to *you* precisely. We mustn't think like this. Thank you for your letter, it was reassuring to hear that Strindberg has left Paris, the poor sick man. It was terrible to think that he was a close friend of yours. He must have been quite a handful, and rather dangerous too. We have been right in the middle of Nansen fever. Nansen looks very well, now has a rather serious, slightly melancholy expression and has put on weight. Your devoted K. Bjølstad.

* * *

Munch has taken up graphic art, he uses jet black lithographer's Indian ink, uses pastel and scraping tools, sees that the lithograph can express the *Frieze of Life* in art nouveau-like lines and surfaces. He uses the colours unrestrainedly, exploits the natural patterns in the grain in his woodcuts, has them printed by Clot.

A frieze must not always have the even uniformity that so often makes friezes and decorative paintings so dreadfully dull. For example, a frieze can have the same effect as a symphony, rising in the light areas, falling in the darker ones, now loud now soft, the notes can ring out and reverberate, piercing notes, with here and there the sound of drums.

He tries to portray both mental and physical development, to show woman in all her variety, the mystery of man, woman as both heroine and whore, man's worship of her. It is a poem about love and death, about the transformation of matter. What is it that holds a body together? What causes its components to develop, what happens to the spirit after death. Andreas is dead, but he doesn't disappear physically does he, it is just the matter in the body that is transformed, that becomes other matter. But the spirit?

Graphic art gives Munch new artistic scope. It may also give him a wider public. In his time he will donate over seventeen thousand graphic items to the city of Oslo, and that is only a fraction of his whole output. He prints woodcut on lithograph, lithograph on woodcut, carries on working on the resulting print with oil, crayon or water colours, scrapes and reworks, will start going about with a copper plate in his pocket, etching motifs into it when they turn up, a landscape, a waitress in a wine bar. He will solve the technical and practical problems with great aplomb, will anticipate the principles of cubism long before Picasso.

Paris 1896. Munch makes countless versions of *The Sick Child*. He uses grainy paper which Clot prepares with white of egg. The lithographic stones with the girl in profile lie side by side in serried ranks, ready for printing. According to Paul Herrmann, Munch comes and stands in front of the row, closes his eyes and points his finger at random in front of him: Print grey, green, blue, brown, print yellow, pink, red. And then we'll go and have a schnapps.

Strindberg visits Munch in the studio, experiences thought waves, the continuous thought waves between the two friends, which are sometimes calm and sometimes stormy, not least when Munch takes the liberty, not just of writing Stindberg on the portrait of Strindberg, but also of burdening it with a naked female figure. Strindberg demands that this hated creature be removed, demands that his name be written properly.

But Strindberg suddenly calms down and writes a longish prose poem about eight of Munch's paintings. It is a friendly gesture, perhaps the desire to win for Munch the same sort of attention Strindberg succeeded in attracting for Gauguin's work a year before. He writes: *The Kiss*, the blending into one another of two beings, the smaller of which, in the form of a carp, seems ready to devour the larger one, in the manner of vermin, microbes, vampires and women. Or: The man who gives, who creates the illusion that the woman reciprocates. The man who begs to be allowed to offer his soul, his blood, his freedom, his bliss. In exchange for what? In exchange for the joy of giving his soul, his blood, his freedom, his peace, his bliss.

*

Munch walks arm in arm with Tupsy Jebe on the boulevards. She is twenty five years old, brimming with *joie de vivre* and fearless, has in general no respect for Munch's traumas but takes him firmly by the arm and distracts him from his brooding, will start to bombard him with letters when he begins to avoid her.

She is young and unblemished, tries to make plans with him. He replies hesitantly, cannot say where he will be next week, perhaps in Brussels, perhaps in Åsgårdstrand. But for a short time he walks arm in arm with a beautiful young woman who, at least according to Christian Krohg, is in love with him. She begins her confidential dialogue with him thus:

My dear friend, thanks for your letter. Yes, it's a good job you wrote when you did, for I have recently rained down so many curses and reproaches on you that I was convinced you must be able to feel them even so far away. Had I only been near you, I would have been thoroughly vile, twenty times as vile as many times before.

*

Munch exhibits his work at the Salon des Indépendants, from the beginning of April, in the company of twelve hundred other works of art.

His ideas are beginning to move closer to Henrik Ibsen again. Between the two of them there is understanding and artistic cross-fertilization. Munch is to make the posters for the staging of *Peer Gynt* and *John Gabriel Borkmann* by the avant-garde Théâtre de l'Œuvre. *Ghosts*, *Hedda Gabler* and *When We Dead Awaken* are all plays which in different ways assume importance for Munch's art. What Ibsen gains from Munch is less certain.

Munch shows *Vampire* and *The Scream*. Meier-Graefe had written to him: Send me *The Scream* or similar strong stuff. Strong stuff is all he has. He also shows *Death and the Woman*, and *Madonna*. Yet his works do not seem to have attracted much attention from the critics; however before the Salon des Indépendants closes, he opens an exhibition at the Salon de l'Art Nouveau under Siegfried Bing, the specialist in Japanese and oriental art, kakemonos, bronzes and ceramics. This is a completely new world of decorative *objets d'art* that Bing has brought to Europe. He creates a forum for new art in rue de Provence, demonstrates new techniques, new aesthetic ideas, l'art japonais, which will become important for Munch in his later graphic work, in lithographs and woodcuts. Now he gives Munch the adjoining room, not the main room, because a possible new Munch scandal could harm his fledgling internationalism. For the time being, a 'Gesamtausstellung' of Edvard Munch is just too great a risk, hence the adjoining room where, according to Bing, Munch's work for some reason looks more respectable.

Again Strindberg is among the visitors to the exhibition, and the Swedish symbolist artist Ivan Aguëli writes in *L'Encyclopédie Contemporaine* about Munch's links with literature, with Poe and Maeterlinck, the Belgian writer and symbolist, whose *Pelléas et Mélisande* has already meant a great deal to Munch. The play is an indirect and completely undocumentary portrayal of Munch's affair with fru Thaulow, which he wishes to illustrate. The text has made a powerful impression on him and in 1909 fru Thaulow will translate it from French into Norwegian, a hint perhaps that her affair with Munch twenty-four years earlier also deeply marked her too.

*

But it is not the end of the world, the exhibition does not have to close, Paris is not shaken to the foundations by Munch's presence. Meier-Graefe, who has had great plans for Munch the graphic artist, will be thwarted in his attempt to make them both stinking rich, as he had hoped and counted on. But has Munch ever yearned for wealth or luxury? For years he has made do with quite modest surroundings, has not held court, has not sought to impress or create an impression of false success. He has looked after his concentration, happy is he who has a room, has always had a room, has into the bargain declined the offer to live with his aunt and brother and sisters when he has been in Christiania, has become a man of *pensions* and dining rooms, whence the slightly threadbare impression bordering on the pathetic he often makes on people who do not know him. He has an address, but is constantly moving house.

Dear Aunt: You can't imagine what the studio looked like when I got back, the worst pigsty I've ever clapped eyes on, I could hardly stand it. Then a wonderful idea occurred to me after three days thinking about the situation; I got hold of a brush and pan, and that helped a lot. Now it's quite cosy, I've made a divan out of a painting box and a few rugs.

*

He does not lose contact with his family, but always keeps Aunt Karen informed of where he is so that her letters can reach him.

Dear Edvard: Laura is a full-time student at the Ljan home-crafts school. She is in extremely good form. It's remarkable how well she's recovered in just one year. We firmly hope that weaving will also make her want to earn something herself. I've never been so hopeful about her future as I am now. She is much more easy-going, mixes with other people, is not shy about conversing, walks to Ljan at half-past six every morning, returns in the afternoon, designs patterns, studies a little Spanish, and then reads Goszner. We have no money problems and are not short of anything. We've got a new stove in the sitting-room where the veranda is, it's a lovely room. This summer we'll be having the young office clerks again. Our rent here is 280 crowns and we might be able to let part during the winter. Things are rather uncertain of course, but we manage very well.

*

They survive by means of legacies, music lessons, moss pictures, renting out rooms, and what Munch produces. All the time he must ensure that he earns enough money. He pays a flying visit to Christiania in order to execute his very first decorative commission in the hall of Axel Heiberg's Villa Franzebraaten in Lysaker, paints a mermaid who looks down a touch coquettishly from her perch high up under the ceiling in the stairway. The picture is painted with an ironic distance which Munch otherwise never displays in relation to women.

Meier-Graefe's miscalculations are only too readily apparent. The Parisians do not queue up to buy Munch's graphic art. It takes more than this to become part of this city's artistic establishment, even if Munch does attend Stéphane Mallarmé's Tuesday salons and also produces a portrait of him, and an etching which the poet acknowledges is a good likeness.

* * *

In the autumn, Munch fetches up with Alfred Hauge, with whom he still shares a studio at 22 Universitetsgaten, and will continue to do so.

To begin with they are probably with Jæger in Belgium. Now the former leader of the Christiania Bohemians is quite sure how to win three million francs at the racetrack. He has worked out a cast-iron system, meanwhile placing his works in safe keeping with The New York Life Insurance Company on Boulevard des Italiens, and has revealed the truth about the reserve fund, the director's own private hoard of money.

Munch in Blankenberge, three ruffians and visionaries, three thread-bare Billygoats Gruff, each with his vision of how to get rich. Unhappy Jæger, made for lobster and champagne, women and philosophy, who once in Christiania sat, head in hands, saying: hell and damnation, hell and damnation, who fell to the ground and was kicked in the head by Hjalmar Christensen, who could not stand the sight of him.

Now he flits with his friends from paddock to bookie, knows which horse to back, knows with total certainty. Munch has to borrow money from Hauge, poor though he is. It must surely be possible to make money, to make gold.

Or to make the world revolution.

*

Back in Paris, Strindberg has left. It is time Strindberg was admitted to hospital, lost as he is in the universe, naked in a barren room. The doctor and poet Marcel Réja slips Munch into a syphilis clinic. Munch portrays a man with Strindberg's features. He sits naked in front of the doctor, showing his armpits which are covered in rashes and sores. The other patients pace up and down in the background with large boils on their torsos.

Munch remembers what he *saw*, Strindberg had an acute attack of his skin complaint two years earlier, huge burns after sulphur experiments, when he claimed he had produced not gold but coal. He burnt his skin, inhaled quite different poison gases from those he associated with Aspasia. His friends organized the disastrous fund-raising effort to pay for the treatment. In an extension of the clinic theme Munch makes the lithograph *Women in Hospital*, in which the patient who is consulting the doctor is fully dressed while the others are naked.

* * *

Tupsy Jebe is away visiting Trondheim.

My dearest: I'm ashamed of myself, here I do nothing day after day, can't sit still, play for five minutes, sing for five minutes, read for five minutes. I'll probably be going on a little trip to Røros with mummy and daddy, no doubt very boring, it's such an ugly place. I must tell you about the rumours which are flying about me here, would you believe they're saying that Heyerdahl and his wife are going to separate, and that H. is going to marry me! Even though I have absolutely no inkling of it myself! You don't need to bring anything with you when you come, any painting things and a few pairs of socks you can borrow from me, and you're not exactly down to your last penny, are you?

*

She hopes Munch will follow her, but he remains in Paris. He is making graphic portraits of prominent people, reworking earlier motifs in a creative burst, starts work on the programme for the staging of *Peer Gynt* in Paris. Ibsen himself follows everything at a distance, touchy beneath the rebellious exterior, wears his heart on his sleeve, has a huge amount of hair. Hair all over, long thick side-whiskers which, according to Lugné-Poe, spread out like fans, framing the bitter mouth. His eyes have an indeterminate pale colour concealed behind gold-rimmed spectacles. His brow is broad and powerful, as though all his thoughts and plays could come tumbling out of his head at any moment. All the same, he is small of stature, completely dwarfed by other people. Pink cheeks, a kind of melancholy kindness, which adds a conciliatory note to the grim overall impression. And a distant, youthful, lively voice which he uses to inform those around him that he likes to be addressed as 'doctor', this man who spends a great deal of his time unmasking hypocrisy, meaningless conventional gestures and fossilized rules, and who himself cannot have a conversation without first running a comb through his hair, who cannot write with anything but a gold pen, who is almost manic about what is proper and correct. He takes Paris by storm, without actually being there in person. Meanwhile Munch, according to his friend Alfred Hauge, is making dreadful sketches for the programme, drawing Peer Gynt up in the air astride a goat while Solveig stands there wringing her hands after him. According to Hauge, sentimental, unattractive rubbish. Instead, his friend gets him to use one of his *own* pictures, *Woman between Pine Trees*. In fact, it is a foretaste of the woodcut *Two Women on the Shore*, the old and the young, Mother Aase and Solveig, Aunt Karen and Inger, stages in a human life.

He has reached the point where there is nowhere left to run to. Drawing inspiration from Maeterlinck, he lives in the constant awareness that in every person's life there is a moment of death, that in the depths of every face, even in twelve commissioned portraits of Axel Heiberg, there is a death mask, the human being on the threshold of the final mystery.

Les Fleurs du Mal, *The Urn*, women's faces resembling skulls, paraphrases on the Salomé theme. Oscar Wilde's play has been staged in Paris the same year. It is the last stage in the forward march of vampirism, woman as an absolute harbinger of death. But Munch also devotes time to compassion, to sorrow, provides Gunnar Heiberg with a conclusion to his play *The Balcony*: What is this sorrow against the fact that one day I shall die?

His contact with the poet and doctor Marcel Réja is pivotal. He discovers the art created by the insane. When Réja lets him into the hospital, he sees the most gruesome fates that can befall people. All vanity is extinguished, all scruples have vanished. The greedy, living plant which feeds on the human heart suddenly sprouts, grows, puts out branches in all directions. And beneath all vanity and tumult, it spreads out its branches of darkness and silence.

Only death awaits.

* * *

Dearest friend: Well, now I've been and confessed and you should feel terribly flattered I think, but time is hanging very heavy. I got to Trondhjem, but can scarcely recall how. I feel as though a gigantic hand has torn me away from everything I'm attached to, where I feel happy and have the desire to do something. I feel how differently from me all these people think, and I'm weak, you know, terribly weak, to be able to put up with all this. Scold me if you like, no doubt I deserve it. Poor Edvard, all this nonsense must be boring you to tears. One shouldn't bother others with one's own worries, but when I come up here I become a totally different person, silent and downcast, stupid and dull. Isn't it awfully hot working in the studio just now? I like the idea of your doing etching and lithography, my dear. You paint such awful stuff. What a cheek, eh! You're probably turning purple with rage. Your devoted Tupsy.

*

Munch moves, perhaps back to Norway, perhaps to Germany, Belgium or France, in any case distances himself from her, is clearly not ready for a new affair. He waits, observes, hesitates. But Tupsy Jebe is young and fearless. She does not give up without a fight.

They make a double engraving together. He portrays her lying in bed, waiting, as though ready to make love. It is a highly erotic picture, whereas her portrait of him is completely neutral. She has him sit holding a cigarette, his left hand against his chin, distant, unattainable, thinking like a philosopher.

Dearest: Have lost my wallet containing 16 francs, as well as no love letters from you. I'm sure it's beautiful at Åsgårdstrand. Come to Bretagne soon, or it'll be too late. I've got such lovely Turkish tobacco I can offer you, otherwise not much fun apart from my excellent company, and that's surely good enough. Are you painting large pictures? Drop me a line, can't you, and tell me a bit about what you're doing. *Alors, au revoir!* Warmest wishes from Tupsy.

*

Munch has five hundred crowns too little, is short of money again, Jæger's system has not delivered the goods. He has had to borrow from Alfred Hauge after the disaster at Blankenberge, turn to his good customer Olaf Schou, a factory owner, to ask for a loan, has to have money for his work, which he thinks will be important, or at least marks the first steps towards reproduction, an art form not yet known at home in

Norway. He imagines what it would be like to have a loan, his studio is full of half-finished works, he refuses to speak of anything unpleasant, such as the prospect of starving to death, because in Paris people do simply let you starve to death if you haven't any money.

He spends the autumn and winter in Paris, is a regular at Charlotte's Crèmerie, Lilas and Bullier, delights in the boulevards and the hurly-burly of life which, in this city, always holds so many associations for him.

*

And Tupsy Jebe writes: My dear. Is it so terribly wonderful up there on the moon or wherever it is you are now that you forget about everyone else? May one ask what you are thinking about, faithless man? Are you happy and in good spirits? Tell me a little about my successor or substitute. My dear, very old Edvard. Müller is very pleased with the tapestry. He went away for a week and gave me the run of his house, including loads of bottles of wine, etc, so you should be glad I haven't become a drunk. I silently drank a toast to you and sat poised on his finest furniture, smoked cigarettes stretched out on his chaise longue and did my best to enjoy myself as much as possible, stuck with my own company as I was . . .

*

He allows himself to fall under her charm, intelligent and talented as she is. And she's so young. And incredibly funny. He can have a laugh with her. Have a laugh with a woman! There certainly haven't been many such occasions. She must remind him of Dagny Juel. Or Oda Krohg. Where on earth did she get her self-confidence from? At *her* age, he had crept about Christiania, felt himself the target of every glance, hadn't even had the courage to kiss. But here she is, an officer's daughter from Trondhjem, who paints and etches, while her brother Halvdan is on tour with Delius in Florida. She's a gift, but even presents can be a mixed blessing. Now he is being bombarded with letters from a twenty-five-year-old woman who drinks absinthe, smokes Turkish cigarettes, who has learned in record time all there is to know about sin, who wants to be with him where he is, but where he never is because he has other things on his mind, because he can never say where he is going to be in a month's time.

*

Dearest: I wonder whether one of these days I may not really lose my temper with you. I feel so alone, wouldn't you like to sit here with me and share a moment of bliss together? Or if are you *anderswo engagiert*, you can go to blazes. Yes, you see, here I sit all on my own thinking about you and about that time a year ago, about Paris and about all that is bright and good, and then I think I feel even more lonely.

Where are all your pictures? Are you going to have an exhibition in Brussels? Why do you assume we're still just as good friends as before? Do you spend a lot of time with Borghild? How am I going to get away from this place? There are crowds of Norwegians here, each one worse than the next, they do nothing but booze, I can't stand the sight of them. Are you going to come soon, Edvard? It was terribly sad about the food shortage, you must look like a ghost now. And when I've become so terribly fat as well! *Les extrêmes se touchent.* Could Mag and I read you a little French or German when you come? You'll be able to earn lots of money and become a rich man. Now I've sat here staring at you for so long that I've forgotten to write anything. I have the tiny little etching I made of you on the wall in front of me. How can you have that horrible picture of me on your wall? I'm surely not as ugly as that, am I? So you call me a butterfly, do you? I read your letters with a large pinch of salt. Dear Edvard, I just cannot credit that I could ever have been so incredibly stupid as to believe you would come here, even though you promised to. Well, don't bother then, if you don't want to. I won't cross you. I'm sure there are girls a-plenty in Braunschweig, or wherever it is you want to go to. You really are a meanie. If I believed you, I wouldn't write like this. But you're a liar and you're no better than all the other wolves I'm surrounded by here and who try to ruin me in all possible ways. In any case, why should you be anywhere except where I am? Can you explain that? Did you receive a card from me here? Here we are staying with Krag, who makes a fuss of us. We eat at the Ferkel, the scene of so many of your binges. Oh yes, I've heard all about it. It interests me greatly. We are here with an Italian painter who, in spite of *die kurze zeit* is already in love with me. We spent all yesterday at the exhibition, the Italian came with us, he's from Sicily and we're perhaps going to visit him there. Wonder whether they'd let me take you with me! Helge Rode reminded me very much of you. Heavens, how phlegmatic you both are. He said practically not a word. Now you mustn't be angry, because basically you're so terribly sweet. I've been carrying this weird and wonderful letter round with me in my pocket for a few days, but have now suddenly decided to send it anyway, you silly. Yesterday we heard the same sort of music as that time in St Cloud. Do you remember the little sketch I painted which I was so fond of last year, when we had such a falling out? Would you believe that my father has torn it up because there was a naked woman on the back of it? You can imagine how much I miss it. Wasn't that a disgraceful thing to do? What are you painting at the moment? Are you coming soon? I've suddenly lost my thumb. Do you think it's dangerous? It was cut off by my knife. I just wanted to say that you are a real meanie. To be continued ...

Have you absolutely no intention of replying to my last letter?

He replies to her in no uncertain terms. He wants to lay down the conditions *himself*. Then she replies:

Dear Commander, thank you for your invitation for a trip to the country, however, I must unfortunately decline immediately as its rather irritable tone does not *appelliere* to me. I had thought you wanted to spend Christmas with me, but as you are engaged, I may as well accept an invitation to spend Christmas Eve in Paris at Krag's home. I still *deploriere* that we do not understand one another when we write letters. For seven nights and seven days the effect of your letter has been so frightful that I thought silence the best policy. Time heals all wounds, the one on my mouth included, we hope. Tupsy.

* * *

It is 1897. Engineer Andrée sails up to Spitsbergen in his balloon and out over the sea planning to reach the North Pole, with August Strindberg's godson on board. After crashing, they manage to reach Hvitøya, where the remains of their skeletons are found thirty-three years later. Gauguin paints *Where Do We Come From, What Are We, Where Do We Go To?* and Munch makes a new version of *Separation*, the double portrait, *Paul Herrmann and Paul Contard*, *Mother and Daughter*, an etching of *Obstfelder*, a woodcut of *Kiss*, a lithograph of *Mallarmé* and *Funeral March*. He dines at Jonas Lie's, sees Bjørnson's *Beyond Our Power* at the Théâtre de l'Œuvre without being moved and prepares for a fresh encounter with the Parisian public. He is to exhibit ten paintings at the Salon des Indépendants from the third of April to the thirty-first of May.

He has moved house to 60 rue de Seine, a practical address so long as he uses the printer Alfred Léon Lemercier, whose graphic printing shop is at number 57. Now he also has a room which can be heated, while he continues to rent the old studio in rue de la Santé to store the paintings. However, he has not paid the rent and is afraid the landlord will confiscate the pictures intended for the exhibition.

But Munch has a plan. One day he comes to the studio with Paul Herrmann. His friend remains out on the pavement. Munch scoots past the landlord as soon as he enters the building and dashes up to the studio. There he opens the window and throws the selected paintings down onto the street. A landlord is not entitled to confiscate any of a tenant's property if it is outside the house.

Herrmann stands on the pavement to catch what is thrown down to him, collects up the pictures as Munch dashes down the stairs, past the open-mouthed landlord and out onto the street. They make a quick get-away. In the coach they inspect the works of art. There is now a hole in *Three Stages of Woman*, but it is not a calamity. A picture must be able to stand a few knocks. They glue the picture back together on the way to the exhibition.

*

It is the current version of *The Frieze of Life* that Munch now exhibits. *Summer, Moonlight, Kiss, Three Stages of Woman, Jealousy, Death in the Sickroom, At the Deathbed.* Not a complete version in other words, but a whole wall at l'Indépendant, in a total exhibition of fifteen hundred works.

Reactions are mixed. There is no scandal, yet neither is it an obvious success, even though thirty years later Munch seems to remember being given pride of place in the exhibition, and that the attention he attracted elicited comparison with Manet's first exhibition.

The Parisian press writes: This time, Munch is rather bizarre, sees the world as very ugly. Brutal harmonies, syntheses of inadequate lines. All of this is rather crude. But in *La Plume*, which reproduces a picture of the lithograph *Death in the Sickroom*, Yvanohé Rambosson concludes: Munch's paintings are the most interesting in the entire exhibition.

Dear Edvard: It hardly seems fair that when you have so much else to contend with, you should also be lumbered with sending us money. So there's to be an exhibition of your work in Brussels, is there? We wish you all the best for it. Then you're coming home. It will be strange to see you again. Though time passes quickly, it still seems to me that there are a lot of things which feel as though they happened many years ago when it was actually just yesterday. It also seems to me quite a long time ago since you used to come and visit us during that sad time in the gloomy flat down at the local shop. Your devoted K.B.

*

Munch is on his way back to Norway. Paris has not given him the fame and honour Meier-Graefe led him to expect. At the end of May he comes to an arrangement with his printers Clot and Lemercier about storing the lithographic stones while he is away. A few months before, he hadn't had a clue how to scrape together enough money to leave the city. Now he sets off for the Gare du Nord. It is spring in Europe. He stands in a railway station with a bulky printing press which he has planned to bring home to Norway, stands in front of the railway officials negotiating a price, understands that he cannot haggle, that the freight price is not for discussion, that it is simply beyond his means. The printing press must remain behind in Paris, like all the other things.

He has no idea where the money is going to come from, but that is nothing new, he's been through it before. He boards the train, minus the lithographic stones, minus the printing press, but is alive, is not insane like Strindberg is, will soon make a woodcut of Strindberg's brain. What does he find inside it? A naked woman. He sits on the train and feels the power of the moon, the logic of the tides, feels ebb and flow. Feels flow.

* * *

He is sitting on the steamer from Christiania. Then he hears an unfamiliar voice:

Isn't that Munch?

Yes, it is.

My name's Adolf Hansen Bollerød. Don't you recognize me? From Åsgårdstrand.

Oh yes. Munch does recognize him after all.

I have a little house in Åsgårdstrand, says Bollerød.

A house? asks Munch expectantly.

Yes. It's for sale.

*

Munch buys a little house, unpainted but, according to Aunt Karen, with a lovely view of the sea. He has shown graphic works in the black and white exhibition at Blomqvist's and in La Libre Esthétique in Brussels. This must have brought in something, even though there is no record anywhere of large sales. But money enough for a house, a tiny little house in Åsgårdstrand, almost on the shore, between forest and sea, with a view of the stones, the Medusa's heads, with a view of his own life. A house in Åsgårdstrand. For something between eight and nine hundred crowns. Two hundred crowns cash down payment. The rest according to their agreement.

Now he owns his own life, his own past, has his own memories right in front of him. He is not yet thirty-five years of age. An enormous printing press remains behind at the railway station in Paris. He can afford a house, but not the shipment of almost two hundred kilograms of iron.

* * *

September 1897. Munch has an exhibition at the Diorama in Christiania, 41 Karl Johan. As usual he turns up totally unruffled, bringing eighty-five paintings, thirty-five lithographs, nine woodcuts, twenty-five etchings, five zincographs, as well as thirty catalogue items consisting of studies and sketches. The foreword to the catalogue is from the pen of the French critic Edouard Gérard, who certainly carries more weight than Andreas Aubert and is French into the bargain, a fact calculated to impress the upstanding citizens of the capital. The scandal in Berlin is history now. And the twig painters are also no longer really as influential. There are limits, even in the case of Munch, who suddenly starts to attract at least lukewarm understanding and calls forth comparison with the obscure dramatist Maeterlinck. Now people know

156

what symbolism is, now they can stand in front of the pictures and nod, conveying the strong impression to other visitors that they are initiates, that this is something they understand. *Transformation of Matter*, *Three Stages of Woman*, *Death in the Sickroom*. Hm. These are pictures that have already been exhibited and torn to shreds by the critics before, yet don't they gain by further examination? Isn't there something deeper here? Something one hadn't originally budgeted for in one's own beauty-conscious mind? But which now seems quite acceptable?

Dagbladet writes: It is lack of familiarity with Bohemian culture that accounts for the observer's embarrassment when confronted by some of Munch's strange pictures. We have no desire to know that the human being is unclean, a prisoner of the senses, that he suffers in love, suffers in hatred, in fear, in jealousy, is turned to Ashes by moonlight and the kiss of the vampire. Yet it is true that the human being screams with Angst at the impending judgement day, at the horrifying endlessness of this world, a prospect it scarcely dares acknowledge. Most women must surely protest against Munch's paintings. Everyone who believes in life's innate goodness must do likewise.

Munch is summing up several years' work. The National Gallery decides to buy the portrait of that enemy of society, Hans Jæger. The Museum also buys *Night in Nice* and *Self-Portrait with Cigarette*.

*

Just round the corner, Munch still shares a studio with Alfred Hauge. The two painters each have their own frugal room off the studio. Munch has not come back home in order to live with his aunt and sisters. He has made a logical choice: aloneness, a room he can lock, the freedom to have breakfast or to skip it, but at least it is his own choice, not the family's expectations about a shared life burdened with obligations. And Aunt Karen understands this. He needs his *own* rooms, and is living in a draughty studio in Universitetsgaten with one of the last survivors of the Bohemians.

If it gets too cold, he moves to the Grand.

*

The same autumn, Gunnar Heiberg's play *The People's Assembly* opens at the Christiania Theatre. It is dedicated to Heiberg's mistress Oda Krohg. Frederick Delius has written the music. He paraphrases Bjørnson's and Nordraak's national anthem *Yes, we love this land with fond devotion*, performs it in the minor key, changes the entire vision of proud Norway, of all that rises forth, into a funeral march, alters the trumpet fanfares and the hope for the future to a funeral dirge in the minor key. Fru Milly Bergh is among the audience and is moved, so moved that as much as ten years later she writes a letter to Delius thanking him for the experience, the scandal, the performance, the upshot of which is that after a short time and violent protests, the piece has to be performed *without* music, which means that Frederic Delius, friend of Norway, has to take the score back with him to the continent. Edvard Munch makes the lithograph *Funeral March*.

*

1898. Puvis de Chavannes dies, Mallarmé dies, Taine dies, Moreau dies, Rops dies, Boudin dies and Dagny Juel almost died when, a few months before the New Year she gave birth to Iva.

Fantin de Latour paints *Andromeda*. Space comes a step nearer, as does a new century. Munch will paint *Ibsen at the Grand Café* and *Fertility*, an etching of *Helge Rode*, woodcuts of *Fertility*, *The Voice* and *Women on the Shore*, and a lithograph of Przybyszewski. He will never finish *Ducha*, will never finish *Stach*. He gave the Pole a copy of *Madonna with Foetus* coloured by hand and with a personal dedication. Stach wrote:

There are moments when woman ceases to be a vampire. At the moment she gives herself fully and completely to a man the uncleanliness is washed away and her destructive impulse and shame disappear without trace, her face shines with the awesome beauty of conception. There are moments in a woman's soul when she forgets herself and all around her and transforms herself into a formless, timeless and dimensionless creation. At that moment, virginity is conceived in her: *Madonna*.

*

Stach's words: I have tried to portray the individual's real life together with his fall from grace and his slide into the abyss.

Munch knows that his friend is now turning his own writing into lived life, in other words, doing the opposite of what Munch himself is doing. Stach is summoning the dark urges to the surface, the endless series of volcanic eruptions, with a tragic awareness that everything he does, he must do. He has created his own hell from his own sexuality, will soon deceive Ducha with two new women, start long-term affairs with them, as though Marta Foerder has merely made him even more aware of his own destructive urges.

Munch knows that Ducha and Stach are on their way to Paris and later to Spain, Playa del Mera, heaven knows why they are going there. They have lost touch with their surroundings, have become lonely with one another, have grown together into a wound and use *Tranquillity*, Ducha's family home in Norway, to lick the wound. They sponge off the family when neither of them can earn enough through art. Yes, Munch sees what can happen. That is precisely why he bought the house in Åsgårdstrand. He wants to have control over his life, even if the tide is turning in his favour, even if the sap is rising.

Munch talks to the walls in his diminutive house in Åsgårdstrand. If there are powers that can hear me, answer. Is it possible to live a life without loving?

He paces up and down in a tiny living room. Now he has finally said no to Tupsy Jebe, said no to her youth, to her concern for him and her loyalty.

The stove gives off a clammy warmth.

Munch knows that the father of the man who sold him the house was bedridden in this room. Old Bollerød. He fell victim to consumption. Munch knows that Bollerød's father and two of his sons as well died of the same cause. He knows that the old man lay in this room for a year, his bed along one of the walls, while his daughter-in-law and the three children squeezed as close as they could to the other walls. Bollerød was as bowed as a violin. Munch can still hear the echo of his cough, like something being rattled in an iron bucket. The tuberculosis bacillus, the one that mowed down his own family, which broke down his mother, his sister and his brother. The red spot of blood on the white handkerchief:

Father, the stuff I'm coughing up is so dark.

But he escaped. Now he sits alone in Åsgårdstrand reflecting on life. In so many situations he has felt the urge towards loneliness, has bought this house from a fisherman who wanted to move into the city. It is his own past, a little town which lies in a bay overlooking the fjord at the foot of low-lying hills. Yellow, red and white wooden houses like a row of teeth. The sea laps against the stones and pebbles of the shore.

Munch owns a house, a sheltered garden with a hedge which runs right down to the shore, to the boulders and pebbles, which are both white and multi-coloured. He has a sitting-room and a kitchen, windows with small panes and a kitchen painted blue with a large old-fashioned hearth. It takes up almost half the room.

He is not the sort for ostentatious fine furniture. The living room consists of a table, a couple of chairs and a wide double bed. This is to be his home, for half the year at least.

He has had the stove put in to get rid of the cold which has penetrated deep into the walls. It is not large or elegant, but it is his, not just as property he owns, but as lived life. It is his trees, his shore, his forest, his own stones and stars, the ones he has been painting for years. Now it is suddenly close to him in a completely new way. For the very first time, he has committed himself to the future.

Now he sits in his house thinking about fish.

They live out there in the sea, spawn and die.

He thinks of fishermen on dry land, dark and swarthy, walking with bent backs to and fro on the shore seeing to the nets, the fishermen, who pull up the fish in a threshing white and silver mass. Yet they are not just a mass. They are individuals. They are countless heads, eyes staring vacantly out upon an entirely new world into which they are suddenly hauled up, before being thrown down into the boat to the hunchbacked fisherman with the wooden leg who is always drunk. Countless heads will be eaten and transformed into another substance, will become part of the human organism, will be flushed out again over the earth, will become land animals, flowers, bushes and trees.

Who was she, that woman who gave him the yellow flowers thirteen years ago? For him she was a mystery. She seduced him with haunting music, her laughter was something he had never heard before in any other person. Milly Bergh, Admiral Ihlen's daughter, one of that breed who turn heads and set people whispering after them on the street, at the theatre or at concerts. She whom Per Krohg will later include in his large-scale society portrait at the Grand Café. Who makes the world's darkest, strongest coffee and who knows the art of composing a menu. Who is the author of a cookery book called *Interesting Food*. The woman who, according to C.J., has a scintillating mind which leaves the air quivering behind her wherever she has been. Now Munch sits in his own house, thirteen years later, shakes his fist at her, feels rage and hatred, wants to avenge that faithless laughter. He is in a terrible state. Until, that is, he is calmed down by the memory of her eyes, the naked neck, the bared arm, the hips which had once swayed in *his* honour.

He had walked deep into the forest with her, had seen phalluses everywhere, tree trunks which resembled gothic churches. Sacred love! His deep-seated urges for once at one with the military doctor's Christianity. The branches looked like the roof of a church, a succession of spires. Is it possible to live life without love? He owns a house, owns his own memories, a past, remembers how her eyes grew large and dark, hollows which for a moment reminded him of skulls, before they emerged from the forest onto the shore. The moment when she stood there before him in the moonlight, when she could have walked straight out into the sea and disappeared into the depths, when he experienced the actual transformation, when everything suddenly turned to gold. The seconds before she turned towards him, and the time had come at last.

*

He puts some wood on the fire in the kitchen.

A large blazing fire. The flames crackle up towards the chimney.

Yes, the tide is turning in his favour. A delicious warmth flows out towards him. The flames are fanned by oxygen. He sees living creatures in the ashes. Just like in St Cloud that time. In the coal and wood embers he sees the white snakes of ash. Twisting and turning convulsively, as though in fear of death.

It was just like this when, as a child, he would be about to go to sleep, hands folded and would stare out into the dark room. He would see hell before him then. Would he awaken like one of those contorted bodies and be cast into hell's fiery furnace?

Munch paces up and down in the square room with the low ceiling, asking himself whether he has any right to be part of the dance of life. What has he actually lived for all these years?

He has carried the memories within him, has not managed to tear himself free from the point of departure. Strindberg was convinced that Munch was having an affair with Dagny Juel, but it was perhaps because she did *not* go into the forest with him that Ducha grew close to him.

* * *

Dear Munch. We had been thinking we might come down this week. But then my brother from Spain absolutely begged us not to come down until he has travelled south himself. He can't do without us. We're such good company for a booze up, as he puts it. So it can't be before Thursday. Then it would be lovely to make a little trip to Åsgårdstrand and château Munch. I'll have a large canvas and stretcher at the ready and shall put on my finest light blue dress, so some art will most likely come of it, and we'll find a shady sheltered spot in the garden where we can fill and empty our beakers to the background accompaniment of crickets and corncrakes and the lapping of the waves on the shore. Isn't that lovely? I have quite incredible expectations of château Munch. Fare well. Your Åse Ng.

* * *

He has bought a revolver.

He thinks it is great fun to shoot at a target in the kitchen. He stands there with a shiny little pistol, an even smaller lead bullet, feels how futile reflection is, indeed all species of philosophy as compared with the fact that when the little bullet strikes the heart you are dead. Are you really dead and gone? Is there no hereafter?

The coffee is ready.

He smokes a cigarette, drinks his coffee. There is a ghostly flickering from the fireplace. He thinks: have I the right to love as animals, plants, fish do?

A terrible bang.

His eardrums are completely deafened.

He feels a burning, stinging pain above his eye, stands up bewildered, is holding the revolver in his hand.

In his thoughts he had fired a shot.

Was it only in his thoughts?

But the bullet has singed his eyebrows.

Munch walks over to the oak beam.

There he sees it.

The bullet has bored deep into the rock hard wood.

*

One day Munch is sitting in the home of H., a university graduate. He sees red flushed faces. Flowers and wine. It is a party. Suddenly there is a wax-faced man standing in the doorway.

He has a thin face with hollow cheeks, jet-black hair and a beard. Munch immediately sees that he is in the final stage of consumption.

The dying man's wife is sitting on the sofa.

I think the wind'll probably turn cold soon, she says in a flat, expressionless voice.

The woman is pregnant. The father of the child is H.

The wax-faced man dies soon after. He lies there on the brink of death and sees his wife's condition. In these circumstances death is welcome to him.

The following year, his widow is married to H., the undergraduate.

One day she is standing by the paraffin lamp. She stoops. A flame sets light to her clothes.

Screaming she darts about the room, is transformed into a living flame. Holding a blanket, H. throws himself upon her.

She is in hospital, hovering for a long time between life and death.

But she survives, her face and large areas of her body covered in burns.

Then they flay him. Cut the skin from his body. His own skin gives new life to the widow's burned skin.

But the scars remain there for ever.

Whenever she gets warm, large red blotches come out on her face and neck.

* * *

So there he sits, the thin painter E., in a restaurant with the fat little Høst and Gunnar Heiberg with his peevish, sharp, twinkling eyes, the drooling mouth, the thick sensual lips, a cross between a pig and a toad. Heiberg has a nose for women. Has plucked Oda from under their very noses. What dimly-lit rooms did he visit in Berlin?

Lovely, says Heiberg glancing at two ladies.

Which one do you mean? The little black-haired one?

No, I mean the little red-haired one.

Not for me, says Munch. He recalls that Høst has told him about her, she is his wife's best friend. Her name is frøken Larsen. She apparently gives fru Høst a daily massage.

Let me introduce the painter Munch, says H.

Tulla Larsen. This is the painter Edvard Munch.

*

You make such a good motif with your red hair, he says, without actually thinking of a picture, more for something to say.

Oh do I, would you like to paint me? she replies, quick as a flash.

Yes, why not? Come to my studio, says Munch. Then I'll paint a sketch. Shall we say tomorrow at midday? 22 Universitetsgaten, the same studio as Alfred Hauge.

It is autumn 1898. What dwells in the mind of a man? Munch opens the door for Mathilde Larsen, born on the tenth of August 1869, the eleventh of twelve sisters, the daughter of P. A. Larsen, the wine merchant, who for so many years has supplied the population with wine, supplied bottles to the Grand and to Gravesen's, everything Munch has consumed.

Tulla Larsen comes into Munch's studio in Universitetsgaten. She has attended Nikka Vonen's cookery school for young ladies in West Norway. She has also been in Berlin, and has apparently studied graphic art. She is wearing a simple black dress. He paints her standing up. She says she has an apartment in Homannsbyen, tells him that she is twenty-nine years of age. Munch paints a simple portrait of a standing woman in a black dress. Even he thinks it a dull painting.

Well, that's it, he says, accompanying her to the stairway. I'll let you know if I decide to go ahead. I was almost going to ask you for a kiss.

Were you really? Why didn't you then? she says and turns on her heel.

*

A few days later a written invitation arrives to a party up at Holmenkollen. Munch attends it and finds himself seated next to Tulla Larsen. Wine, champagne and sumptuous food are served. It is autumn 1898. The Przybyszewskis have gone off to Cracow to become leaders of the peacock Bohemians. Strindberg is living in Lund and visits the young poet Emil Kléen, ill with cancer, in hospital. Hans Jæger is travelling round Europe drumming up funds for the printing of *Confessions*, *Prison* and *Despair*. As he stands in a huge patrician mansion on Holmenkollen Munch sees that people are dancing, that a dark woman's leg is raised so high that her petticoat is showing. He feels his senses are aroused by the champagne.

Go on, dance, fru H.! says frøken L. By Jove, if she isn't dancing the can-can just like they do at Bullier!

The dark one carries on dancing while the red-haired frøken Larsen cheers her on. After midnight, everyone is in ebullient mood thanks to the champagne. Munch looks at fru H. What a lovely shift. But it is

Tulla Larsen he finds himself sitting beside during the sleigh journey home. As they approach the streets of the city, she whispers:

Couldn't we go up to your studio?

He pretends not to hear. Perhaps he recalls Strindberg's characterization of red hair, his own picture *Cheveux Rouges*: Showers of gold rain down upon the hapless subject. Kneeling before her darker alter ego, she begs for mercy, begs for the mercy of being destroyed by needle pricks, golden cords which tie her to the earth and to suffering, bloody rain which pours down over the madwoman, who courts unhappiness, that blessed unhappiness of being loved, which is to say, of loving.

No, he does not wish to take her with him up to the studio for the night. He is thinking of the picture he calls *Three Stages of Woman*, the one Strindberg calls *Sinner/Manly/Mistress*, is approaching the fusion, the merging into one, the kiss, the sacrificing of the soul. He wants to paint *Fertility*, first calls it *Autumn*, then later *Fertility*, two strong robust individuals in profile, in the country, under a highly symmetrical, leafy tree. But in the sleigh that night are two tense, nervous individuals in an icy sinful city.

He soon sees her again. Tulla Larsen and Edvard Munch are each separately invited to various parties, as though fru H. is matchmaking. It becomes impossible not to run into one another, suddenly they are meeting one another all the time.

He lives in an airless little room adjoining the studio. He has a mattress to sleep on and a reeking paraffin stove. He yearns to be away, yearns to be back in Paris. His soul is in turmoil, the atoms in his body are realigning. Again he stumbles into a party already in full swing. Dinner is almost finished and a lot of alcohol has been consumed. He sees both the dark one and the red-haired one. Now he wants to concentrate on the dark one. He sees her great deep shining eyes. Listen, she says, in a confidential tone, as though about to take him completely into her confidence. For a long time they gaze into each other's eyes. Then the red-haired one goes about with a hurt expression. He is not going to be left in peace with the dark-haired one. Frøken Larsen asks her friend to accompany her to the garderobe. Munch is also invited. What does she want to show him? Frøken Larsen has taken the lead. She wants to show him her friend's naked skin, to show him the underclothes a woman wears for a party. He stands there looking, at a loss what to do. Fru H. has started to take her clothes off.

Come outside for a breath of air, says frøken Larsen suddenly.

They only get as far as the stairs. He is terribly aroused. She notices it. They kiss one another passionately. He feels powerless, surrenders, becomes half of his own kiss, of the paintings, the etchings, the fusion of two people into one. She has him now, the red-haired one, though it was the dark one he wanted. He has never been any good with women who have long noses and thin upper lips. But the kiss is just the beginning. Now he feels her hands, the demanding hands. When the party is over, she accompanies him and Hauge out onto the street. They walk across to the Grand.

Frøken Larsen, says Munch. It's late. Thank you ever so much for this evening. Now I think we'd better go our separate ways. Shall I accompany you?

But she does not move.

He tries to go on his way, to signal that the party is over, that he wants to go home to bed.

But she just stands there.

Shall we take a room at the Grand? says Hauge at last. Couldn't we sit and talk, the three of us?

Yes let's, says Tulla Larsen firmly.

*

They sit in the small hotel room discussing art, discussing people that interest them. The wine and the talking make them tired and sleepy. Perhaps we should all lie down, Hauge suggests.

She lies between them on the bed, moves very slowly and carefully up close to him. He feels her touch. Their lips graze.

Then morning comes.

They agree to meet again two days later.

*

She comes up to his studio. He knows what's going to happen. They kiss passionately. They lie down on the mattress. Hours of love-making, what he is later to call surrendering to the inevitable, tasting the bitter fruit, an entire winter of nightly dissipation and debauchery in the little room with the reeking paraffin stove, and now and then, when finances permit, the Grand.

Now he has found the red-haired woman he has always sought after, at least in his paintings. Does she know that she has embarked on an affair with a painter who even refers to himself as a neurotic, a person who has weak nerves, a nervous complaint which can sometimes take the form of irritability, mental and physical fatigue, the feeling of being incapable of work, depression, the imagined illnesses of the hypochondriac and also compulsive behaviour. Munch suddenly lies gripped with fever in Christiania. It is March 1899. He has had to rent a room at Gravesen's after two drunken orgies involving long sleigh rides. He has come down with a serious attack of bronchitis.

*

Seeing his condition, Jappe Nilssen sends for Doctor Koren. Munch is given some medicine and becomes drowsy.

He lies there dozing when there is a knock at the door. It is half-past eleven in the evening.

In comes Tulla Larsen. And Skredsvig, drunk as usual at this time of the day. Then it is champagne, cigars and cigarettes.

Skredsvig sings for Munch. Tulla Larsen laughs with her red lips. Munch glimpses curly red hair through the haze of cigar smoke, starts to drink as well. Tulla shouts:

Sing some more, Skredsvig, sing some more!

Skredsvig launches into song, Munch feels ill, his heart starts to pound. Eventually, he says that he must have rest.

She hesitates, but at last does as he bids.

Hmm, goodbye then, my prince.

It is three o'clock. He lies there hot and sleepless. Palpitations. Fever. He feels that he absolutely should not have drunk anything.

The following day Koren calls again. Then Jappe. Then it is straight to hospital.

After his illness he goes out to Nordstrand, to Aunt Karen and his sister Inger. His sister Laura is also out there now. She is not well, seems cut off from her surroundings. For much of the day she sits inactive, staring vacantly out into the room, which in all its bareness symbolizes her lack of interest in her surroundings. Just as depressing is the view through the curtainless windows. The fjord is grey and colourless, everything seems deserted, uninhabited, the only hint of life being the tulips on the table. The atmosphere of gloom is further emphasized by the colours. The bright red tablecloth accentuates the woman's mental condition, the carpet's indeterminate pattern is as formless as the woman's troubled, erratic thoughts. His sister Laura has withdrawn deep into herself now.

Munch employs his time exploring his feelings for Tulla. He does not forget Nietzsche's advice: If you seek out women, do not forget to take your whip. He is a friendly man of few words, wants peace and solitude, but always opens the door if people knock long enough. Tulla Larsen is knocking at the door. Munch has fled to Nordstrand, knows that it takes time to recover from such an illness. His brother Andreas never recovered. Munch feels tight in the chest, tired and ill. He paints a little, reads the cards she sends him, realizes he must get even further away from her.

He decides to go to Berlin and Paris. This is the only way he can put some distance between them, place himself beyond her reach. The only way he can finish it, so that she will understand.

* * *

A short time later he moves into Hotel Cöln in Berlin. He experiences the liberating feeling of having escaped. It is late April, sunshine alternating with rain. Just like the sudden changes in himself. Now at last the time has come for coffee and brandy at Café Bauer. He looks forward to being alone, to being able to work whenever he chooses, and to meeting old friends again.

Two days later Tulla Larsen checks into the hotel.

I've come to stay at your hotel, she says. Surely you don't have any objection?

He is flabbergasted. What is he to say?

Well, all right then, just for one night, he stutters. But everyone will see through it of course. I've told you I need peace and quiet. If you absolutely must be in Berlin at the same time as me, can't you take a room in a pension instead?

I should damned well think not, she says categorically. Not for all the tea in China!

Her room is on the ground floor, while his room is on the first.

The following day he tells her in no uncertain terms that she must not stay at the same hotel as him. She digs her heels in. Then he says there is some business he has to attend to, something he needs to be alone for. They agree to meet at a restaurant later that evening. She can dine alone if he does not turn up.

He arrives late.

She sits there waiting and has not yet eaten.

I shan't eat unless you're there, she says.

This is hopeless, he says flatly, explaining to her that he's going to be meeting some friends before very long. For two years he's looked forward to seeing these old friends.

Then the tears start to fall.

It is the first time he has seen her weep.

*

He stays with her until late into the night.

He awakens in his own bed.

He has not slept much. He feels wretched. Gets up and goes out. A biting wind. It blows straight through his clothes. His bronchitis gets worse. He is nervous, drags himself exhausted along the streets. He wants to be alone, as in earlier days, to reflect on life, to experience that feeling of freedom and solitude right in the middle of a lively café. To be absolutely alone.

When he returns to the hotel she is sitting there waiting for him.

He looks at her. A stranger. A greenish, ravaged face. The skin sticks to the bones of her face like wax. At first he feels fear. Then his anger mounts. She's not the poor little girl she pretends to be.

*

He threatens to leave her, to go away, make himself scarce.

Then she says: If you go, I'll go too.

He feels impotent, knows that she is not going to let him go, try as he might. Then he completely loses his temper:

I've seen all your different faces, he says. Yours is an evil one. I'd tread carefully if I were you.

He says goodbye, tells her she can go wherever she likes for all he cares.

As for him, he knows where he wants to go: Anywhere. So long as it is away from her.

*

Is a mere individual going to bring him down? He tries to recapture the sense of his former equilibrium, walks the streets, tries to remember, comes home late. There is a light in her room, he feels he must at least go in and say goodnight.

She is lying on the sofa, her face swollen with weeping. He thinks she is angry, but she collapses weakly into his arms. He embraces her, feels her warm skin. His feelings are torn between sympathy and desire. He came to Berlin to feel free, he came to work and see his friends. Now he sits in a room in Hotel Cöln and sees that she is clinging to him. Her body is far too warm. She does not look well. She is coughing a lot. He also feels steadily worse himself.

*

Together in his room. He feels tired, ill and out-of-sorts, has started drinking even in the morning, not moderate amounts either but to excess.

They are together every single evening now. He has three and a half thousand crowns in his pocket, has sold *Spring* to the National Gallery, later writes that he did so when befuddled by champagne, an intoxication created by an ageing virgin, the man lacked the courage to play Joseph.

Paris, how to get to Paris, perhaps Italy would be better. Now he has neither whip nor defences. She is stronger than Tupsy Jebe, is experienced at least, and knows a thing or two. She is the three women he has already created in *Sphinx*, *Three Stages of Woman*, the woman he will soon create in *The Dance of Life*: tall, with a gaunt face and ferrety little eyes. Her golden hair looks like a halo. Her tightly pursed lips form a curious smile.

An inexplicable feeling of fear comes over him.

A shudder.

That evening he dreams he is kissing a corpse.

They are sitting in a café together.

Suddenly she says: Do you remember you dreamed that you kissed me, that you kissed death's clammy lips?

Yes, he says.

There was probably something in it, you know. I'm having such terrible coughing fits. I keep on bringing up blood in the mornings.

He gives a start. A fatal disease? Something very dangerous at least. He has bronchitis, is very vulnerable. Is she a carrier of the old arch-enemy, the consumption bacillus? Those millions of unseen enemies, germs which have brought death and unhappiness to his family.

He looks at her. Is this the smiling face of death?

His own eyes are like beacons, a long, bright beam of light trained on the past, or ahead onto what is to come.

Sudden presentiments. He has always had an inkling of the future, has thought of certain people just before bumping into them in the street. It is many years since he painted *Love Kissing Death*.

So they are ill. Both of them! Which means he can't leave her. He soon realizes that they must travel together, find somewhere further south, travel towards the sun, like the time he took the train to Nice. He must take care that there is no catastrophe now. They must travel together, to Italy, to Florence. He must turn his plans upside down, luckily he has money.

By now he should have been in Paris printing at Clot and Lemercier. But, when all's said and done, she's ill, perhaps even more so than he. Dying, as she puts it herself. Coughing up blood every morning. He cannot leave her in the lurch now.

* * *

He knows that he has a strongly developed talent for studying facial expressions, deciphering people's characters, good as well as bad. Later he will write that it was just this quality which may have instilled in him a feeling of impending doom at an early age, will write that her various inherent qualities were bound to be his undoing. He has seen many women who have any number of shifting expressions, but claims that never before has he met anyone who so clearly has just three.

She can wear a look of the deepest sorrow, among the most expressive he has ever seen, like the weeping Madonnas of the Pre-Raphaelites, a look which pulls his heartstrings, making them contract with sympathy. But when she is happy, he has never seen such radiant joy, as though sunshine was suddenly lighting up her whole face, a smiling face which can irritate him because there is no room in it for his own suffering. She is always glacially indifferent when he feels most unwell.

Then there is the third face, which frightens him. This is the fateful face, which makes him an observer of his own destruction. The face of the sphinx, in which he finds all the dangerous characteristics of woman.

* * *

They set off together for Florence. Sickness, drinking, unhappiness.

They rival one another in suffering. He sees that her eyes are small and ferrety, she flits about like a wild creature, he attempts in vain to plunge his eyes into her soul, seeks in vain to dominate her will. Here in Italy she strikes him as ill and rebellious. Florence is a disappointment. A freezing wind blowing down from the mountains combines with stifling heat from the sun. He feels steadily worse. Things cannot go on like this. There is not an ounce of strength left in his body. He takes to his bed.

*

She thinks she sees that wonderful, all-embracing love concealed somewhere beneath his pathological timidity, in the silence between all the words, in his distant look. She dreams of that uncommon love which burns with a great flame.

They have strolled about in Florence, observing the love of other people, seeing the birds on the wing, watching flowers open. But neither of them has drawn any strength from it.

During the long hours, in his sickbed and especially during the sleepless nights, he reflects on what has already happened. Does he love her? The answer is no. She is beautiful, she awakens his desire, she is wealthy and independent. He thinks they may perhaps grow together, but she is strange, he doesn't understand her. Why, that evening together with the dark fru H., had she virtually handed her to him on a plate up in the ladies' dressing room, shown her off, a friend at that! Isn't she lovely? she had said. Why did she open her friend's bodice? Did she love him then? Why had she unbuttoned the plump little dark one's bodice, shown him the pale, bare arm which was revealed, the golden breast which nestled hidden within the silk petticoat. And yet was *this* the reason he had kissed her, there on the stairs. He had been aroused by the dark one, had been carried away.

Later she grew even more puzzling. For example, that time in the street when, deathly pallid, he had almost collapsed. He was quite unprepared for her glacial tone. And what about the night scene at his sickbed, with Skredsvig, when, laughing, she had danced *Swan Lake*? Her laughter was always cold when he was ill.

He lies ill in bed in Florence, is now sicker than she is. There is much he does not understand.

Go somewhere else, he begs her, get well, for God's sake let's both get well!

* * *

She departs reluctantly for Paris.

She feels banished. He remains behind in Italy, lying in bed. His old friend fru Vullum drives him up to Fiesole, the Etruscan town. They sit him at a window, with a view of the Arno, he can gaze down at the city with its massive cathedral, Brunelleschi's masterpiece, the distinctive cupola and Giotto's bell tower which he has seen in countless Romantic oil paintings, the Uffizi and the Palazzo Pitti, the great painting collections, Michelangelo, Verrocchio, Masaccio, Raphael, da Vinci. He sits at a window writing to Tulla in Paris:

My dear, I'm dropping you a line today too, more or less just to say hello, so there will be none of that baring of the soul which we both find so awkward. Let me describe the view: my feet half wrapped in a rug, propped up on a stool, and bathed in the rays of an Italian sun, a false, perfidious sun colder than ice. Then there is the window, with all Florence behind it, that lovely Florence which I do not actually visit, like another Canaan, like a symbol of my life, of the promise it holds for me. Framing Florence's white buildings: above are frightful thunderclouds, rain and wind, and below is freshly sprung foliage. If only I could get well enough to leave this horrible country, or, more precisely, this horrible climate, but I shall probably not be well enough to leave until it is high summer. Goodbye, my dear friend, drink a glass of absinthe for me in Paris, and be happy that you *can*.

*

She replies immediately.

To Edvard Munch, Ristorante Bellagio, Regresso Maiano, presso Fiesole, prov. Firenze (Florenz), Italia.

My dear friend: Thank you for your letter which I received yesterday, in bed of course. There is no point in getting up when one has lost one's voice. During the night I was running a temperature. My pulse was 110. What do you think of that? But today I feel better. Oh you poor chap, still just as weak as I am, but luckily out of bed a little, so presumably well enough to be able to walk about a bit more now. It's good to hear that you've missed me a bit. I constantly see your room before me wherever I go, see you lying there while I sit here, medicine bottles and tea tray, newspapers and a hundred other things strewn about, I can see your various expressions altering with your mood, I long for you so, would rather see you for two minutes than all these people who sit with me or have been up to see me for hours on end the last few days. Just imagine, though I hardly dare say it, just imagine if you were to come here for just a few days. But I shall not try and persuade you, you know best what you can manage, but I can't put into words how much I should love to be together with you here, right here, just for a short time. I am so tired now. A thousand greetings from your Tulla.

*

He notes a weakness in one lung. This is not influenza, not bronchitis, not something which will disappear just like that. He has not an ounce of strength left in his body, tries to get up but is forced to go straight

171

back to bed. He reads her letters from Paris. The Segelckes and the Diriks are visiting her, the Nørregaards have just left. She writes that she has lost her voice after an eventful day and night. She is in the company of Obstfelder, Delius, Gunnar Heiberg and his beloved Oda, things are no doubt building up to a violent quarrel between them. Lively nights here, there and everywhere. Coming home at five o'clock in the morning, promises to better her ways, is off to Grez sur Mer. To Delius.

*

He doesn't know what to think. This hectic partying. It makes him feel uneasy. So many unreliable people. Including Heiberg, the skirt chaser. Hadn't Munch forbidden her to see him, quite apart from his feelings for Oda? But she writes:

My dear, why aren't you and Heiberg friends? We spent the whole of yesterday together, he tells me *so* many curious things, you've no idea what a strong impression he made on me, I've seldom been so surprised by anyone, but there we are, he sent his best regards to you by the way, you were the general topic of conversation of course. Everyone felt sorry for the poor sick fellow in Florence and thought it was callous (hmm) of me to leave you. Why don't you like the people who are actually your greatest admirers? Why do you push them away?

*

He reads open-mouthed with surprise and becomes terribly dejected. So this is how she carries on, is it! He has demanded of her not to spend any time in the company of Heiberg and the others, and that is the very first thing she does, up and about all night, falls ill again, then a little hint about falling in love! G.H. Those lecherous little snake's eyes of his. If *this* is how she chooses to part company with him it's the best thing that could happen. But all the same. He writes back: I've always thought Heiberg's way of seeing things would suit you down to the ground.

Then he receives a letter which brims with longing. She regrets everything. Now there is no further mention of Heiberg at all, it's Munch and only Munch. Yet in the next letter, she has been on the spree the whole night and is suddenly in bed running a high temperature. He feels a mixture of sympathy and goodness knows what. How will it all end? He sends her further remonstrating letters. Then she replies that they absolutely insist she accompanies them on a bicycle trip. After a few glasses of whisky fru Diriks just wouldn't take no for an answer and today she's expecting a visit from Heiberg, that is, if he hasn't gone out to see fru Krohg at Grez. He is terribly amusing, almost fascinating at times, but never mind, it would all take too long to tell you . . .

He lies in bed in Fiesole, feeling as though he is walking in his sleep on the roof. With a sure, calm step he walks without seeing or hearing.

Then someone calls to him, louder and louder. He wakens. He falls down from the roof, down from his dreams. Don't do this to me! he shouts. I am walking peacefully in my dreams! It's my life, this is the only way I can live!

But she is calling from Paris:

You mustn't be angry with me. I'm so well now, never cough. Thank you for the lovely flowers, at first I thought they were butterflies, you must really have been taken with me, your walking companion, that day we visited the Roman baths together. Why do you discard things you have written to me? That's just the sort of impulsive letter that should be sent. I'm sure that's just the sort I would probably have liked best. Then you stop in the middle of a really interesting sentence, though that's just typical of you. You're afraid of long reflections, but I must tell you that Heiberg absolutely does not strike me as attractive, quite the contrary, indeed less and less so the more time I spend with him: the first few days he took me by storm, though all we did was talk about you and nothing else the whole time. I think it's interesting to hear what he thinks of you, even if we don't see eye to eye on this point. He gets worked up, more worked up than at any other time, when he gets onto the subject of you, every nerve in his body is tense, I see he admires you but also bears a little grudge against you for something.

* * *

Munch travels via Pisa along the coast to Rome. His uncle P. A. Munch is buried there. He studies art, shivers in a cold hotel room with stone floors, and now the three and a half thousand crowns have almost run out. He studies Raphael with an eye to decorative art projects back home, writes to Tulla who is in Grez. She replies: Yes, of course you do tell me a little bit each day, even when you are travelling. Thank you for every telegram you send me. I've thought about you so much the last few days. As for me, I've been in Paris since last Tuesday with fru Mowinckel and fru Krohg who, between you and me, has now left Heiberg. You can well imagine I've witnessed a battle the like of which it would be hard to imagine. Everyone was worked up and at each other's throats, not least fru Krohg. The last round was at the Pantheon on Wednesday evening between eleven o'clock and one o'clock. It was awful and really upset me. I've come out here today, where Per Krohg and I are now alone, and let me tell you, it's a relief to be on our own. I've become incredibly hardened here in Paris, that's a fact. Thanks to a certain person, I can now put up with the most incredible insults. I have the distinct impression you think it a really bad thing that you've fallen in love with me, but if you're in love with someone, the last thing you think about is whether it's suitable or not. You're simply in love, regardless of whether you each make life intolerable for one another. Don't be angry with me for saying this and remember to send me a few lines every day of your journey.

*

He sends her further letters, he is still very weak, on his way back to his past, to Åsgårdstrand, via Paris, and writes to her: I'm so sorry to hear that it's rainy weather for you. Wish you had the sun on your face. It pains me that you are sad, but how can things be any different from what they are? You're reasonable enough to understand that. I wonder whether I can still paint. I've probably forgotten how. Have you still any copper plates left? You must really try to etch a landscape, you know, I'll get hold of some plates, and later on I'll explain all you need to know about etching.

He is back in Paris, inspired by Raphael, by the art in Rome, tells Meier-Graefe that he now wants to return home to Norway and create decorative art for large walls, the conclusion to *The Frieze of Life*: *Virginia Creeper*, *Melancholy*, *Golgotha* and *The Dance of Life*. At about the same time, Meier-Graefe, in his *Contribution to a Modern Aesthetic*, writes that there is no concealing the fact that a setting in which typical pictures by Munch fitted in naturally will never be possible, or even desirable.

* * *

Where on earth would he fit in naturally?

In a life shared with Tulla Larsen?

With his family at home in Nordstrand?

*

He is his pictures. Many years later he will say to Rolf Stenersen: Remember, all I have is my pictures.

Now he is returning to the scenes of his past, where the pictures are conceived. To Tulla he writes: You know all I've done and sacrificed to be with you, I've seriously jeopardized my health and have done so many times that it's doubtful whether I'll ever recover, I've put all my work aside, you must not be impossible, my dear, you must not ask for more.

*

He feels he must choose between work and love. Yet he puts off the decision. He keeps on writing to the one he claims he wants to put behind him.

She replies: How can you think that I'm trying to deceive you! Why do you always accuse me of lying, especially when those involved are only insignificant individuals who happen to cross my path. Don't you realize that I can't stand your being suspicious of me in any way at all? If I go out one evening, it's because I need to, because I must have a bit of a change instead of always having you on my mind. It's not a hankering for entertainment but melancholy if anything. I take this seriously, for me it is deadly serious and you *must* try not to be suspicious of me.

But he is suspicious of her. Heiberg! Why did she ever get involved with him at all. He muses about his old friend: Gunnar H. has a pointed slightly lopsided belly. With it he makes his way slowly but surely towards his goal. His nostrils are always flared trying to catch the scent of a bit of skirt for the taking. If he detects a chink in a marriage, he sails in bows first, moors securely in the chink, guzzles, does not budge. And Sigurd Bødtker, the dog, the poodle, fetches him the game. Look, here comes Gunnar H. sailing forth with his fat little belly, his little piggy eyes blinking, yes, he's a cross between a toad and a pig, even down to the voice, sometimes a croak, sometimes a slurp. On occasion his face can even be moved, by a painful emotion somewhat akin to empathy. It then adopts the expression of a person relieving himself. He lives off nothing but maggots, always sniffing about for a hint of decay in a marriage. With his cunning little eyes he weighs up when a husband is too tired and the woman dissatisfied. A little wedge which splits them apart. Then he sits between the two of them. Always ready to be amusing, always smacking his lips at table, praising the lady's cooking. Always ready to taste the fare, the dainty dish of marriage.

* * *

Dear Tulla: You must be at Drøbak now, have no doubt also found accommodation, which can't be that difficult, you don't know anyone else in Drøbak, you say? Yes you do, it would have been lovely to see you again, but I'm doing my level best not to think of you, I have to do all I can to ensure that I can paint. If I don't get well during these two months, then I'll never be well again. I'm taking quinine, iron, arsenic tablets by the fistful, which should help. Here in my château life is wonderful, sitting in the garden or lying in a hammock, always with a canvas at the ready so I can cheat fate and at good moments paint a few brush strokes. The Lies, the Dons, the Vogts never come here now, having seen my contorted features when they did appear they probably think I'm mad. Thank you very much for the letters, surely you can see that I love you, that's just what is so wrong, I don't think I'm suited to love anyone or for anyone to love me, I'm so ill-suited to sharing my life with anyone, which became only too clear during the time we were together, I'm impossible, only fit for painting pictures.

*

Munch, on the threshold of a new century, writes to Tulla Larsen about the necessity to make a choice, about what is on his mind, about her beautiful letters, has to assure her that he loves her, and in the next sentence has to ask her not to come down to Åsgårdstrand, not there, not until he says so, and of course not for any length of time. She must accept that, for some time to come, he will do whatever he must to answer his calling, get ready for the exhibition, the one he has for so long been waiting and hoping for. This, my dearest, is an absolute condition. But he asks her nicely to be a dear, to be a darling and fit in with this which simply has to happen, his decision is irrevocable. He cannot go about like a living corpse and not get anything done.

Munch writes and makes a sizeable ink blot as though to illustrate the strong words, himself describes them as strong words, but writes that he has no alternative but to say them, as he does not know what will happen if she goes against his will. He hopes at long last actually to finish a painting and concludes his letter with a quotation borrowed from Ibsen: A kiss and a hope that the miracle may happen.

* * *

Munch spends the summer in Christiania and Åsgårdstrand. It is the summer when, ironically, he will paint the double portrait of Åse and Harald Nørregaard. He forces her to look straight at him whereas he paints her husband in profile. There is defiance in her face. A strong, challenging look, almost angry. He must have looked similarly defiant as he stood behind the easel. They are friends, but they also share a past. He remembers the details, down to the smallest ones, that she would not hold his hand, remembers the southerly wind that blew her long flaxen hair over her eyes the day before the wedding, remembers that he stood behind the pillar in the church and felt that his life's greatest happiness was perhaps disappearing at that very moment.

*

He sits in the garden at Åsgårdstrand talking with Frederick Delius and Helge Rode about the transparency of the body, about telepathy, about X-rays and the mysterious rays from space. This is itself a meeting in space, on the globe they call the earth. Three people exchange ideas about hidden worlds and about the puzzle of life. Simultaneously, all three of them are working on a dance motif, Rode on the play *The Dance Goes On*, Delius on the symphonic poem *Life's Dance*, Munch on his own painting *Tulla Larsen in Three Stages*, in white, red and black.

Munch himself dances with the red-haired one as Gunnar Heiberg licks his chops over an unidentified woman in white close beside him.

*

Eventually he sees her again. They have a lot to talk about. He says: You must realize that in me the capacity for great passion is dead, the poison of consumption filled my childhood home with sorrow and fear of life, strangled belief in life and childhood happiness, devastated my home. Just remember that.

He sits there trying to explain to her yet again that work is and remains his great passion. He says:

Mark my words, I shall never marry.

Tulla says brusquely: I've had a letter from Dagny Juel. She asks me to be nice to you, just as nice to you as *she* has been.

To this he replies: Dagny was nice to me because she let me be. Because she left me in peace.

*

She cannot leave him in peace.

Doesn't he understand that when he's constantly in her thoughts, regardless of where she is, then eventually she is bound to begin to fathom him, or at least grasp *something* about him?

She cannot stand meeting him in cafés, cannot bear that it is so painful during the short periods she sees him. Will he really not meet her? He thinks: Why doesn't she get hold of some books, why doesn't she develop her mind, why doesn't she develop an interest in something?

But her passion has focused on just one thing.

She writes: My dearest: Would like to have telephoned, but was so afraid of disturbing you, apart from which I hoped you'd send me a little letter today as I didn't receive one yesterday or before either. I have applied myself so well the last few days, made woodcuts and drawn everything I've come across. But it's impossible for me to get the wax to stay put on the copper plate.

He reads, feels weak, dizzy, tired, feels the sickness eating its way deeper and deeper into his lungs.

It is a doctor who finally realizes how serious it is: incipient tuberculosis.

This is his first trip for a long time north of Christiania, up along the lake and the river to Gudbrandsdalen.

He has received strict instructions from the doctor:

Kornhaug Sanatorium, Fåberg.

* * *

Balzac asked: Which will be the victor, will disease conquer man or will man conquer disease? Nietzsche said: There can be no higher wisdom without the experience of sickness. This is the prerequisite of greater health. In other words, sickness and madness are the condition of greater mental activity.

Munch is in Kornhaug Sanatorium as the Boer War in Africa enters a new phase. A new century, a new way of feeling. Ibsen's *When We Dead Awaken* is performed for the first time in Stuttgart. It is the year of *The Dance of Life*, *Virginia Creeper* and *Melancholy*, three paintings each with an element of madness, painted by an artist with tuberculosis.

He has inherited the weaknesses of both father and mother. A weak chest and poor nerves.

Laura is in a mental hospital. He is in a sanatorium.

Then he paints himself on the cross, naked and exposed, butt of the crowd's scorn, object of their veneration. Yet at the same time, in the foreground: his own profile amongst the crowd. While a hideous woman clad in the garb of death and with a face contorted in a frightful grimace lays her hand on his shoulder, seals his fate, makes clear his choice: He can take either of two paths. He must choose between loneliness and love.

But both paths end at Golgotha, end in death.

*

He receives a letter from Aunt Karen.

Dear Edvard: When you are lying sleepless, don't concentrate on any one thing, but let your thoughts wander from one trifling thing to another, don't linger on anything. I've tried this. What about taking quinine? Might that not be a good idea? You mustn't think of sending us any money, another 400 crowns came today for Laura. We've saved 360 crowns partly from what you've sent and partly from gratuities Inger and Laura received for Christmas. Now you can see that we've more than enough. You don't need to think any more of repaying the first years. In a few days we're going to visit Laura and send you her greetings, Inger sends you her best wishes, if you're in difficulty you can borrow from us.

*

He is a fugitive from a woman. She is wealthy. She has a will of iron. He has had his picture taken together with her by a street photographer, letting her set off the exposure, letting her use her left hand to release the mechanism in the form of a rubber balloon attached to the camera by a tube.

She stares into the camera with an ambivalent expression, he is looking to the right of the camera with a distant, almost defiant air. Behind them is a scene of tropical vegetation, a sort of ironic paraphrase of Adam and Eve in Paradise.

He spends a long winter in Kornhaug Sanatorium, reads in the paper that there is snow in Capri, that three million people are starving in India, that Puccini is preparing for the opening of *Tosca* in Rome.

And Tulla Larsen feels homeless in Berlin.

My dearest: It is terrible to think of this protracted illness which will not let up, aren't you taking any medicine? Presumably you still don't know when you'll feel strong enough to risk coming down here. January 2nd. Do you remember it last year?

He probably does remember most of it, her beautiful face, her flowing red hair, but he avoids all amorous expressions, wants to prevent her from believing in a future life together for them, yet nevertheless thinks: have higher powers determined that they will spend their lives together?

In an obscure side valley in Norway he goes through hell, a rigorous cure in a sanatorium, enforced idleness for between seventeen and twenty-four hours a day, all of them in a sanatorium chair parked on the sun veranda and well wrapped up. He feels like a horse which has been ridden into the ground. She is in Germany and asks him why he cannot come.

It is eleven years since the attack of fever at Dörnberger's, ten years since the hospital in Le Havre, five years since Andreas died of pneumonia. He himself has had countless minor bouts of fever, colds, as well as serious attacks of influenza. He still feels ill, anxious, listless.

Ibsen's *Ghosts* opens at the National Theatre. The wine merchant's daughter writes from Berlin, finds his letters unfriendly, emphasizes that she is serious, that she has staked her whole life on him, that she can therefore easily come to grief. Sitting in a sanatorium he recalls the life they have already had together, love's bitter-sweet irony. That morning in the café, for instance; they had lain in each other's arms all night, the whole night simply belonged to one another. Then suddenly, sitting at a table, they were strangers, couldn't even look one another in the eye. He had said it again, if one cannot really love for a lifetime, or, like me, cannot marry, then as friends we still ought to be able to let each other feel something of that wonderful enigma.

Was it then that he began to think he would never be rid of her? As she had intimated, she might end up taking her own life.

In that case could they possibly live as he might perhaps have been able to live with Ducha? Each with their own private life, each with their own work, each with their own room. And yet as lovers, as friends? He writes that she has held a greater place in his heart than anyone else. In Berlin she tries to understand a man who speaks with two tongues, who thinks of marriage as a friendly liaison, without any obligations.

She reads his dreams: that she gets a printing machine for etching. He wants to get books for her, perhaps they might even have some kind of a home, but it depends on his own work, his own health, his urge towards loneliness regulates his life. My dearest: Life is surely not just a feast of love is it? He is writing from the sanatorium, wants to give her guidance on how to be healthy. She writes that she has been seriously ill. She must have fresh air. He is persuaded that having a cold rub down is not good for the nervous or anaemic. He finds it maddening that she jeopardizes her health with cold water. Where sickness is concerned he starts to act like a doctor, an elder brother. He has learned from the military doctor's decrees, from Aunt Karen's advice, she must wrap up well and keep warm.

But he cannot come to visit her, is too ill himself, it may take as much as a year. She replies: My dearest one, I've suffered a lot recently, I've fought the hardest battle of my life, the possibility of letting you go, for your sake, I've been close to despair, have begged to be allowed to die, to save you, but have not been able to do it, cannot give you up, I must be yours, even if I'm away from you a lot. You're the only person in the world I think it's worth living and breathing for. I fully understand what you mean by a marriage without obligations.

He replies: My dearest, for the time being we must both try to rest. I don't want to go into further detail now about what we must sort out later on. As soon as I can I shall try to meet you.

*

They are inextricably bound together, he a patient in a sanatorium in Gudbrandsdalen, she in Germany where she has gone to work, is etching in a room in Potsdam, the whole table cluttered with all kinds of acids, her hands black with tar.

She has been in the company of Obstfelder and the Vogts, there are piles of books lying about, *Niels Lyhne*, Carlyle, Jonas Lie, Vilhelm Krag, Dostoyevsky. Is he satisfied now?

She is trying to do as he says, listen to his admonitions, but simply cannot get him out of her thoughts, asks him not to be cross because she writes so often. What she calls her outpourings about one thing and another.

He accepts all the words, all the sudden changes, like the spring weather that time in Florence, glacial winds and rain, or burning hot sun. She is steadily being worn down by the uncertainty, the obsession, while he has endless sleepless nights, the bed an enemy, at the sanatorium together with sick people, some of them will not pull through, will succumb in the end. The cough, the blood that is brought up, discoloured handkerchiefs, death in the waiting room, eyes without hope. And all the time, her letters, more and more despairing.

He replies: So you find my letter harsh, do you? Sooner or later you must be made to see things clearly. Think a little for once. I remember letters I wrote you during sleepless nights to make you see reason. It is odd. You with your health, your energy, your thirst for love, are nevertheless cold in a way. I've often said so. I who am cold, contemplative, had to warm *you*. I did not leave any the stronger for your embraces.

* * *

Blood. Pumping blood. Pounding hearts. Who is that knocking?

A nurse comes with the post. A telegram from Tulla in Germany. She writes that she is going to die, is fatally ill, has been to the doctor and learned that she is in an advanced stage of consumption.

He is flabbergasted, reads, tries to understand. But before he has collected his thoughts, a new telegram arrives:

Have taken poison, have been unconscious the whole night. Come straight away. Still hope.

He leaps up.

She's really gone and done it!

He drops what he was doing. Has to save her, cost what it may.

Then he receives yet another telegram. Don't come, it won't help! Don't come, it'll be your undoing! But I've loved you unto death! Dreadfully sorry for all that's happened. Yours till death.

* * *

But he does go. Back to Germany. Berlin, Mittelstrasse.

She says: The pictures, do you remember *Vampire*? You asked me whether I understood the motif. It's the culmination of love, you said.

Yes. It was a warning. Now do you understand what I meant?

She nods.

Here is *Jealousy*, he adds. Here's a picture which shows that love goes hand in hand with death.

She does not say anything.

Yes, you understand it now. Now we will build on what we have learned.

*

She goes about with a tired, frightened expression.

He has come to her, used her money, as she asked him to do. She is wealthy. P. A. Larsen's daughter. She sent him money. For he was broke.

That was the fateful moment. He stood there with *her* money in his hand. He spurned the doctor's advice and packed his bags.

It is spring 1900. He is in Germany living on her money. It is humiliating, but he has no other option.

He came to Berlin and went straight up to her room, where he found a shirt.

Whose shirt is this? he asked.

Just R.'s shirt, she replied. R. forgot it. It's of no importance.

R.'s shirt in her drawer?

He was filled with jealousy. A terrible suspicion invaded him.

*

She weeps her heart out, weeps in his arms. Both of them are ill.

We must get better, he says, we'll travel south.

They are living in a hotel in Dresden. He feels tired and weak. Drinking the whole day. Then lovemaking. He feels even more drained, but feels the happiness of being near her. He possesses her completely yet is jealous and suspicious. She had written: There is so much in the past that you must forgive me for, everything was so new to me, the terror of having a child, you've no idea how I suffered when I left you, you

must remember what things were like at home, there was so little understanding about anything, I have never needed to lie to my mother. That
time I asked you whether you had syphilis, which I'd heard rumours
about, even then I was so determined to be yours that I wouldn't have
shrunk from either death or a fatal illness. When you upbraided me for
believing you would pass it on to me, all I can tell you is that I had not
known any man intimately, and had no idea how far a man's responsibility went. Do you really think unmarried women, whether young or even
slightly older, understand such things? In any case, I'd never heard that
word or disease mentioned until two years ago. I've never acted coldly
in any respect, the only thing I've been sure about and felt in my heart
of hearts is that for me you are everything. I can't imagine how I could
possibly live without you.

*

Days in Germany, reconciliation and fresh wounds, she in tears, he
despairing, tired, ill, drunk. He thought the alcohol would put some
body into him and provide some relief from his bronchitis. They are
inextricably bound together now. She harks back to their old discussion
about marriage. He had once written that it would be madness for him to
marry because of his extreme nervousness. Yet suddenly he asks: Will
she blindly do what he asks of her without questioning it? Does she agree
that everything must be absolutely out in the open, that there must be
unrestricted freedom in everything, for example if, for his health's or his
art's sake, he has to go away from her as soon as they are married?

He speaks to her, is overcome with euphoria. Does he know that
lack of oxygen induces euphoria, that it is lung disease that can make
him suddenly elated, like a crew of balloonists who ascend to too great
an altitude and in their elation throw out ballast instead of letting out
gas, that even people hanging on the gallows – in a word, he tells her,
the events of the past few months have made a strong impression on
him, almost transformed him. Suddenly he feels he can see a strong man
behind all these things. If love is not felt as love of life, it is worthless.
He speaks to her, it is a possibility after all, quite apart from the money
question, he has asked her to send a few hundred crowns to his sister
and aunt, he wrote that she must have three thousand crowns ready
when he came to Berlin. Now he is there, reads in the paper that the
métro in Paris is open, apparently a new underground communication
system, hears her talking about marriage, begins to talk about it
himself.

All right, he'll give it a try then!

What does she think when she hears these words, these so-longed-
for words? For she has heard him correctly, yes, he is saying marriage!
She jumps up immediately, is going to arrange everything, get the

papers from the mayor. They are there before he knows where he is. Further discussions about the marriage settlement, the freedom he must be able to expect. Then suddenly she says:

You know I have a lot of money. We will have to have a separation of property.

He hears what she says. She knows that he does not have any money, that he is living off her now. But that's *her* fault, isn't it? All the lost work, all because of her. And there she is talking about separation of property? So she doesn't trust him? This infuriates him. Separation of property? No question of it. No marriage then. He jumps up incensed. Won't hear another word, lies awake the whole night.

The following day he is just as furious. He says unequivocally that there is no longer any question of marriage.

In any case, he cannot find the papers.

* * *

Then he receives the news of Obstfelder's death. My goodness. Obstfelder. Already! No one was there in his final hour. It all happened so quickly. No one had any inkling that his physical condition was hopeless. It started as an ordinary cold. But the cold lingered on. Suddenly he developed swallowing problems. Tubercular pharyngitis and laryngitis. In other words, pulmonary tuberculosis. The noblest of souls, who wandered about the world with rucksack and violin, who had written poems about everything he actually wanted to paint, which had provided a defence against the accusations of madness. Over-sensitive Obstfelder, dry-humoured, laconic and desperate. Among the wrong people, in the wrong country, in the wrong world. Three years younger than Munch himself. My goodness, Tulla. Obstfelder!

*

And what of his own lungs? He distinctly feels a weakness there which makes him anxious. What chance does he really have? And she is not well either.

Perhaps the south will have a beneficial effect on both of them.

They go to Como, on the other side of the mountains. They are met by spring. New life. A touch of the Mediterranean in the southerly wind.

But the days follow the same pattern. They have both learned to drink. She is the daughter of a wine merchant, and Munch himself has also contributed handsomely to the sales. Tired, ill, drunk. Passionate sex. He reads in the paper that the heavenly sphere at the Universal Exhibition in Paris has collapsed. Nine deaths. Is it a warning? He feels even worse.

One evening they are sitting in the Diavolo restaurant. Devil, appropriate name. After all, he is acquainted with the devil, is following in

Strindberg's footsteps, gets drunk and nasty, says harsh things. All the suspicions, what was she actually doing with the Romanian's shirt in her drawer? Did they actually have an affair? And what of the weeks alone before his arrival? The consumption which vanished? He sits in a restaurant beside Lake Como and comes out with the nastiest words he can think of, she's a wealthy ageing spinster, what kind of riff-raff is it that she's surrounded with, swindlers, whoremongers, drunkards, whose seed is spent, people who no longer have any sense of the continuity of life, who loudly proclaim that nowadays love is a stimulant. Incidentally, did she know that she looks like a cat? Those cold eyes. Less soul in them than in a cat's. He once had a cat himself, a white one, in Paris. He put it out into the street. Should have kept it. More soul in it than in her eyes.

Munch is inflamed by the alcohol. The spirits fuel his temper. Suddenly he sees enemies everywhere. Her worst faces are terrible, repugnant. This cold Madonna from Homannsbyen, the wine merchant's daughter, does she know that she is drinking away his income, that she is supping from the treasury of *art*? At this she gets up and goes, leaves the table, the wine, the slander. He remains sitting where he is, has done everything in his power to get her not to love him any more. But it was she who got up and left him and suddenly it felt so empty at the restaurant table.

Later, when he goes up to bed, her shoes are not in their usual place outside her room.

Then his fury subsides. What has she done! He has visions of her body floating in Lake Como, he tosses and turns in bed, with the most terrible imaginings. My God, Tulla! With her boundless vulnerability, her fundamental loneliness.

He does not get a minute's sleep.

When morning comes, he gets up and rushes down to the dining room. There she sits at a table calmly drinking coffee.

* * *

Is this the hell he is going to commit himself to for a whole lifetime?

She's the one who has the money after all. What power.

We can get married at the consulate in Nice, she says.

All right, so we'll go to Nice, he says, tired.

They arrive there just as Nietzsche's death is announced. Heavens above. Yet more death. Zarathustra who wishes to sing, even when he is suffering. If only he could hear the voices of the hidden helpers, those who love the higher being: You who are isolated today, you who stand alone, one day you will be a people, from you who have chosen yourselves shall a chosen people arise, and from that people, the superman.

He spoke to Strindberg about Nietzsche that time in Berlin. He learned to understand Zarathustra's son, Zarathustra's creator: I love the person who creates something outside himself and then perishes. It was Nietzsche who pointed out that the human being is the only creature which laughs, because the human being suffers such torments that it has to invent laughter. Humiliated, neglected, reviled Nietzsche. Who else could Munch identify with? He went blind, his soul was destroyed and gradually he went insane. He could say that it was the day after tomorrow that belonged to him.

Munch is in Nice, thinks about Nietzsche and talks to Tulla Larsen about marriage.

*

He wakens tired, ill and out of sorts and by morning has already started drinking.

She has been to see the consul, says that they can go there and get married whenever they like. But he avoids her, walks the streets, the stifling air makes him feel even more miserable. At night in the hotel, sexual excesses, despair, when will he be able to begin to paint again? His chest is hurting once more.

*

Then a particular morning arrives.

Quiet as a mouse he packs his bags, travels to Switzerland, Hotel and Pension Motta, Airolo, Ct. du Tessin. Up in the mountains. To a more beautiful town, to purer air. He wants to go high up in the mountains, there he is suddenly one day on the platform of the funicular, wants to get away from this hell, this degradation. He has left her. Done a bunk. Silently packed his bags. Run off like a cur.

He wants to buy a ticket for the funicular.

Name, asks the ticket conductor.

Name?

Yes, your name and passport.

What d'you mean? Munch feels violent anger welling up. Why do I need a passport to go up to the top of the mountain? I've never heard anything like it! It's completely mad!

He walks to the hotel, his head is swimming. Shortly after there are two gendarmes outside his door. They escort him down to the gendarmerie. He has assaulted a conductor on the funicular, has he? There is no arguing. He is thrown into what he will later call a filthy hole of a prison. He remains incarcerated there for one or two days. Later he cannot recall exactly. But in any case prison.

To have to stare at a wall day and night.

So *she* is not the only one who is after him now.

* * *

But you treat me like an enemy and don't even want friendship, a lot could have been avoided if you'd let us stay in Germany, but you wanted me away.

Tulla Larsen has tracked him down and sends desperate letters.

My dearest, have a little sympathy for me, believe me when I say that I'm doing my utmost to be and become better. You must be willing to talk to me. I shall go away from you at once if you wish me to. I suffer unspeakably from all your despair. I knew you must have been ill, somewhere or other, I could feel it. You could easily have been dead. Or I could. And we wouldn't have known a thing about one another. I could now accept a good many things I didn't understand in Berlin and Dresden, but you completely took the wind out of my sails that day in Nice.

*

He doesn't know what to reply. Instead he writes to his sister:

Dear Inger, thank you for your letter, things are so difficult that I've hardly had the energy to write. Now at least there's a solution of sorts. The doctor has examined me, has firmly impressed upon me the need for caution. I've no choice, there's a weakness in one lung. X is the same. She knows what part she's played in my illness, but wants to push through a hasty marriage, speaks about her future. I just laugh at it all. Seriously though, I think she must be mentally ill in some way. When I heard she'd written to you, I said to her: I can well imagine the fine phrases. For she's excellent at insinuating herself, and now she wanted to use you as she has previously used my friends. But don't imagine she would be interested in you or anyone else unless her own interest was involved. Greetings to Aunt.

*

He has taken flight again, avoided marriage. Tears and despair. But one way or another he has escaped. He may have promised to see her again, *she* may at last have had enough. He virtually drags himself back to Christiania, is still sick, takes a room in a *pension*, or sanatorium, at Ljan.

It is a two-storey yellow wooden house on a hilly slope, with ugly carved wooden embellishments, ridiculous animal ornamentation, the sickly-sweet yellow colour looks sad against the dark green pine forest. In a draft novella Munch writes about the house which gazes darkly out over the fjord with wide-eyed windows. He has no peace of mind, paces to and fro in the two rooms, the epileptic proprietor is bedridden with paralysed legs.

He sees his sister Laura again. Writes: I sat the melancholy creature at the flaming red table with the window behind her. The idea was to make her large and powerful and monumental in her black, silent, eternal sorrow. This is how Laura sat in the hospital. She did not recognize him. He spoke tender words to her. She did not understand them. Her black eyes were lacklustre. Vacant and unmoving they stared into space.

He makes sketches of Laura in hospital. Then he returns to the yellow house. He hates the bed, where he lies waiting for sleep to come, but it does so only for brief moments, and he awakens immediately thereafter, then lies waiting for morning to come. These are the long night hours with what he calls a thousand terrible thoughts. When the winter sun approaches the horizon and shines in through the window, his room is lit up by red and yellow flames. He walks down the stairs and sees two light-blue staring eyes. The epileptic.

Out on the road he meets the madman more and more often. A flapping cape about his shoulders, he draws nearer, walks straight at him, whispers into his ear: Next time I'll shoot them.

* * *

He exhibits his work at the Diorama. Old graphic works, old pictures which have already been shown before, an exhibition almost of defiance.

And it attracts no attention.

Nor does he, as he fails to appear. But he sees storm clouds on the horizon. The epileptic proprietor is dead. One day he meets the consumptive shop owner, who is always coughing and spitting. At the same time he is contacted by an acquaintance in a dark-brown house in the vicinity. Come and visit me, Munch. I only weigh a hundred and ten pounds now, like a child. I spit blood all day long.

*

A new year. 1901. Queen Victoria dies and Munch's picture *By the Shore/The Lonely Ones*, which Olaf Schou had bought, is lost in a shipwreck. That winter, Munch will paint *White Night*, which he will later call one of his best pictures. He will paint *The German*, *The Frenchman*, *Albert Kollmann*, *Kollmann and Sten Drewsen*, and also make an etching of *Dead Mother and Child*, a woodcut of *Evening*, a lithograph of *Holger Drachmann* and *Sin*. But he is still sick, still isolated, plagued by insomnia, by memories of the storm which he thinks lies behind him. He fell from the roof like a sleepwalker, woke up and ran among people with a wound in his soul. To begin with his desire had no object. He remembers her cold remarks about his being sickly. He remembers the repellent things, the indecent jokes. But what difference does it make now?

Is sympathy a weakness, was he worthless because he could not bear to see her suffer? She who even when she was quite small ran wild in the backstreets of Homannsbyen. His thoughts come in an avalanche, he cannot stop, has to write it down, all those letters she sends to Aunt Karen and his sister Inger, a malicious red-haired bit of a thing. She was forever setting the boys against one another, pulling her girlfriends' hair, was always full of tricks, screaming when she did not get the doll she wanted, then received an allowance when she was fifteen years of age, an extremely large amount of money, went out into the world and continued her back-street life, intrigued and lied, cried her eyes out when she did not get the big doll Munch, if he'd really loved her she would have rejected him.

But it's over now he thinks, furious, as the memories wash over him. It's over, it *must* be over.

*

He paints the earth in the grip of frost. *White Night.* A harmonious picture. The nearest pine and fir trees are incorporated into the square format with powerful synthétique stylistic effects. A dark blue mass silhouetted against the moonlit snow. The snow shines through scratches and points, creating small shining suns in the darkness which captivate the eye. On the ground in the middle distance stands a small cubist house shining white in the moonlight. Down towards the fjord the pine forest is a jagged fence marking the perimeter. Behind this Munch has looked out over the frozen fjord. Imprisoned under the layer of ice it lies there with its huge watery surface. A low island can be glimpsed in the hazy distance and above it two or three pale stars twinkle in the foggy air.

*

Then he hears rumours about what she is saying somewhere out there in Europe, that he has used her money, he who was born ill and in poverty, whereas she is a spoilt rich man's child. So she's talking about him. It makes his blood boil, he is sure she is undermining his reputation in Germany. She is an actress in the theatre of life. He tries to remember that he was frightened by that face from the very outset, tries to remember that he felt it his duty to allow himself to be tormented by her until the crisis was over.

Munch treads in Strindberg's footsteps. It is 1901, the winter when, after many months' separation, Dagny Juel and Stanislaw Przybyszewski are reunited in Berlin and move on to Warsaw. Only a few months until Vladyslav Emeryk will point a revolver at Ducha in the Grand Hotel at Tbilisi. In Ljan Munch feels his own hatred rise, his hatred of Tulla Larsen, and simultaneously his sympathy, which will inevitably propel him towards actions still in the future.

* * *

Dear Munch: Tulla has been up to see us several times this Christmas. She's very calm now and seldom mentions you, a good sign in my view. No, just leave her be, and I hope things will take their natural course. But if ever she feels a little bit of hope, the whole thing will soon flare up again. She knows that you have nothing but friendly feelings for her. She has asked whether she can buy some of your lithographs which are at our place. She wants to give one or two as presents and keep one or two for herself. Be careful now and don't get out of your depth. Farewell, dear Munch, and write again soon. Your Åse Ng.

*

Aunt Karen and his sister Inger are spending the winter in Fredrikstad. Dear Edvard: If only you could be well again. I sometimes dream that you're so much better, I also think God will see to it that you can work with the same will and strength as before. Are there no clothes that need repairing, I haven't been able to see you, as I've been afraid you didn't want me to, but many times I've been anxious you might be ill, so it has all been rather worrying. My cough is somewhat better now, though I've got a little bronchitis after my trip, but I have to be careful, so I take cough powder in the evening, which also helps me to sleep, the weather has been terrible this winter. Aunt Karen.

* * *

At last spring comes. The frost disappears from the ground. Munch can hear birdsong again, feel the warmth of the sun.

And she is not there. He is alone with himself, is going to spend a summer in Åsgårdstrand, almost uneventful. At last he feels well.

It is the summer when the first works by the Spanish painter Pablo Picasso are exhibited in Paris.

While the winter was cold, the summer brings tropical heat. A temperature of thirty-three degrees in the shade is recorded. Munch sees people gathering in couples beside the boulders on the shore. The fjord lies shrouded in a blue veil, golden sailing boats glide along slowly on a gentle breeze, long waves draw themselves up to the stones and break, the moon rises from the sea.

He tries to live a regular life, sits in the garden, where undisturbed he can pursue his many reflections, his conflicting thoughts, his sudden longing for her, his violent hatred.

*

In *Morgenbladet* under the headline *A Sad Case* he reads: The board of the National Gallery has just purchased a new picture by Edvard Munch, a landscape sketch which took its place in the collection on Friday. There is no gainsaying that the picture is as unworthy of representing Munch's landscape art as it is of hanging in the gallery at all. It *is* nothing and it means nothing.

* * *

He jumps out of his seat.

Ducha dead!

Shot in Tbilisi by a lover. Ducha! It's a long time since he last saw her. He accompanied her down to the steamboat in 1898, when she had been to visit her ailing father at *Tranquillity* and was to follow Stach to

Cracow. Just like before they had talked about everything that interested them. She never complained about her existence.

Munch sits in his garden at Åsgårdstrand as the images well up in him. There was never any unpleasantness between himself and Ducha, only trust and understanding, and now and then a little irony.

She could explain things to him, take him by the arm, confide in him, encourage and comfort him, calm and inspire at the same time.

He is asked to draw a portrait of her for *Kristiania Dagsavis*, but he cannot bring himself to do it. He is too deeply affected by what has happened.

*

The announcement of Ducha's death mingles with his thoughts about Tulla. He sits on the shore, hypnotized by the long shining waves which come racing in against the stones and break, one after the other. They reflect the white clouds. A bright glittering surface.

Ducha shot in Tbilisi.

But under the narrow lines of the waves he sees green stones, strange dark shapes. A warning about a new world out there beneath the surface of the water.

*

Kristiania Dagsavis 29 June 1901:

A quiet man? Yes. Edvard Munch has become a quiet man. He has now become the symbol of contradiction which he felt compelled to be. Proud and dignified, he has kept his distance from the crowd, indeed even from the little band of supporters who have proclaimed his art with fanaticism.

Munch has lived up here in Christiania again for a year. But he has hidden himself away in a pension in Ljan and the set at the Grand or the regulars on Karl Johan have not so much as glimpsed his irascible profile. For during the past year Munch has also been a sick man.

* * *

He exhibits new paintings at Hollændergården. But despite the purchase by the National Gallery he has money troubles. The same autumn all the pictures he owns are pawned at Wang's Auction Rooms as security for various loans. There are no prospects of further sales and he cannot go to Tulla Larsen.

Friends ask him why he is no longer with her. With her, a Madonna. Why does he not love her?

Peace, is his reply. Leave me in peace.

In the paper he reads that Toulouse-Lautrec, a year younger than himself, is dead.

* * *

He comes to Germany at the beginning of November.

Hotel Janson, Mittelstrasse, then Hotel Hippodrom, Charlottenburg, then Lützowstrasse.

Dear Aunt: I've now got into my old routine down here and am living a peaceful existence. It was difficult in Christiania where I just know too many people. It's a good job I got away quickly before all the money had run out. I'm hoping to get down to some work here, and am due to have an exhibition in February, hope to sell something then. I'm showing a couple of pictures in the Nordic Exhibition in Vienna, as far as I know just four of us representing Norway, Werenskiold, Eilif Peterssen and Krohg, apart from me. Quite fun in a way. The two I have there are among my worst pictures. X is calm now, I hear from the Nørregaards, and attends parties at their home as well as elsewhere. She will scarcely be able to get up to the same tricks as before in front of so many people.

*

Munch has rented a studio for three months. It is time for a fresh attempt in Germany. His choice has vacillated between Germany and Paris, but in Berlin he is better informed about the art world.

He hires the red-haired model, a fact which will later cause people to believe that it is Tulla Larsen he is paraphrasing in the lithograph *Sin*. In a photograph of Munch's studio, the model stands naked in front of an upended version of *Woman/Sphinx*, a hint of the psychological stocktaking of the events of the past few years.

The Berlin Sezession had acquired its own premises in Kantstrasse three years earlier, as a direct result of Munch's own scandal in 1892, when the city's radical elements banded together in protest against the older generation. The painters Ludvig von Hoffmann, Leistikow and the young, dynamic art dealer Paul Cassirer now invite Munch to exhibit his entire *Frieze of Life*. The spacious entrance hall is the setting for twenty-two pictures 'aus dem modernen Seelenleben'. Munch places *Golgotha* in the middle and the series 'Love and Death' on either side. Now he is exhibiting his life, proving that he has remained faithful to his vision in the Montagnes Russes twelve years earlier, when he decided to depict sacred, decisive moments. He portrays death in childhood, Sophie in the chair, the mother in the bed. Then he depicts the web of love. His own Medusa's hair has wrapped itself round his own memories. He chains fru Thaulow to himself forever, also captures Aase Nørregaard with the separation motif, weaves the sufferings of others into his own, like the time Jappe Nilssen was rushing about with the pistol in Åsgårdstrand. He paints himself at the lowest point of an attack of angst, forces Tulla Larsen to wear the women's masks he claims to have seen in three versions of her face.

191

The pictures hang in Kantstrasse, in the massive entrance hall, framed in white, differing in colours and sizes, but linked together by particular colours and lines, horizontal and vertical, the vertical lines of the trees and the walls, the horizontal lines of the floors, the ground, the roofs and the crowns of the trees. The wavy lines of the sea soothing like lullabies, the sad grey-green tones in the death rooms, the scream of fire, the blood-red sky and the clang of the reds, the vivid reds, yellows and greens.

The subtitle of the left wall is 'The Growth of Love', *Red and White*, *Eye to Eye*, *Kiss* and *Madonna* are among the pictures hanging there. On the front wall he has assembled pictures under the title 'The Flowering and Disintegration of Love', including *After the Fall*, *Vampire*, *Jealousy*, *Sphinx* and *Melancholy*. On the right-hand wall, the theme is 'The Angst of Living', including *Scream*, *Fear* and *Virginia Creeper*. On the rear wall the theme is 'Death', with pictures such as *Death Agony*, *Death in the Sickroom*, *Death and the Maiden* and *Dead Mother and Child*.

The review *Kunst für alle* records that a blend of the brutal, Nordic love of colour, the influence of Manet and a bent for reverie has resulted in something quite unique.

* * *

The circle of Scandinavians is small. He constantly receives fresh reports of what Tulla Larsen has said about him.

It is at this time that he makes the acquaintance of the mystic and art lover Albert Kollmann, the priest's son from Mecklenburg who himself wanted to be a painter but who became a merchant instead and was also dubbed The Devil. Later Munch will paint a double portrait. Himself as Peer Gynt and Kollmann as the button moulder.

But the button moulder is friendly, a sensitive patrician, a passionate, warm-hearted ascetic, a man who finds losing at chess as unbearable as the sight of clashing colours in a painting, a man who cannot stand Prussian reserve officers, a man of few words, a vegetarian and teetotaller, a passionate admirer of Cézanne, hypersensitive in any confrontation. He is quite capable of standing up and saying: '*Die Luft ist dort nicht gut*' before making his exit.

He becomes an indefatigable admirer of Munch's art, a man who will later sit for hours on end in the galleries where Munch's pictures hang, completely lost in them, a ghost from the age of Goethe, with an old Italianate face. Later Munch will give him much of the credit for his increasing popularity in Germany. His enthusiasm will win Munch friends and admirers who each in their own way will play a decisive role in his further career abroad.

One of them is the eye specialist Max Linde from Lübeck, who will purchase Munch's *Fertility* and write the book *Edvard Munch und die Kunst der Zukunft*, and who is Munch's first patron. He wants Munch to paint him a frieze with motifs from the Norwegian midsummer night. He owns a house with extensive grounds containing sculptures by Rodin, where Munch can sit and rest his nerves. Another is Gustav Schiefler in Hamburg, a stickler for order, a lawyer, botanist, statistician, letter-writer. He will play a decisive role in the cataloguing of Munch's graphic works. There is also the stocking manufacturer Herbert Esche in Chemnitz and a little man with a hat, Munch's future biographer, Kurt Glaser.

All of them are people who wish him well, who experience Munch's work as an explosion of feelings and revelations which shakes them to the depths of their being. Kollmann's enthusiasm is passed on to the others.

So Munch attracts fresh attention in Germany, but meets with silence in Norway. He sits in the grounds of Linde's house, thinking: can this be all there is? He has encountered recognition and resistance, but what of it?

It is with mixed feelings that he returns to Norway to work that summer, returns to Christiania, to the garden in Åsgårdstrand, the jasmine and the lilacs, and a young, spirited girl. Her name is Ingse Vibe and she is Tupsy Jebe's spiritual sister, just as youthfully matter-of-fact, just as cheerfully confident in life. She reminds him of his youth, of the time when everything was possible. Yet so much still lies ahead of him.

* * *

And what lies behind him suddenly resurfaces again.

1902, the summer of the fires, forest fires in Sweden, forest fires in France and some twenty miles south-west of Åsgårdstrand the town of Larvik burns, two thousand people being made homeless.

Munch sits in his garden. Even in the stones there is will, the will to form, crystallization. He continues to reflect on the stuff of his conversations with Kollmann. Theosophy, somnambulism, spiritualism, hypnosis, telepathy. The earth is a cell and human beings are bacteria on its surface. God is in us and we are in God. He is seized with a mystical-religious ecstasy, strolls about in his flowering garden and sees procreation, archetypes, the bee and the flower, the bird which guards the nest, hears Ingse Vibe's warbling laughter.

He observes the profuse, luxuriant unfolding of life, thinks that it is the fundamental law of life to multiply, to bear fruit. So might it be possible after all? A young girl like her. There is no depth to her, she surrounds herself with her own cheerfulness. No, it is beyond his grasp now. All he has is his pictures, he took the decision that time long ago, is not suited to carrying on the family line. His sister Inger is the only healthy one. The remaining brothers and sisters are either dead or suffering from illness. It is far too great a chance to take to multiply, to become part of the cycle, the transformation of matter.

But in his literary writings the longing is clear. The pictures are not always enough. They cost him great existential renunciation, besides which, in more prosaic terms, they also cost him a loan of eleven hundred crowns from the Folkebank, with Fridtjof Nansen as guarantor, so that he can redeem the twenty-five pictures he has pawned to Wang's art dealers, which Wang threatened he would sell in a forced sale. His own paintings! The only children he has.

Things will suddenly become difficult for him at Åsgårdstrand. He has become more short-tempered. Now he regards von Ditten, the elegant boulevardier with the gold-rimmed spectacles, as a long-legged irritating individual. Munch has previously met him at a fancy dress ball. In Munch's eyes von Ditten is doubly stupid. He has chopped down all the trees in Åsgårdstrand, most probably to improve the view of the sea from his imposing villa on the southern side of the town. Munch lives in a hovel in the working class part. The two of them are completely different types. After their confrontation at the artists' fancy dress ball Munch had von Ditten up before the conciliation board because he had called him a cheat, and had alleged that Munch had stolen ten crowns from a waiter. But Munch himself did not attend the board's meeting.

Instead he is in Åsgårdstrand, has acquired the habit of drinking alcohol at breakfast, has begun to experience changes in both body and mind, has come through an emotional inferno, pulled himself up again and run away from a scene of the past, gone back to Germany, exhibited *The Frieze of Life* in the city where he caused the greatest scandal. Too many extremes. Suddenly there is an imbalance. Now he carries a revolver. That is the sort of weapon people carry in Åsgårdstrand. The romanticism of gunpowder. Munch and Hauge are already experts at target shooting.

There are some people who attend national rifle competitions with Krag-Jørgensen rifles. In Åsgårdstrand a revolver is good enough. Munch stands down on the shore plugging away at a target at the place where, seventeen years earlier, he had felt the power of fru Thaulow's dark eyes. He shoots at his own past, is still not sure whether he has chosen the right direction. He is regarded as a polite, shy, introverted almost aristocratic person, a man who knows how to talk, but who is usually tongue-tied when himself exposed to rudeness. Now he shoots at targets, tries to hit the points in his past he is most horrified by, tries to destroy what is the very basis of his pictures. The aggression, everything which hung in the air when he left Tulla Larsen, or when Milly Thaulow suddenly became fru Bergh. A slightly more harmless enemy is therefore welcome. But suddenly seven young men stand outside von Ditten's garden gate, people von Ditten first thinks are ruffians from Horten or Moss, or at least teenage girls whom von Ditten, with his fine night binoculars, can observe as they shout: von Dit, bandit, is a silly git. They are standing in front of a garden gate which, by Åsgårdstrand standards, is ridiculously large, built of cement, sea sand and iron which is embedded two feet deep in the ground. The heavy iron gates are carried by seven ruffians fifty yards away and dumped on the road. Von Ditten's neighbour Ragnar Næss marches out with his shotgun.

*

At eight o'clock in the evening Edvard Munch comes to the council hall guardroom. As soon as von Ditten catches sight of Munch, he flies into a rage. He is convinced it is Munch who is behind all the pranks.

Now I've got you, Munch! So *you're* the one who's behind it all! But I have left some papers with the police. They prove that you stole …

Say that once more if you dare!

You stole ten crowns from a waiter, I said. Think I didn't see you, Munch?

A young girl suddenly sticks her oar in, stares at Munch with unconcealed expectation. Give him one, Munch!

Munch lashes out.

This is the first in a series of punch-ups, which in letters to Aunt Karen he calls a box on the ears, in his diary, a few punches in the eye, or which von Ditten will call a blow to the upper arm and a blow to the lower arm. A punch-up in the council hall guardroom, with the whole neighbourhood as witnesses.

Von Ditten calls for the police.

No, to my manner of thinking this be a private matter, says police constable Pedersen. Called him a swindler, you have, and now he's blacked your eye for you.

*

Munch and Bødtker go home to Munch's house and drink.

The garden fills up with young people.

The living room fills up with young people.

Eyes shining with admiration.

They want to fête Munch. Three cheers! they shout.

Munch surveys the tightly-packed throng; then becomes embarrassed.

When I get worked up there's nothing I can't do, I suppose, he mumbles. I'm usually very timid. Be off with you all now.

* * *

Munch paints *The Ladies on the Bridge*. And he chooses his model with care.

Look at me, will you, fru Åse Nørregaard! Now you're married to Harald. My own lawyer. What was in your mind when you were still frøken Åse Carlsen, when I asked you to hold my hand? You said no, do you remember? But was it really so much to ask?

Once again Munch forces Åse Nørregaard to look him straight in the eye. There is colossal power in her character, the new age woman, proud and independent, not neurotic and clinging. Is it mere coincidence that Munch paints her like this, at this precise time? Just when in Christiania Christian Krohg is interviewing Gina Krohg about the emancipation of women and lets her sing Munch's praises for his obituary of Dagny Juel.

Munch paints the stages of woman. He paints the strong mature fru Nørregaard. And he paints young girls bathing naked and full of the joys of spring.

* * *

Then he is wakened with a start from his reveries among the blackcurrant and redcurrant bushes.

There is someone up at the house. A woman. With head bowed.

Tulla!

He gets up, walks up to the gate, sees that it is a stranger, no, not a stranger actually, but Tulla's friend, frøken Dahl. A spiritualist with a red nose. Apparently she lives with Tulla now.

It had to happen. Six months. But nothing is forgotten. Tulla Larsen cannot possibly be forgotten. He has fixed her to the canvas, in white, red and black, and with bowed head, strikingly beautiful in her sorrow. I know why you've come, he says.

You must go to her, replies frøken D.

Munch feels his heart pounding. But he cannot flee. He must hear what she has to say.

Come in and sit down.

They sit beside one another. He glances expectantly at frøken D.

Yes, she says. I've come from Tulla. You must go to her in Drøbak. Her condition is very . . . serious.

How do you mean serious?

Morphine.

He replies that it is impossible, there has to be an end of it, he cannot . . .

Tulla loves you, says frøken D.

This exchange has already taken place countless times in Munch's mind. He knows every word he will say. He has constructed a whole system of defences. He knows so much about her now. The rumours have got under his skin, like an infection. She is still going about with the toad crossed with a pig. And what about that Romanian, and perhaps worst of all, the accusation that Munch has sponged off her, that he has cynically tapped her for money.

Frøken D. sits there in his own home. He has let her in of his own volition, could have said no, that he was not free, that she must leave immediately, but he has let her in, has always had a weakness for the weakness of others, *her* weakness, the bombardment from that quarter, that he must become the meaning in her life, that he above all, the introverted neurotic Edvard Munch, shall take her in his arms, carry her towards what is meaningful, the love he does not feel, the realization of a vision he has never had, not even artistically. For between man and woman in *his* world there is always a loser, one who is betrayed.

You must come to her, says frøken D. again. She loves you.

Munch hears Tulla Larsen's voice through her friend's words. Yes, but the whole thing's become impossible now, he says. He tells frøken D. that it's over, it was such hell, that he's been completely off the rails since the time he met her almost four years ago. Nevertheless he is curious:

Is she still speaking of marriage?

No, no, not that, says frøken D. with a grief-stricken, confidential look.

Suddenly she bows her head, so she has come all the way to Åsgårdstrand to say that Tulla Larsen is desperate, that she is taking morphine, that Munch is all she talks about, that it is a matter of life and death.

Then he must either think that sympathy is a human failing or he must feel that he still desires her. For he *has* desired her, cannot but acknowledge his urges, even when hatred gets the upper hand in memories and literary jottings. So he takes his time with frøken D., argues and analyses, but is starting to give ground, perhaps without realizing it himself yet, tries to convince her that it's obvious he cannot meet Tulla Larsen anywhere, that it is inconceivable that, at least *voluntarily*, they should resume the hell they both went through when they were together.

It is more than eighteen months ago now. No more will he be arbitrarily imprisoned by Swiss gendarmes, or have to waken in the morning and wonder what he had actually been up to the previous evening. He has gained a new foothold, has struck up acquaintance, perhaps even made friends, with important people in German cultural and financial life, people who are willing to give him work, to do what they can to ensure that his financial situation is no longer catastrophic. But nothing is certain! No genuine security. The episode with von Ditten. He could turn up at any moment, in other words.

I have a feeling something terrible may happen, says frøken D.

Munch sits in the garden.

The sickly thoughts seep into his mind like a rising tide. Imperceptibly but inescapably and with overwhelming force, the silhouettes, the play of the lines, alters. He knows that she has lived a fast life in Munich, that she has met Gunnar Heiberg again, with his pointed lopsided belly, with his croaking, snorting voice. He knows that she has been a regular visitor to his rooms, spread rumours, saying that he had sponged off her, used her money and then abandoned her like a bounder, that she has even written to Aunt Karen and his sister Inger, told them that he has behaved like a bounder, a contemptible bounder who deserves to be spat upon.

Ruined years.

He thinks of himself as a wandering minstrel in front of the rich woman's door. Admits that he had said: open your door. Admits that he had said: you are beautiful. Admits that he had felt: I am tired and lovesick.

She had fed him from the table of her love, he had eaten of her heart, but the food was poisoned, he sat at her table in the company of Death, Sickness and Poison.

He sits in the garden, observes the strong colours of summer, bright green against bright blue, bright yellow against bright red. Women in loose-fitting garments, young girls everywhere, like butterflies, sticking their heads into his garden, saying hello, giving him long poems about the sea:

When I gaze down into the sea, life's mysteries I seem to see, life's mysteries deep and, high above, the lovely mirror of the sky, O thou mystery! Thou sea, thou life! Unfathomable –

Young girls, fifteen-year-olds, with eyes and looks which remind him of a lost world, their experienced innocence, surrounded by clumsy, cocky, naïve, strutting boys. He sits in his garden as von Ditten puts his house on the market, thinks about when he walked here with Tulla Larsen, spring, the flowering, the celebration, before autumn turned nature the colour of a bloody scream. Cannot make up his mind, self-loathing or hatred, is she a black angel. Even in the stones there is fire. If you strike a stone, fire spurts out of it. The unreleased power, the power between himself and Tulla. He sits in the garden, allowing himself to be torn apart by his thoughts, by regret, despair, sympathy, pain and hatred.

She had not given him time. Wasn't it just time he had asked her for? Time to get well.

Bødtker is suddenly standing in the garden.

A dark, grim face.

The theatre critic Sigurd Bødtker, the poodle with the wagging tail. Munch's loyal second.

I know why you've come, says Munch. Let's sit down and talk.

Bødtker walks down into Munch's garden. Munch hears his excited yapping voice and listens intently.

Listen, Munch, you must talk to her, she's at death's door, leave right away if you want to see her, go to Drøbak, I'll come with you. Don't hesitate!

Bødtker sits under the lilacs. Munch feels the words sinking in to him, filling him with inertia.

Drøbak. So that's where she is, four hours by boat, The City of Free Love, where the so-called Post-Bohemians disport themselves during the summer. Oda gathers them together in her house, Krohg himself lives in a hotel, copies his old pictures to earn money for her court, constant parties, champagne flowing, Christian Krohg, formerly such an imposing fellow, a touch foppish perhaps, in any case now he is a slimy, soft-horned snail who carries a brothel on his back, a brothel with pimps and procurers, a brothel where Tulla Larsen also has a room. That rich, pampered girl from the back-streets of Homannsbyen, a malicious red-haired bit of a thing. Who threw her money about in Germany, everywhere, on people who might have become her hired assassins, a deranged Romanian among others.

You see, Bødtker, I'm at the end of my tether. Had I loved her, she would have thrown me over. Do you get it, Bødtker? Her face tells you everything, don't you see, Spring Woman, Whore and Sorrow. I've been frightened of this face from the very start. It's true, I *was* willing to marry. I wanted to help her over the worst pitfalls, the madness of love, her love for me, the consumption, which placed her life in jeopardy. I fell ill, madness again raised its ugly head in me. *She* recovered from her illness at least.

So you see, Bødtker? She and she alone had the right to love! When a man kissed her, he was no more than her plaything, whom she had the right to destroy, so she tried to get a Romanian to shoot me. I was always the injured party. And who is she with now? A toad, or a pig? I saw life's Medusa's head at an early age, Bødtker.

* * *

He is on his way to the city of free love, says goodbye to Kollmann who is there visiting him, who has stood somewhere between the trees, like a button moulder, a friendly Mephistopheles.

Munch on his way to Drøbak, cannot resist the pull, despite all his horrible thoughts about her. The truth is not what he says, but his feelings.

He arrives in Drøbak, and frøken D. comes rushing towards him, stumbles on her long skirts. A flushed, hysterical face:

Oh God, Munch, it was a good thing I met you. I've just come from Tulla now. I must talk to the doctor immediately.

Munch feels a stab of fear, visualizes her grief-stricken, despairing face. He stands on the jetty at Drøbak one day in late summer and asks how she is.

Oh, she is very ill in bed, Munch. I thought she was going to die. She's been vomiting all night.

Go to the doctor, says Bødtker, we'll cast off in half an hour.

*

The boat lies at the jetty. Sudden gusts of wind come from the hills, a strong northerly wind. On board are Munch, Bødtker and frøken D. Munch hears her breathless, hysterical voice. The boat cuts through the water like an arrow.

Keep still, Munch warns them. He is sitting at the tiller. He feels that the wind is unpredictable now. It wouldn't take much for the boat to fill with water.

Oh, I'm not afraid, says frøken D.

Oh, aren't you? says Munch. Who admits to being afraid of death? Had it not been for the fear of death most of us would have killed ourselves.

I think we are the ones who will be drowned, says Bødtker suddenly. Not her.

Munch starts at these words. Will he see her alive and well after all?

What if she's dead, says frøken D. gloomily. We'll have to see whether the shutters have been opened when we get nearer. She was lying in the dark when I left her.

Munch feels a stab of pain in his heart. If she's lying there, silent, stiff and white, dead on account of him, without his being there to comfort her, what will he do then?

Fear grips his heart, the boat cleaves swiftly through the water. He manoeuvres in an arc towards the squalls. At last he can see the little cluster of houses, are the shutters closed or not, has she got up, there he sees the house, the shutters are closed, so she's still in bed, has he really murdered her?

A man is pacing up and down impatiently in front of the house. He peers at the approaching boat. It is late summer 1902, Munch sits in a little boat and sees frøken D. jump ashore, dash up to the strange man, talk to him, how grave they both look, is she dead, Munch runs after them, is she dead, how is she, oh, she's lying just as she was before, so she's not dead. It is the power of the moon, he has never tied himself like this to any person before, fru Thaulow placed herself beyond his reach. Tulla is the only one not to have accepted his *no*, he cannot reject her, has come to Drøbak because he feels for her, has tightened the bow, that almost unbearable feeling, all those summer nights in the garden at home in Åsgårdstrand, on the other side of the fjord, if ever anything were symbolical, with the water between them, the dismal grey house, so she is lying in there behind the closed shutters, he goes into the darkened room, sees that there is a bed in a corner, sees her pallid face, the garish red hair, he takes her hand, the first time for one and a half years, feels her skin, remembers all the love they have had, all the tears they have shed, the joy and the despair, now they are together again.

How are you? he says softly.

*

She lies in bed, says she cannot manage without him.

They could have got married, in Dresden or Nice.

He sits on the edge of the bed, holding her hand, speaking softly to her.

Things are going to be better now, he says. You must try and be happy again. All those days he has been away from her, a year and a half, what was she actually doing all that time? There are two empty bottles of morphine on the table. Someone opens the shutters, he holds her hand, speaks softly to her.

Do you think you could try to get up? Eat a bit of something?

Yes, perhaps I could, she whispers weakly.

*

Frøken D. has produced coffee and food and a bottle of wine, Tulla Larsen is sitting in her dressing gown, Munch can see she is pale. Another wave of feelings rises in him, not naked desire, but tenderness.

The mood almost becomes cheerful.

How can she get up again like this. And so soon!

What strength of character, says Bødtker.

Munch hears the sound in his voice, his admiration. Then he starts to joke with her himself. So the morphine wasn't as bad as all that after all, eh?

She falls silent, says suddenly that she must lie down.

Bødtker begins to talk of heart failure, which can result from morphine poisoning. She has taken an overdose for Munch's sake, has wanted to die for his sake.

Again Munch sits on the edge of her bed, feels her pulse racing. Softly she asks him to say a prayer, says that she will never weep again, is delirious, hears dark music, d'you hear it? Look at my hands, suicidal hands, she lies for a long time, eyes closed, then her mouth begins to move again. Munch bends over her and listens. What's she saying? What are the first words he can make out, she's saying, my God, isn't she saying, isn't that *Heiberg* she's saying? Gunnar Heiberg? Isn't she saying that he's too fat? Isn't she talking about Bødtker too? And about Kavli, Arne Kavli, the painter, is it his name she's saying? She's delirious. Poor soul. He caresses her. Poor little Tulla. You're going to get well again, perhaps it was Gunnar Heiberg, perhaps Kavli. Poor soul that she is. What rubbish. What utter nonsense.

He is alone with her now, sitting at her bedside far into the night, notices that she becomes calmer, mumbles that she is tired. Soon her breathing becomes regular and she falls asleep.

*

He leaves her, but not as he did last time, not like a cur and not for ever. Leaves her for a week, then comes back to fetch her, is going to do all in his power to make a new life for the two of them.

He has sat at her bedside, has been making plans, they will travel to England, away from all their old life, he cannot bear to see her like this, the drawn face, the compliant voice, yes, she wants to come with him to England, tired and listless she lies there listening to him, he scrutinizes her face, can he read her through her soul, after all she's the first person to have placed her life in his hands, has shown him her pain, has not been too proud to stand before him naked, vulnerable and helpless.

He has asked Bødtker to make the conditions crystal clear to her. He is not marrying under any circumstances, she must take him as she finds him, when he comes back they will be joined as one, not in matrimony though, but according to certain laws, perhaps as a result of a higher power, she will put behind her all the old things, become his friend, his partner for life, someone who can count on him, even if he is away, someone she can be sure will move heaven and earth to help her, she must be in absolutely no doubt that she cannot trespass on what he calls his kingdom, where he must be alone, the kingdom of his imagination, the inner sanctum. She must also be in no doubt about his need to be alone, about all his idiosyncrasies. She cannot penetrate into the fortress of his imagination, but of course she can live in his cottage in Åsgårdstrand, stroll about in his garden, all the external things, it is his life that is at stake, she must understand that, Bødtker will surely have said all this, when he comes back to fetch her, these conditions have no doubt been made perfectly clear, perhaps time will help them, blot out the sympathy.

Perhaps love will come.

*

A week passes. Perhaps Munch goes back to Kollmann at Åsgårdstrand. Perhaps he goes to Christiania to get hold of some money, whatever the case he comes back to Drøbak, genuinely comes to fetch her. His fate is decided, everything is clear, his whole life is at stake. He walks along a track, there is a sheer drop down into the fjord, or is it hell, death? He arrives in Drøbak in the evening, there is a letter from Bødtker: Come round if you'd like to, or come tomorrow, we're having a big party at the hotel.

But he is no longer part of the Bohemian set, is not particularly popular after all that has happened, the fact that in Paris Oda was with Tulla, Gunnar Heiberg, Christian Krohg, various people he may have spoken disparagingly about. No, he won't go to the party at the hotel, he'll find another hotel, then he has a terrible suspicion: Is it all a miserable hoax?

The following day he meets her at Bødtker's home.

He sees she is excitable and nervous, recognizes the symptoms, but now he *is* here, isn't he. She wanted to die because he wasn't here. Why unhappy *now*?

He hears Bødtker's voice, the poodle, that excitable yapping voice of his:

So you're thinking of going abroad together and getting married.

Munch starts.

Getting married? He stares uncomprehendingly at Bødtker.

Tulla jumps up, her face red, goes out to the kitchen.

Munch sees that she is unbalanced, is afraid of what she might do, listens for sounds, she is still capable of anything.

Listen, says Munch, you promised to tell her my conditions, did you tell . . .

No, says Bødtker, it was impossible. She wouldn't be able to bear it.

Tulla comes back in.

Munch is agitated: Do you want to come over to the other side of the fjord with me or are you staying here? I won't ever marry, but I'll do anything else.

I think a lot of what Tulla says is right, says Bødtker.

Surprised, Munch turns to the poodle. Is Bødtker on *her* side?

All or nothing, says Munch. The steamer leaves in an hour.

*

The suspicion! That terrible possibility. The longing to get away, to be alone. And yet: what does she do when he's not here? Who is she with? Even after a fatal dose of morphine she was muttering about Heiberg, Bødtker and Kavli.

Munch stands on the jetty. The steamer has arrived. He waits. She was only supposed to be fetching some clothes. But she's been away an hour. Only minutes till the boat leaves. Munch feels anxious, this is not how he had imagined it would be.

What's taking her so long? Is she having second thoughts? Is this not what she wanted after all?

Here she comes at last, rushing down to the jetty with a little travelling bag.

You were ages, he says.

She doesn't reply.

What's the matter with you? he asks.

They sit there on a little steamer without speaking. What can they actually say? She has summoned him. They have gone through yet another trial of strength, can feel each other's nerves. He has laid down his conditions.

Now they both sit there silent on a steamer.

* * *

They take the inland road from Horten to Åsgårdstrand.

His own landscape. He can see the wavy lines, fields and meadows, the white-painted houses, the bright red barns. It is as quiet as a Sunday, and he walks again at her side, tries to hear his way through her silence, asks her from time to time how she is. She replies softly. Might it be possible, after all that has happened, that they are no longer enemies, that a completely new love, more sincere, more truthful, could grow from the ashes. For a year and a half he has tried to live alone, it didn't make him more serene, he has been involved in a brawl, has lain sleepless, has allowed himself to be aroused by laughing young girls who have brought their poems to show him.

It is evening when they arrive at Åsgårdstrand.

They stand in his garden.

He glances round. No longer late summer. Already autumn. A hint of red on the trees.

He should have been in Berlin, had planned a trip to Germany, instead here he is in the garden with Tulla, soon to leave for England.

They go into the house.

They are met by chill, damp air.

He walks over to the hearth. Lights the fire. A big, blazing fire. They are pale and frozen stiff. They sit down beside one another in silence. Staring into the fire.

He has nothing to say.

No words cross her lips.

*

They go to bed in separate rooms.

During the night he gets up and goes in to her.

Are you cold? he says. It's freezing.

He lays another blanket over her, puts his arms round her, just as he would a child. My God, how he wants to comfort her! She lies in bed listless, heavy as lead. A child. Yet he feels just as ill, just as much a child. He sees that they bring out what is weakest in each other, what is most helpless, most unfit for life.

She has dozed off. He caresses her. Mumbles: What on earth is to become of us, Tulla?

Then he goes back to his own bed.

* * *

Will we manage to forget? Will we try to get to know one another as friends?

The question hangs in the room. She is in his house. It had to come, after the tears, the embraces.

Too much past.

Manage to forget?

She says: I'm not so sure, Edvard, I don't think ... There's so much sympathy for me from my girl friends ...

He flares up, feels as though he is going to black out, an intolerable look on her face, that strong hint. So *that* was the main thing! *Her* pain. *Her* pride! Tulla Larsen the victim!

You're just play-acting, he says. You take to your bed as though you're at death's door, pretend to commit suicide!

How dare you! she replies, furious.

But now he is watching her, noting the smallest detail, her tone strikes him as dry and unfeeling, her gestures as mechanical. Is she acting now, under his very nose? He feels his anger rise, a boundless anger.

Look here, he says. What was all that about? In Munich. The Romanian who was going to kill me. You pestered the life out of my aunt! And all those other things? You've driven me to the end of my tether! I'm going far, far away! You'll never see me again!

*

He leaves her, storms out onto the road, needs a drink to cope with his inner turmoil, buys a bottle of brandy, is in his own landscape, sees the forest he can walk into, the shore, the stones, the sea. Out there on the massive stone fru Thaulow once sat. Like a mermaid. Then he waded out into the sea, went after her, out to the stone, sat down beside her. Afterwards he fell ill. So he is easily led, sometimes acts impetuously, whether from euphoria, from lung disease, or from lack of air. When the balloon is already far too high above the earth, he sends it even higher, more flame, more gas, until it is too late, till gravity can no longer touch him, till he floats in empty space.

But he has not fled, cannot flee from Tulla Larsen, not after what has happened, instead returns with the bottle of brandy.

*

Then something strange happens. Something he can never get straight in his mind. As soon as he opens the door it is as though an alien power seizes him. He feels literally as though he is seized across the back, as though powerful hands force his muscles to contract, to expand. A terrible tiredness.

What he is describing is actually a mild stroke: The feeling of disappearing, at the same time as electrical impulses were twisting my face, my arms, my back, in contortions. I had the sensation of being forced to the ground, then I half-fell half-sat at the table, with my hands under my head.

A stroke? That heaviness, a terrible tiredness, heaviness, the body being twisted, the sensation of being forced to the ground. In any case, he sits at the table, notices that she is in the room, that she stands there tall and unmoving in the kitchen, a cold grim face, but for Munch the faces blend together, not the face of sorrow, not the face of the nun, the Madonna, but the Medusa's head, the mollusc, the jellyfish's head, the tentacles.

She is standing behind him. Just beside the bowl of fruit.

He cannot see her, can merely feel her cold eyes on his back. He writhes as though having convulsions, feels as though about to fall off the chair. Then he seizes the bottle of brandy, downs a few glasses.

Now it's his turn. His tears. He sits head in hands and weeps, cannot hold back the tears for the impotence, the despair, for everything that has gone wrong in his life so far.

The whole time she stands there behind him, silent, her eyes glued to his back.

Would you like something to eat? she says, placing the bowl of fruit on the table.

No, he says.

Can do nothing but drink, glass after glass, moving his head backwards and forwards, weeping like a child, thinking of all that has gone wrong in his life, all those he has made unhappy, one of whom is standing behind him, one who is directly affected by his weakness, his inability to say yes or no.

There is nothing but the sound of weeping, of the bottle being poured into the glass. Hour after hour. He sits at the table. Drinks huge gulps.

She stands there right behind him, in the doorway to the kitchen. Does not say a word.

Dusk begins to fall.

*

She puts her face close to his head.

What's the revolver for? she says.

He does not reply, clasps the revolver tightly between his fingers.

Then she asks him if it is loaded.

He does not answer, stares vacantly ahead.

She asks him again, more insistently now: Answer me, is it loaded?

A colossal bang.

He is no longer shooting at his own memories. He is shooting at himself. Not at his heart, but at his hands, the ineffectual, impotent hands.

The room fills with smoke.

Munch stands up. Blood pours from his hand. Confused, he peers round, lies down on the bed, tries to hold his left arm up in the air.

She paces up and down like an automaton. As though nothing had happened.

Eventually she fetches a bucket, washes away the blood, presses an already blood-red handkerchief to her breast.

He looks at her from the bed. Registers the cold expression on her face.

You ass, he says. Don't let me bleed to death. At least fetch a doctor.

Munch lies in the National Hospital in Christiania.

There is no one who can threaten him. He is almost happy, lies in bed and tries to explain to himself the strange state he was in before the pistol went off. He lies there and relives the realization that she had not changed, that he could not go through that hell all over again, that he could neither send her packing nor manhandle her, neither live with her nor be without her. Lethargy, lack of willpower. But it was another kind of will which intervened, his own deep, violent protest perhaps, or *her* hateful, almost contemptible will.

His arm in a sling, he had taken the steamer over to Christiania. He could feel the violent pain, kept taking swigs of brandy on the boat. Physical, not mental or emotional pain now. He had thought of her the whole time. And what if she killed herself? He had written letters to Bødtker, asked him to track her down, make sure she did not harm herself in any way.

A thought surfaces in him. Had he ruined her completely? Had he seen into her soul?

He remembers what she said, the tone of her voice, all those things he could not believe, an empty show. Had he instinctively realized that she had something up her sleeve, that the entire reconciliation was *her* revenge, her desire to make him bend to her will yet again, to make good the humiliation, to spit in his face, so that the whole world could see that it was not he who had left her, but she who had left him. In other words, that she was the stronger, in spite of everything.

He lies in the hospital, tries to find answers, feels the throbbing in his hand, the anxiety which steals up on him: will his hand have to be amputated after all? Afterwards – he tries to remember, she had thrown herself round his neck in tears, had wept uncontrollably: Yes, you're the only good person I know. The embrace. To weep in her arms until he can weep no more. Listen, we'll go to Paris. We'll forget all this. I'll do my damnedest for you. We'll paint together.

Cloudy memories.

What actually happened at Åsgårdstrand? He lies in hospital and has pulled the dressing off. The morphine is doing its work. He suddenly becomes delirious. Tulla, Heiberg is repulsive you know. Just imagine if you'd ended up with him. Just imagine treating a woman like that.

He hears her voice from a long way away.

But it's only his left hand that is injured, after all.

My goodness, what a comfort you are, he murmurs, woozily.

He thinks he can see Bødtker. At any rate, he can hear his yapping voice.

Listen, let's all go together. Come with us, Munch, won't you?

What are they talking about? A trip? To Paris?

The doctor comes out: You mustn't stay here, you people. Munch is not well.

A cloud of fog envelops him. Then he is alone again.

*

The strange feeling of semi-contentment in hospital, before the operation, with his arm in a sling. He is in the large public ward, cannot afford greater luxury. There are two long rows of beds. Beside him is a farmer with cancer, his face waxen yellow. Patients from other wards come visiting in the evening, limping in on crutches. Munch knows that the bullet passed through two fingers, shattering them, around him patients shake their legs to and fro in the hope of stimulating their circulation. Some of them laugh, try to see the funny side of it all. Munch lies in bed waiting for the operation, sees the porter arrive, a black-haired older man with a pale sinister face. The porter pushes a trolley under the patient, fetches him for an operation, without a word. Soon it'll be Munch's turn. He is fetched for the operation, is rolled into a theatre with galleries on both sides. He understands that the operation is not just an event for himself and the doctor, for he has spectators, waiting as though at the theatre. Suddenly he recognizes faces, young students he recalls from the cafés, from Karl Johan. There they stand now, observing him. He hears the professor ask whether he wants an anaesthetic, whether he wants chloroform. But Munch is afraid to accept the offer. He remembers all those nights of palpitations. An anaesthetic would perhaps dull the pain, but it might also kill him. No, he is anchored to the pain, sees no other alternative but to go through this fully conscious.

He sees that they have taken out their scalpels. He follows all the movements in the theatre, the spectators' eyes, the professor's hand. Then he feels the scalpel moving through his own flesh. It scrapes against the bones. He can see blood gushing out, sees the fingers hanging like an empty glove, swollen and bloody. But he is silent, completely silent, refuses to cry out, clenches his teeth. The bullet has fragmented, Munch sees that the bone protrudes in a mass of splinters, inside all this red there is a chaos of bone and lead, elements of his body, elements of a bullet which is going to be removed, so that only flesh remains, the remains of a finger joint. They snip, prick, cut. He has been on the operating table for one and a half hours. Then he hears the doctor say:

There we are, finished. I don't think his hand can take any more now.

* * *

At long last he emerges into the street, can drive up Karl Johan if he likes. He is very weak, feels his hand throbbing, a deformed monstrosity.

A long way off he suddenly sees a tall, red-haired woman and a tall slim man walking on the pavement.

Tulla!

His heart pounds. It *is* her! She is walking along the pavement with an unfamiliar man! No, not unfamiliar. Frøken L. and Kavli! Arne Kavli, the young fashion painter. Fifteen years his junior. The blood rings in his ears, in his throbbing hand, he feels the suspicion he has had all along: that everything that happened was a game, something they had conjured up, to test him, see how far he was willing to go. Something that wasn't quite right. Her strange remoteness after the shot.

Kavli!

Kollmann comes. He has very good news. Money from Germany. But Munch does not listen to what he says.

Why aren't you listening? asks Kollmann.

Did you know that Tulla Larsen is with Kavli? Munch replies.

Kollmann looks at him anxiously. But women are *like* that, Munch! You must try to forget.

He begins to drink heavily, has to drain the glass straight away, immediately pouring another to calm his nerves. He knows that it is a crippled limb, a monstrosity, this hand he used to use for everything, a helpmate, which made it possible for him to play the piano. Now it is ugly and useless. He feels a stab of pain whenever his hand comes into contact with various objects, furniture, tram windows. Bottles of wine, spirits! He pours one glass after another, wants to forget, deaden the pain, but wakens with a start in the night. Impossible to sleep. He lights the lamp, thinks about his crippled limb. It does not give him a moment's peace. So frøken L. and Kavli are bound for Paris. Kollmann tries to calm him, he realizes that the shot saved her, that it killed off his flame for her, that her own flame burned more strongly, the vampire's, the desire that only blood can satisfy.

Munch avoids people, cannot sit in the same room as others and eat, is himself just a piece of meat, a crippled hand, people would surely have found it too repulsive.

Autumn 1902. Munch in Christiania, he whispers her name in hatred. He sits in a restaurant, drinking. Suddenly he sees that people are staring at him. Why are they staring like that? He glances around him. Then he discovers that he has raised his hand high in the air. He has sat at the table and shaken his fist at her, without realizing it.

*

He resumes his strolls round the city.

These streets he knows like the inside of his pocket. Jæger's streets. Now they are his, and he feels as wretched as Jæger was in 1888, no, even more wretched. One day he is walking down Karl Johan when he sees a coach approaching. He catches a glint of red. Oh yes, he sees that the colours are right, outlined by people he seems to know very well, the creatures of free love. Yes, it's Sigurd Bødtker and his wife, a black beard round his mouth, a yapping poodle and a bitch on heat and, naturally as night follows day – Gunnar Heiberg, the toad, the pig.

Munch stands in a doorway, realizes that the moment has come, that they really are off to Paris, all of them. Tulla Larsen and Arne Kavli! He could have killed the pair of them! It could all have been over. They could have had their obituaries. The whole thing was just a crude put-up job. He has destroyed himself for a woman he never loved. He follows them, finds a place where, undisturbed, he can observe the massive steamer with the towering funnels bound for the Continent.

The smoke belches out, the passengers come up on deck, wave to their friends and relations, a mood of anticipation. Then he sees frøken L., tall, slim, radiant, with her flowing red hair, a golden halo! The red also stands out on her lips, those well-formed thin lips of hers. Now she is smiling at Kavli, holding him by the arm in a most intimate manner, as Gunnar Heiberg makes some witty remark.

Munch turns on his heel, walks away from the harbour, back into town. He finds a bar, orders wine, downs one glass after another, then raises his hand again, holding it high in the air.

Contemptible! he cries. Riff-raff!

He starts to attract the attention of the other customers, alarmed at his violent outburst. A waiter comes up and seizes him by the collar, propels him through the bar, kicks open a door and throws him out into the street. He hurtles full length, flies through the air, tries to break his fall with his right hand. But the injured hand collides violently with the cobbled surface. There is blood everywhere.

*

Good God, he realizes he is on the slippery slope, teetering on the edge of the abyss, the path he has taken is much too narrow. These painful events, sights, thoughts and characteristics. Are there nothing but painful images in him? Is the whole thing no more than a play he is directing himself? His hand throbs with pain. Yes, perhaps he really *is* ill, but who *are* this rabble who have finally succeeded in bringing him down, who rise up in anger to avenge a rich young woman of thirty-three, to exact revenge on him because he, a poor minstrel, dared to have an affair with her? Who on earth are this bunch of whoremongers and drunkards who hold him in such contempt?

It is three weeks since the shot in Åsgårdstrand. Frøken L. is already on a steamship together with a young painter. Munch walks the streets, in search of restaurants. Nothing but wine and spirits from P. A. Larsen the wine merchant will soothe him.

* * *

Truth. Photography. X-rays. His own damaged hand, immortalized by the Christiania X-ray Institute before the operation. The bullet can clearly be seen, at an angle of almost ninety degrees to the splintered lower joint of the middle finger on the left hand.

September 1902. The bandage is removed. He shudders. His own slender well-formed hand has become a deformed monstrosity. His well-formed, refined fingers. Crippled, ugly, useless. A revolver bullet, 0.22. Now it dawns on him that he is not just a painter. What about the piano? True, he was never as accomplished a player as Stach, could not make Chopin come to life, but as long as he can remember he has tinkled away, not always when it suited others, certainly not always when he was sober either, but all the same. He has nevertheless regarded a piano as a necessity in any future home. He certainly can't play the Revolution *étude* now.

*

But only two days after being discharged from the National Hospital, on the twenty-fourth of September, he is in the firing line once more. From the pistols of the press. He exhibits his work at Blomqvist's again, opens the floodgates, lets them see what sort of work he has been doing. It is a total anticlimax, none of the recognition there was in Berlin, not even any visitors, just a few uninterested souls. Until the second of October, that is, when an anonymous reader's letter is published in *Aftenposten*:

> Dear Editor: I called in at Blomqvist's to see the Munch exhibition. This is not art. It is trash. It is filth. To exhibit such pictures makes a mockery of the public. Because if one exhibits such works, it must be because one thinks that the two are compatible – the art on display and the public which comes to see it. This is a mockery. Because the public is not so stupid that it thinks this is the real thing. Some people laugh, but most are indignant. And rightly so. One *should* be indignant at such stuff. The public should have enough self-respect not to put up with such art. And if there is nothing else we can do, then we must strike. I appeal to anyone with an annual subscription to Blomqvist's to cancel it.

And the editorial board of *Aftenposten* adds: The above letter has been sent to us by a gentleman who is highly regarded in the community. The wider public is of the same opinion as the honoured correspondent.

The cartoonist Ragnvald Blix, who is already influenced by Munch, draws a cartoon of the exhibition for the satirical paper *Tyrihans*, depicting an empty gallery where the artist's shadow is the only spectator.

Subsequently, as a consequence of the reader's letter, people fairly pour into the exhibition. But now the public are photographed by the artist himself! Munch with a Kodak camera, with an exposure of one-twentieth of a second, a roll of film with four, six or twelve pictures measuring nine millimetres by nine. The camera stands on a polished table top, which reflects the works on display and the roof structure, and Munch would also appear to have moved a light object in front of the lens, presumably in order to manipulate the effect of the light.

He is tired now, is no longer as able to rise serenely above the criticism. He wants to paint a picture measuring two metres by one metre showing how the stinking manure of *Aftenposten*'s decorated editor Amandus Schibstedt is spread on the garden of art by his lowly minions, as he puts it in a newspaper interview. Munch cannot bear it, no more manure, please, no more contempt and malice. Now he is a cripple, has been brought to the brink of his own universe. He has fallen into the abyss, but has managed to get a finger-hold on a ledge of rock, knows that there is a way up the cliff wall, but cannot yet see it. Stinking manure, meanness and malice. It is ten years now since he was called a complete maniac, it is sixteen years since a twig painter yelled humbug! right into his face. Aubert has kept him at a distance with his avuncular pseudo-understanding. Munch is now vulnerable to absolutely any perfidy, sees enemies everywhere, Tulla Larsen's friends, penniless post-Bohemians or wealthy pillars of the middle class.

Then Christian Krohg enters the arena again, magnanimous, goes straight to the heart of the matter, cuts through all the verbiage, writes an analysis in *Verdens Gang* and points out that the public do not accept Munch because they are looking for a photographic likeness, thinking in black and white, because they have a yardstick, which is likeness, a yardstick Munch falls so far short of that all yardsticks become redundant.

* * *

Dear Munch: I'm so sorry I wasn't at home when you called. If only you'd telephoned beforehand, I would have given sewing school a miss. I wrote a long, formal letter to you a few days ago, but threw it into the wastepaper basket. You can have a bit of nonsense instead. And I'm well qualified in that department. Incidentally, there's something I have to say, which is that it was a little mean of you when you said that your exhibitions were less good when I was present. I really felt like a relative of King Lear's youngest daughter when you said that. You see, I'm not one of those who blurt out their enthusiasm straight away, which strikes me as somewhat disrespectful. I always fall silent when something moves me. How an audience, as soon as the curtain falls, can begin to wave its arms and legs about and clap and call out is a mystery to me. I must always have peace and quiet and it is off-putting when there is someone beside me. So I think, dear Munch, that you were mistaken in this. The amount of inner joy I have derived and continue to derive from your art you can probably not fully appreciate and I'm endlessly indebted to you, I think, both spiritually and materially. Well, there you have it. Another time you mustn't speak such twaddle. Not all people are alike, and in my opinion, despite all the knowledge of human beings you say you have, you don't understand me, for one, very well. You understand one kind of person perhaps, but there are so many kinds, my dear friend. Incidentally, I think the T-kind is rather strange. Don't you? Åse Ng.

* * *

It is autumn in Christiania. Munch strolls about with his camera. One day he asks Aunt Karen and his sister Inger whether he can take a photograph of them.

Scenes of the past. As though he wants to see the patterns in his life. He walks in through the doorway to Pilestredet 30b, to where it all began, his mother's death at Christmas 1868, when he was five years old.

At the foot of the large double bed he had sat on a child's chair and watched the tall female figure who blotted out the dim light filtering in through the window. He had sat there listening to her speak, his mother, a woman who, in photographs, most closely resembles her daughter Inger in her features, the dark, serious eyes, the erect carriage. She asked her children whether they would be sad when she was gone. She asked them to promise to follow Jesus their whole lives, then they would meet her again in heaven. Munch had sat in the little chair, not quite able to grasp the meaning of her words, hearing only the tone of her voice. He saw the dark figure at the window, did not know what was actually supposed to happen, merely knew that it was sad, so he wept.

Munch walks into the courtyard at Pilestredet, photographs something which is not there, one hundred and twenty millimetres by eighty-nine, collodion printing-out paper. Not a soul to be seen, only the courtyard, the walls, what he will call the contours of a white swan, something barely visible, yet the symbol of art's ideal, purity, whereas the artist himself must plunge down into the depths, into life, must become soiled. The transformation of earlier events, Christmas 1868, when large snowflakes fell without ceasing, as snow can only fall when one is a child. All the candles inside, on the Christmas tree. The air was heavy with the smell of wax and burnt pine needles, his mother sat on the sofa in her large black dress, silent and pale, waiting for something Munch had no inkling of. The military doctor paced up and down, sat down suddenly and spoke to his wife. Munch saw his mother smile, saw that tears were running down her cheeks. Everything was so quiet.

Now he is back where it all happened, autumn 1902. He photographs the naked trees. The leaves have fallen to the ground, there has recently been a gale. He stands beside Aunt Karen and his sister Inger, has them sit on the steps outside a house in Olav Ryes Plass, where they lived from 1883 to 1885. It was then that he had painted the portrait of Inger and started work on *The Sick Child*. Now he photographs these two women whom he never fears, whom he loves unreservedly. Not once have they let him down. They have defended him at all stages, against all attacks, critics and enemies. They have tried to understand him, all his idiosyncrasies.

When, once, she had been asked to become his stepmother Aunt Karen had said no. Nevertheless she lived with the military doctor until his death. Munch asks his aunt to sit like the dark female figure in the woodcut *Two Women on the Shore*, asks his sister Inger to stand, as in his own vision of woman's first stage, the stage of spring, falling in love, *joie de vivre*. As though to tell of a love she has perhaps never experienced.

He uses his family as props in an illusion of already lived life. They are willing accomplices. Finally he photographs himself, lies alone on an iron bed. Medicine bottles or alcohol stand on the nearby table, at any rate there he lies, in hospital, in a *pension*, barely visible. It is perhaps an early study on the theme of Marat's death, the ultimate victory of woman over man.

He lies on the bed staring listlessly into the camera lens.

* * *

Munch in Dr Linde's home. He can hear Enrico Caruso singing *Vesti la giubba* by Ruggiero Leoncavallo on a scratchy gramophone. Extreme cold throughout Europe. Aunt Karen tells him about the blizzard at home in Christiania. The anarchist Rubino fails in his attempt to assassinate the King of the Belgians. Munch sits surrounded by Rodin sculptures. His hand throbs. His middle finger is appreciably shortened, the operation not an unqualified success, he will probably lose a nail. He has his picture taken with bandaged hand. The healthy fingers stand out in contrast to the clearly amputated middle finger, as he etches a picture directly onto a copper plate. He has his picture taken in front of the sculpture *The Age of Bronze*. There is still a hint of defiance in his eyes, but above all the face expresses helplessness, emptiness perhaps, at any rate boundless vulnerability, as though at any moment he might jump up nervously from the chair, incapable of controlling his feelings.

Kollmann takes all the decisions and Dr Linde adds the finishing touches. *Edvard Munch und die Kunst der Zukunft* is a copiously illustrated monograph with colour plates produced with sophisticated printing techniques. Munch is a guest in the upper-middle-class home of an eye specialist rolling in money and awash with children and servants, who is one of his greatest admirers and his patron. And Kollmann shadows him, is always in the vicinity, can suddenly pop up out of nowhere, always at the right moment, guides him, slips him money when he needs it, keeps him at his work when he is seized with a desire to run away from it. It is autumn 1902. Jæger has at long last got the last two volumes of his trilogy about his love affair with Oda Krohg printed by a firm in Brittany.

* * *

Just before Christmas, Munch is again living in Berlin, Hotel Stadt Riga, Mittelstrasse, then Hotel Hippodrom am Knie, Charlottenburg. It is now that he really comes into contact with Landesgerichtsrat Gustav Schiefler, who will buy his graphic art and embark upon the cataloguing of Munch's entire graphic output.

His aunt writes, informing him that Dedekam has become an art critic on *Morgenbladet*. He speaks of Munch as the greatest colourist. Just as musical people never sing out of tune, Munch never puts a false or clashing colour on the canvas: It is interesting to note that Werenskiold is strongly influenced by Munch, so this is very much a case of the genie having influenced the master.

*

Dear Aunt: I've had one bout of influenza after another this winter. This time it was my throat and ears that were affected. From here I'm going on to Paris as I'm to exhibit some pictures there. I shall be living on the outskirts of Paris, at Delius's house, and will lie low for obvious reasons. My finger is doing quite well, even though I've had problems with it the whole time. It's no thing of beauty now, short and almost rigid. My exhibition at Cassirer's was praised everywhere, the same pictures as I had at Blomqvist's. I hope to get to my house early. I shall ask Inger to send 3 blackcurrant and 6 redcurrant bushes and three dwarf apple trees to Åsgårdstrand. She can find out about this at Olsen's on Storgaten. She could address them to Henriksen the fisherman and ask him to plant them in suitable places. I shall see to it that Laura receives the book by Linde, if this is a good idea for someone so nervous. I'm glad to have put Berlin behind me, all the fiddling about with pictures and engravings was starting to get me down. On this trip all I'm taking with me is a little holdall and a rug. Things are calmer for me now and I have more time to write. Greetings to Grønvold from me. He's a droll fellow.

* * *

In literary jottings, Munch writes: Madness is again rearing its head in me. All of a sudden I go completely berserk. I sometimes fly at people and want to hit them.

He plans a detailed literary description of the pain he felt when his hand was injured, and then – hell and damnation – that Tulla Larsen, who, after destroying a painter regarded as the best in the land, goes and shacks up with a *mediocre* talent! Arne Kavli! A crude fashion painter. The bosom friend of poodles, toads and pigs! Tulla Larsen's *own* circle! A menagerie bought for a song. Barking, whining, slurping and slobbering. The Post-Bohemians! *Now* she is interesting, a woman people talk about – what a frightfully sad story, that business with a wretched genius – he was a martyr to his art whereas *she*, she is a generous patron of art, floats about Paris buying a picture or two now and then. Munch is furious, cannot regain his composure, is en route for the same city as she is, the menagerie of the Post-Bohemians.

*

He never tires of Paris. Here he becomes known as that perennial Scandinavian ghost. He shows eight paintings in the Salon des Indépendants, from the twentieth of March to the twenty-fifth of April. He keeps back his highly provocative *Hearse on Potsdamer Platz*, exhibits *The Enchanted Forest*, *The Girls on the Bridge*, *On the Veranda*, *Summer Night*, *Inheritance* and *Madonna*.

What did he think of Paris? That it had greater scope? *Inheritance* immediately draws large crowds. He knows the sounds only too well from before: laughter or cries of disgust, the red child with the diseased skin, the mother dressed in black. Sad, tragic, hideous. The critic Félicien Fagus cannot make up his mind. He writes of the clumsiness, the platitudes, the incredible errors, the mother whose lap holds a gelatinous foetus, its colour that of a shroud. But he also writes that, in *Madonna*, Munch displays all the qualities of a true painter. A superb presentation of flesh and bestiality.

Karl Eugen Schmidt writes that when it comes to heaping cacophony on disharmony and brutality on tastelessness, the man from Norway has no peer, overshoots every target and slips deeper and deeper into chaos.

Or the Leblond brothers, who consider that the savage precision of the portraits and the witty choice of colours in the imagined scenes combine to give the impression of a Chinese Norway.

Flesh and bestiality! Chaos! Cacophony on disharmony! A Chinese Norway! Meant as a description of his own inner state of mind.

He is in *her* city, so she is there at the same time, somewhere or other, among the poodles, toads and pigs. It is 1903, the year Munch also comes into contact with the influential gallery owner Commeter in Hamburg. Pissarro and Whistler die, Munch will paint *Dr Linde's Sons*,

Village Street with Burning House, Country Road, Åsgårdstrand, make etchings of *The Girls on the Jetty* and *Holstentor, Lübeck*, lithographs of *The Violin Concert* and *The Brooch*. The woman playing the violin and wearing a brooch is called Eva Mudocci.

Jappe Nilssen has already written to Munch: here in Paris there are two ladies, the pianist Bella Edwards and the violinist Eva Mudocci, Eva M. is unhappy. Bella Edwards has total power over her. They're a couple. Now I have a proposal and a request for you. They are coming up to Norway to give concerts. Couldn't you take Eva under your wing, flirt with her a little, so that her feelings may become natural?

But they meet in Paris.

She stands by a piano holding the violin in her hand, its almost human curves, the waist. At the piano sits her accompanist Bella Edwards, Grieg's secret friend. Eva Mudocci stands holding the Golden Emiliani, a genuine Stradivarius. Her real name is Evangeline Muddock, but an Italian-sounding name is essential for her career. So she is an English woman with an Italian or Spanish-sounding name, who has lived mostly in Germany but would like to be Scandinavian because Grieg and Ibsen are.

Munch meets them after the concert. They sit talking in a Parisian café. Eva Mudocci tells him that she and Bella Edwards live in a small apartment in rue Las Cases. She listens to Munch's many ideas and associations and thinks he is 'brilliantly witty in a dry caustic way'.

For his part, Munch sees her as a Madonna made flesh. He already dreams of painting her portrait. The perfect portrait. Perhaps he will actually manage to get his mind off Tulla Larsen.

*

The next time he sees her, he is standing outside the door to their flat in Rue Las Cases holding a massive lupin half as big as himself. He has invited himself to tea.

The power of the moon. He will later write about how Paris suddenly makes a powerful impression on him. The city of spring, of life, of love. Eva Mudocci. The lady with the violin. When she plays, he is filled with a sense of beauty, harmony, with the pure feelings he yearns for.

Dear Eva: To some extent, nervousness is an expression of strength. In recent years, I have waged a major mental battle which will never cease. As you have seen, I have periods of feeling immensely strong and then sink again into the deepest despair. As I have told you, I do not wish for happiness. When I complain, it is merely self-torment. I do not know where it will all end. I have the impression of being on a little ship without a helmsman, and the ship is being propelled rapidly by the current into uncharted waters.

*

He is fleeing his past, gives full vent to his fascination, bestows on her the words he has always longed to say to another person, without fear of betrayal. Yet Munch's love for Eva Mudocci is just as much his love for the portrait of her, the pictures he knows he can create. Madonna! Her thousand-year-old eyes, the reminder of generations now dead, generations to come. Munch in Paris or at Grez, fleeing the Norwegian colony, completely absorbed in a woman who perhaps reminds him of a vision, who recreates the dream.

*

Lieber Edvard: Yesterday evening I could not come to visit you because when I left you my thoughts were not quite clear. Also, when I was with you, despite all the living feelings, it was as though death had taken up residence in me. Then it suddenly dawned on me what had happened, from beginning to end. I suddenly felt I loved you and *wanted* to believe that you also loved me. That is why this loathsome quarrel flared up between us. Now I understand better. I'm proud of my feelings, they explain everything I've done. Whether you've behaved badly towards me I don't know. You probably didn't mean to hurt me. You wanted a spring flower for yourself, through you I wanted to attain a happiness I'd never known before, I wanted to bathe and fortify myself in the fire of life, wanted you to lead me into this state of being. And you could have done so but you didn't and so far no real fire of life has shown you how. What was beautiful for each of us in its own way is not much fun when it's like this. Eva.

*

Liebe Eva! Another blizzard, after the spring flowers. That evening at Lilas, you were completely changed. Why? I've no idea. *I* haven't changed, I'm ill and very nervous of making a slip, but what can I do about it? So I shall no longer write to you in the evening, I shall write on good paper and if possible more clearly. You see, I just want to fit in with you and of course you are free to dictate when I speak to you. Unfortunately it's only of an evening, in a café, that I'm in the mood, and in a café you have to take writing paper along with you. I think we should meet in happier circumstances. Days when events and circumstances do not conspire to overwhelm me. Then I shall also paint a beautiful portrait of you. I have an *idée fixe*: that your experience has been the same as mine and I have the *idée fixe* that a Norwegian plays a role in your life. Dein Edvard.

*

Dear Edvard, today Rasmussen arrived with an umbrella and said it was from you – heavens above! – so much trouble over a stupid umbrella! I wish you hadn't done it, it was so unnecessary, I should like to have given you a scolding and boxed your ears and broken the umbrella again! I'm so happy that you like my music, so do come along sometime, it isn't virtuoso stuff, but I think you like that anyway. You're certainly musical, you who are an artist to the depths of your being, with strengths and weaknesses, the beautiful and the ugly, but do you know what a child of pain music is? How one suffers, how for weeks before an important concert one is sick with nerves, and on the platform can scarcely see or hear, one could die of fear, yes, I'd love to play for you if we could meet in happier circumstances. Eva.

*

Munch knows the forces, the passion which, in his case, in his body, has been poison and which Eva Mudocci now describes using other words. He is in Paris, the city where there are other Norwegians, enemies on every street corner! Thoughts of Tulla Larsen steal into his mind. He has not managed to put them behind him, is certain that poodles, pigs and toads can move to attack at any moment.

Then Eva M. writes: I'm writing yet again, even if you haven't, and am doing so for two reasons, first, I often feel sympathy for you. Rasmussen always wants us to come with him to places where the Norwegians are, and I get sick and tired of these ever-dramatic, hysterical faces, tired of the people, even of *the names* of these people, I understand why you flee them, that you want to live in peace alone. I can't understand what it is about the Norwegians, who are one of the finest peoples on earth, one of the cleverest and most talented and at the same time, in a way, so weak, so wild, so lawless. I don't mean lawless in the usual sense, for one ought to break the laws one has created oneself, but there are natural laws, basic laws and it is just these laws that the Norwegians break and that's why they become so unhappy and hysterical. It's perhaps because they don't understand their own culture. The old, the wild strong blood jars with the modern ideas of the age, full of yearning. The other reason I'm writing is that I don't feel well. I should so much have liked to sit beside you. Eva.

*

Liebe Eva! Yes, the Norwegians, and I'm a Norwegian myself, even though I have nothing to do with my countrymen when I'm abroad. I'm sorry there are so many of them in the Latin Quarter, and right next to my studio. I don't know whether I should come back here this autumn. You're right, there's great power and a good deal of uncouthness in us. This is why we go under as individuals, and the women even more so, as the men are always closer to the culture or allow themselves to be absorbed into it. The beautiful relationship between man and woman in the old culture, the half-sensual, half-spiritual, is of no use to us. In us, the overriding element is that great, powerful natural will and it is this that brings us down. Why don't you go out into the country instead of getting worked up about Norwegians? Why not? I often feel for you the kind of love one feels for a sister, and I should like to press your head to my heart. What do you mean when you speak of the great gulf between us? We are like one another in so many ways, even if our pasts have been different. We both come from nervous stock. Dein Edvard.

*

Lieber Edvard, I'm not as impolite about your people as you say. I didn't say they are without culture, how could I have said that, their culture is perhaps like froth on stormy waters, I think that the wild blood from ancient times has changed little in the Norwegian nature, while the blood of other nations has become weaker, thinner and colder, perhaps precisely by virtue of a civilization which has grown up over thousands of years. During this time, the Norwegians have adhered to their character. Then suddenly there is a stream of the most modern ideas and these foreign elements have a terrible power to captivate and drive people down all kinds of false paths. It's hard to say what I feel, I love Norwegians, but I see how dangerous you are, for each other and for all those you come into contact with. Perhaps in a thousand years, when all other nations lie dead and impotent, you will stand where the front-ranking nations do now. Your people are still young, they have simply had a long childhood, and of course if you don't all destroy one another, as you say. So, I said and meant nothing impolite. And you've gone and worked yourself up again. Dear child, if I am to be your sister, then I should look after you better than you do yourself. Never in my life have I met a man who takes such poor care of himself, that much I have learned about you. You get worked up and then, to make sure you get even more worked up, you sit – I'm quite sure of this – in cafés drinking brandy and God knows what else until 10 o'clock in the morning and then you're like death warmed up, driven to exhaustion by your fevered imaginings. Eva.

* * *

Munch is back at Dr Linde's estate, surrounded by Rodin sculptures and north German respectability. He paints Linde's portrait, the eye specialist whose life is so well ordered, who has bought *Fertility* and is himself a paragon of all that is healthy and natural.

Munch writes to Eva from Dr Linde's house: Liebe Eva! Here the spring is fantastic, cloudless sunshine, longings and desires. We met one another in unfavourable circumstances. Perhaps, and I really believe this, we will meet at a later date when everything is different. I shall go to your concert, read your music, just as I read your eyes. *Du bist ganz Musik*.

*

She reproaches him for writing letters to her on dirty notepaper: You say that men and women don't understand one another? Is that why you write so illegibly? It doesn't matter if you write bad German, but please do try to write a little more clearly! Reading what you have written makes my eyes water. I'm ready to admit that my handwriting is hard to read, but what about *yours*! And at least write on clean notepaper. Yours smells musty. Shall I send you a packet of writing paper? Spring green and smelling of violets? No, not that, but clean, just clean, like your nails! Poor boy! Now I've scolded you enough, if you find it hard to write in German, write in Norwegian, I'm able to read a little Norwegian, and would learn some from it. Were you mad in Paris? You were certainly ill, we're all mad from time to time and that's fine, in moments of madness one achieves what one cannot achieve otherwise, and that is the whole idea, isn't it? You say it's dangerous. Perhaps, but for many people a dangerous path may have more appeal than the humdrum path which people have to tread every day of their lives. Rather heroic pain any day than prosaic contentment.

*

Munch replies. She mustn't take it amiss, but actually that is all the paper he has when suddenly finding himself in some café or other and feeling the urge to write to her. He is sensitive, easily hurt, even the most innocuous words hurt his feelings.

She replies: Dear beast, my dear sweet idiot! Can't I have a little joke with you any more, that's how I am, I have to joke so as not to quake in my boots at the sheer horror of life. Apart from which I'm your friend, which gives me the right to tease you. I'm not asking anything of you. I'm nobler than you, I place two kisses on your snakelike eyes, two kisses to make amends so we don't both act so foolishly again, all right? I'd forgotten that what can be said with a laugh can't be written, even though, on the other hand, there's no laughter that can explain away harsh words with a jest, I therefore kiss you too once on the mouth so that we can really make up, as children say, all right? Mein Lieber, it pains me when my words hurt you, and I don't want this to happen any more, you are yourself and are not meant to belong to anyone else, don't give it another thought, I didn't mean it, now I kiss you again, once for each word which has hurt you. Is that all right now? The weather is unsettled. There has been a storm with thunder and lightning. Bad weather fills my thoughts with evil spirits. I thank God, or the gods, for the sunshine. I love sunshine like a cat does, constantly seek it and never find it, because darkness is stronger than light. If only one could believe in Pan. Guess what, two days ago I saw Pan. He was sitting on the spire of St Clothilde's church and was playing his pipe for all he was worth.

*

Munch replies, thanks her for the photograph of herself she has sent him. It is a lovely photograph, but has no expression, gives no hint of her character. He wants to paint her. The perfect portrait.

Meanwhile he sails Dr Linde's boat. On the sea he shakes off his past, all the painful memories. He is ill. He asks her to greet the quiet square in Paris, beside St Clothilde's church.

It is summer. Time he was going home.

Back to the fjord, to the cottage. To Åsgårdstrand.

* * *

It is midsummer evening.

Munch sits on the hotel veranda and sips his whisky and soda. Åsgårdstrand is shrouded in a white dreamlike veil, with the simple white houses, the violet-tinged water.

Munch is pale. This is where he shot the pistol, this is where he touched rock bottom. He is driven towards his past, has no need to hold his ruined hand up to the light to remind himself. Blackcurrant and redcurrant bushes and dwarf apple trees cannot dull the pain, any more than can friends, who come bringing alcohol and install themselves in his garden, surrendering to the sun, the scent of jasmine, the moonlit nights.

His friend Gierløff, who later recalls that Munch paints the reflection of the moonlight, has a monopoly of the moon, remembers a seal which hauls itself up onto a rock, with shiny head and wet eyes, remembers the waves from the swell, which come chasing in, rounded and glittering, remembers the long nights, brilliant white seagulls, a sandpiper which strutted about on the beach, an innocent little herring on the surface of the water, a pair of ducks which came paddling round the headland. Munch's world. Munch's idyll. His friend Gierløff's golden memory.

Meanwhile Munch paints *Self-portrait in Hell*.

* * *

He takes off his clothes, removes the last protective layer, photographs himself stark naked in his own garden, in profile. Right hand outstretched towards the light, his sunlit torso forming a contrast with the dark background, as in the *Portrait in Hell*.

Strindberg has paved the way, has even shown him where he could plunge down into the abyss. He has already done so, is on a ledge, can see both his salvation and hell, photographs himself, studies his naked body with wonder, the pale body, the tanned face, the close-cropped hair. As though after a self-imposed asceticism. A cleansing.

He photographs himself inside his own house, the room is in sharp focus, not least the carved chest he has received as a gift from Tulla Larsen. But he himself is hard to make out, indistinct, and intentionally so it would appear, like a commentary on his own existential situation. He writes: The camera is no match for painting, since I cannot use it in heaven or hell.

He has sent four hundred crowns to Aunt Karen at Son. Has decided to hold yet another exhibition at Blomqvist's later that autumn, despite the fearful prospect of Schibstedt's reeking manure.

But newspaper critics have never been able to stop him. The last time, they got him to waver, but that was just after the shot went off, and that is already almost a year ago now. He is also starting to get a surprising amount of commissions for portraits from Germans.

*

Dear Aunt: There was a steady invasion of Christiania-Bohemians who would come in of an evening, get drunk and completely upset me. Some of them came from frøken L.'s crowd and were ill-intentioned. Incidentally, I've now realized that I must give Christiania and most of the Christiania crowd a wide berth, make a complete break with the circle which, with frøken L. in the lead, has done me such rank injustice and embittered my life. I also clearly see that I must make a determined effort to shake off the nervous weakness resulting from the years of persecution at the hands of this evil female. I have now understood that these dramatic episodes have simply been a pathological consequence of the years of torment. I want to find a completely peaceful spot where I can paint undisturbed. I continue to receive the most flattering letters from Germany, in Weimar efforts are being made to have me back, I've got two commissions there, and I also have a commission for a portrait from Chemnitz in Saxony. But I shall not go until my nerves are in better condition.

* * *

September in Lübeck, in the grounds of Dr Linde's home. Munch paints Dr Linde's four sons. They are playing in the grounds, and are then summoned to say hello to the foreign guest. Curious, but a little shy, they pose in front of the white french windows of the conservatory.

He immediately sees how he will paint them, the first impression, the individual characters of the four sons; in the left half of the painting, the youngest of the brothers in a sailor suit forms one unit with the eldest. In the right half of the picture the most obviously independent one stands alone. He stands legs apart, leaning back nonchalantly against the door frame, holding a straw hat with red ribbons in his right hand. The next youngest son stands in the middle, hands folded.

Munch writes to his aunt that he feels strong, is living like a prince, explains how the protracted influenza the previous winter was a consequence of all the hospital episodes. Dear Aunt, had it not been for all the artistic encouragement, my final sacrifice for frøken L. might perhaps have broken me for a long time. Could you ask Inger to buy some beautiful flowering plants for my garden, they can be sent to Larsen, manager of the Co-op.

Later that autumn he is in Åsgårdstrand. The season makes him think of Tulla Larsen. The colours are the same, blood-red skies, like that time the shot went off. A young girl, Petra, has started to run errands for him, buy groceries, take care of all the practical things.

He writes to Eva Mudocci: Greetings from my home. Emotional storms and the life in Christiania have severed our spiritual links. Do you think of me?

He has kissed her letters, writes that he sees her white cliffs, or breasts, somewhere in the distance. In deeply erotic letters to Eva Mudocci he tells her that her picture hangs over his bed. Munch asks why he has not had any letters from her, should he also include her among his enemies? She is two different people, and that frightens him. He writes that he feels stronger, though is restless and nervous. She replies that she has written two letters. Why has he not received them? And then she wants to say something nice even though he doesn't deserve it because he has insinuated that she *too* is his enemy. Lieber Edvard: You are one of those people who have either friends or enemies. Most people call the most insignificant and run-of-the-mill acquaintances friends and do not know any different, you should count yourself lucky you've experienced either category. By the way, what do you mean when you say I'm two people? And why are you afraid? You need have no fear.

* * *

Eva Mudocci travels to Denmark with Bella Edwards and holds a concert in Copenhagen. Munch is still in Åsgårdstrand, drawing a flower, writing: here I am, this flower is no good, I should so much have liked to be at your concert. Instead he goes to Christiania. Exhibition at Blomqvist's according to the familiar pattern: thirty-six paintings, twenty-six graphic works.

Aftenposten and its editor Schibstedt are poised to attack:

Two ladies were standing at Blomqvist's in front of Munch's pictures and one of them said timorously: It can't be *dangerous* to say that one doesn't like them, can it? But the other took the bull by the horns and rashly replied: Heavens no, I for one am not afraid of saying so.

Verdens Gang two days later: As always at first sight Munch seems forbidding, the exhibition has so far been visited by crowds of people, who by all accounts are laughing heartily and having a very jolly time of it.

Morgenposten the same day: There are a good many works of interest in the popular art salon. In the afternoon when people are out strolling there are also crowds of spectators who smile with pleasure, laugh in despair, or snort with indignation at having to pay to see such rubbish among the other fine, beautiful works. If you are a professional critic, then you take it all in your stride, you simply stop looking at the rubbish and writing about it.

Tyrihans three weeks later: We dropped in to have at look at Munch the other day. First we observed the public. It was a very mixed bag. Some upstanding citizens, whose artistic sense had not kept pace with the times and who with visible repugnance hurried from one master-piece to the next. A few stubborn humorists who had not yet abandoned hope of bringing out the ridiculousness of the situation. And a few neu-tral types who contemplated the most glaring splashes of colour with a gentle smile. But we pressed on. Over there in front of No. 10, *The Operating Table*, stood just the lady we were looking for. The one who understands the very essence of it all. We sidled up to her and listened to her expressions of enthusiasm, she turned to a young female friend who did not yet look quite so firmly convinced that she understood it all: Have you ever seen *death* so strikingly close? Do you understand that this is the artist's soul emancipating itself from his feelings of pain at the horror of death? This is how Munch sees death! Behind us we heard one of the upstanding citizens mutter a gentle Upon my word! We continued to study the painting seriously to see whether we could possibly detect any emancipation, but despite our best intentions all we could identify was a group of orang utans which were observing three murderous looking gorillas with quite alarming serenity.

* * *

Berlin, Hotel Stadt Riga, later Lützowstrasse 82.

Dear Jappe: I've taken up skating to keep fit. When I fall I hit my left hand, so it ends up looking like a bunch of purple grapes. The monks' liqueur, Bénédictine, can be obtained courtesy of P. A. Larsen.

Kollmann is in the vicinity. Munch feels that they share a similar fate. They are both orphans from a middle-class background. They have had their pictures taken in front of gravestones in a courtyard in Berlin, as though to draw attention to their feeling of closeness to death, to a world invisible to the naked eye.

Schiefler visits Munch at Lützowstrasse in November. There are no chairs, so he has to sit on a chest. They discuss Cassirer. Munch is hav-ing another exhibition in Paul Cassirer's fashionable art salon, where Dr Linde's book on Munch was presented in January the same year, and led the influential art critic Rosenhagen to comment that Munch was one of the strongest talents in modern art as a whole. Now Munch shares the main room with Goya, a hundred years older than himself, who painted portraits of people with a hint of serious mental disturbance.

Munch sits on a chest talking to Schiefler about the effects of alcohol. He says that when he gets an idea, but hasn't the strength to capitalize on it, he uses alcohol. He tells his new German friend about his background, the influences on him, speaks about his friend Hans Jæger, who literally had to go to prison for his art, talks about Ibsen and about women who inflict themselves upon men and then you cannot get rid of them.

This is the winter Munch will paint his *Salome* picture, in which Eva Mudocci is suddenly the model for the woman with the Medusa's head. The man in the picture is Munch, pathologically thin, whereas Eva Mudocci is a smiling contented Madonna, allowing her hair to flow down over the man's head.

*

It is then that Eva Mudocci suddenly starts addressing Munch in a very cold, formal manner in her letters to him, presumably deeply hurt, and also offended by his remoteness, by words he has not said or perhaps has said. It is the winter when Munch will carry the unwieldy printing stones there, making the excuse that he has other matters to attend to, the winter when he will write to Jappe Nilssen that he is living with Eva Mudocci, but that he does not know what to write about *that* specifically, the winter when he will ask the violinist about her true sexual orientation and thus insult her beyond measure. She is clearly offended that Munch does not reply to her approaches, and when they meet she is so angry that she cannot find words. Munch has said some catastrophic things to her: *Das ist nicht normal*.

Then she writes: Bitte lesen durch! Du bist nicht mein Freund. Du bist es nicht wert! I've been far too patient with you, did not believe a word of all the ill I heard about you from all quarters, I only thought the best, but now I'm beginning to think I was mistaken, to think that your bad manners can actually be put down to schlechte Natur. Recently you said you wanted to comply with my wishes, I wish you could be just a little polite. I should have said this earlier today when we met, but was too cross.

Munch receives several glacial letters, refuses to meet her in a café, and not in the evening, yet meets her all the same, tries to paint her, but fails in the attempt to paint the perfect portrait. But he makes the lithograph of her, *Madonna* or *The Lady with the Brooch*, delivers the heavy lithographic stone to her hotel and writes, on a slip of paper: here's the stone. What a weight off my mind!

It is the winter when it is announced from Paris that in October Tulla Larsen married the young Norwegian painter Arne Kavli.

* * *

Dear Jappe: You ask whether I have recovered from the wound which the united company of champagne-swilling Bohemians and the champagne-selling bourgeoisie so carefully inflicted on me, well, the answer is that I have not recovered, that treachery smoulders away somewhere deep inside me, and when I've drunk so much that the wound is laid bare, I really get down to work. I'm glad I'm going to Weimar, as I've challenged three people to a duel with pistols. I also feel the cold joy of power in that Germany is conquered for my art and at least that has fostered interest. I'm now to paint Count Kessler in Weimar and all that remains now is a commission from the Duke. I must say, if I am to be ruled, I would rather be ruled by a duke than by a common shopkeeper from Homannsbyen. The braying monkey Nils C. Vogt called Homannsbyen the launching pad for Norwegian girls out into the world. Your good health! I'm drinking white wine and eating oysters. In other words, everything is all right. You were so very nice this spring in connection with Miss Eva Mudocci. In parliament, Georg Sverdrup, in a serious debate about the union with Sweden, suddenly said Loving shepherd, eh? I'm painting and drawing and living with Eva M., but I'm not sure. Write something about this, can you. I'm a fugitive from a bloody battle.

* * *

Munch sells eight hundred graphic works at the exhibition in the Gesellschaft Hamburgischer Kunstfreunde. He has avoided having to sell his house at Åsgårdstrand by compulsory auction, thanks, among other things, to an advance of fifteen hundred marks from Cassirer.

He is now forty years of age, is going to paint *The Linde Frieze*, *Adam and Eve beneath the Apple Tree*, *Young Girl in the Garden*, *Count Harry Kessler* and *Dr Linde*, will print the etching *Washerwoman on the Shore*, as well as various prints and variations on earlier motifs.

It is now that he throws himself into the life of the bourgeoisie, counts and barons. He exhibits at the Sezession in Vienna, a city which will often devote a great deal of attention to him. He travels to Weimar and meets Count Prozor and his wife, visits this couple in a huge villa where they sit representing Russia in frock coats. He visits Nietzsche's sister, Frau Förster, in the house where the philosopher spent the last years of his life.

At least one letter a week is exchanged by Munch and Schiefler. After all the years in Germany, he now has influential friends who give him all possible backing. But he is not balanced, and there is reason to suppose that he has plenty of alcohol to hand, explaining to friends that it is necessary for painting pictures. At the end of February he is back in Paris, back to *her* city, which also became Milly Thaulow's city for a while.

* * *

When summer comes he is in Åsgårdstrand with friends, by the fireside, in the garden with a view of the sea, the shore below the house. The light which floods in, both from the sky and from the reflection of the

sky on the surface of the sea. Large quantities of alcohol. He can lie dozing in the sun for hours. Intoxicated, he can open the door to the studio,
where he always manages to work, as he smells the heady scent of the
jasmine.

Munch lives in a house, a cottage, a little château, which he has ironically called the home of happiness, where as time passes there are a fair
number of marks on the walls from revolver shots, where he recognizes
young girls who have grown a year older than last time, girls he can
paint and offer a painting in payment, but they are not interested. They
back away, preferring something pretty. At the same time, Cassirer
obtains a contract for Munch's graphic work in Berlin and Commeter
obtains a corresponding contract for Munch's paintings in Hamburg.
Schiefler continues his work on a catalogue of Munch's graphic art.

Åsgårdstrand with Petra Book, a conscientious young girl, daughter
of the gardener with the morello cherries, the one who later, in *The
Freia Frieze*, will be painted with a scythe. And also the more calculating holidaymaker Ingse Vibe, who knows how to catch men.

Åsgårdstrand, the town with four lame cobblers, where he can carry
paintings through the streets without attracting attention. As everyone
is on Munch the painter's side, even if they object to being offered daubings instead of money. Here there is a boat he can sail, like Odysseus, for
a change of perspective. He paints three cocky young lads sprawling on
the road right outside his own house, and observes a little girl standing
with her back to them, visibly uneasy and embarrassed by all the attention. In Åsgårdstrand there are people right outside the walls of his
house. It is another summer of photographs, experiments in the garden
with a self-timer in front of the huge picture entitled *Bathing Boys*, sun
and nakedness. Nothing concealed or covered up, everything laid bare.
He still has close-cropped hair. It makes him look vulnerable yet also
aggressive.

He has a revolver as a bookmark.

* * *

Dr Linde not only needs a portrait of himself in sailing dress, he needs
pictures for the four sons of the house, a frieze with motifs from the
Norwegian midsummer night.

Lieber Herr Munch: I'm very pleased that you already have some
sketches for the children's rooms, please choose children's themes, in
other words, themes which correspond to the life of a child, so no loving
couples or people kissing, children don't understand any of that. I had
thought it might be best to go for landscapes as they are neutral and
children themselves invent landscapes.

* * *

Christiania lies enveloped in a blue light. When the day is three hours

229

old, Munch sets up his easel in Studenterlunden near Rosenkrantzgate. The city seems deserted. Munch stands painting, sandwiched between his friends Ravensberg and Gierløff.

But people there are, hidden in narrow alleys, behind curtains, a group of four or five pale and, according to Gierløff, drunken youths comes along, they pause, sneer derisively, make sarcastic remarks as Munch concentrates on the tall poplars midway between Karl Johan and Stortingsgaten.

Suddenly there is a crowd. Floozies, tartish office girls and young ruffians are drawn to the place where Munch stands painting. The people of the night make offensive personal remarks about his artistic achievements. Munch acts like a magnet to the unbalanced. At last he is ready to work, but is surrounded by people who are ready to have a go at him with their bare fists. Munch realizes that trouble is brewing and wants to quit the scene with as little fuss as possible. Then PC 91 turns up, his helmet askew. He looks Munch straight in the eye, and as Munch subsequently finds it necessary to write in the paper: He addresses me discourteously and refuses to go away.

Piperviken police station. A sudden gust of wind. Munch spills oil paint on his clothes. Nothing really seems to make any impression on him. He has a picture in his head, is probably whistling the tune about Napoleon and his army as he observes a red-faced detective superintendent in the absent-minded manner which is a sure sign that a fresh motif is becoming visible to his inner eye.

Name and address are taken. Then he is discharged. Back out of the police station. Easel, painting and paint box. Munch has no intention of abandoning the task in hand. He returns to the poplars in Studenterlunden. The light can still be used. He intends to work until six o'clock. PC 91 stands on the pavement and observes him with rapt attention.

* * *

There has been an 'incident'.

He is already highly nervous, is able to write calmly to the newspaper albeit with trembling hand, explains the business in Studenterlunden to all and sundry, but does not feel more secure as a result of these events, recognizes the symptoms, must not fall now, may experience the same feeling of madness. What was it he had discussed with Nietzsche's sister in Weimar, a highly subjective experience of nature, how he can feel intense melancholy, for example in the spring, in the light, in the sun, the feeling that all other people are surrounded by life, but not him.

He comes to Dr Linde in Lübeck, has painted pictures featuring light, the light of the Norwegian summer night, but not light enough, has been told not to paint people kissing, no dark urges for four boys who are still innocently ignorant. Munch comes with parts of the frieze, with landscapes, a summer's day which has not yet had a couple of lovers in an embrace painted onto it, a frieze without sex or urges, blood-red skies or consumptive girls, adapted to suit an impossibly rich eye specialist and his four sons. Dr Max Linde, his kind benefactor, will in a few years get into serious financial difficulties and be forced to sell his extensive collection of contemporary art, including Rodin, Monet, Signac, Degas and Munch. But at this stage, in August 1904, he cannot use lack of money as a pretext. Nor can he offer any clear artistic justification when he later rejects Munch's proposed frieze, a work Munch had reckoned on receiving three thousand marks for, money he has already spent. Dr Linde will turn him down in the politest possible manner, regrettable, not suitable, no further justification than that. But here is the Norwegian summer night, and as Munch understands it this does not just mean poplars in Christiania, it means above all the scenes of his past in Åsgårdstrand, forest, shore and sea, and man and woman somewhere between the elements. Moonlit dance by the sea, the eternal dance, man and woman who find one another, two by two, some of them sad lonely ones, those who will not find love, others who do. Youth by the sea, boys and girls gazing intensely out towards the waves, perhaps not the most soothing illustrations for a middle-class nursery, girls lost in amorous yearning, swarthy men sitting close by, as though all are aware of the colossal forces somewhere between sea and forest.

In Dr Linde's grounds it is very warm. Munch can feel his host's eyes upon him. The peace at Dr Linde's home has so far done him good, but it is impossible to sit in the grounds among Rodin sculptures and enjoy himself now. Munch is presumably thinking about money, knows that he has lived on advances, the astronomical outlay on materials, something he has never been frugal with, and apart from that his lifestyle, the cafés, money to support the family, as well as Laura.

Money has never meant anything to him other than as a means to exist. He is frugal, a chest can serve as a sofa. Munch is planning an exhibition in Copenhagen on the first of September 1904. A retrospective. He sits in Dr Linde's grounds reading *Tyrihans*, three copies of which he has been sent from home, a cartoon of 'The Battle in Studenterlunden' and the poem 'June Night on Karl Johan', freely adapted from Edvard Munch, to the folk melody 'To Drive Water, To Drive Wood'. Munch reads about himself as a caricature in a satirical magazine. Dr Linde observes him with concern. He sees that Munch's ability to concentrate is weakening.

Don't meet your compatriots, he says. Try to stop drinking.

The following year he will write to Munch that the unpleasant effect of alcohol is that for a time the nerves are on edge as though they have been lashed by a whip. In the same letter he advises Munch to live in permanent abstinence.

* * *

August 1904. Dr Linde accompanies Munch to the boat. All the pictures for the Copenhagen exhibition are on board.

The boat glides out of the harbour. Evening descends over the sea.

It is golden, shimmering late summer.

At home they are excavating the Oseberg ship. Munch peers across at the Danish islands. What was it Eva Mudocci had written? Suddenly he thinks of Olav Tryggvason, King of Norway from 995 to 1000, the great-grandson of Harald the Fair-Haired. Over nine hundred years ago that king had sailed on Viking raids in these waters, exactly nine hundred and four years before he himself sailed north. Munch stands on deck and sees the sun set.

Olav Tryggvason, on his way from Vendland, in September of the year 1000 – his foes were called Svein Tjugeskjegg, Olof Skötkonung and Eirik, son of Håkon Jarl – would then be betrayed by his countrymen in league with Danes and Swedes. Murdered, destroyed, thanks to his new religious ideas.

Munch stands on the ship and keeps a weather eye open for the enemy. How many people are there, out there over the horizon, who wish *him* the same fate? He goes down to his bunk, feels uneasy, the rasping under his breast, the stabbing pain. It is the fear again. Is fear a substance, a metal? Munch lies in his bunk, with all his pictures on board, which he feels like a heavy mass filling his body. It rises slowly up to his heart.

He is aware of the slightest sound, the slightest creak the boat makes, he feels the swell, the rotations of the earth, the primeval rotations, up towards his heart. He tosses from side to side, thinks of Olav Tryggvason who sailed the same route and who was slain at the battle of Svolder, thanks to a conspiracy of Norwegians, Swedes and Danes. For new ideas. Then it was religion, Christianity, for which King Olav was prepared to die. Munch gazes out through the porthole. He can see the cliffs a long way off. But why is the captain heading straight for the cliffs? Is he mad? The boat must be on the wrong course! And the captain? Can't he see the cliffs? Doesn't he now what he's doing? Munch lies down again, tries to rein in his nerves. Closes his eyes. Straight for the cliffs. All he can see is the cliffs. Then he leaps up. His heart is pounding. He gets dressed at the double. Dawn is breaking in the east. He dashes up onto the bridge.

Hey, helmsman, we're heading straight for the cliffs!

* * *

Copenhagen. Munch goes ashore, sees that the crates of paintings have arrived and are standing there on the quay in the early morning light. It is only five o'clock. He checks that the crates are intact and goes along to the customs house. Formalities, papers, signatures. Then he walks into town, to Café Bernina. He feels he has hardly slept a wink. Now he takes a corner seat with coffee, bread and a dram.

The brandy helps. The day lies before him. Then Knut Hamsun walks in. The poet has been on the town. It is still very early. Hamsun walks across the floor without seeing Munch, who for his part and with a hint of *schadenfreude* notes that Hamsun is bow-legged. Munch calls him over. They drink a glass.

Why didn't you come to the wedding, Munch? I invited you. God damn it! Oh, by the way, Thomas Krag is here.

They sit chatting like this for a while. Then Hamsun leaves the table and goes off to get some sleep.

Munch goes on sitting there.

A big man with a black beard sits down beside him. A face he does not know. The fellow introduces himself. Haukland. The Norwegian poet Andreas Haukland. Oh yes. Munch recalls having read about his book, lambasted as smut, so he must be talented.

Please, let me treat you to a glass, says Munch.

They sit there in the Café Bernina, it is the twenty-third of August 1904. In a week's time Munch will present seventy-eight pictures at *Den fri* exhibition. Haukland is well away. Munch feels drawn to him, lambasted as smut, certainly very talented then. Munch tells him that he has come to Copenhagen to hold an exhibition.

I'll send you a ticket, Haukland. And I also buy your books by the way.

Haukland does not appear particularly interested.

Can you lend me a bit of cash, Munch?

Munch presses three crowns into his hand. Then he goes along to the gallery, sees that the crates of paintings have arrived and that all the preparations are going according to plan. After that he goes over to Rådhusplassen, to the pavement café outside the Hotel Bristol, takes a seat at a table. He suddenly feels very tired. It is now seven o'clock in the evening.

Then he recognizes Haukland's face.

The writer is drunk now. He takes a seat at the table. It is small. They sit close together. Munch feels that he can't be bothered to talk to the man any longer. He had an almost sleepless night on the boat, apart from which his thoughts are on his retrospective exhibition with over seventy pictures.

A withering blow to Munch's left eye. A fist with an iron ring on one finger.

Haukland lands him another punch.

Munch struggles to get up. More punches. Five or six iron-fisted punches. His hat goes flying across the pavement. Munch notices that his face is smeared in blood, running from eye, nose and mouth. He can't get a word out. Staggers backwards. People gather round. Someone calls the police.

Fight between Norwegian artists outside Hotel Bristol! The author Andreas Haukland attacks the painter Munch! *Politiken*, 24 August 1904: People sitting enjoying a coffee outside the Hotel Bristol at about 7 o'clock yesterday evening witnessed a very strange sight. At one of the tables sat two Norwegian gentlemen who to all appearances were quite peacefully enjoying a couple of Danish lagers. Suddenly one of them stood up and, with a well-aimed blow, sent his companion's top hat flying, following this up with a number of punches delivered with all his might straight into the victim's face. Mission accomplished, he calmly stuck his hands into his pockets and prepared to go on his way. The other gentleman, who had taken the beating with staggering composure, meanwhile struggled back onto his feet and was handed his battered hat by one of the waiters. Herr Wilkening, the proprietor, who arrived on the scene, on questioning the gentleman who had remained behind, was informed that his companion had struck him, a somewhat superfluous observation seeing that his face was streaming with blood.

* * *

The town hall bells are ringing. Munch sits at the Bristol talking to Gustav Essman who has reputedly himself been in a duel with Edvard Brandes, after he had gone to Helsingør and attacked his colleague with a dog whip. Essman, who will soon be shot at a literary *variété* at the Hotel Dagmar by a masked lady who then takes her own life.

Yes, well, says Essman. A bit of bloodletting's good for you. It happens in this city. Twenty fights a day. But mainly in the backstreets though, not on Rådhusplassen or in the big cafés.

The papers are full of headlines. The shock, the humiliation, the embarrassment. Norwegians in the metropolis. Mad Vikings. The Danish press has a field day. Isn't it high time the Norwegian colony put its house in order?

Munch drinks.

He recalls that the police had not let him wash his face. Smeared with blood, he had accompanied Haukland and a constable to the police station. A little boy had run along on the other side of them, fascinated and staring intently up at him.

Do you want Haukland arrested? the deputy chief constable had asked. No, Munch had replied. Just let him go.

Now Munch sits at the Bristol and knows that it is a week until the exhibition opens. But he has no energy to think about pictures now. He goes to his room and lies down to drink.

*

So, writes Hamsun in the paper, the case is closed. Haukland was fined forty crowns. However, the fact is that anyone who knows Haukland and Munch is convinced that the former would not have struck the latter unless he had given him some reason. Indeed, it is strange how difficult the painter Munch appears to find it to go about the world without coming into conflict with both private individuals and the police. And he a former State scholar, his name having for many years featured in the cultural budget. It rather depends on who mixes your red wine, how often it has happened and whether in jest or with malice aforethought. Now it could be that Haukland would have put up with far more from another, less imposing man than Edvard Munch before letting fly with his fist. The genius, the maestro, ought over the years to have learned to exercise angelic gentleness and patience in his dealings with everybody and absolutely not provoke a writer. His genius is fundamentally why in the past we have supported his inclusion in the cultural budget. Let us see a little something for our money!

*

It is a public analysis of Munch's personality. Hamsun tries to make out that it is really Munch who is the guilty party. At the time it was said that Munch's innocent eyes were wet with tears after the assault. Munch innocent? Munch in tears?

Then Krohg also takes up his pen, in *Verdens Gang*, under the headline 'One on the Nose':

> Not since Olav Tryggvason many years ago at the palace in Stockholm struck Sigrid Storråde in the face, has any of the innumerable similar acts since committed and committed now on a daily basis in the three Scandinavian countries achieved such notoriety as the blow administered by one Norwegian to another outside the Hotel Bristol in Copenhagen. The persecution of herr Haukland as a result of this minor event has attained huge personal proportions. It is an out-and-out witch-hunt.

*

Then Haukland also takes up his pen. In *Socialdemokraten* he writes: I have now lived in Copenhagen for a year. Throughout this time I have never caused any trouble whatsoever. Nor have I done so in Norway. Then I met Edvard Munch. When we were walking across Amager Square together, he suggested we should go into a wine bar there for a drink. I replied that I did not have time as I had to go up to an office to collect some money of mine there. He continued to press me and we went in. As we sat there, he absolutely insisted I accept a German five-mark piece as a loan from him. I said there was no need, as I was going up to the office anyway to get some money. But he absolutely insisted I should take it. So I put it in my pocket and went on my way. As I walked along, it occurred to me that Munch had told me that a man in Berlin once offered him a two-crown piece, and Munch said that he had taken it as the worst insult he had ever received in his life. It began to rankle with me that Munch had intended to insult me with the five-mark piece. Later that day I ran into him again outside the Bristol and gave him the five marks back. He then remarked that I probably needed it more than he did, which I took as an insult. The whole time we sat together on this occasion he was unpleasant. And when I mentioned my parents in passing, he spoke of them disparagingly. This was when I stood up and hit him. It was impetuous, but a shameful assault it was not.

*

Munch lies in bed drinking.

One day, two days. What is he to do? Pistols? A duel? Has to go to the exhibition. Opening in two days' time! Drewsen has promised to help him hang the pictures.

Finally he forces himself to go out. Into the gallery with his swollen face. He notices the looks. Everybody is eyeing him. They have read the papers. They know. A journalist turns up:

My God yes, I've been assaulted too, Munch. Don't let it get you down. By the way, can you lend me five crowns?

*

The exhibition's going to be good, says Drewsen.

What are we going to do about Haukland? says Munch.

Hmm, says Drewsen.

A duel with pistols, says Munch.

They walk about the gallery together. There hang all the pictures. Excellent. Looks excellent. But Munch can't concentrate. Punched in the face. Drewsen stands there talking to his fiancée. It's going to be brilliant, he says. Hope so, says Munch vaguely. But what am I going to do about Haukland? The pictures hang there in front of him. They no longer mean anything.

The Bernina, he says all of a sudden. We must go to the Bernina, Drewsen!

*

They sit in the cab. Munch and Drewsen. Munch has purchased a cane. But it is far too light. There was no sturdier one to be found.

236

Here he comes! shouts Drewsen suddenly. No, over there, Munch. On the other side, between Krag and another chap.

Munch follows Drewsen's gaze. Then he sees Haukland. Let me out! he says, nervously clutching the stick.

Careful, Munch!

Munch clutches the stick tightly. It is far too light, far too spindly. But he raises his arm and walks straight across the street. Haukland extends his hand.

Mr Munch, may I offer you an apology?

Munch hears what he says, has excellent hearing. An apology?

What? he says. Then he lashes out with the stick, one blow after another, but without any force.

Haukland wrests the stick from Munch and snaps it in two with his bare fists. Then he stops Munch in his tracks with a huge punch in the face.

His hat is sent flying over the pavement once again. Munch staggers. He is bleeding heavily.

Haukland dashes up the steps to the hotel.

Munch stands there flabbergasted and feels a stinging in the eye. Humiliated again. Drewsen comes over to him.

Why didn't you hit him harder, Munch?

* * *

Dear Aunt: You'll probably have been alarmed to hear of another little fracas. It's not as serious as it sounds. It was just a drunk who was rather unpleasant and who has been fined. I'm coming home in a week's time, maybe earlier.

*

Dear Edvard: Thanks for your card. We fully appreciate that you've had trouble with a drunk. We know you too well to believe what appears in the newspapers. We do think it was awful that you laid into him later, but he must have insulted you on that occasion too. But don't get involved in any more fights! We're quite sure you didn't speak ill of his parents. Nothing could be less like you. You must do your level best to calm down and not get worked up about all this tripe that they write. We don't take any notice of it, but we've been terribly worried at the thought of your being exposed to such awful things. Your devoted Karen Bjølstad.

*

The exhibition in Copenhagen. Seventy-eight pictures, *Politiken* writes that Munch's pictures are drawing more people than any other one-man exhibition in the city.

The Danish critics: He is trying to scream, to let out a full-throated yell. But all we get in these paintings is a throttled croak, so that almost everything in them quivers in a kind of incredibly turgid paralysis, which confuses, tires and irritates the spectator. *Scream* is, no mistake about it, an artistic howler of the first rank. It is on that painting's flaming red clouds that some tactless individual has written in pencil: could only have been painted by a madman.

*

But Munch has already left town. Away from the humiliation. Home to Norway, to Åsgårdstrand. Fruit on the trees. Vegetables in the soil.

Back to the land of the Vikings. He was not slain at the battle of Svolder. He came back home. To Åsgårdstrand.

Just a stone's throw away they are excavating the Oseberg ship. Back to the past. This is how his uncle, the historian P. A. Munch, had researched forgotten things. Suddenly they became visible again.

Munch walks over to Oseberg and watches the Viking ship emerge from its clay grave near Vadlastrøm, by the edge of the moraine, the long ridge of glacial boulders. A ship which lies in clay soil, with oars sticking out on both sides, ready to put to sea. Munch walks about in the past, talks nineteen to the dozen among people he feels at ease with, feeds them his own theories about the Viking age, about the Oseberg ship, lives in what he will later call the only nice house he has ever lived in.

* * *

Dear Aunt: I was in Horten when the earthquake struck. I was on the first floor of a hotel, still in bed. I had the impression that the bed had suddenly started to slide. It's hard to explain all the strange sensations as the quaking increased, but I shot out of bed and when there was a huge crack, a creaking and groaning in all the beams, I thought the house was going to collapse and was almost on the point of dashing outside half-dressed. Still, I carried on getting dressed. On the roof I could hear the rattle of falling masonry and I looked out of the window thinking it was a hurricane. Yet the sea was calm. A dog howled as though possessed. At last I had got my clothes on. And it was all over. Everywhere the town was in a commotion. I walked to Åsgårdstrand. Everywhere chimneys had fallen down. Here in Åsgårdstrand of course everybody thinks that the end of the world is nigh.

* * *

Munch exhibits ninety paintings at the Diorama. Eighteen subjects from the contemporary life of the soul. Also five lithographs and drawings.

Eva Mudocci is in town too. She is interviewed in the newspaper by Christian Krohg. Munch is too tired to meet her. He is possessed by the thought of frøken L. The miserable conspiracy which has destroyed him. Everywhere he meets people, and his bile rises. He realizes that cities are not good for him.

Later, Eva Mudocci writes from Paris:

I've sent you a letter. As you don't write, I'm not sure you've received it. With all my heart I wish you would write. It would have been good to know that you're still my friend, that you don't believe lies about me, just as I don't believe any ill of you. Please do write, I consider you my friend, write to me please. Eva.

*

At the same time as the exhibition at the Diorama, Jens Thiis is on show at the Hals brothers' gallery and gives a lecture on Munch's art to a half-empty hall.

Under the headline *The Truth about Munch*, Vårt Land writes:

How can they have the audacity to present us with such stuff! How is it that there is not a howl of indignation at the breathtaking effrontery? For it is nothing less than effrontery when we are offered stuff such as this. Edvard Munch's exhibition is the most insolent, most pitiful, most preposterous that the Decadents have put on so far. And that is saying something. What are we to make of this chaos of poisonous colours, of crude and yet childishly contorted figures? Is this to say that there is nothing praiseworthy in these many pictures? Yes, for in this exhibition there is categorically *nothing*. There is not a line, not a form which is properly caught, not a colour which does not jar. As for composition and narrative, the less we say about those the better. Apart from being devoid of talent, his art is so provocative and full of ballyhoo that one is simply bound to protest. This is the truth about Edvard Munch, and anyone who cannot see it is blind.

* * *

Munch goes back to Germany. He has not seen Aunt Karen and his sister Inger in Christiania, nor visited Laura.

Dear Aunt: I caught a touch of influenza when the north-east wind set in. I didn't forget your birthday, but didn't manage to get a letter off to you in time. I'm travelling down to Dr Linde with his frieze. That miserable woman has also made sure I haven't been able to profit in peace from the luck I've had. It's the same old story with this woman: the haves shall steal from the have-nots, and take even the last lamb.

He comes to Lübeck with the frieze. It cannot have occurred to him that it really will be rejected. The specialist's wife may perhaps find the subject matter too gloomy. Rumours about the set-to in Copenhagen may have blackened his name. In any case, he does not receive the money he had been expecting. He sits dejected in Dr Linde's grounds. Turned down! And by his own patron!

The rages become more and more frequent. If he could only control

239

himself. Drink has had a calming effect and still does so in the morning. But in the afternoon, whereas before he used to become heavy and drowsy, he now works himself up into a state.

Aunt Karen writes from Nordstrand before Christmas:

> You've been ever so kind, Edvard, especially with all the serious problems you've had to cope with. You sent money, so I was often very anxious that you might be getting yourself into difficulties, and you asked me in a letter to go to Dr Arentz. You asked me most insistently to do this to collect your credit with him. And you desperately needed it yourself. Oh yes, I can think of a lot of examples, I've kept all your letters which show what a difficult time you had becoming known, so it has certainly cost a great deal to make a breakthrough. Tonight there's such beautiful moonlight here. There is such a lovely view from the windows, Bundefjord is down below us. It must also be quite strange to see the old city of Lübeck by moonlight. The ships in the harbour. Our thoughts were with you a lot on the twelfth. Perhaps you'd forgotten it. Now Christmas Eve is fast approaching. Happy Christmas from your devoted Karen Bjølstad.

*

Christmas in Lübeck. Christmas in a brothel. He hides away in filthy dives surrounded by women for sale. Turned down by his patron, though still receiving board and lodging. He paints a new self-portrait, reads in the papers that New York is to have skyscrapers. More frequently he notices small episodes of numbness. Especially during the night. His legs and arms go numb.

That wretched woman. It's as if she's behind everything. Frøken L. The red-haired one. It was her fist in Copenhagen, her words in the newspaper, her doing, the rejection of the frieze. A conspiracy. What rumours she has spread! He needs alcohol, needs money. What is Dr Linde's reason for his rejection? So his wife can sleep peacefully at night, or a conspiracy? Someone has ruined his reputation, sown doubts about his morality. The very idea that he could have sponged off her. Off her! She who has robbed him of his peace of mind, his concentration, his equilibrium. That period when she plagued him to death. He was ill, she had asked him to come. He had used up everything he had been paid by the gallery. Three thousand crowns. Had no money left. Let her pay when she asked him to come. What rumours has she spread? He has been in Berlin. Hotel Stadt Riga, Mittelstrasse. Has seen Kollmann again. Then Lübeck once more. Bourgeois peace. Vast grounds with Rodin sculptures. A dissatisfied patron and his lady wife. Not up to the mark. Something wrong with the pictures, or with him personally.

Then he suddenly goes to Hamburg, leaving behind a crate of graphic prints which Schiefler has his eye on. Giebfrieds Hotel, Koppel 9. He celebrates New Year's Eve with fireworks, champagne corks, more alcohol. It is now 1905. There is a terrible storm in the Baltic, ten people perish. Munch has rented a tasteless single hotel room. The beginning of a new year. What was the previous one like? Even the finest nerves are affected.

He drinks with Giebfried. A wreck in the morning. Fills himself with alcohol. A sudden attack. Does not calm down as time passes, as he used to. He demolishes the room in the evening, believes he is being attacked by his compatriots.

From the street he hears voices. Who is that talking? Does he hear the name Munch? Is that Munch they are saying? His own name? Is it the dog's voice he hears? The whining poodle? He goes down to the hotel café, sees there are many serious drinkers there. Giebfried talks about his wife who is in a sanatorium. Apparently she has DTs. Munch does not remember how he eventually lands back in his own bed.

But he awakens the following day and knows he has an appointment. He has accepted a commission to paint the portrait of a lady. Fräulein Warburg. What he will later call one of his best pictures. An excellent picture. He paints it in the space of two mornings. Completed in five hours.

As he paints he keeps his spirits up with alcohol. Fräulein Warburg stands before him in a white dress. Munch paints calmly and straightforwardly, with rapid brush strokes. A fine job, he says to himself. One of the best.

Then he goes back to the hotel. He spends the evening with an American doctor. In the restaurant, Giebfried has a little canary in a cage. It sings all the time. Munch suddenly becomes livid. Violent hallucinations. When he recovers consciousness he is lying on the floor and looking straight up at the faces of Giebfried and the doctor.

The doctor looks at him anxiously.

This is going to end badly, Mr Munch.

Munch gets up and looks about him. He is surrounded by broken furniture. Upholstery in tatters everywhere. Kaiser Wilhelm's bust lies in smithereens on the floor.

*

The next morning he is wakened by Giebfried, who brings him some port.

Drink up, Munch. It'll calm you down.

He feels the numbing effect, knows that he must get to work again, put the finishing touches to the picture of the banker's daughter,

Fräulein Warburg. When he has finished, he has his picture taken in front of the portrait, with glazed eyes.

In the evening, he visits Schiefler. For Twelfth Night his children are putting on a performance in picturesque costumes. Schiefler notes that the performance makes surprisingly little impression on Munch. The painter is lost in his own world.

Later that evening he goes to the hotel. The thought of Tulla Larsen hits him with full force. Should she be allowed to destroy him totally? He went to her from his sanatorium bed because she said it was a matter of life and death. He had also wanted her to reflect a little about his situation. Above all he wanted peace. She had coughed up blood, she said. In Munch's case things were very tight at home. A sister in a mental asylum. A brother's help was certainly needed. She had ruined two years. Munch sits at Giebfried's getting himself more and more worked up with drink.

Button up your waistcoat, says his fat host out of the blue.

I'll leave my waistcoat as it is, Munch replies.

Button up your waistcoat.

Another voice this time. The captain's. The one who will probably accompany the Emperor to Morocco.

Button up your waistcoat, Mr Munch!

Munch flares up. How dare he? Come outside! he shouts, fuming with rage.

They stand outside the hotel entrance. Munch is holding a fist under the captain's nose. He could have hit him now. Given him a good thrashing. The captain takes out a card and hands it to him. Leaves the scene without so much as a word. Giebfried comes out into the street, hands Munch his overcoat and orders him: Out!

He walks out into the streets of Hamburg, wanders aimlessly about, looking for an open café. Brandy. Great waves of rage surge through him. He finds a place. Drinks brandy. Afterwards, he makes for the Alster Pavilion. Finds another café. More brandy. Finally sits dozing over a glass.

Dawn starts to break. Munch goes back to Giebfried. Now he lets him in.

He collapses into bed, sleeps until late morning.

Giebfried wakens him with port. Munch begins to rouse himself.

You're challenged to a duel, says Giebfried. The captain has left for Morocco, but he'll be back in a couple of months.

Nonsense, says Munch. I just lost my temper, that's all.

Giebfried looks at him anxiously.

Drop him a few lines, he says at last. Apologize. That should do the trick.

A visiting theatre group, *Judith* by Hebbel. He is murdered by the
woman. Interesting. Ibsen must have learnt from him. Munch in
Hamburg. On the binge for three days, yet painting one of his best portraits ever. He has written to the captain. An unreserved apology. He
asks the captain to understand that the whole thing was the result of
illness. He is tired and weak. Tries to remember everything that happened, but can't get the sequence of events straight. He realizes he must
get away.

*

A portrait exhibition in Berlin at Cassirer's. Munch receives an advance
on the sales. Commeter and Cassirer are big names in the German art
gallery world. But the former is a disappointment. He cannot sell
Munch's pictures.

Otherwise there is progress on every front. Great progress. He is
invited to Prague. A result of his breakthrough in Vienna. He exhibits
seventy-five paintings and fifty graphic works. He will assume decisive
importance for such artists as Gerstel, Schiele and Kokoschka. He is
revered as the great master by the young artists of Bohemia. A mystic
with a barbarian instinct. A very important painter. But the general
euphoria leaves him cold. He does not see. Does not hear. He has got an
idea. A play, *The City of Free Love*. On the tenth of February he writes
to Ravensberg from Berlin, requesting the following notice in *Verdens
Gang*, which he dubs 'The Enemies' Newspaper', because all Tulla
Larsen's friends write for it:

> 'Besides painting, Edvard Munch has also devoted time to litera-
> ture. He has already completed a comedy. It is called *The City of
> Free Love*. The plot is that a poor bard and a rich princess both
> hear about The City of Free Love at the same time, which leads to
> a great many comic complications.' This is penned and signed by
> the maestro in Prague, 10 February, anno 1905. I think this little
> notice will nettle these people a bit.

The City of Free Love. A play by Edvard Munch.

> The Bard has roamed through many lands, is wearied by grievous
> sufferings, thirsty after lying in the arms of love and being warmed
> by its fires. The great passion he has sought in vain. Thus begins
> the play about The Bard and the Dollar Princess, which is accom-
> panied by drawings of the other protagonists, various sorts of ani-
> mal: pigs, dogs, tigers, kangaroos, queen bees and witches. Munch
> gives vent to all his hatred in a caricature, the play about The City
> of Free Love, where the Dollar Princess reigns supreme, where

they carouse all night and sleep all day, where marriage can be arranged without a priest or any other nonsense, where, moreover, marriage does not last more than three years under pain of punishment, and where marriage can also be contracted for two or three days. The city where the lap pig, the spitting image of Gunnar Heiberg, is gilded and carried about like a pet god. Ladies are allowed to take turns at holding it in their laps. The Dollar Princess, who could just as easily have been the daughter of a wine merchant, declaims:

Oh piggy sweet/How can we meet/The price you bear/Is much too dear/A thousand crowns we cannot meet.

The Dollar Princess is not without her charms for the poor Bard. But he is ill, lies writhing in agony with diarrhoea, asks the nurse for a chamber pot, cannot embrace the Dollar Princess!

I'm ill. Don't touch me!

The Princess becomes hysterical, white as a sheet with scorn and indignation. The bard is ruining her love life.

Oh woe is me – but are we not in the City of Freedom? Is love not free?

Then the pig comes in with a chain: Tie him to the Dollar Princess!

But the Bard snaps the chain and makes off. Then preparations are made for a procession in the town square. The poet, Billygoat Gruff, witches burned at the stake, various trade unions: the cuckolds', the drunkards', the politicians' and, not least, the bastards' union, all led by the pig: Dear friend, lend me your wife and I'll free you from strife. Boo hoo hoo, is all the Dollar Princess can manage, adding that fond embraces are no longer to her liking unless she can have revenge. Revenge on the Bard who would have none of her! She kisses the pig and strokes the kangaroo. All beg money from her:

Dear maid, lend me a crown and you can sit on my throne.

And the Princess generously hands out money as the queen bee puts forward proposals for revenge. For she knows that the Bard is said to be so very kind-hearted. They therefore set a trap: the Dollar Princess lies down as though dying and screams for help, they dig a grave in front of her, he then falls into the grave and is killed.

The Dollar Princess claps her hands, ecstatic with joy because the Bard – an artist – is suffering the torments of unhappy love for *her* sake. Meanwhile the Bard, who has fallen into the grave, says: Yes, by all that is dear, it was an unhappy love.

The play continues with a lunch in honour of the polar explorers, a lunch costing sixty thousand crowns, consisting of twenty dishes and twenty types of wine from P. A. Larsen's wine cellar. But the Bard has no money to buy any food and tries to get back ten crowns which the Chairman of the Discovery of the North Pole had once borrowed from him. This proves difficult. It is pointless making any demands unless one is a member of some union or association.

The play now becomes a paraphrase of Norway's situation before the dissolution of the Union. War against Sweden, to be or not to be? The Pig and the Dog, in other words, Heiberg and Bødtker, whip up the mood:

We want war! We want war!

Meanwhile the Bard is arrested by the chief of police, has created a stir in the street, made a mess on the pavement, besmirched the ladies and gentlemen of the city with his blood. He is an anarchist and a danger to those around him. There is a trial. The Bard is accused of having kissed the Dollar Princess, of *not* having kissed the Dollar Princess, of not having wanted to chain himself to the Dollar Princess, he has fallen into a grave and engaged in indecent behaviour, on the same occasion shouted, splashed blood on various ladies' clothes. Everyone in the courtroom cries out:

Shame, shame, he dared to humiliate the woman!

The judge asks: Why did you not marry her? The Bard replies: I lay with her because I did not want to marry.

Then the modern Moses speaks, is summoned to give counsel in the difficult case. By his horns and his beard it is plain for all to see that couples first lie with one another and when tired of one another they marry.

The Bard thus recognizes that the freedom to love is confined to women alone.

There then follows a paraphrase of *Lovely the Earth Is*.

* * *

Dear Munch, As you will see, your stay in Prague is described by *Verdens Gang*. Everyone has seen the article and is talking about it, so I think it's doing you some good. Well, it must have been fun for you to be down there and meet with understanding and respect in all quarters. Here of course the chosen ones are few, yet I still believe there are more of them than you think. I often meet quite young people who enthuse about you unaware that we're good friends and who, it turns out, have great understanding of your works and are very fond of them to boot. I think you attach too much importance to what a few mean-spirited editors and a few down-and-out hacks think and write. Times have changed. Now people don't say a word when your name crops up. So there has visibly been a great change for the better. I only hope you're not embittered. I gather you see T.L. in Heiberg's play *Love's Tragedy*. That's something that never occurred to me even once. I think it was Oda the whole time. Fru Dybwad was the spitting image of her and Eide did his utmost to look like Obstfelder. This was according to Gunnar Heiberg's specific wishes. He had even asked Eide to come up here and ask to see your lithograph of him. And there can hardly be any doubt that it is the tragedy of their own love. Now we're looking forward to summer and to coming to visit you at Åsgårdstrand. It would be fun if you painted my picture again. Thanks for the photograph. It's excellent, even if you aren't wearing the expression I'm fondest of in you. You look a bit stern, which is not always the case. Well, do take care of yourself and keep on writing. It's so nice to hear from you. Greetings from Harald. The children are asleep. Yours Åse Ng.

*

Sick and nervous Munch returns to Hamburg. The cold joy of success is no match for the despair. His nerves are still taut. He is drinking steadily, is troubled by insomnia.

Schiefler invites him to dinner. Munch arrives early, is very tired, is offered a sofa in Schiefler's office. When the steak is ready, Schiefler writes in his diary, Munch comes and sits slightly away from the table, not until the dessert does he move nearer. Schiefler takes it as a sign of his nervous shyness that Munch needs time to feel at ease.

He has brought further graphic prints for Schiefler's catalogue. The old motifs from the past, from Åsgårdstrand. Schiefler relates that Munch loses himself in memories. Many minutes' silence between every sentence, as together they examine the prints, people on the shore, the *Kiss* motif, *Two People*. The unutterable loneliness in a scene from nature.

Schiefler has great empathy with Munch's art and an understanding of what drives him. He invites him to the opera to see *Carmen* and to the Schauspielhaus to see *Frau Doré*.

Munch tells Schiefler about his affair with Tulla Larsen, but is so agitated and nervous that Schiefler cannot follow him. At dinner in Schiefler's family home he makes a violent attack on womankind in general, nevertheless taking care not to insult his hostess.

* * *

Must have peace. His one and only thought. He takes the steamer to Kristiansand wishing to return home to Åsgårdstrand, to his own house.

It is 1905. Amalie Skram dies. Boström's dependent nation principles. The break between the governments of Norway and Sweden on the seventh of February. The Special Commission. Then Christian Michelsen's new coalition government. Løvland in Stockholm, the dispute about special consular status for Norway. The question of

Norwegian independence, the impending threat of war. The war of defence. The pig or toad Heiberg is a warmonger, together with Nørregaard, Admiral Sparre, Castberg, Georg Stang.

Meanwhile Munch ends up with the roué Thomas Stang in Kristiansand. A supply of alcohol. High spirits at the club. Hysteria of another kind. The hysteria of nationalism. The hysteria of the Separation. A general booze-up for the cause of Norway. Jingoistic cries late into the night. Munch with friends who suppress his own neuroticism, but do not cure it.

* * *

One spring morning he awakens in Åsgårdstrand. The whole garden is in bloom. Dazzling white cherry trees. Lush green grass, a light blue fjord.

The whole town is festooned with posters. The Union with Sweden is dissolved. Everything they had yearned for but not dared to believe in.

Munch gets out of bed. His heart is pounding. The alcohol courses through his veins.

Then people start thronging to his house, the painter Karsten, the only person he can really call his pupil, who has hung around him the last few summers, and frøken Vibe, who is scarcely a nubile young thing any longer, but a woman with lovers, including a philanderer from the border guards and also an actor.

Munch is nervous about how he is going to behave. Just so long as nothing happens. No attack of rage now. Excited, ecstatic people are coming with talk of freedom, with talk of war. Karsten is certain that, if war it is, he will join up.

Munch listens. He has not been in a war, never did his military service. At that time he had one haemorrhage after another, he feels bound to explain, was too weak. But you can plainly see the bullet holes in the wall, he is a good shot, has shot off a finger, he's a sniper, ha ha, so he can shoot but not fight. In a war he would be no use. If he were to fall, he would not be able to stop himself.

Munch's speech is disjointed and nervous, he is drowned out by the others. The thing is not to drink too much. The others sit there chattering and drinking. Should they enlist? Now then, Munch, are you going to enlist? Ingse Vibe laughs. He has told Schiefler about this young woman who had often visited him in the studio. Suddenly it became too much, Munch tells Schiefler. It seems he had thrown her out. But then she became so insistent and pressing that she had put her foot in the door so he couldn't close it. In other words, completely the opposite of the story going the rounds in town, that Munch, dressed up to the nines, had invited her to a party, that she had presented herself, but there had not been any party after all. Just the two of them, that at one point he had asked her whether she would marry him, saying: an old man and a young woman can produce very gifted children. Now she is back in Munch's living room, in the little room with the stove and the bed. The sun is sparkling down on the fjord, everywhere fruit trees are in blossom. Munch feels the anxiety, knows that he must not have too much to drink. So Karsten is going to enlist if there is war.

Then the party sets out in a boat across the fjord, making for the hotel on Larkollen. Munch is at the helm. He sees Ingse sitting there surrounded by all her suitors, the actor, the border guard. Her yellow curls blow about in the southerly wind.

They go ashore on the other side of the fjord, enter the hotel and sit in a room next to the dining room. Munch will not go in. He says he is shy, afraid of people.

But the bell rings for dinner. Munch hears the sound of the chairs. It is the middle classes taking their seats. The sound of knives and forks, of voices.

Then he gets up, curious about who is in there. Someone he knows perhaps. But he is afraid to go in. He bends down and peeps through the keyhole.

A push from behind.

Ingse's foot.

Munch goes flying into the room, falls with a crash onto the floor, tries to stop himself with his hands, feels a shooting pain, hears Ingse's laughter somewhere behind him. He feels as if he might faint.

Then he sees the row of faces frozen in amazement.

In a fury he grabs hold of Ingse Vibe, throws her across his knee, spanks her over and over again, does not come to his senses until he notices that everyone is standing round him wide-eyed with shock.

Oh my God. I've done it again!

Another attack. He's gone too far. A new scandal. Yet another subject for gossip. Has tanned Ingse Vibe's bare behind, laid into a lady.

An attack. What do people really know about attacks?

* * *

Munch stands in the garden and does his best to paint bright, spring pictures, seventh-of-June pictures. Tries to calm down, to paint fruit trees and flowers.

But he is not alone. Karsten is there too. The talented Karsten, his only self-confessed pupil.

Strange chap, that Karsten. The large broad-brimmed hat, always at a rakish angle. An irresistible subject. A full-length painting of Karsten with white suit and pipe and a hand in one pocket. The playful expression. His mouth forming some gibe or other.

Then Munch suddenly realizes just what they had been saying, he has not done military service, has not been a soldier, but he has shot, three years ago he used to do a lot of shooting, shot at the wall in the next room, shot into the beam by the hearth, shot off two fingers, could shoot off the head of a nail from ten metres.

Shall I shoot the cigarette out of your mouth? he says all of a sudden.

Why not? Karsten answers and stands ready.

They stand in the garden, Munch takes aim from six metres away.

Then he shoots, knows he will hit the mark, shoots at Karsten's face, from six metres away, shoots the cigarette out of his mouth.

Brave chap, Karsten!

Afterwards he thinks: madness.

They persecute a man until he goes mad, then they exclaim: he is mad. But Karsten does not exclaim anything. He just stands there. Munch feels the fear, the heaviness that rises from below, will rise right up to his heart. Later, in a clinic in Copenhagen, he will point to a spot and say: there!

Karsten and Müller. One whisky and soda after another. What's Karsten talking about?

The impending war. The war with Sweden. To defend the nation against a superior power. The war of defence.

People must enlist. Karsten enlists. Müller enlists. Why doesn't Munch enlist?

Now, Munch, aren't you going to join up? The war, Munch. It could be any day now. Aren't you going to join up?

One whisky and soda after another. The little room, Karsten, Müller and Munch. Munch sits, head bowed, hearing the questions being fired at him. What is he to say? Hasn't he explained this before? Then Karsten takes a bottle, lifts it and makes as though to strike Munch's head, but stops just short, repeating this action over and over again.

You're not going to join up with us? Are you afraid, Munch?

Munch takes Karsten by the shoulders, propels him towards the door, pushes him out through the door which opens onto the garden and the fjord, the only door he uses, as the door into the street is always firmly locked. Now it is Karsten who is on his way out, over the little veranda with the steep steps. Munch writes that he thinks of his left arm, must protect his hand, take precautions. He propels Karsten before him, his mouth no longer about to make some gibe. Munch tries to push him off the veranda, down the steep steps, but Karsten is holding on to him. Down they both fall, first down the steps and then down the steep, stone-strewn slope leading down to the fjord. There they lie; Karsten, in a white suit, tries to get up. Munch gets up first. He raises his foot, kicks Karsten in the eye with his left heel, feels the pain in his left hand, crushed, broken.

Karsten staggers out of the garden in his white suit, blood pouring from his eye. Müller follows him. Munch walks up the steps and back into the house. Feels a violent pain in his hand. He sees Karsten and Müller come up to the window facing onto the road, Karsten in white, Müller in black. It is a June night, the trees are in blossom. Munch is seething with rage, can see nothing but the two men who are standing outside the window.

Then he goes to fetch a shotgun. He loads it and pushes the barrel through the window shattering the glass. His finger is on the trigger, he shouts, threatens, shakes with fury.

Müller stands in front of Karsten. Then they slowly retreat along the road.

Munch is alone with himself again. He puts the shotgun down on the bed.

That's the last straw. His hand is hurting. Not even Åsgårdstrand is a viable proposition any longer. He knows that sooner or later it will all go wrong. He must get away, now, immediately.

He travels to Copenhagen.

* * *

Lieber Hr. Landrichter Schiefler! I'd like to have shown you the journal of my crimes. In it I openly describe my state of mind and how I cope with it, how reason and will are eclipsed and another will takes me over. It seems to be that when alcohol weakens the first will, blind instinct takes over, and I live in my fantasies, always thinking I'm confronted with the same enemies as harmed me before. I've tried everything I can to control this, but with no success. So I must try something else. Ihr ergebener Edv. Munch.

* * *

The referendum on Norwegian independence on the thirteenth of August shows that 368,208 voted in favour of the Government's position, with a hundred and eighty-four votes against. No women were allowed to vote.

Dear Aunt: Thanks for your letter. I can well imagine that it has been an exhausting time for you all recently. It looked as though there might be war any minute. Now things look better, but one can't really be sure. I must say I've seldom been so surprised as when the news came that the king had been sent packing and the country was free. It is also miraculous that there wasn't war immediately. It has made a strong impression everywhere abroad. The fact that it all went off just as smoothly as dismissing a kitchen maid, a very stylish revolution, the Danes are saying. But this approval and the little smile from abroad have also deeply wounded the Swedes, which is scarcely surprising after all. Nor is it surprising that they should do something to save face. Thank you for the flag and the book. I hoisted the flag when our warships anchored off Åsgårdstrand, flags flying from every vantage point. The flag covered almost the entire house as the flagstaff was so small. I had to leave Åsgårdstrand as too many people turned up. Wouldn't the two of you like to come and stay in my house? The garden is full of berries. You'll find a way to get in somehow. Since I have the key, you'll somehow or other have to break open the door, I need a new lock anyway. There are a lot of letters there which I know you two won't read. Put them away so no one else can see them. There are also books which a gentleman of a certain age might read, but which would probably be rather strong stuff for Inger, nervous as she is, e.g. *From The Christiania Bohemians* and *Sick Love*. Take care of these, will you, Aunt. There are heaps of berries, I hope. I had a word with Fridtjof Nansen. He thought everything would turn out all right. It's not a bad idea to make some concessions to the Swedes. The whole thing has been amazing I think. Never before has anyone obtained their freedom without blood-letting. I'm only afraid the Swedes may trick us, as they did before. Here I'm managing to relax. I feel well. I shall probably rent a house in the country in Germany. I need to get away from that nasty business and from the Bohemians and have a really long rest.

* * *

Munch in Denmark. A refugee. He will stay away from Norway and Åsgårdstrand for four years. He is bent upon curing once and for all what, in a letter to his aunt, he terms the nervous prostration which has built up over many years. And she writes that it is clear that his nerves need to be brought under control systematically after so many years of painful persecution.

It's a sheer miracle that you haven't buckled under, she writes. There is a higher force.

Aunt Karen, who regrets that Norway did not declare itself a republic, and who supports Munch in everything he elects to do, even if this means that she almost never sees him.

Munch prepares for exile. He opens an exhibition in Copenhagen, in Amagertorv. In *Politiken* he reads that it is already a long while since the Norwegian painter Edvard Munch caused a stir. If people still feel anything for him, it is probably disgruntlement at the fact that he no longer gives them the cheap thrill of feeling annoyed. In Copenhagen at any rate there is great indifference towards him, so great indeed that it is possible to visit his exhibition in Amagertorv without encountering a single person in front of his paintings. By virtue of their ever more unfinished, not so say shoddy condition, his paintings are still among the most provocative works modern art has to offer. And also, alas, among the most depressing. As everyone knows, it was his folly to seek to portray the unseeable. Feelings, thoughts, expressions and dreams in shapes and colours, with neither basis nor model in reality, but which exhausted reality by virtue of symbolic naïveté. He did not pull off this miracle. He was not a god, not even a genius.

*

The review in *Politiken* is painstakingly edited and reproduced in *Aftenposten*. An obituary. Edvard Munch is laid to rest as an artist in Copenhagen, as rumours abound at home that he has done a bunk from the political upheavals, fled like a coward from the threat of war.

* * *

In autumn 1905 he is back in Germany. He will paint Esche's children in Chemnitz, three portraits for three thousand marks, while the wild animals, the Fauves, are exhibiting their work in Paris, Henri Matisse among them, with a new, powerful style, strong bright colours and clear-cut contours.

Munch is living in Thüringen, not far from Weimar, where he has many friends. Frau Elisabeth Förster Nietzsche, Graf Kessler, Van der Velde, Professor Auerbach and his wife. He paints the portrait of Friedrich Nietzsche, monumental yet decorative, portrays him as the poet of Zarathustra among the mountains, in his cave. He stands on his veranda and looks down into a deep valley, as the blazing sun rises in the sky. According to Munch he stands in light, but wishes to be in darkness.

Munch in Thüringerwald, hoping that the mountain air will be beneficial to his nerves, sudden numbness in his feet, arms and tongue, the feeling that it will get worse, until his whole side is paralysed. Then it will be his arms, then his tongue, then death.

*

The Death of Marat.
Munch and Tulla Larsen, autumn 1902.
In the summer of 1793, the twenty-five-year-old Charlotte Corday killed the French revolutionary leader Marat, killed him with a knife as he sat in the bathtub.

Munch paints *Still Life/The Murderess* and later *The Death of Marat*: a woman stands naked, with red hair, a bowl of fruit on the table, just as at Åsgårdstrand three years earlier. The man lies covered in blood, slain on the bed.

*

Munch wants to see a bull slaughtered, wants, as he puts it, to experience the event *through every pore*. He accompanies the slaughterer into the cowshed, sees a well-fed animal which the slaughterer embraces, all the while addressing it as *chéri*. Munch feels minor symptoms. Numbness.

The slaughterer leads the huge beast into the place of execution. Munch watches the slaughterer thread a rope through an iron ring in the ground, tie the end round the bull's horn and pull. The bull falls to its knees, its head forced to the ground, two great dark eyes look out into the room.

Munch sees a hammer with a long shaft, hears a dull blow, sees the same pair of eyes as the blood pours from its head, watches the slaughterer take an iron pole and thrust it into the hole in the bull's head, watches him rotating it in the bleeding brain.

The Death of Marat. The doomed bull.

The slaughterer takes a dagger and plunges it into the animal's heart. A thick stream of blood gushes out. The slaughterer holds a glass under it and then drinks the warm blood.

Munch paints the bloody Marat, himself as a corpse, Tulla Larsen as the murderess, paints Tulla Larsen seen through Arne Kavli's eyes. Woman as the pillar of salt, and the bowl of fruit, like a still life by Cézanne, and the woman's many hats.

The slaughterer slits open the bull's stomach. Intestines, heart and kidneys are taken out. The head is cut off. The skin is removed. The fat and tallow show up white and pale yellow, the meat red and blue-violet.

What's that moving there by the backbone?

Munch sees a little white string, moving rhythmically back and forth like a beating pulse.

Just nerves, says the slaughterer.

* * *

He receives a letter from Eva Mudocci and writes back.

Liebe Eva: I was so glad to hear from you. I wrote for some time but did not receive any reply, tell me how things are with you, what you are doing, are you painting, playing the piano, are you happy? Are you engaged? Is Paris beautiful? Have you seen Delius? I do not hate the people you think I do, the ones I hate above all are a lot of Norwegians who have been despicable towards me; you've spent quite a lot of time in the enemy camp, by the way. *Dein alter Freund Edvard Munch.*

*

She replies straight away.

Lieber Edvard Munch: Your letter came today! And I'm so happy, I've read it over and over again and each time I laugh with joy. You've no idea what a tonic it is for me after a long year without a single word from my friend. I wrote, but when I didn't receive any reply, I thought you had no desire to write, so I preferred not to either, for a whole year

I've been on my high horse, but in the end I *had* to write. What shall I tell you? What I've been doing for the past year? I've been undertaking a long study, guess what of? For the most part you – you – you – your work, your art, your self, everything I did not understand has now become so clear, I understand, I understand. Yes, I have been in the Enemy camp, but never have I heard anyone say the slightest ill word about you. Am I engaged? No, whom should I get engaged to? I had only scorn for all those in the Enemy camp. Me engaged? You with your delicate soul, and you think your soul is sick? Your nerves perhaps, but your fine, noble soul? You poor, beloved, wonderful friend.

*

She writes from Paris and Copenhagen, says that she can come to see him, alone, in mid-January. But it is still December.

Munch in Bad Elgersburg, Thüringerwald. He is living in an inn, receives a visit from Schiefler. Munch meets him at the railway station. Together they walk at sunset to the old palace, the health establishment where Schiefler is going to live. Munch tells his friend about his nervous problems, about things he has done which he cannot remember, terrible things, he speaks again about the woman, frøken Larsen, about everything that happened three years earlier, shows him new etchings, subjects which strike Schiefler as semi-humorous. Salomé tearing a man's eyes out.

December in Thüringerwald. Ibsen lies ill in Christiania. Munch asks a relation who is looking after the playwright to convey his greetings. White snow and clear sky. Munch and Schiefler go for walks in the forests and mountains taking a copper plate with them. Munch makes an etching of the waitress in a wine tavern.

Fresh air. Heart to heart with a friend.

Munch knows he must avoid the social round in Weimar, must try to calm down. Perhaps next year will be better. On New Year's Eve he stands down in the valley, between the mountains looking up at the clear winter sky with all the stars.

* * *

The reunion with Eva Mudocci is a disappointment. They meet in Elgersburg for just a few hours, she is travelling through.

Lieber Edvard! I'm sorry I wept, but you should know that this was largely due to fatigue, that is the last time you will see me weak.

Two days later: *Lieber Edvard*: It was absolutely not a success that I visited you, was it? Not just that you were so nervous and agitated about everything that's happened to you, but also that I was so tired and worn out after the journey and wasn't in a good mood either. I'm so concerned for you, write soon, I think about you all the time, I think you know what I mean when I say that I must make myself free, free to think only of you, all I can think of is you, whether we meet again or not, I live for you, I want to help you, do not be afraid!

* * *

It is 1906, Munch will paint *Self-Portrait with Wine Bottle*, paint the peace won at such cost, with the bottle at arm's length.

More and more often he notices small attacks of numbness, especially at night. Arms and legs become numb. During the day he feels a heaviness in his right leg, it drags a little. Then there are all the curious attacks and strange ideas.

He is sitting in the spa restaurant, is taking breakfast with an old guest. The Dutchman.

Munch suddenly says that he can hypnotize people, the Dutchman wants to see a demonstration. He mixes a bowl of mustard, pepper, tobacco ash and vinegar.

Eat this! says Munch to the Dutchman, looking at him with a forbidding expression. If you don't eat it, I'll shoot you on the spot!

The Dutchman leaves the same evening.

*

Munch in Thüringen. Frau Förster Nietzsche has introduced him to her friend, the director of a psychiatric clinic. Doesn't he want to request admission? Admitted to a psychiatric clinic like his sister Laura? No question of it. A spa, but not a sanatorium.

Bad Kösen, the hotel with the ironic name: The Bold Knight.

*

In Bad Ilmenau he paints *Self-Portrait with Wine Bottle*. His posture, the limp hands and the look of resignation intimate that all strength has left him. It is as though the narrow room is pressing in upon him, emphasizing his feeling of unease. The strong red and green colour contrasts behind his head further emphasize this impression.

Dear Aunt: I know I haven't written very much recently, I'm well, have recovered from my influenza and I hope that this protracted nervous prostration will subside, today my friend Director Schiefler from Hamburg is giving a lecture about me, a large exhibition has opened there. Politically things seem to be going quite well, even though relations between France and Germany have been very tense and continue to be so. Well, it started last year back in Norway, for me there is something of the fantastic about it, the time when my severe neurasthenia was at its worst, which meant that I saw everything almost as though in a dream. Of course, it's unpleasant that I can't be in my little idyll in Åsgårdstrand, but when I think of the terrible state I work myself into up there ... Inger must see to it that things are planted in the garden. I've got a boat down there, so Inger can go rowing.

*

Lieber Edvard: You asked me whether I was engaged, and I said no, what I told you about was over *long ago*, it was very short-lived, no longer than a few days, I couldn't carry on, because I wasn't in love, looked upon it as a huge, terrible sin, so I made an end of it. You see, I was born with two ideals, one of them was to become a great artist, the other was to meet a great artist before whom I could go down on bended knee, someone I could love and have children with so both personalities could carry on in the stream of life. For many years I went about like a nun and lived for my ideals, then at last you turned up, but I was so inexperienced, so silly and innocent that I was at a loss what to do when the time finally came, I didn't understand you and didn't even understand myself. That time you left Paris, I was still shy. Then there was the time in Berlin, when I became steadily more stupid, apart from which I was pursued by what you had said, I mean, that I was not normal, and then, because I *wanted to know if it was true*, I did what I've just told you. Now that all that is over, you must be wondering why I'm writing this, I'm writing because I want to be free of all this, never think about it again, I want to be free, calm, cool and content and better able to be your *friend*, someone who can perhaps really help you, so be my friend, please, write, let's meet, we two friends, always let me know how you are. Eva.

*

Ibsen dies on the twenty-third of May. Munch is working on the decor for Max Reinhardt's production of *Ghosts* at the Kammerspiele, Deutsches Theater. He keeps on feeling these alarming stabs of pain below the breast. Port in the morning has a calming effect. Half a bottle. Then coffee and a little bread.

But his anxiety returns. He has to go out into the street, to the first restaurant. A dram, two drams. It helps for a little while. But the anxiety returns, imperceptibly, like a rising tide. Steals into him. The feeling of just having lost something. Keys, his notebook, but never his wallet.

Max Reinhardt wants a frieze for his new theatre. Munch starts to make some sketches, taking as his starting point the love motifs from *The Frieze of Life*, using the shoreline from Åsgårdstrand as a uniting, unifying background.

Munch, in Berlin, is visited by the Nørregaards. Åse and Harald. The joyful warmth of reunion. Late nights living it up as in the old days. They think he looks better.

* * *

Lieber Edvard: I'm so pleased to have your letter, I see that you are writing in a much calmer and less nervous manner. Dear, dear friend, old friend! How you write! Your play gladdens and interests me a great deal, I've thought so many times that you ought to write a book.

Munch in Berlin, with *The City of Free Love* in his luggage, oaths and bile, toads, pigs and dogs. *The Death of Marat*, monstrous women, conspiracies, thoughts which destroy so that he does not notice any real improvement.

The Reinhardt Frieze, reworkings of scenes of the past.

Ingse Vibe writes from Åsgårdstrand: You've missed your chance. And neglected me. God only knows how much I miss you. I seem to remember a walk to the bathing hut!

Later she writes from Jelka Delius's house in Grez: You must come here soon, then we can make a fire in the hearth and have a party.

The murder of Marat is burning away inside his head, colouring his thoughts red. Back to the past. Not just the murder, but the beginning, the kiss, the seduction, couple on the shore and *The Lonely Ones/ Summer Night*, painted with tempera on unprepared canvas. At the same time as the sketches for *Ghosts* and *Hedda Gabler*. Hedda with the revolver, Osvald with the illness. The sizes and dimensions are the same as in *The Linde Frieze*. But Munch no longer needs to make allowances for children. When he paints with tempera, he achieves an inner glow which, beneath the matte surface, creates the impression of the intense light of midsummer night. A huge undertaking, a frieze which is designed to go round the entire auditorium of the theatre.

Schiefler visits Munch in Bad Kösen in September and notes that various women give him the eye.

He is a slim man with a sensitive expression, a convalescent who will not allow himself any rest, and who has already made substantial progress with *The Reinhardt Frieze*, a frieze which will never be used, since the auditorium will be rebuilt some years later and the pictures sold privately owing to the theatre's financial difficulties.

Munch also talks to Schiefler about the play, about *The City Of Free Love*, talks about marriage and monogamy, the need for a wife to keep order.

But he confides in Schiefler, who again notes this in his diary, that it is a terrible thought that the door opens every morning and it is always the same woman who comes in. He adds that it is also an intolerable thought that this woman, a woman Schiefler understands is not just any woman but a quite specific one, that this woman would shine like a beacon in his company. Munch tries to give an example, but again speaks of his own past, is driven towards the darkness, cannot break free.

* * *

The Tsar dissolves the Duma, Dreyfus is rehabilitated, Cézanne dies, Frits Thaulow dies, picture telegraphy is invented. It is winter in Germany. Dear Aunt: I'm living very carefully, going to bed at nine o'clock, have taken up skating on the doctor's advice.

But in Weimar Munch uses the camera for further self-portraits reflecting his own fate, variations on the motif *Self-Portrait with Wine Bottle*. He sits slumped in a room with his travelling bag behind him as if to underline the feeling of homelessness. A weak figure, withdrawn into his own melancholy and loneliness. In November he writes to Schiefler: after a long period of rest, life is running smoothly and peacefully, like the gentle River Saalech, and the stormy periods in my life are like ancient towers with ravens circling round them. However, I must always remember that there are terrible precipices or waterfalls, in Berlin it was particularly awful, I realize I must be resigned, be careful, I get a lot of sleep, that helps.

*

He celebrates Christmas in Saalech and the day before Christmas Eve sends a letter to Jappe Nilssen, sends him the first hectographs from the subsequent *History of Suffering*. The bloody hand at the top of the letter. He writes that for the last few years the tree rings have been ominous, the pig Gunnar Heiberg and the ladies' club at the foot of the page, and on the reverse side: a magpie shot in the wing in Thüringerwald, the snail Krohg with Oda's brothel on his back, as well as the pig and the poodle. The latter, Sigurd Bødtker, is holding its paw out in front of one of P. A. Larsen's wine bottles.

The same thoughts over and over again. Munch is now completely convinced that they made a fool of him that time he was summoned to Drøbak. Now he cannot but believe that Tulla Larsen was already having an affair with the painter Arne Kavli even then. Heiberg and Bødtker were her henchmen. And to cap it all: Heiberg had an affair with Tulla Larsen in Paris while Munch himself lay ill in Fiesole, sending her passionate letters.

* * *

Munch returns to Berlin with a sense of foreboding.

He knows that he will again have the company of his cousin Ludvig Ravensberg, the baron, an accomplished socialite, the man who is a master on the trapeze and observes a regime of rigorous physical and spiritual hygiene. The man Munch sometimes accompanies on car trips in the middle of the night, with a bottle of champagne in his lap. Back to Berlin, the city which laid the foundations for Strindberg's inferno crisis. Ducha and Stach. So many memories.

*

But it is 1907. The year he paints a new version of *The Sick Child*, the portrait of *Walther Rathenau*, *Zum süssen Mädel*, *Desire*, *Amor and Psyche*. The etching *Portrait of a Woman/The Countess*.

Munch in Berlin, Habsburger Hof, will hold an exhibition at Cassirer's gallery at the end of January, will paint the German industrial magnate and statesman Walther Rathenau, the son of the founder of AEG, who writes to Munch that he has half an hour spare on Thursday and an hour on Friday, that Munch will probably need a large canvas, as his height is six feet and two inches.

But first, the dress rehearsals of *Hedda Gabler* with Max Reinhardt. Schiefler comes to town, has received a letter saying Munch feels ill, this time quite a serious dose, but is back in town *in Feuer!* But he assures Schiefler that this time he will be *extremely* careful, try to live a regular life, following the doctor's advice, will not see a soul, not even go to the theatre.

A few days later Schiefler travels from Hamburg to Berlin and meets Munch, who is now occupied with the rehearsals for *Hedda Gabler* and asks Schiefler's wife for advice about the colour effects. Orange, blue, mauve. When later they are about to eat, Schiefler notes that Munch seems highly nervous, will not eat, cancels the appointment to show them the exhibition at Cassirer's gallery.

Schiefler visits Munch the following day in the Habsburger Hof and finds him in bed. He explains that the previous evening he had got worked up and drunk too much; once again he starts talking about Tulla Larsen and about Gunnar Heiberg's role in the whole affair, how the Almighty has united the pig and the toad in Heiberg.

It is now that Munch more systematically makes the pencil drawings of Tulla Larsen and her animals. At this stage the drawings are merely the result of his own attacks of rage, drawn in a daze and yet with a kind of awareness, as he puts it, like the postcards. Fresh onslaughts which he continues to send to his enemies at home. Postcards containing such strong language that the recipients threaten to sue him.

Life no longer flows calmly. He shows Schiefler the new version of *Marat*, a completely new technique, with pronounced broad vertical, horizontal or diagonal lines or strokes often as much as a metre in length. The surface is broken up, and what Munch calls an element of pre-cubism finds expression. The pictures *Amor and Psyche* followed by *Consolation* and *Murder*, in other words, *The Murder of Marat*, as cubism makes its appearance in France with *Les Demoiselles d'Avignon*, as the painters Emil Nolde and Ludwig Kirchner begin to show an interest in Munch's painting. *The Murder of Marat*, with the woman Munch calls The Countess as model, and her brutal spouse.

*

Munch leaves for Stockholm in April, has received a commission for a portrait from the magnate Thiel, who will also buy a number of his pictures, promises twenty-five or thirty thousand marks to be paid in instalments. He is swept up again into the social whirl, meets Prince Eugen, meets his Finnish colleague Gallén again, who says that the

Swedes feel as though an arm has been amputated after the dissolution of the Union. Munch mentions to his family the prospect of a visit to Norway, but instead goes to another Åsgårdstrand, rents a fisherman's cottage in Warnemünde, am Strom 53, after a visit to Lübeck. He is now suffering from major back problems and heartburn, writes that *The Sick Child* is being painted by a sick painter.

*

And the whole time Kollmann is there. Just round the corner, hidden in the wings, suddenly emerging, slipping Munch a little money when he cannot afford to pay, turning up unexpectedly on railway stations and in restaurants.

Kollmann. Button-moulder. Angel, or devil.

At any rate, an indispensable shadow.

* * *

Munch in Warnemünde. He has engaged a housekeeper, in a desperate desire for an ordered existence, sea air, health and the recovery of his strength.

He has been feeling depressed, tries to talk to Schiefler about how he actually *sees* people, what mental pictures he actually has of the various personalities.

He tells him that he often sees people surrounded by an aura, a sort of colourless flame, has a theory that he is able to reveal the process of metabolism, and can see the transformation of matter in the organism and in nature. Just when Schiefler discovers that Munch is a hypochondriac, Munch talks, in his fisherman's cottage, about the overall unity in nature, about the legacy of Goethe and Spinoza, God in all life, not just the links between humans, plants and animals, but also the links with what is termed inorganic nature, with the process of crystallization, a verbal torrent that lasts until late into the night and continues the following morning, including observations about the purity of the female.

Munch between illnesses, the horror of illness, elation and depression, has already represented his mood swings as being as dramatic as the outline of the Himalayas, visits the doctor who no doubt finds it difficult to come to any precise diagnosis, but who settles on stomach catarrh.

Munch in Warnemünde, refreshing dips in the sea, paints bathing men, with himself and the lifeguards as models, strong, naked men who emerge from the sea, as though ready to go straight to work, a pictorial vitality which is achieved by using the colours themselves as building material, a system of oblique brush strokes, a majestic, powerful and frank apotheosis of manhood, so audaciously direct that later in the autumn the picture is rejected by Clematis art dealers in Hamburg, for fear it might be reported to the police. Sea air, summer in a place where almost no one knows him.

His will to work returns and with it new and bitter presentations of the relationship between woman and man. A new version of *The Frieze of Life*. The shoreline at Åsgårdstrand replaced by the interior of a brothel. Almost without exception the women are red-haired, some motifs are seen as though through a wide-angle lens, striking distortions, a provocative and febrile use of colour, the man debased in the presence of woman, through his desire, his hatred and his jealousy.

The woman's glacial callousness is manifest. It is completely impenetrable. The man is trembling with desire, longing, despair, he plays many different roles, comforts and understands, but the woman is absorbed in herself. As in *Amor and Psyche*, bathed in sunlight whereas the man melts into the shadows, is drawn towards the darkness. Apuleius's story: Amor leaves Psyche at sunrise, she has broken her promise not to see who he really is.

Lifelines, life paths, leading to the definitive version of *The Death of Marat*, woman and man in the same situation, she naked and rigid, he also naked and prostrate, a motif he will later say it took him nine years to give birth to, in other words the time from the first nightmarish winter with Tulla Larsen until the summer in Warnemünde.

The painting is one of their children, the progeny of himself and the one he terms the beloved maiden.

Later he asks Gierløff to tell the enemy that this painting has been born, baptized and is on display at L'Indépendant in Paris. *The Death of Marat*. Intense, aggressive, crude. The naked truth, seen from Warnemünde in the summer of 1907. The bowl of fruit has been removed and the dead or dying man's blood is concentrated around the hand. His arm hangs limply down from the side of the bed.

*

Munch in Warnemünde. Edvard Grieg dies. Baden-Powell founds the scouting movement. Munch has hired Rosa Meissner, and sometimes also her sister Olga, as models.

Rosa Meissner, a dark blonde, a professional model from Berlin, a woman he will paint with red hair. She poses, for both painting and photographs, for the picture *Weeping Girl*, a variant of *Psyche*, obsessed with one single thought, love. Suffering and restless in a room with an empty bed.

How many threads there are that go back to Tulla Larsen! All that hatred cannot have been disgorged without just a hint of compassion, memories of a woman who created her love out of defeat. How sure is he of her betrayal. In Warnemünde the compassion seems to mingle with the hatred. He is working on his first sympathy motif, *The Sick Child*, as well as the portrait of *Old Man in Warnemünde*, two human lives each at different ages, yet nevertheless both in the antechamber of death.

He has his picture taken in front of these paintings, with *Children in the Street* on the left and a detail from a painting on the right, a solitary wine bottle, the symbol of his loneliness. Munch in Warnemünde, with softer features, longer hair, a more patently vital and engaging *joie de vivre*, working on studies of the hideous, humiliating consequences of desire. And the consequences of sympathy, studies of everyday life, the individual midway between light and darkness, the thin veneer of reason.

As Munch himself will put it: the influence of alcohol exacerbated the cleavage of the mind or soul to the limit, to the point where there were two states, reminiscent of two wild birds tied together and pulling in opposite directions, threatening to disintegrate or to snap the tie. Beneath the violent cleavage of these two mental states a terrible inner tension gradually arose, an intense inner conflict, a frightful battle in the confines of the soul.

*

Strindberg is in Sweden writing *The Ghost Sonata* as Munch tries to sort out his life in Warnemünde. This maddening neurasthenia, as he himself calls it. Auditory and mental hallucinations. What he construes as thoughts mingle with what has actually occurred. The experience of the split personality, walking beside oneself.

And what is this business with the joiner, the grimy little joiner? Why had he placed his hand on Munch's chest as the two of them were talking? They are packing pictures, the joiner and his son, pictures which are to be dispatched, Munch recalls the joiner's hand, feeling its way over his jacket. His notebook! The one with the important sketches, the bull being killed, Drachmann who is soon to die, where is it, he can't do without it, Munch knows it was in his pocket, until just a few seconds ago. The notebook. It's absolutely vital. Nobody is going to leave until it is found. Munch in Warnemünde, the joiner and his son, Munch looks high and low, they *must* have taken it, the joiner and his son, he can still recall the movement on the street, the hand placed on his chest. Munch feels in his pockets, no sign of the notebook, goes on looking. The vital sketches, impossible to imagine that it has been lost. No one is going to leave! Then he suddenly puts his hand into his pocket, clutches something unmistakable. The notebook! There it is! Has it been there all the time? It's not possible, he felt in his pocket countless times, all his pockets. The notebook wasn't there. Now he stands there with it in his hand. Happy. Embarrassed. A joiner and his son. Has held them prisoner. Certain that the notebook had been stolen.

In the evening: glass after glass. Large quantities of alcohol. Until he passes out. Collapses into bed.

*

Munch naked on the shore, at his easel, working with enormous energy. He visits Schiefler, arrives by automobile, carefully dressed and wearing a purple tie, comes with the bathing picture for Salon Clematis, wants to exhibit it, naked men emerging from the water. He is breaking new ground, ground no one has trodden before.

Later, in November, he meets Schiefler at a ladies' club. Meets Aubert again. Munch has met him before in Berlin. There he stands, the critic who in 1885 wished Munch's *The Sick Child* had been rejected, who thought the painting an abandoned, half-scraped out sketch, venturing to suggest that the painter had run out of steam while working on it, that the painting was not a painting at all, but a half-finished mess. Aubert, who wondered whether at that time Munch was hoodwinking his public, as a painting could sometimes change from one day to the next, for during the night Munch would continue to work on pictures already on display. The man who called Munch's pictures sloppy and rough but who nevertheless always left the door ajar where the painter's talent was concerned, a touch of genius, etc. Now there is Andreas Aubert in Fräulein Schapire's home in Berlin, entertaining Munch and the others present by holding forth on the genius of the work of the German Romantic painter Caspar David Friedrich, absolutely the greatest German painter of them all, so obviously the greatest, without any doubt, and Aubert is living in Hamburg specifically in order to study a work by this painter. And to add insult to injury, Aubert seems to think that Munch is the greatest *Norwegian* painter, absolutely, beyond any doubt, his morbidity, his gloominess apart, that is. For, as Aubert says to Munch, he can't abide morbidity, gloominess and sham decadence. What he wants above all is to be a cultivated aristocrat in the service of art.

Aubert: I don't like members of the demi-monde.

Munch: Do I not smell of patchouli?

Aubert: Do you?

Munch: Herr Aubert, don't you know that I come from one of Norway's most cultured families?

* * *

In Warnemünde he has so far been in control, but Berlin is always harrowing for him.

Hotel Hippodrome, Charlottenburg am Knie. The scruffy hotel boy, the dapper little host, the many large rooms no one lives in, flirting with the hotel maids, drunk every evening, often until he passes out. Girls, a strangely lonely place, a six-storey brick building, musty. Munch on one of the upper floors, accompanied by a girl, given a dressing down by a woman, a woman, from a brothel perhaps? Bastard, she said.

*

Herr Ludvig Ravensberg, painter. Stensgt. 1. Christiania. Norwegen: Dear Ludwig: Would you be so good as to find out whether the heavy stones depicting the heroic deeds of the Bohemian rascals are being well cared for at Petersen and Waitz's. You must tell him I shall soon be printing a run. It's very important. I've rented an old fisherman's cottage in Warnemünde. The sea air is lovely. For the information of that pair of pimps GH – SB, let them know that they appear in hell in my frieze, naked at the syphilis doctor's, their bodies covered in sores. It can serve as a timely warning. How is life in the Enemy camp? Greetings to yourself and Gierløff. Yours Edvard Munch.

*

Just before Christmas, *The Reinhardt Frieze* is ready for hanging in the theatre. Continuous work, he works non-stop, drinks, wishes to be left in peace, ends up going out with people. Christmas 1907, a man comes up to him and says:

Mr Munch, how is your hand?

Munch replies: Do you know me?

The stranger nods: I saw you at a concert five years ago.

Munch replies: I'm sure I was very drunk, wasn't I?

The stranger nods again: Yes, you could say so.

Tactless! Provocative! Munch feels the anger surge through him. How dare this stranger ask him about his condition, his *hand's* condition, his crippled limb, the eternal reminder of his humiliation.

Schiefler visits Munch at his hotel the following day. Munch is still highly agitated, having only returned from town at five or six o'clock in the morning. No sleep, he is again starting to talk about that terrible woman, about her henchmen, about frøken Larsen, letting himself get worked up by the old thoughts, again and again, this sly, shameless, decadent, provocative bunch, this clique consisting of a set of down-and-out literati, drunken progeny of the well heeled, a red-haired, spoiled, malicious bit of a thing. And a total stranger who comments on his maimed hand, asks him about his deformity! With thoughts such as these Munch starts the new year, 1908, the year of his downfall, and his resurrection. He is on a journey of the mind. Violent swings, the deepest gloom. Then suddenly exhilarated: Herr Schiefler, did you know I've become a *friseur*, I paint nothing but friezes now. And I have dry points on the brain. Mr Schiefler, do you realize that I can't go to the opening, after all you know what people say, either I'm mad or my pictures are.

A new year for Munch. He is working on the triptych *Three Ages of Life*, will paint *Mason and Mechanic*, and a new version of *The Lonely Ones*. Travels to Paris with *The Death of Marat*, exhibits it together with what one critic will call this whole pack of *fumistes*, of charlatans, by which he means Munch and his companions Braque, Derain and

Rouault. Munch steers clear of the Norwegian colony, is shy, feels secure only when alone, but then he is prey to persecution mania, the old thoughts, the conspiracy. What was it the doctor in Kösen had said: first come the minor bouts of numbness, then larger ones, to begin with in the arm, dizziness, a variety of physical and mental phenomena, then in the end you have a stroke and are completely paralysed, or you die. It is 1908. Munch meets Blix and Karsten on the boulevard, has as a matter of fact never had anything against Karsten, invites them up for a glass of wine, is bursting to tell them that he intends to paint a picture, a massive picture, of heaven and hell:

Gunnar Heiberg will be seated next to the devil. And he intends to place friends and enemies at various points in a hierarchy of his own devising rising up towards heaven. Blix bursts out laughing.

Munch is furious: I know you're a friend of Heiberg!

Of Karsten too, Blix replies. But if I may venture to hope for inclusion in the picture, I don't mind sitting next to Heiberg.

It's too much for Munch. Far too much. The old rage, wants to wring Blix's neck. Ragnvald Blix. A miserable cartoonist, a man who will later say that it will be a long time before he forgets the madness he glimpsed in Munch's eyes. Karsten stands between them. It is probably at this time that Munch walks the streets at night, drunk and despairing, in a daze, following women into louche houses, later writing that his conduct towards the chambermaids at the hotel left something to be desired. In a large dance hall, he was also rough with a waitress, or something of that order, probably overstepped the mark a bit.

*

Ludvig Ravensberg: Dear kinsman: Alarm must have gripped the faithful flock in Norway when the news came that the mighty commander had appeared in Paris plumb in the middle of the Enemy camp. Of such stuff are heroes made. Fear and alarm was nothing new to them. The news also brought dread and ruination into the Enemy camp. I sat in the dining car to give myself courage and sustenance from the delicious food and the wonderful grape juice. But the enemy was at large. I shall tell you about the other events on a later occasion. Meanwhile, to hearten the bold little flock, ask Gierløff to broadcast the fact that I am showing my picture *Marat is Murdered* at L'Indépendant in Paris. This will also strike fear into the Enemy camp.

*

Dear Aunt: I'm steering clear of the Norwegian colony, I've had enough of it. There's a lot of snow here just now. Here and in Berlin there's been a terrible epidemic of influenza, in Rostock, which has a population of sixty-five thousand, at one time there were a thousand deaths a month. This time I didn't catch it.

Ravensberg: Noble kinsman: I am anxiously waiting to hear what effect the news of my battles has had in Christiania. I closed my letter by relating to you the tense moment as I left Berlin. Kollmann with my army. The pictures rolled up and ready. I shall later tell how the enemy was already at large, poisoned the wine and in Cologne stole the large roll of pictures. I shall later tell of the attack in Cologne as well as the battles at the Pantheon, Boulevard Michel, at Lilas, rue de Seine, and of my fortress, Hotel du Sénat. The enemy had appointed an awesome commander by the name of Eide. He is a general and has an even more awesome ability to calculate the square root of his enemies. I shall not anticipate events and tell you of all the unburned witches the enemy has in its army. But many greetings to you and the faithful few from your friend and kinsman Edvard Munch.

*

Back to Germany. Spring in Warnemünde. Here he receives news of her death. Åse Nørregaard. The strongest of them all. She whom he already knew as early as 1889, when a gust of wind blew her flaxen hair over her eyes, she who became his friend, a woman he could have shared his life with, a woman of whom he later wrote that she could have been the greatest joy of his life, a series of small coincidences at that time, at Nordstrand, at Bekkelaget, at Ljan, the days before the wedding. Strong and tall. It could have been her and him. Munch and *The Lady on the Bridge*, always *en face*, like a challenge, or a reminder. She could have been fru Åse Munch. An innocent cold, influenza perhaps, of the sort he has had so many times himself. Sudden pneumonia.

Åse Nørregaard, thirty-eight years of age.

Death in May. Munch sits with his panama hat in Warnemünde and watches an ice-cold spring sun sink into the sea, writes to her husband Harald: You know I know what you've lost. You think you have lost everything, spring and summer and no words can comfort you. You also know that I have lost my greatest female friend.

*

Ravensberg. Noble kinsman: Thank you for your letter. I may well take a stroll some dark night, muffled up in a cape, for secret discussions. Tell me, have you not heard the howls from the Enemy camp? Have my shells had any effect? I think the scoundrels CK, GH and SB are on the run now. It's good to have a safety valve when giving that pack of rogues a damned good hiding is not an option. Believe you me, SB was certainly told where to get off in ten postcards. Now it's clear for all to see what a rotten little scheme they cobbled together just for the sake of some cash. The girl was rich enough to fork out 20,000 crowns to have me, poor devil, destroyed. I'm now in the process of writing a long book about the whole affair. That pack of rogues have such bad consciences that they daren't raise a finger. That is, if they don't pay someone else to have me murdered. They must be beside themselves that the Corpse is spitting.

* * *

The restless summer. In London Emmeline Pankhurst and her daughter are forced to go to prison in the battle for women's right to vote. Munch tries to regain his equilibrium, strolls about in the streets, paints the lives of people by the shore, the drowned body they carry up out of the sea, paints *The Worker and the Child*, paints *Mason and Mechanic*.

It occurs to him that he has really never had peace and quiet for work. Always sickness, fleeing from his thoughts, or financial hardship. He has had to paint in between everything else, has become accustomed to seizing the moment, blotting out everything else for a few brief hours or minutes, capturing the motif as he sees it. Calm, rest, regularity are what he hopes for. His German contacts are working for him. Gallery owners in all the major cities. Berlin, Hamburg, Dresden, Breslau, Munich, Cologne. But when Schiefler comes to visit him in July to have his portrait painted, there has been a deterioration. Munch tells him that he has had a further attack of neurasthenia, sent postcards with extremely insulting text and drawings to Christian Krohg, Gunnar Heiberg and Sigurd Bødtker. Krohg has now sought legal advice and through his lawyer asked for an explanation and an apology. The thought of a possible court case does not make Munch any calmer.

He writes to Gierløff: It is one of my dreams for the future, when my health has stabilized and my purse is full, to come to somewhere near Christiania (Holmenkollen) and throw one hell of a party for the few people I count as my friends, of which there are only a handful. Here by the sea I hope that I can become what I was before, admittedly as an ageing gentleman with silver in my hair. To the consternation of friends and foes, my postcards apparently landed in the most magnificent Christiania spring. Now it's done I'm glad I told those gentlemen a few home truths. The method, the postcard, is not to my liking, but unless one wants to knock the stuffing out of them all and end up in clink for it, what other option is there. As I wrote to you, I had thought of starting with monumental caricatures. When I had dispatched John the Baptist's head, the anger took hold of me and I simply dashed off the postcards. I gave them such a dressing down that Thommesen must have thought he was leader of the world's biggest pack of scoundrels. They had no sympathy for me, and I was driven to madness.

*

Munch drinks cold beer on an empty stomach. His stomach reacts, impossible to eat, just glass after glass. A constant bath of alcohol. Schiefler notes that he never stops returning to the subject of frøken L., the same old story, nothing new, just gets himself worked up, the thought of the conspiracy, the ruined hand, the finger stump.

He has alarming stabs of pain in his heart, feels dizzy when he stands up, tries to remember whether he had been impatient with the bellboy at the Hippodrome? New episodes, a whole series of events, signs, people who are not what they say they are, detectives perhaps. Receives a letter from Sherlock Holmes in Norway, lives in a house with a housekeeper whom he calls 'die kleine Perle', a woman who, he writes, wanders about with Madonna eyes and love sickness.

Why does the proprietor ask him how he likes women? What does he mean? A very leading question, suspicious, a hint of something else. Munch becomes uneasy, sees a policeman visiting the proprietor, soon after the proprietor comes with a stranger up to his room, saying he wants to investigate the tremors in the house.

Nonsense! Pure invention! The proprietor is no longer to be trusted. He knows something. May be an envoy of the enemy. The threat from Krohg. A lawsuit. What actually had he written on the postcard? What had he drawn? To Heiberg he had written: Will you allow me to use your likeness as an advertisement for P. A. Larsen's the wine merchant's?

Munch is in Warnemünde and feels the ground is giving way. There may be detectives in town. Spies. Schiefler has left. Munch fears arrest, decides to go to Copenhagen, hastily packs.

The police could turn up at any moment. He says to the proprietor:
I'm leaving tomorrow.
You mustn't do that, the man replies. You're too ill.
What does he mean? Isn't he up to deciding where or when he wants to go himself? Can't the man hear what is said to him? He's leaving tomorrow, he says. For Copenhagen. This is certainly no place for me.

*

Fährdampfer Prins Christian. Warnemünde disappears in the sunshine, the long row of small houses along the river and the shore, the large hotels. And with it peace and stability. Now he is not certain of anything.

Who is that strange chap with a bird's head, spindly birdlike legs, a bird's wings and a cloak? Black hair and thick eyebrows. It is just a disguise. Not human eyes but falcon's eyes.

*

Out to the open sea. Munch goes to his cabin. Beer and a dram. Eats a little too. Beer and a dram. Is safer now. The railway over the islands to Copenhagen. Why on earth is he going to Copenhagen? Enemies there too. Haukland. The newspapers. Has been buried alive by the newspaper *Politiken*. Now the bird with wings comes flying into the carriage.

The strange bird-man in the compartment. Detective with the head of a bird. Munch scrutinizes him at length. It is early morning. Pale sallow faces everywhere. *Guten Tag*. *Guten Tag*. Excuse me, are you on your way to Copenhagen? To Helsinki? Where do you come from? The Esperanto meeting in Berlin. Oh yes! No coincidence! So the stranger is interested in Esperanto. Esperanto unites. Does Munch know Esperanto?

What is your occupation, asks Munch suddenly.

Psychiatrist, the man replies.

Exactly, thinks Munch. That stands to reason too. A sign. Not just a coincidence.

I suffer with my nerves, says Munch. I'm extremely nervous. Have been for a long time.

Munch sits in a railway compartment talking to a psychiatrist. An analyst from Vienna. A detective then. Can the detective advise him, help him, he suffers terribly with his nerves, but also from drinking and alcohol. So can he give him some good advice, should he have himself admitted to a clinic, a sanatorium? The fear of madness. Laura at Gaustad, at the Women's Hospital. Impossible to forget the screams. Impossible to forget the silence.

Better to say that you've drunk too much, says the Esperanto man. If you say you have a nervous disposition, you will just be moved from one institution to another. God only knows when you will get out.

*

He arrives in Copenhagen in late August, just as when he came from Lübeck four years ago.

Is someone whistling at him? Munch is convinced he can hear a whistle. That chap over there. Didn't he whistle? Munch turns round. First left. Then right. Isn't that someone whistling? The chap there, right behind him. There's someone yelling. How can they know ... Is there someone who *knows*? Someone who knows that he has arrived? Is it in the paper? Munch buys the papers. Skims through the columns. The grouse-shooting season has begun. They will be out shooting game. Nothing about him, to say that he has come. Unless the language is coded. Another language.

Munch in Sjælland. Copenhagen. Taarbæk Badehotel, at Klampenborg, the Railway Hotel in Helsingør, Hornbæk Inn. As Jens Thiis is in the process of beating his rivals in the battle to become director of the National Gallery, Munch feels that stabbing pain below the breast every morning.

A surprising pain. Surely fear cannot take the form of a dagger? Can fear be solid and stab? Isn't it a dull pain, no a *solid* one, the one he has felt more or less his entire life, ever since he was a child?

Nicotine. The tobacco plant's cremation; the resulting smoke eats into the channels of the arteries, swirls about in the labyrinths of the brain – intricate workshop of thought – and in the passages of the heart. Even the finest nerves are affected. Munch writes that he can feel it, the finest nerve of all is affected, the very nerve of life. Yes, it is the nerve of life. He can feel it. It is burning now. It is burning up.

Copenhagen, September 1908. Whisky and soda, cigar. Whisky and soda, cigar.

In the evening: the masses in the streets, pale in the electric lights, sallow as ghosts. They walk past him. He can see straight through them, behind the masks.

He walks up to a complete stranger and gives him a dressing down. Didn't he say something? Oh yes he did, he'd better not try it on. Munch could plainly hear him. Yes. Plainly. In the restaurant he can hear it plainly. They are talking about him. Those people over there. Aren't they, Mathiesen? The poet from Norway, fat as a pig from food and drink, a gifted psychological poet, a little perverse.

Shall we have a drink, Munch? Yes. Let's. They drink. Munch and Mathiesen. Whisky and sodas and cigars. They drink themselves senseless. Munch awakens with a start, does not know which hotel he is in, does not know when or how he got there, all he can see is the Norwegian writer's broad back beside him in the bed.

Tickle my back will you, Munch.

Munch feels the nausea rising, as usual has to get out of bed and be sick. The beginning of the day. Vomit and port. Mathiesen for company.

What about a drink now, Munch?

Of course they are going to drink. Wine, the only thing that can deaden, for a few brief minutes. The nerve of life is burning up. Well, let it burn up then. The pain, the fear, everything. Then it is over. The rolling black ball. Fear. It rolls and stops at each vulnerable place. Now a sickness, now an impulse, action.

*

The train to Taarbæk. He can hear his own footfalls against the pavement. A loud clatter. As though they are loose. Like a clown? Visit Goldstein in Taarbæk. Once it was St Cloud. How is Goldstein now? In St Cloud Goldstein had wanted to kill him.

*

Noble kin! Now it is time for the heroes to arm themselves. The brave chieftain is in peril. Like a knight without fear or reproach in postcards he has handed his enemies his own weapons, saying: strike this noble breast. And the Enemy strikes. So give me news as soon as possible. Convoke the faithful forthwith and arm them to the teeth. By the by, noble kin, not a word about this letter, but put all my war letters in safe keeping. Greetings from your friend and kinsman Edvard Munch.

*

When Munch awakens on Goldstein's sofa the next day, he feels dizzy, notices that his legs will not support him, his hands will not grip. Paralysis. No feeling in his hand, no feeling in his left side. Limps on his right leg. Goldstein's look.

We're moving, he says. To town. To the doctor.

Out of the question, Goldstein!

There is terror in Munch's eyes. Has the Enemy sent out its secret agents?

*

Badehotel, in Klampenborg. Where he licked his wounds in 1905 too. No Goldstein now. A hotel room. Munch in Taarbæk. Totters about. Drinks, sleeps, drinks. A large desolate hotel. He paces the corridors at night when he cannot sleep, when nobody can see him. Has to practise walking. Sends a short letter to Schiefler. The only fixed point. Writes that he may go to Stockholm, writes that rage is a beautiful thing which should be used for artistic purposes, but alas! his creative drive is in a blind alley. *Viele herzlich Grüsze an Alle, Ihr Edvard Munch.*

The following day Munch sets out along the road to Copenhagen.

There is a cholera epidemic in St Petersburg. He puts one foot in front of the other, fights against the paralysis, limps his way to Copenhagen. His tie is askew, his hair tousled, his shoes unpolished and his clothes unbrushed. Wants to have a rest in a restaurant, but is turned away. Tramp, vagabond.

Munch comes to Copenhagen on foot, September 1908, limps into reception at Hotel Wied, rents two rooms on the first floor, wants a view of both street and courtyard. That is the safest policy. He is convinced they may attack at any moment.

*

At night he drinks, drifts off briefly to sleep, then reawakens.

He hears sounds. There is someone talking. He is not afraid of gas, like Strindberg. He is afraid of voices. Norwegian voices. What was that? What is that he can hear down there in the street?

Munch.

Somebody saying his name. They are speaking louder now.

There he is. Don't let him out of your sight.

Munch rushes to the window. Not a soul to be seen. It is as silent as the grave. But surely he heard voices, didn't he?

He walks over to the bed, lies down again.

Munch. Edvard Munch.

The voices. Clearly Norwegian!

Now we've got him. Do you have the revolver?

Unmistakable. A woman's voice! Other voices. He gets up again. But as soon as he goes to the window, there is deathly silence.

Night in the hotel. Outside is a red car. That must be where they are hiding! Or else in the courtyard.

He goes into the other room. There are Norwegians out there. Now they are coming to take him. He is surrounded.

If only he had had a revolver.

Voices everywhere. He clearly hears a man say:

Woman baiter.

He rings for service. What is all this racket? The man cannot give an answer. Fetch Goldstein, says Munch. For God's sake fetch Goldstein! Meanwhile a telegram to Gierløff in Norway: Please come as soon as you can. Extremely urgent!

*

Then Goldstein comes, like a dark angel. It is the third of October 1908. Goldstein leans over Munch in his bed. Munch lies there frantic, tired to distraction.

Listen, Goldstein, it's despicable of them to attack me when I'm ill, get me a revolver.

Goldstein gets him a doctor. At long last. Munch's very words. A ten-year-long inferno. Now he says:

I can't take any more. Goldstein, get me to the psychiatric clinic.

* * *

A white room with morning sunshine streaming in through the open window.

Outside, in the corridor: a young nurse who is reading at a small table with flowers on it. Inside, in Munch's room, a nurse who, when Gierløff arrives, looks up and smiles like a lily of the valley.

Gierløff later writes:

In the white bed Munch. Barely awake, tired, casts a quick glance at the door, smiles weakly and whispers: Here lies Hamlet, and there comes Fortinbras from Norway.

Then Gierløff says: Good morning, Shakespeare, what on earth have you been up to this time?

Munch replies: I've had it. Can you sort out my affairs for me?

By the eighth of October Gierløff has already written a letter to *Dagbladet* in Christiania: A quiet, ever so quiet house, tucked away down a quiet, ever so quiet street on the outskirts of Fredriksberg. It is a psychiatric clinic, Kochsvei 21, Professor Jacobson's clinic. It is there that I find Munch.

Gierløff writes a letter to the paper, pours oil on troubled waters, no one must get the idea that Munch is seriously ill. Not ill at all, has been admitted to the psychiatric clinic almost by chance. Some trouble with his leg. An article which has but one aim, with Munch's connivance certainly: Not to give his enemies in Norway the feeling they have won. Not to let them believe the Danish press: Munch mentally ill!

But Munch himself writes of strong sleeping draughts, says that he slept for eight days, with a nurse sleeping in the same room, on a sofa.

*

Norwegian painter mentally ill! Edvard Munch in a psychiatric clinic. The unstable artistic temperament! The Norwegian painter Edvard Munch admitted to a psychiatric clinic. *Aftenbladet* 5 October 1908:

It has long been apparent that the Norwegian painter Edvard Munch was heading for a nervous breakdown, and now one of his friends has arranged for him to be admitted to Professor Jacobson's psychiatric clinic here. Edvard Munch is still only 45 years of age. Opinion is strongly divided as to the extent to which Munch should be regarded as a genius, but he has at any rate succeeded in attracting attention to himself, and no mistake about it, through his ruthless painting style and his drastic mode of expression. There is something of the Willumsen about him in his avoidance of the ordinary. But whereas Willumsen favours the ethereal, Munch plumbs the depths. He is the painter of the poor and the despairing, and he tells of need and misery at their ugliest.

And in the newspaper *Vårt Land*: The highly controversial Norwegian painter Edvard Munch was admitted in Copenhagen yesterday to Professor Daniel Jacobson's psychiatric clinic in Kochsvej. His admission was partly arranged by a close friend, but was otherwise completely voluntary. As this will certainly provoke a lot of discussion, we would point out that Munch finally decided to have complete rest. His present condition can perhaps best be described as a nervous breakdown, which has been brewing for a long time, but which however is of a transitory nature. The Norwegian painter will in all likelihood succeed in finding peace and rest in the quiet clinic. Afterwards, his friends are considering arranging a trip to the mountains for him, so that he can make a complete recovery. Not just here in Norway, but also in Copenhagen, Paris and Berlin, the forty–five year-old Edvard Munch has been highly controversial ever since he first emerged as an artist. His bleakly pessimistic view of life, his contempt for all the accepted rules of painting, have made him bitter enemies everywhere and naturally ardent supporters as well. Most particularly, those canvases in which Munch has portrayed human need and misery without the least attempt to tone them down have been the subject of controversy. In his landscapes, by contrast, even people originally hostile to him have found great beauty. Munch has been familiar to us since as long ago as the 1888 exhibition of Nordic art in Copenhagen. One of his very best works is *Spring*, a young consumptive girl sits doomed at the window gazing out onto the awakening spring landscape. It is not just as an artist that Munch has attracted attention, but also as an eccentric. His clash in a café here in Copenhagen with the Norwegian writer Andreas Haukland is still fresh in our memories.

* * *

October 1908. Munch has recovered from his paralysis, is receiving massage every day. But what of the voices? What are they talking about outside the door? He is to be moved south, they are saying. Munch glances at the window. Is it locked? The last chance, if everything gets too much. Are there bars on it?

Munch in hospital, which he describes in a letter to Schiefler as a prison for refined criminal aristocrats. He lies there listening for voices in the street.

But he can hear them no longer.

In the next room is the Danish writer Anders W. Holm, who notes that Munch has pinned the lithograph of Strindberg over his bed with four drawing pins. For a time he also has the lithograph *Sick Girl* hanging in his room. Holm keeps on asking a nurse to enquire of Munch whether Munch will visit him. He describes Munch as exceptionally friendly and affable. If Munch cannot visit Holm in the next room, he sends the nurse with four or five paintings instead, so that Holm will have something to look at.

Dear Aunt: As you must all already be aware from the greetings I sent you, I've had myself admitted to a psychiatric clinic. I hope that here I shall be able to put an end to the unbearable inner turmoil from which I have been suffering since those troubles I had. I only wish I'd done it long ago, then I would have spared myself and you and many others a lot of unpleasantness. The doctor is good and the people are nice. I have a bath every day and am to eat as much as possible to put a bit of flesh on my nerves. Otherwise, I've been well and have painted a good deal. The cure is in full swing. I'm having electrical treatment, massage and baths every day. The doctor says I've had too little electricity and in general am very debilitated, which is hardly surprising after all. The strange thing is that, physically speaking, I've become the healthiest individual imaginable and can stand both cold and wet. The Order of St Olav medal attracted a lot of attention here at the clinic. The nurse thought it such a lovely brooch.

He has been made a Knight of St Olav, an irony of fate, a sudden act of friendliness from his own country. He sees a lady on the same floor as himself: she paces up and down, up and down. Munch knows what this is. The turmoil he has experienced himself, which can only be deadened by pacing, up and down. One day she is gone. The door to her room is open. There stands the bed, there is the table with a flower, there are all her small possessions, books and knick-knacks.

They find her in the black pool.

* * *

The Art Association in Copenhagen arranges a major exhibition of Munch's works in November. In *Danebrog* Frits Magnussen writes:

> Now he returns, an idol, with a reputation of almost European stature. One must therefore be permitted to tell him a few necessary home truths. Edvard Munch cannot make up his mind what sort of artist he wants to be. One minute he explodes on the canvas in a wild delirium of colours, jettisoning form and draughtsmanship completely, the next minute he is absorbed in intense fevered imaginings *à la* Rops and Stuck, then turning his attention to a detailed psychological portrayal of the individual, all the while spreading such a chaos of palette scrapings around him that one cannot tell one end of the picture from the other. Edvard Munch is a dangerous man. Dangerous for the young. The fact that he can be taken seriously at all is purely the result of his innate talent, even though he treats it with utter disrespect, and it is doubtful whether he will ever make the mark in the history of art to which his inherent gift entitled him.

* * *

It troubles Munch that this Doctor Jacobson may gain a false impression of his state of mind. The depression is the result of most unusual circumstances dating back six years.

Munch makes a pen and ink drawing of himself in the chair with the doctor and nurse while undergoing electric shock therapy and writes: Professor Jacobson giving the famous painter Munch electric shock therapy and charging his fragile brain with positive male and negative female energy.

There is the usual conflict between doctor and patient. First a long period in bed, then, little by little, the various cures, heart massage, electric therapy, pine needle baths and electric light baths. After breakfast, fresh air therapy. Well wrapped up, he is placed beside open windows. He writes to his Aunt that he has a very nice room, has started to paint, eats in his room when he feels ill at ease eating with the other patients. Writes of excellent, friendly nurses, lets himself be ordered about by young and old:

Aren't you up yet, Munch? It's time for your fresh air cure.

*

Dear Aunt: I know the St Olav award was well-intentioned and indicates a friendly attitude, but I'm not exactly in favour of such decorations, and I think I may well have declined it in the past. I've just been interrupted by the girl bringing me the little round breakfast table. I now walk and drive during the daytime. I hope I'll sort out most of my problems here, but a complete cure for my nervous trouble is highly unlikely, as it is in large measure inherited from father. He suffered greatly from palpitations and nervous anxiety. I'm really longing to see and paint Norwegian scenery and would very much like to come and visit the two of you in your lovely rooms with the beautiful view. But I've little desire for Christiania, perhaps in spring I shall rent a place somewhere near Kristiansand. One thing that has changed is that I now have to use a lorgnette. It's a nuisance.

*

Who is mad, or most right, who is strongest?

Inside he is like a glass of cloudy water. At Doctor Jacobson's the glass is gradually becoming clearer. What will be left when the sediment has finally settled?

Dear Jappe: Many thanks for your letter. Obviously I'm glad I have the friends I do, especially when I have so many real and imagined enemies. For me the crash was bound to come. That day at the Grand six years ago, you remember, you surely noticed that I was affected, and since then I've lived in constant tension and nervous anxiety, which in the end had to find a release. And it was quite violent when it finally came, after a trip to Sweden and four days spent with Sigurd Mathiesen in alcoholic paradise. I've had a thorough psychiatric cure, and probably also suffered a small stroke. Part of my brain was damaged through incessant thinking about one single thing.

*

He still thinks about only one thing, to the editor Anker Kirkeby he laments the fact that tobacco and wine have been his enemies, that it is a pity that wine, which comes from the sun, should be so dangerous.

Then it breaks over him like a tidal wave: the desire to work. He recalls what Dr Linde and Schiefler advised him to do: make drawings of these sick thoughts, as he already has done, but systematically now, as part of his convalescence, or as a conscious new graphic series.

At last. Alpha and Omega. The first and last letters in the Greek alphabet. The beginning and the end. Man and woman. Dedicated to Schiefler. The summing up. The health cure. The definitive settlement. The final postcard. Once and for all if possible: to have done with Tulla Larsen. To have done with Heiberg, Bødtker and Krohg. Complete sets of eighteen lithographs, twenty copies on Japan paper, five copies on grey board, twenty-five copies on white board. There are as many as three copies of some of them on dark, greyish brown paper.

*

Alpha is the man, Omega the woman. They live in paradise. Alpha loves Omega. At Veierland they sit together in the evening, leaning on one another, looking at the yellow pillar of the moon. The remembered scene is the shore between sea and forest. In the forest there live strange animals and plants. Munch writes the fable, writes about a great dark cloud which billows up from the sea, just as it had in 1885, the first time he had visited fru Thaulow in her house by the church in Borre. A cloud which throws its shadow over the island. Then Alpha calls to Omega, but Omega cannot hear him, she is sitting with the head of a snake between her hands, staring at its flashing eyes, it has come slithering up through the ferns, up over her body.

She sits with the snake in the rain, does not hear Alpha calling. Later Alpha kills the snake, but now Omega is walking among the animals. She meets the bear, feels the creature's soft coat against her body. Then nothing is ever again as it was before.

Omega is driven from one animal to the other.

She meets the poet hyena, his coat is rather bedraggled, her usual words of love do not work on him, but Omega plaits a laurel wreath with her soft small hands and crowns him, puts her sweet face up against his sardonic muzzle. Omega on the island, going from animal to animal, not afraid of the tiger, but rests her small hand in its jaws, fondling its teeth.

The tiger and the bear are done for. They are in love with Omega, they know the scent of the pale apple blossom which is Omega's favourite flower, the one she kisses every morning when the sun rises. The tiger and the bear meet on the road. They tear one another to pieces.

Then Omega clings to her Alpha again, does not understand what is happening, sees all the other curious unsuspecting animals observing her. Alpha can see that Omega's eyes change colour from light blue on ordinary days, to black, with flashes of carmine when she beholds her lovers, when she conceals her mouth with a flower.

Her favourite occupation is kissing. She kisses the ass by the river and does not notice when Alpha fetches the ostrich and nuzzles against its neck. Omega feels tired and sorry that she does not own all the animals on the island, sits down on the grass weeping bitterly. Then she gets up and runs wildly about.

Then she meets the pig.

Omega and the pig look at one another.

One night, as the yellow pillar of the moon rocks gently in the water, Omega flees across the sea on the back of a deer to the light green mainland. Alpha is alone again on the island.

But not completely. One day Omega's children come and flock round him, a new species has sprung up on the island. Now they gather round Alpha who they think is their father. There are piglets, baby monkeys and cubs of beasts of prey and other hybrid offspring of humans.

Then Alpha runs along the shore.

Heaven and sea are red with blood.

He hears cries in the air and covers his ears.

Earth, heaven and sea quake.

Alpha is overcome with a great fear.

*

One day the deer brings Omega back.

Alpha is sitting on the shore.

She comes towards him. Alpha feels the blood ringing in his ears. His muscles tense.

Then he strikes Omega dead.

But when he sees her soulless face, he is alarmed by its expression. For it is the same expression it was wearing that time in the forest, when he loved her most!

While he is still looking at her, all her children and the animals on the island set upon him from behind.

They tear him to pieces.

*

The new species carries life on.

VI

> Human fates are like worlds, like a star shining forth in the darkness. (EDVARD MUNCH)

A whole life has come to an end. A new one can begin. But when Munch arrives in Kragerø in 1909, he has distanced himself from events. He has thirty-five years left to live, and will fear all who try to intrude upon his solitude.

*

There are moments in the life of every individual when all stands out in sharp relief, both what has been and what can reasonably be expected of the future.

Munch will live a life alone in large empty houses. He will paint and think in the present, but live in the past and the future. Will think that the language of a flower is its scent. Will try to get closer to the earth. Not just walk on the surface but live in a declivity of it, at the bottom of the atmosphere, like life on the sea-bed. Live a life surrounded by unseen forces, live in anticipation of the crystal kingdom, the certainty of one day being able to surrender to the earth, of being transformed, of becoming the stuff from which plants and trees grow. Reach upwards to the sun. Open out like the petals of a flower in the morning. Just that. Not look in any other direction.

*

But first there is the long winter in hospital.

Dear Jappe: A curious feeling to return to the hurly-burly of the world. I have become partly reconciled to the monastic existence in my room. *That* too has its charm. Having the world at arm's length. I seem to have a tenacity all my own. Yes, I must exhibit in Norway of course, but it won't be like before. My pictures are painted in foreign lands, and not as they were before in the same spirit as at home. And my old truculence, or to be more precise, keenness for a fight, has gone. I did not, like Sinding, leave the country in high dudgeon. I was simply hounded out. Dear Jappe, I would love to talk to you at length. Well, well, the time of alcohol, of mingled joy and sorrow, is over for me. A strange world is now closed to me. I can't see how you have stood it for so long. I have to get used to my room. That has its charm too. Its peace. And then there is reading. Women I leave in heaven, like the old Italian artists. The rose's thorns are too painful. I'm starting to enjoy women as one does a flower, breathing the scent and marvelling at the beautiful petals without touching them. At least this way one is not disappointed.

* * *

He takes walks at the zoo with his friend Helge Rode. He marvels at life's profusion and sees new pictures taking shape.

You must let me paint you, Doctor Jacobson. A life-sized portrait. I currently have exhibitions in Breslau, Munich and Cologne. I shall soon be having a show in Christiania. So long as I can paint I don't feel ill.

But is that legitimate, Munch?

I've been faithful to art, Doctor Jacobson. Now we shall see whether it is faithful to me.

He places Jacobson up in his room, models him like a sculpture.

Yes, like that. Keep still now.

But is it legitimate, Munch?

Yes, it is legitimate, for when he is painting, he is in charge. He feels that he has dominion over the doctor just as the doctor had dominion over him.

Let's have a drop, Doctor Jacobson.

Are you sure?

No, no. It's just that I too wanted to say something.

His capacity for work is still there. While it continues to be strong, there must still be hope. He places the doctor, imposing and feet wide apart, in a fiery inferno of colour. The Doctor stands firmly planted on both legs, hands by his sides, in a full-length frontal portrait. He looks extremely self-satisfied, is accustomed to making the diagnosis, to sealing the fate of others. Munch thinks there is something slightly ridiculous about him as he stands there with his all-too visible authority. He paints the doctor's portrait in red, violet and gold.

What colour shall I paint your beard, Doctor Jacobson?

That's madness, Munch! It doesn't look like me at all!

But don't you see how the door opens and the doctor, the day's ray of sunshine, comes in to the poor patients?

Perhaps, Munch.

Aren't you a little bow-legged, Doctor Jacobson? Who will buy this picture I wonder?

* * *

He paints *Self-Portrait at the Clinic*, without a cigarette. He is sitting by the window, his back to the observer, is still not ready to go out into the world. His nerves. They come in waves. Violent palpitations. The old symptoms.

But the alcohol has gone. The hangovers with it.

There is something aggressive, almost impatient, about the subject. As though a decision has been taken. As though he is merely waiting for its implementation.

*

Dear Munch: It occurs to me again that you *must* arrange an exhibition here in Norway. You owe it to the mother country and to all of us who are your friends here. And then you must bear in mind that your exhibition would take place in quite different circumstances from before. Whereas before all the papers were *against* you, now they would all be *behind* you. Even *Aftenposten* adopts a highly respectful tone when referring to your triumphal progress around Europe. As for me, life is unmitigated misery. I no longer see anyone. Whole weeks pass without my ever exchanging a word with another soul. We're getting old. My God, what an age it seems since I was young. All my old friends have gone away, scattered all over the world. Some have become so middle class and wealthy that they are lost to me. Others are permanently at rest and completely dead. All there is left is a middle-aged man of letters chewing over his fate. *Merde!* Your friend Jappe.

* * *

It is March 1909. While Munch is in the clinic, Jappe Nilssen and Jens Thiis arrange a major exhibition at Blomqvist's, featuring one hundred paintings and two hundred prints.

Dagbladet writes: Munch's exhibition at Blomqvist's is drawing throngs of rapt onlookers. The gallery is full the entire day, and even people who until quite recently looked upon most of Munch's pictures as strange, incomprehensible artistic runes are now making a serious effort and stand before each picture at length. It is obvious to anyone familiar with the Christiania public that no exhibition for many many years now has been so remarkable, so rich, has so caught the interest, gripped and impressed people as has this one with its spirituality and beauty, the exhibition has all the majesty and power of high summer. With this exhibition Edvard Munch takes his place as a *master* also in the consciousness of the wider, educated Norwegian public.

*

Dear Edvard: You can imagine what a joy it was for me to see that you have triumphed against all odds. I could see this in all your new works. To think that you could attain such power. It was interesting to see the people you know at the clinic. Inger was quite enraptured by the portrait of the Director. We have been happier than we can say at all the good reviews. It is so fine that everything is coming out at last. Now people can see what you've had to contend with. I'm writing just these few lines. I imagine you'll be receiving a lot of letters now. Your devoted Karen Bjølstad.

*

In Christiania, Munch's friends have secured sales to the city's wealthy elite. The business magnate Christian Mustad has made purchases, as have the art-loving Roede brothers. Also Ravensberg, Jappe Nilssen,

Gierløff and Thiis. This means they can cable to Copenhagen: You've sold pictures to the value of sixty thousand crowns.

Munch cables back: Arrange a lavish party in a private room at the Grand. Every conceivable delicacy.

Munch speaks to them by telephone at eight-thirty. The rest of the evening the telephone stands on the table with an open line to Kochsvej. He has a great deal to talk to them about.

* * *

Ørebladet 31 March 1909: Public quarrel between Jens Thiis and Christian Krohg. A high-profile libel action in the offing? National Gallery Director Jens Thiis and the painter Christian Krohg have not been on particularly good terms in recent years. They were rivals for the post of director of the art museum and the fact that Thiis was appointed did little to calm herr Krohg who, despite his good-humoured nature, can also be a quarrelsome fellow. Then came the Munch exhibition. Hapless Munch! Not only does he raise the whole temperature of the debate about the power of his paintbrush. He also causes a clash between two of the leading figures in our small community of artists. As already reported, Thiis spent a total of 10,000 crowns at the Munch exhibition. He was authorized to do so by his Ministry. A committee helped him to select the best pictures. Thiis set the ball rolling for the sale with a speed and energy which flabbergasted both Krohg and others. Now Christian Krohg is chairman of the committee of pictorial artists. And it is being said that the committee of pictorial artists is being bypassed in the appointment of the members of the buying committee. In *Verdens Gang* herr Krohg alleges that, in the presence of a number of people, and at Blomqvist's gallery, herr Thiis spoke in such terms of Krohg personally that Krohg considers he must give herr Thiis an opportunity to account for his comments. In front of me, Krohg continues, I have statements from two named and well-known figures, indicating that, on that occasion, herr Thiis said among other things that I was a scoundrel, who from *professional jealousy* of Munch had intrigued in the Ministry against the purchase of some of Munch's paintings, and also that: Krohg always acts only from the worst motives. So we will see what herr Thiis replies. It is all most exciting.

*

Doctor Jacobson advises Munch not to cut himself off.

But he still sometimes feels over-excited. Over-irritable. For a long time now during his breakdown he has been writing what he calls war letters to Ravensberg. Has written of battles, sieges, fortresses. A whole army of bastards. Or of pigs. Now he wants Ravensberg to look after the letters. He is thinking of issuing them as a book.

But for his part Ravensberg only sends victorious bulletins from

Norway, good news, the huge success at Blomqvist's, recognition by the general public, tries to get him to understand that the pictures of his enemies are highly exaggerated.

*

A farm with a garden? Munch writes. A place by the sea where I can receive my friends? Nobody will convince me that my flowering tree would not be undermined by a thousand voles nevertheless.

In the midst of his friends' elation in Christiania, Munch is in hospital processing the memories of his breakdown. He recalls the terrible siege of Hotel Wied, recalls the great throng's war cries outside the fortress, all their mean little plans, how they sat ensconced in a blood-red automobile which emitted wild cries, how the Enemy disguised themselves first as workers, then as policemen, tried to catch him off his guard. At Jacobson's clinic he dreams of buying a yacht with great white sails and of storming up to the bare cliffs, of crushing the Enemy at one fell swoop.

*

For it is still war.

He can hear the clash of swords at home. He can see the arrows like a cloud in the sky. He hears the din of huge blows. His friends! The noble skald Gierløff, the knight Dedekam, Jappe Nilssen and not least commander Jens Thiis, director of the National Gallery, with his qualities as general. Now they sally forth in spotless, shining armour, crushing the Enemy in a mighty battle. Yet the danger is not yet over. Assassins and cunning spies are at work, seeking to undermine the brave army. Voles and moles are eating soil fit to burst.

Munch greatly regrets that he cannot himself come and take part in the battle.

Now he is dreaming of a flying machine, the huge airship *The Eagle*. It is only a few months until Louis Blériot will fly across the English Channel. Peary reaches the North Pole and in Germany a cure for syphilis has been developed. So everything is possible.

But Doctor Jacobson says that Munch suffers from excess courage, his courage must be reined in, or it will burst his insides.

But will he listen?

The same day as Aunt Karen writes about her impressions of the exhibition, Munch sends his cousin Ravensberg the following order accompanied by an illustration:

I hereby declare that, owing to his misdeeds, old Krohg's beard shall be regarded as outlawed, so that it can be set on fire wherever anyone encounters him, in church, at the palace, in the committee, or on the lavatory. Under my seal E.M.

*

He leaves his room. Walks along the corridor. Down the stairs. Out into the hall. Walks out into the porch.

There before him lies the street. Lilacs on both sides.

He carries on walking. The street is not very wide. But when he comes out onto Vesterbro, the pavements are larger. There is room for several vehicles to pass. He makes for the zoo.

He notices that the street becomes wider with every step.

He pauses. The street pauses too.

But it is already too big.

A large crossroads lies ahead of him.

He walks along the walls of the houses. His heart is pounding. This road has become a lot larger since last time. It is spring. Light pours down from the sky. Far too much light. The dark crowns of the trees shine a delicate green. Far too few trees. Far too little shade. He feels the dizziness. Must not fall now. They would come running. A fresh attack. He would be moved to another room. There would be yet more reports in the newspapers. Mentally ill again. Mentally ill for good this time. Like Laura. Inevitable relapses. A person alone in space. Alone with his shadow. Far too much space. His body which feels too large. And yet too small.

An open door. He walks into the courtyard. His heart is pounding.

If he falls now, no one will see him.

* * *

Dear Munch: As far as I gather from your last letter, you won't be coming up here then. Goodness knows whether this isn't just foolish of you, Munch. If you successfully got through a stay here, you would be strengthened for the *rest of your days*. Perhaps you remember barely a year ago after my break with Oda, that I myself wasn't in particularly good shape for anything. If I now look back soberly on that period, I think I was actually half-insane and cannot understand how I was allowed to walk about freely. But all that winter it was crystal clear to me that if I could only get back to Paris, the city of *my* pain, if I could survive a stay there, where every street and every house, every smell and every person were memories, painful memories for me, I would be home and dry. And I had the courage to try it. I went there. Would you believe that for eight days I paced up and down outside the Café de la Régence without daring to go in, that I sat in a bar just opposite every single lunch time and looked across, but felt as though I would fall flat on my face as soon as I was over the threshold. So I took the plunge one day, and did not fall flat on my face. On the contrary. I did more. I took a room in the very hotel we had once lived in, took *the very room* where I had once known happiness. Of course it hurt like mad the first night, I readily admit, but it didn't kill me. On the contrary. I cheered up. And when I left Paris, I was a new man, who had cast his suffering aside, who had distanced himself from his memories and who in the future had no intention of letting himself be dragged down by them. Word of honour! I owe the whole lot to that trip to Paris. So it is on the basis of my own experience that I advised you to come up here. But of course you know best how much strength you have and what you can cope with. I won't advise you one way or the other. Your friend Jappe.

*

Dear Jappe: Let me try gradually to explain my position. Nobody I think fully understands what I have had to endure in Norway all these years. Up to a point my situation can be compared with yours some years ago. It was bad, but different. At least you were in love. And in a way that suffering is now an accepted, natural thing. But I had that terrible suffering without being in love. It was planned persecution. And it was not just *one* person who was involved. I stood alone against the thousand, and the thousand cast stones. I have felt just how defenceless a person is, and how impossible it is to obtain justice. And I have come to realize that there is no justice but that of might is right, of the herd. I would like this to be clear for the few people who really are my friends. I'm convinced that the many would still like to see me destroyed. And what an easy matter that would be. I have felt and understood that it would be easy to get rid of me, who have been so careless. During the three years people regarded me as more or less intimately associated with her, out of compassion I allowed myself to be torn to pieces and pestered until I was half dead, in order to get her back on her feet again and make the inevitable break bearable. When I had thus sacrificed myself to the limit, and she *had* got over it all and was in the arms of someone she was actually in love with, and who gave her comfort, the thought that I was actually living at all was intolerable to this person, so they dreamed up what will for all time be a disgrace to those involved. The drama of 1902. Bødtker is ill, they say, so I shall not punish him. Anyway, it seems his conscience does not trouble him. The Salomé of the moneyed aristocracy danced and gave out gold, and I had to give more than my life. I was hounded and pushed to the very brink of madness. As I've already said, nervous agitation, anger and sickness have merely led me to do some stupid things which have only harmed me and made these people's triumph all the greater. I have no alternative but to accept the inevitable. Struggle on as best I can with my shattered life. Thanks for your long letter. Many thanks also for all your efforts and your untiring work. I owe you a huge debt of gratitude for the success of the exhibition. Your devoted Edvard Munch.

*

To get rid of his nerves is an impossibility. But what about eliminating his enemies? He is thinking of an island near Kragerø or Fredriksvern. Open sea is best. He must leave within the fortnight. Otherwise he will never get out. Doctor Jacobson cannot forget what Munch has painted during his stay. Sane people do not paint green faces. Sane people do not place their doctor in a fiery inferno of colours.

But Munch wants to be off. The main battle must take place while he himself is present. Perhaps as early as the autumn. The Diorama Gallery. The light is better than at Blomqvist's. He thinks of Jæger. Every single painting transformed into a bomb. Shell them to pieces. The news that Jæger had returned to Christiania had gladdened him. He had written to Jappe Nilssen: I don't think Jæger is afraid of giving these half-baked Bohemians of very humble origins a piece of his mind. Let him throw the bomb. He will throw his own paintings into the faces of the Enemy, he must build himself up for the great battle, find a place by the open sea.

Ravensberg, dear kinsman. Do you know of anywhere near Larvik?

Or two days later: Do you know of anywhere near Skien?

He needs support. Someone who can assist him, come and fetch him, ensure that everything goes according to plan, keep a weather eye open for the Enemy, keep a special lookout for red automobiles.

A large, attractive red farm with a garden. Is there an island which might be suitable? Is there a beautiful spot with open sea and pine forest?

A further attack now might mean that he was incarcerated for good. He suddenly has revelations of new dangers. The button moulder is called Kollmann, but his own name is Peer Gynt, and in letters to Ravensberg, Christiania becomes another name for Hægstadtunet. There the people of Hægstad stagger about the worse for wear after all they have eaten and drunk and he feels sure they are in pursuit of him.

No, it must be a suitable house with a large garden, where he can devote himself to rest and fresh air and pottering about in the garden. A fortress on the coast. Inside the fortress walls, in the castle garden, he can play host to the brave warriors who have fought his battle. Lounging on the grass with a luxurious table prepared by Petra the Second. Wit and joy shall be the order of the day. Would Ravensberg be able to come down and help him at short notice?

*

He comes to Norway without knowing where he is going to live. It is spring 1909. Ravensberg has been to collect him from the clinic. He notes that Munch is still very weak. During the ferry crossing to Kristiansand he mostly sits quietly by himself. He who would otherwise have been talking nineteen to the dozen with his friends.

*

White, idyllic Sørland villages. Sørland in May. Tulips and white narcissi, the scent of lily of the valley.

He is on a trip with Ravensberg. Looking for somewhere to live. Kristiansand is too large, too dangerous, too many cigar shops. The temptations of drinking sessions with Thorvald Stang. And what about Lillesand, what about Grimstad, what about Arendal?

Ravensberg stands beside him on deck as they sail into Kragerø. He sees how the town rises up in terraces from the sea.

They book in at a hotel.

In the evening they take a stroll and discover Skrubben, two large houses linked by a bridge. The sea lies before them.

He sees the sparkling blue fjord, Stabbestad's long, low ridge of hills in the late evening sun. In the mouth of the fjord the large granite islet lies glowing red and warm, like a freshly lit port lantern in the first hint of twilight, enveloped in silence.

It is a piece of untouched nature. White granite cliffs and grey rocky outcrops with small green fields in amongst them. Lonely pines point skywards. In winter, the sun would probably rise in the middle of the sound, straight out of the sea, in the distance behind the outermost red islet.

* * *

Bergen *Aftenblad* 5 June 1909:

The Committee of the Art Association felt obliged to hang everything that Munch, in his unparalleled conceitedness, has ventured to send. If we confer the name of art on vulgarity without a word of protest, we are giving it public recognition. Since when have ugliness, stench and filth been accepted in the realm of art? Soon any miserable wretch will have the right to lay bare his stinking spiritual life in the halls of art. And the more absolutely he does so, and the more he stinks, the truer it is and the more he is entitled, not to compassion, but to admiration. Ugh! Murderers are locked up and protective measures are taken against anarchists, while others are permitted to spew forth their slimy poison over life's fundamental values and our children are at liberty to enjoy it unhampered.

*

And the Stavanger newspaper *Vestlandet*:

Farewell, prophet! Art is useful when it interprets common human feelings and ideals, makes everyone think and feel like a human being, when it makes us see what can form the stuff of happiness. None of this have I managed to find in the work of the prophet, this trailblazer, one of the world's great men, a Mohammed! He is so realistic, these miserable charlatans say, they find reality in him, the reality which consists of bright red breasts, violet backs with leprous colours, green beards, dirty petticoats and whole families of degenerate infants. You can keep it. It is the emperor's new clothes in a new version. And other artists are too spineless to do anything but say yes, amen. What if people think me stupid, they secretly sigh to themselves, then they cast their eyes towards heaven and cry: Oh how lovely, how artistic. And the people also stare their eyes out trying to discover the art. But they cannot find it. Yet they earnestly pay twenty-five øre, anxious to do anything but appear stupid. Farewell prophet!

* * *

Dear Edvard: Thank you for your postcards from Arendal and Kragerø. They were so welcome and it was lovely to hear from you. Now let me wish you a most enjoyable and happy summer. I hope you've got yourself a nice sheltered house, as there has been a nasty cold north wind. We lit the stove today. You say you're going to send us money, but you recently sent us 400 crowns. It's too much. You have so many expenses. What must all these exhibitions of yours cost and the travelling and storing your works! Kragerø looks like a nice lively little place. There will certainly be plenty of oysters and mackerel. Inger sends her greetings, as does Laura. Your devoted Karen Bjølstad.

*

Summer at Skrubben. In Bergen, Rasmus Meyer has bought ten paintings, including *Jealousy*, *Three Stages of Woman*, *Karl Johan*, *Dr Rathenau* and *Summer Night in Åsgårdstrand*. *The Morning After* and *The Frenchman* have been purchased by the National Gallery in Christiania. Munch has opted for isolation. The opposite of what Doctor Jacobson advised him. But to Schiefler he writes that the large unpopulated spaces have a calming effect on him. Inga Stærk prepares food with devotion. The garden is a riot of flowers and bursting with apples. To Ravensberg he writes that he is painting and reasonably happy. But fresh waves of nerves soon break over him.

Eva Mudocci has announced her arrival.

*

Concert in Kragerø. The hall of the craft workers' association. Sunday the first of August at six o'clock in the evening. Beethoven's Kreutzer sonata. Chopin, Corelli, Sarasate and Paganini. Tickets from fifty øre to one and a half crowns at Møller's bookshop.

*

But Munch is not there. He is sitting in his house up on the hill. He sends a letter down to the hotel and invites them to tea the following day.

288

Eva Mudocci and Bella Edwards walk up the steep slope to Skrubben. They see two large houses. So that's where he lives.

Eva Mudocci knocks at the door. Time passes. Then she hears his footsteps. Munch opens the door and gives them a warm welcome. An emotional moment. She thinks he looks unwell.

There is so much she cannot say and which it is too late to talk about now.

The tea is ready. There are radishes and cold potatoes on the table. He has decorated the table with small candles. They are served tea by Stina Krafft, whom Eva Mudocci calls a big peasant lass. In the middle of the meal Munch calls her in to tell her that her forefathers were kings in Norway.

Later Munch stands with Eva Mudocci and Bella Edwards in the garden. He shows them the tall stakes on which he has impaled the turnips. He tells them that each represents the head of one of his enemies, so that he can shoot at them whenever he feels like it.

*

In the moonlight he accompanies them down the steep hill to the hotel. He knows they will be staying one more day and invites them to another visit the following day, if they would like to come.

*

Again the two women walk up Barthebakken to Skrubben.

They knock at the door, but no one opens it. Then they carefully open the door and step into the spartanly furnished house with the ugly wallpaper, the ugly floors, the impersonal furniture.

Munch? Are you there?

He is in bed. The bedside table is covered with medicine bottles. He says it is influenza. He always catches it when autumn comes. He cannot shake off his bronchitis either. Now he is lying in bed trying to avoid the bacilli. Doesn't want to catch anything else. There is a cholera epidemic in Rotterdam. Several dead, apparently. Where was it Eva and Bella had come from, by the way? Isn't Kragerø also full of germs?

Then they leave him.

Everything is arranged. They can consider themselves his guests, he has already paid their hotel bill.

They take their leave.

Over forty years later, one spring day in 1950, at The Meadow Nursing Home in Sutton, Surrey, behind a screen in the large ward with all the sick, old people in it, Eva Mudocci remembers that once, on the second of September 1909, she had her last melancholy glimpse of Edvard Munch. Carried the memory of him away with her and, as she wrote, kept it sacred down all the ensuing years.

* * *

November 1909. Back to the Enemy's fortress. Christiania. Hægstad-tunet.

Munch drives all over the city in a car. He finds that Christiania has not changed after all the years he has been away. The centre still has a small-town look about it. Only parts of East Oslo, with the long streets and the rows of tenement blocks, smack of a big city in appearance and atmosphere.

He sees that the royal standard is flying over the royal estate at Bygdø. He notices the Abel Monument with satisfaction and he sees that the pictures in the National Gallery are perfectly hung.

This is the Enemy's city. Previously the Enemy was mainly called Heiberg and Bødtker, apart from frøken X. Now it is Krohg. So is Krohg going to build a palace right in the middle of Stortingsgaten? Is he going to make everything in the garden rosy for himself, sit on the throne in the middle of the palace with the Academy, The Artists' Committee and the Autumn Exhibition under him? And what of Queen Oda? Does she have dominion over it all?

There are many questions that remain unanswered. However, in a letter he reports that his combat vehicle hurtled into the ranks of the Enemy. The Enemy fled terror-struck.

* * *

He visits Åsgårdstrand again.

I shall tell you a story, or remind you of a story. There is an enchanted castle, as usual. A woman comes to it and meets a prince, as usual. Then you remember that he says: I am leaving now. You must not enter those three rooms. He leaves. And while he is away, she goes first into one, then into another and finally into the last and most important room.

Then everything disappears. For what is the innermost room? Everything the prince has lived for, dreamed of and defended. He could not have explained this to her, she would not have understood it.

Perhaps he *had* explained it hundreds of times, to no avail.

*

Château Munch. The garden and the fjord in the November light. How small it seems, château Munch. At Skrubben there are twelve rooms. Nothing happens in them. In Åsgårdstrand, in the living room with the hearth, in the kitchen with the stove, more happened than he could cope with.

He knows that they still gossip about him. He gave Ditten a good thrashing there, put Ingse Vibe across his knee at the hotel on Larkollen and spanked her bare behind. He threw Karsten out and stuck a gun through the window. But was it *he* who called himself a thief and not Ditten? Was it *he* who dreamed up the conspiracy and not

Bødtker? Was it *he* who attacked himself in Studenterlunden and not the police? And was it *he* and not Haukland who caused that commotion in Copenhagen?

But it was *he* who shot himself in the hand.

Perhaps Larsen at the Co-op would understand after all.

* * *

Inga Stærk cooks like a goddess. Ellef chops wood. And safely ensconced behind the counter the beautiful girls flash sparkling eyes towards the street. To Ravensberg Munch writes that he is boldly defending his fortress from a female enemy from Christiania, who has been in Åsgårdstrand several times.

And *Dagbladet* writes:

> Here, in Kittelsen's birthplace, he lives solely for his work, sails about the skerries in a motorboat, draws and paints water colours and, in a spacious room in his studio he has completed a number of large portraits this summer. It is well known that from the very beginning Munch has been racked by illness. It will gladden his friends to learn that he is now well, strong and healthy as never before. His country life in Warnemünde and in Kragerø and not least a long trip in Western Norway he made during the summer, have done wonders for his health. Certainly the fact that he has recently become so much stronger and more robust will also increasingly have set its stamp on his art.

*

He can see the light shifting on the fjord. He can see the sun glinting between the massive crowns of the trees in the garden. In December the horizon comes closer. The sun rises from the sea. From his windows he can see nature's own drama: The Sunrise. The calm surface of the sea, which can conceal all. Even the glow. That which suddenly becomes visible beneath the horizon. The light which struggles forth from the darkness, from the depths. Throws off slime and maggots, throws off death's embrace, spreads out over the surface of the water, intense red, poisonous yellow, like a reminder of hell, before rising, casting off its mortal frame, becoming visible as *another* body, as the sun, liberated and supreme, burning, able to create light. Light! Pours over nature and mankind, has transformed itself into an impregnable fortress, a burning hell, shining over sea and mankind. Creates life!

* * *

He has said yes to a competition, is invited to compete with Emanuel Vigeland, Eilif Peterssen and Gerhard Munthe for the decoration of the new assembly hall in the University of Christiania, which is to be built for the hundredth anniversary in 1911.

The challenge from Puvis de Chavannes. A commission for a decorative project in the Enemy's lair. Colossal dimensions.

He sees the sun rise from the sea.

Life is a bitter sacrament. The entrails of existence are filled with the stuff of decay. Man was a plant which sought the light but which instead stared vacantly out into the darkness of space.

The inspiration from Masaccio and Giotto. Man in nature, in the landscape, in the universe. The expulsion from paradise. The great eternal forces. The sun's overriding power. Zarathustra's sun. Man seeks the light, reaches up like a pillar towards the sun.

*

Ellef and Børre are two old men in Thomesheien. They help Munch with everything conceivable. Master painter Lars Fjeld puts thin paint onto a long piece of string, attaches it tightly to the sides of the canvas, holds it in the middle and lets it snap back onto the canvas, repeats this procedure five or six times making long straight lines and says there you are. Now Munch can begin to paint.

Børre sits as model on a chair.

Munch begins to paint *History*. A distant landscape with an epic air about it. Cliffs, sea and a gnarled giant oak. Beneath the tree sits an old man from the fjords who has toiled ceaselessly down the ages. He sits absorbed in his memories and tells *History* to a little boy. It is intended as a symbolical representation of knowledge acquired through the simple source of all knowledge, *experience*. Experience, which is clarified through memory, as it is handed down from generation to generation. Munch paints Børre. He sees how the eyes of the old, much-travelled skipper flash as something from the days of yore appears in his mind's eye.

Børre the seaman. Odysseus has come ashore. Now he sits on a chair in the garden at Skrubben and is a model for *History*. The historian P. A. Munch's nephew is painting him. It is winter in Kragerø.

Have you been to Antwerp, Munch? asks Børre, as he sits on the chair.

Antwerp? Yes, I have been to Antwerp.

There was a damn fine lass there, in that restaurant down by the quayside.

Damned fine, and no mistake.

Munch?

Yes?

I wonder who snapped her up?

Well, he was a dashed lucky fellow. How long ago can that be now?

It must be near on a half century now, that it must.

I don't think I was born then, Børre.

* * *

The new year begins with death. Death in Christiania. The first war on the rats. The health authorities go onto the offensive in January. Rats are a serious danger to health. Rats can carry infectious diseases. In East Oslo especially the cellars are full of them. The health authorities announce that the war against the rats will continue for the rest of the year and the plan is to destroy a hundred thousand rats.

But Jæger also dies. Jæger is finished, is in Ullevaal hospital, will probably die within the fortnight. It is the seventeenth of January 1910 and Jappe Nilssen writes to Munch from Christiania. Jappe needs money, desperately needs it, needs two hundred crowns. If he does not pay his rent within the week, he will be thrown out onto the street. Jappe Nilssen at 11 Olav Kyresgate. He is one of Jæger's closest friends now. Both have lost in love. And the same woman too. Both have written a novel about their love for her. Both of them feel they are failures in life. To a Swedish girlfriend, Jappe Nilssen writes that he has reached the stage when, tired and without hope, he says to himself: *à quoi bon?* Suddenly one day one is worn out. Tired to death. It is the constant marking time that has eaten away all one's strength. He writes off his own novels as failures. He becomes physically ill at the mere sight of his books.

While Jæger for his part, having completed the trilogy about his love for Oda Krohg and the politico-philosophical colossus *The Anarchist's Bible*, recognizes that his life has been a complete failure, a pointless failed existence. Cannot look back on more than six weeks' real life. Six weeks in 1888. Jæger who writes that he thinks twice a day, once in the morning on getting up, when he thinks: Now I'm going to waste a day. Then again in the evening when he is going to bed. Then he thinks: Now I've wasted it. He leafs through his book *The Anarchist's Bible*, to complete which he expended years of his life. Now he can barely grasp what he wrote himself.

The thought of death has gradually become a close friend.

Perhaps he will last a month. His whole stomach is eaten up by cancer. He can hardly take any food and will ultimately starve to death. The doctors who cut him open said it was the worst case of cancer they had ever seen.

*

Dear Munch! Hans Jæger was very touched by your greetings. Apparently he hadn't expected it, thinking instead that you were hostile to him. He asked me to thank you profusely. He looks most moving as he lies there in his little hospital bed in the large high-ceilinged ward with his long grey beard tumbling down over his chest and his small hands so white, quite transparent and wax-coloured against the blanket. And his eyes have become so strangely large and bright, as bright as a child's. He was hoping to be discharged this Wednesday. Just now Henrik Lund, whose praises he sang, has got him a proper place to live. He had promised that Jæger would at least be very comfortable for the week or two he has left. I'm going to see him this afternoon and ask him to get moving. Jæger himself is taking the whole thing with remarkable calm. Nevertheless, he asks a few questions now and then. But I can't stand it for long when I go to visit him. It's so terribly sad. All those sick people everywhere, half of them condemned to death and bearing its stamp on their faces. And Jæger himself doesn't look very much of this world now either. Death has already set its stamp upon him. He looks almost transfigured. Greetings. Yours Jappe.

*

It is the death of the Bohemian. Munch will never forget Jæger's face. The Bohemians gave Munch life. Jæger gave him his defiance and independence. Confirmed thoughts he had already had, such as that there was no point in kneeling humbly before Christ as his father had done. Jæger, who on the contrary defined Christianity as a *negative* factor in society, together with the old, bourgeois idea of justice and not least *morality*, and through it the bourgeois marriage code. In other words: hypocrisy. While Munch's sister was following Skrefsrud to see which church he was going to worship in, Munch was going about with Hans Jæger, who taught him to listen to his own voice, taught him to live his own life.

*

Munch is in Kragerø painting *History* as Jæger fights for his life in a hotel room in Tostrupgården, directly opposite Parliament. Jappe Nilssen sits with him and can hear the sound of the cars and trams droning past, the sound of people's laughter mingling with his friend's death rattle.

For Munch, Jæger's death is further confirmation that it is the end of an era.

*

Munch himself has no time to die.

He is living in a roomy house with pictures. Portraits, landscapes and sketches for monumental decorations. Outside nature is harsh. He sees people who live off it and in it. Børre and Ellef, Inga and Stina, master painter Lars Fjeld, who can come and correct his work on *History*, pointing out that a branch on the oak tree is too thick in relation to the trunk. Munch listens and asks: How many centimetres thicker, Fjeld? Five? Ten? Kragerø has both coast and mountain. Rocks, curves, vistas. Robust characters who are not easily hoodwinked. Munch blends everything into a pictorial whole, abandons the psychological sauna of *The Frieze of Life* for a cooler approach. In the portraits he looks straight into the personality. His colleague Henrik Sørensen comments that Munch would not have been allowed to paint him even if he had wished to. Because Munch is dangerous. He sees straight through the personality, turns it inside out. Then he hangs it up on a hook and there it hangs for ever.

Munch paints *Springtime Work in the Archipelago*. It is a neutral subject. Man and nature are given equal weight, complementing one another in line and colour. The man and woman cultivating their small plot of land almost merge into the landscape. They are not immediately visible. They are a part of the whole, of the rocks, the grass, the earth. He paints *Winter Landscape*, *Galloping Horses* and *Scrapping a Ship*. Day-to-day life in a small town.

But suddenly fear rears its head again. He paints *The Murderer on the Road*.

Then it is time for another exhibition. The Diorama Gallery in Christiania. Eighty-six paintings and a hundred and thirty-seven graphic works.

*

He exhibits his monumental sketch for the decoration of the University assembly hall. History beneath the tree of knowledge personified by a blind fisherman. Vigeland's and Munch's designs are in competition with Gerhard Munthe. Eilif Peterssen's did not actually receive the go-ahead, but the committee has unanimously decided that Vigeland's and Munch's designs should actually be painted, at the artists' own financial risk and in real-life dimensions, so that they can be displayed in the assembly hall and judged again. If the committee *then* accepts them, the artist may be paid twenty thousand crowns though the committee reserves the right to a completely free hand in the matter.

Then Christian Krohg goes onto the offensive, attacking both Vigeland and Munch head on in *Verdens Gang* on the twenty-third of March 1910. Emanuel Vigeland's design, *Battle of the Dragons*, Krohg writes, is not even worth analysing. Even for someone with no idea of art, it has a completely horrifying effect. As people will have seen, the design shows three horsemen, symmetrically placed, riding merrily along on prancing and incidentally poorly-drawn horses reminiscent of a circus. Two of the riders are stabbing their spears into something which at first glance looks like a sack, but turns out to be a kind of monster, patently intended to represent stupidity or ignorance, and bearing a crown on its head.

And Krohg goes on:

Munch's design was a little more popular with the public and naturally is far superior to it in many respects. But in the *essentials*, which is to say in the idea, the thought, the composition, it is more or less just as misconceived, muddled and naïve as the other one. People are moved by the old fisherman who sits there teaching a little boy the history of Norway. Yet there is absolutely nothing about either him or the boy to suggest that he is doing so. It is not the history of Norway that he is teaching, say the design's admirers. It is the history of the World, it is history in essence. No, on the evidence of our eyes we cannot possibly accept this. A poor fisherman with a patched knee who knows anything about world history is so exceptional that some special explanation is required for one to believe in it. And even if he does know some, it is hardly of the sort which merits the proud and lofty designation: Knowledge. Just as exceptional is the nine-year-old fisher boy listening raptly to a scholarly lecture.

* * *

Dear Edvard: Now Easter is upon us again. The years are rolling by. It is really lovely weather with lots of sunshine, so we've even been sitting on the veranda. In the evening the most enchanting moonlight. I always think of you then. I think it is so lovely that you're living peacefully in your beautiful house in Kragerø while here there is nothing but din and racket, as though a pack of dogs had been let loose. How can artists be so envious? It looks as though Schibstedt and Krohg are in cahoots. Naturally you can't accept this job on such conditions. It would just lead to upset wouldn't it? I think it is so good that you say nothing. Your devoted Karen Bjølstad.

* * *

Dagbladet 5 November 1910:

Edvard Munch has now been living in Skrubben at Kragerø for a year and in those healthy and beautiful natural surroundings has recovered to a peak of health he has never enjoyed before. However, this winter he is leaving to put into practice a long-cherished plan: to acquire his own quiet little farm with an Icelandic horse and all the rural trappings. Yesterday he purchased Consul Juul's splendid great country manor, Ramme, at Hvitsten and will soon be moving in there. Along with the farm there is a large old garden with a hundred fruit trees and three hundred rose bushes, a fine pine wood, a long stretch of shore and mountains. Sheer delight for an artist and for Munch's art. He will also be taking with him the large studio which he built at Skrubben for the decorations to the University assembly hall and will use it to paint the final decorations based on the two designs.

*

He is not allowed to buy Skrubben. The authorities in Kragerø want to hold on to the property. Munch asks if he can just buy the buildings and the garden inside the fence. The authorities reply that they need the site for a hospital. In the local paper there is a heated debate.

But Munch does not cancel his tenancy agreement. Not yet. Just as he links Åsgårdstrand and Christiania to *The Frieze of Life*, he links Skrubben to *History* and *The Sun*. He hangs on to a property for the sake of a few paintings. As long as the authorities will allow.

*

But he *is* allowed to buy the property Ramme at Hvitsten. A hundred fruit trees. The year is 1911. Among other things Munch will paint *Shipyard* and make the woodcut *Snow Shovellers*.

Ravensberg, noble kin: The Count of Skrubben and Lord of Ramme and Åsgårdstrand sends greetings to the proud conqueror of the Capitol. I have raised my triumphant flag on the Diorama Gallery and am opening my exhibition on 1 April. Pity you cannot be there to assist me. The sun is shining in through the castle windows at Ramme as I write you these lines. Snow, sun and mud determine the whereabouts of the castle staff consisting of 3 turkeys, 2 pigeons, 3 ducks and 4 hens. There is also a Nordfjord horse called Rousseau and a billy goat. Have sold the bathing picture in Helsinki for ten thousand frs. Roede is earning an extraordinary amount of money from his cinematograph. I am perhaps going to buy a motorboat. Your friend and kinsman E. Munch.

*

Munch strolls about a property where a previous owner, a rich Belgian, buried his dog Bel Ami in a peaceful little cove. Above the small grave he had erected against the cliff a monument with an animal sculpture and a stone tablet bearing the dog's name, its date of birth and death and in French had written what *Dagbladet* on the twentieth of March called 'the age-old sad and profound epitaph': The better I got to know people, the more I loved my dog.

At the foot of the monument is a trough where the horses can slake their thirst.

*

He is having an exhibition in Christiania again, at the same time as Krohg. Henrik Sørensen also has an exhibition.

The Diorama Gallery in April. One hundred and eleven paintings, twenty-five drawings, one hundred and forty-two graphic works, as well as the Alpha and Omega series and animal studies in lithography.

Krohg is having a retrospective in the slightly more elegant Art Association. The Bohemian has become a bourgeois.

This is the real battle. Munch must feel extraordinary satisfaction at being able to cram the Diorama Gallery full of his animal studies. *Burlesque Loving Couple. Crouching Bird of Prey. The Man and the Ostrich. Man and Woman. The Woman and the Bear. The Woman, the Tiger and the Bear. The Woman and the Snake. The Poodle in the Bows. Omega and the Pig. Omega and the Deer. Omega's Eyes. Alpha's Progeny. Alpha's Despair. Infidelity.*

Here comes Gunnar Heiberg, sailing forth with his fat little belly. And is there anyone who can recognize the rich daughter of P. A. Larsen the wine merchant?

Work has become convalescence. In a letter to Schiefler, Munch writes that he does not feel strong if he does not work. Alcohol replaced by painting.

Before he had to drink to be able to paint. Now he has to paint so as not to drink.

* * *

Karen Borgen sits in front of him at the easel.

Now Munch is no longer shy of women. But in this particular case the woman is a model. He needs a third principal motif for the assembly hall decorations.

As a sixteen-year-old he had drawn a peasant farmer's wife in Hedmark with a child at her breast. That was the beginning of the third motif, Munch tells Thiis. He also says that he bought Nedre Ramme because he needed room for his open-air studio and also to complete the assembly hall pictures. He wants to give the *Alma Mater* motif the same earthbound character as he had given *History* in Kragerø.

He is at Ramme in Hvitsten. This is the place where, in 1888, Jæger played out all his unhappy love affair with Oda Krohg. The place of absinthe and mental breakdown. How many men clawed at Oda's windows just a stone's throw away? Here Krohg paced up and down and threatened to take his own life if Oda would not marry him. It was here that Jæger lived his weeks of real life.

Time has effaced all traces. A lush coastal landscape is all that remains. Silent trees. Cool wind. He will be able to grow asparagus here.

He paints Karen Borgen. *Alma Mater*. Or *The Researchers*. A motif which, according to Munch himself, reflects the Norwegian landscape and spirit, summer and fecundity, the rivalry between researchers, the thirst for knowledge and the desire to achieve. Later he simplifies the motif. Removes some of the bathing children. He is thinking of the assembly hall. The main area on the right or left wall. In each of the two areas at the back stand a young man and a young woman, on the right almost asleep, illuminated by the rays of a new sun, heart to heart, on the left poring expectantly over glowing flasks, both pictures point towards the future in certain respects.

From the mountain to the east of Ramme he can see southwards towards Hurum and Filtvedt. He has found a west-facing cove where he can paint new versions of *Bathing Men*. But Alma Mater sits there with her child. Woman is no longer a threat. Munch is back to the beginning, woman as the prerequisite of all life.

Woman as motif.

*

Dear Thiis: What a lot of flak I've received for keeping Nedre Ramme so I could make studies for the assembly hall pictures! They want it as a bathing place. Which is more important, I ask, that your children should bathe or that Alma Mater's children should bathe? I have another place further away which ordinary mortals can use.

*

Tidens Tegn 8 August 1911. The assembly hall. No one votes for Vigeland. Nor is Munch's work accepted. None of the members of the jury and none of the architects has been able to recommend acceptance of Vigeland's work. The building committee is unanimous on this point. Two members of the jury, Skovgaard and Thiis, recommend that Munch's work should be accepted, whereas Dietrichson does not find it acceptable and the architects advise against it. There will be no fresh competition. The artists are at liberty to submit further designs at their own expense. Vigeland's painting for the rear wall will be taken down, and he has no intention of exhibiting it. Munch on the other hand wants to show his work at the Diorama Gallery. The walls of the assembly hall are to be hung with yellow silk.

*

Dagsposten the same day: The architect Sinding-Larsen today made a strong attack on National Gallery Director Thiis. He accuses him of having been behind the article in *Tidens Tegn* criticising the fact that the architects should serve on the jury and also of having been behind the protest against this by Edvard Munch and Skovgaard. As regards the protest from the board of pictorial artists, Thiis also has a finger in the pie, because, despite the fact that the matter was confidential, he informed the architect Werenskjold that the architects were to serve on the jury. Sinding-Larsen further reports that the painter Vigeland has submitted a written demand that Thiis should step down from the jury as unfit to serve owing to his links with Munch.

*

The Researchers. Alma Mater. A somewhat vaguely formulated motif. The balance between the young bathing boys, which Munch tells Thiis is his speciality, and represent empirical research, and the female figure, *universitas*, against the backdrop of a biological universe. In content an echo of *History*. Munch's own will split in two. He thinks that a work of art is a crystal. As the crystal has life and a soul, so must the work of art. It is not enough for a work of art to have proper external planes and lines. When a stone is thrown at a group of boys, they scatter. There is a regrouping, an event has occurred. It is a composition. To reproduce this regrouping in colour, line and surface is an artistic and pictorial motif. It does not have to be literary, that term of abuse that many use about paintings which do not represent apples on a tablecloth or a violin broken in two.

* * *

Dear Aunt: I have a few hens to spare. Would you two like a couple? Don't really want to kill them, but may have to anyway. I've got a lot of new hens. Write to Ramme, where I shall be going in a few days. Am on a little trip to Fredrikshald. Greetings to Inger. Yours E. Munch.

* * *

November in Kragerø. Munch is at Skrubben again. Restless, impatient in his work. Suddenly the assembly hall pictures have become a mission in his life, just like *The Frieze of Life*. A major work. A concrete manifestation of his philosophical standpoint. While the perspective in *The Frieze of Life* is individual, it is universal in the assembly hall pictures. Nature's laws push the individual into the background.

The first winter storm comes to Kragerø. Munch sits by the stove writing to Schiefler. Together with Johan Anker, Fredrik Stang and fru Stang Lund, Thiis has set up a committee to collect private funds to buy the pictures, or at least the completed *History*, and to *present* it to the University.

*

Lieber Herr Schiefler: I am again sitting in the large house in the little coastal town where I was cast up three years ago by a large storm. Like a fairytale! Well, now I again yearn for large cities. It's a sign that I am getting better. Now I've become incredibly careful. I neither smoke nor drink. Smoking does such a lot of harm. Perhaps I'll go on a trip some time over Christmas, but I'm very uncertain whether I yet want to re-visit the places where I have had hallucinations. Why don't you take a ship via Kristiansand and come here?

Munch feels hardened now. To Schiefler he describes – illustrating it as well – how he stands up to his calves in the snow, shovelling it away. He writes: Today I've shovelled the snow away from my outdoor studio, where I'm painting the pictures for the assembly hall. It seldom happens that an artist's studio is full of snow, I think. But what can one do when the sky is full of it!

He encloses a photo which he calls Master Builder Solness.

* * *

Munch and Schiefler in lamplight. Outside snow falls. Munch is making woodcuts while his friend sits looking on. It is the twenty-eighth of December 1911, and Schiefler writes from Hvitsten to his wife Louise:

This must be the strangest birthday I've ever had. Munch put me up in his own bed, so I should be as comfortable as possible. He slept in the guestroom. So I slept very well right until your little clock told me that it was seven o'clock. Just after that the old housekeeper came to make up the fire and at eight o'clock she brought in coffee. At eight-thirty I got up. In the east reddish clouds could be seen which gives us hope of better weather. I walked through the garden to the shore and clambered up the granite cliff which separates Munch's garden from the fjord and, in the company of a caretaker and a pine tree, looked out on the morning landscape. Now I must break off, as the man who is to take the letter is ready. Pity, as there was so much more I wanted to tell you.

*

The moon over the tree tops. Supper the evening before departure. The pictures for the Munich exhibition are being packed. Schiefler came straight to Hvitsten from Germany. Now he is going to accompany Munch to Kragerø via Christiania. It is the last days of 1911. Munch's terrier Fips rushes excitedly about. Munch has a number of people in his employ. There are two permanent staff at Ramme. The old housekeeper accompanies them on their journey to Kragerø.

Schiefler and Munch walk through the forest down to the jetty where the steamships dock. The others have gone on ahead. After three minutes Munch realizes he has forgotten something. Schiefler plods on alone through the snowbound forest, recognizes scenes Munch has described in his paintings. *Winter Night. Starry Night.* The trees cast delicate shadows on the white moonlit surface. A sleigh suddenly comes towards him along the narrow path. He hears the jingling of bells. Schiefler looks round to see whether Munch is following behind him. But there is only deep silence.

Then he hears Fips barking in the distance. The steamer will soon be here.

As will Munch.

*

It is New Year's Eve 1911. It is the day on which Scott, after shooting his dogs, carries on alone with four men inland from the Beardmore glacier, not knowing that, seventeen days earlier, Roald Amundsen had already won the race for the South Pole.

Schiefler writes to his wife: *Mein liebes Herz.* When we were approaching Kragerø, the passage through the skerries was so narrow that you could touch both sides, left and right. The clear sky had vanished. A cold wind blew snow in our faces when we went up on deck. When we arrived at eight o'clock in the morning it was still dark. Around us, on the islands on both sides of the fjord, lights flickered, but as we were tying up the daylight grew stronger. Munch's factotum was waiting for us with horse and sleigh, and the large retriever Boy, a magnificent creature, was beside himself with joy. Kragerø has some 7,000 inhabitants and is therefore by no means a small place. The town rises steeply up from the harbour towards the hill. On top of it are pines silhouetted against the sky. Everywhere granite, syenite and gneiss protrude from the ground in round knolls, reddish and greyish. And here and there ancient Silurian slate, the oldest formations being much, much older than the Alps. Everything rounded, worn by glaciers again and again. We went off to Munch's house, which lies on a headland. Beside it a magnificent pine towers up. A large house with a great deal of room. He has only rented it, but is happy there. He says: Hvitsten is too idyllic for me, I can't really get going with my painting. Here in Kragerø it is less peaceful and more lively. In Hvitsten the rooms are pleasant, warm and wood panelled. In Kragerø it is not very tastefully papered, it is cheaply furnished, and has bachelor written all over it. All the rooms are full of pictures. The graphic art is in an extra room, of necessity arranged on the floor. This is how he wants it. Comfort might damage his art, which in point of fact always tends to be large in scale. I was dog tired and slept on the sofa while he went for a walk in his beloved Kragerø. Then he came to talk about the accommodation arrangements. He had wondered whether the guest bed was perhaps not a little too narrow, and whether I was content with it. Of course I was. It was as narrow as a chest, indeed as a coffin, but incredibly comfortable. The blankets fitted tightly round the body. Just now we went for a walk together up to the hill between the cliffs which were covered in icicles, through the pine forest, where he played with his dog, hid, let it seek him out, and was happy over the beautiful creature. Then we passed cliffs in streets high up on slopes. The people we met were friendly, young girls and women greeted us with a curtsey, rather lovely – and so back to the house. Hot lunch and a wonderful nap. Since then – after a cup of tea with cakes, the little sleigh was harnessed up, and we sped away with a merry ting-a-ling, first down steep streets, then beside the harbour, and back up the slope across the town. Many times it was quite frightening. Munch himself was a little vexed, because the shaft was not properly made and the sleigh swung about somewhat. Then we drove into a side valley between cliffs, meadows and forest. Then beside mountains, eventually coming out up where we had been for a walk in the morning. We proceeded carefully down the steep road to the painter's house, dinner, a nap – and a further walk through the town. Early to bed, I was a little over-tired. But a magnificent sleep into the New Year.

Ultimately, living in close proximity to such a nervous person can sometimes be trying. But all the same the visit was harmonious throughout, and I must say that my respect for the man and the artist has grown a good deal more. He places his art above all else, his feeling for it being akin to reverence. The thoughtfulness and kindness he showed towards me personally was touching.

* * *

A new year. Munch will paint *Galloping Horse*, *Fir Trees*, *Kragerø* and make lithographs of *Christian Sinding*, *Tor Hedberg*, *T. Stang*, *Snow Shovellers*. The *Titanic* is prepared for her maiden voyage. The suffragettes break windows in London.

Munch feels stronger, is in Skrubben and looks out to sea. A warm south-west wind blows from the continent. Has he the courage to see Paris and Berlin again? He writes to Ravensberg in Rome that he is also yearning for Italy. He wants to clarify his relationship to the world, say to himself: My art is confession. In other words, a kind of egoism. But then he thinks: My art will also help to clarify other people's relationship to the world in their search for truth.

He has received a flattering enquiry from the Sonderbund Exhibition in Cologne. In just one year he will exhibit his work in Vienna, Munich, Paris, Christiania, Cologne, Jena, three different venues in Berlin, and also in Barmen, Gothenburg and New York.

* * *

Copenhagen, Hamburg, Paris and Cologne. The sun is even higher in the sky. Green plants shoot up from the earth. Heralding new life. Heralding destruction. The *Titanic* hits an iceberg and sinks. Munch revisits the old places, walks on the boulevards and feels the sun warm him, while the Bolsheviks in St Petersburg publish the first issue of *Pravda*.

*

The Enemy is almost invisible now. The Enemy is at home in Christiania. Paris is free of toads, pigs, poodles and snails. Munch exhibits a painting and two graphic works at the Salon des Indépendants. Spring in Paris. Spring which always makes him doleful and melancholy. The light has a strong effect on him. People's shadows become sharp and clear. He is back in the city of the vision and the inferno. Transformation of matter. Where is the white cat? Where are the Romanians who played their folk melodies at the Montagnes Russes? And the woman who sang the Carilla waltz? Where is Hans Jæger who lived a friendless existence in Montmartre? Paris. What became of Kalle

Løchen, what became of Hertzberg? Is that dreadful room in rue Condamine just as draughty? And what happened to the concierge in St Cloud?

*

He walks past the terrible rue de la Gaïté, the sombre, quiet rue Delambre. Then he turns off Boulevard Montparnasse and sinks down into a chair outside Closerie des Lilas and opens his paper, reads that Norway and Russia have declared Spitsbergen a neutral area, reads that the author August Strindberg is dead, at the age of sixty three.

*

Good heavens, Strindberg. Baccarat to his honour! Then condemned to friendship with his friends at the Ferkel. There he would sit wearing his little smile, now sarcastic, now childish. Then Paris. He had jumped out of the frying pan into the fire, was about to descend into the deep shafts of hell. Munch sits there remembering a whole stream of images. Their time together in Berlin, the end table at the Ferkel, surrounded by Danes, Swedes, Finns, Norwegians and Russians, lustily extolled by the young German poets. Munch remembers Dehmel who stood on the table and paid tribute to the poet with such gusto that the bottles fell to the ground. He remembers the first nights of the maestro's plays, the exchanges were like the clash of steel on steel, the words delivered with the speed of rapiers. They had the heady fizz and sparkle of the red and white wine on the tables, their glow reflected like small fires all around. He bore his *Inferno* in his hands and offered it up to the public. *Legends*. The strangest novels since *Crime and Punishment*.

*

Munch gets up from the café table, takes out his watch and sees it is time to be getting along.

He takes the train to Germany, to the Sonderbund Exhibition in Cologne, where the aim is to give a comprehensive survey of the most important trends in modern art.

Dear Jappe: I've enjoyed the trip which I think will do me good. The exhibition opens tomorrow. They've given me a very large space. 10 by 15 metres. It's the largest room in the exhibition. The main section will be Van Gogh, Gauguin and Cézanne. 3 rooms of Van Gogh! 86 pictures. Extremely interesting. I'm almost ashamed at having been given such a lot of space. But that was the idea after all. Let's hope they won't regret it. Here there's hardly a varnished picture to be seen. Never has advice been so apposite as in your article on the varnishing of my pictures. Here that is regarded as vandalism. Naturally there's a great amount of *mattissisme* and *cézannisme* just as at home. But I was happy. This time at last almost no apples. The Norwegians will make up for this deficit. I asked a little Hungarian who was hanging his section. Apples? I said. What, he said. Apples? He looks at me pensively, secretively, and then whispered: Back home. We've left our apples in Hungary. This trip has shaken my belief that the country life is the only salvation, and I've got back my taste for large cities. Here the most outlandish things painted in Europe are collected together. In comparison I'm a pure classicist and very colourless. Cologne cathedral is being shaken to its foundations.

* * *

Munch in University hall! Exhibition opened today!

Dagbladet 12 June 1912: It was one of the great openings, one of those which are hotly debated, before, during and after. People arrived in groups, full of expectation, discussing the event beforehand. Would the pictures look good? Would they be suitable for the assembly hall? What effect would they have on its dimensions? If the discussion was already as animated as this in the vestibule, it was certainly no less vociferous inside the hall itself, where the two or three hundred guests gradually assembled, including many artists and architects, numerous parliamentarians, more than a score of professors, the foreign minister and the minister for justice, various members of the diplomatic corps, members of the city council, mayors and the prefect, to mention only some. Opinions were exchanged in friendly and less friendly terms. And just as with all great premières, there were many in favour, many against and almost no don't knows.

*

Then Christian Krohg writes in *Verdens Gang*: It is simply not the case, as certain newspapers have sought to claim, that all criticism has been gagged now that the pictures are hanging in what may eventually be their permanent home. It would also be utterly remarkable if the setting had so great an influence on people's judgement that, although when first shown in the Diorama Gallery they considered the paintings dreadful, when they were shown in the assembly hall, people suddenly considered them excellent. However, one readily acknowledges that the very first superficial impression is slightly more favourable in the assembly hall. This is not saying *much*, and anyway that first impression does not last long owing to shortcomings in the composition and above all owing to insufficient clarity in the conception. If one is to abandon the safety and security of earth and nature, it must be because one is able to pilot one's conceptual aeroplane to great heights and because the engine is superlative. In this case alas the ascent would seem to have been too casually undertaken. The engine powering the imagination did not generate enough speed to keep the aeroplane airborne, so now it lies a tangled wreck on the earth it should never have left and the pilot will no doubt never again hazard such experiments. In the wake of this most recent failed attempt by Munch to decorate the assembly hall, I think an *international* competition should be held.

* * *

Surrounded by ducks, turkeys, pigeons, a Nordfjord horse and various dogs, Munch sits reading Krohg's words. He has already written to Thiis about Krohg, considers that the erstwhile leader of the Bohemians is now revealing his petty and often rather nasty sides. That circle no longer has anything to fight for and has become impotent. It therefore pokes its nose in everywhere. And is as gossipy as a bunch of old women.

He feels the pressure in his eyes.

An accumulation of blood.

He knows he must work. That he must complete *Alma Mater*.

He feeds his poultry, trains his dogs, strokes his horse, paints with his brush.

He is proud of his dogs. As he will later say to Ingse Vibe's son: Wonderful dogs, they're man-eaters.

Suddenly he sees a man coming his way between himself and a white dog. The shadow of the stranger's leg casts a dark patch onto the dog. Long after the man has passed by, the dark patch is still there.

*

Then he receives greetings via the newspaper. Margrete Vullum, who once drove him from Florence up to Fiesole, when Tulla Larsen left for Paris. She realised his physical weakness and mental torment. She found a room for him high up on a mountain where there had once been an Etruscan town. She did not want him to die. Now she writes in *Morgenbladet* and *Tidens Tegn* under the heading 'Christian Krohg':

> We have gradually had to accustom ourselves to his destructive urge. We know he has done everything in his power to destroy Vigeland. We know he is doing everything in his power to destroy Thiis, although anyone can see that love of art breathes from his every pore. We have grown used to it – but is it now going to be Munch's turn as well? Is the mere fact that Thiis is working for Munch's assembly hall all that is needed for Krohg to take against him? Christian Krohg who had such power as the master of realism, and who was nevertheless so broad-minded that he was actually the one who opened so many people's eyes to Munch's singular and uncommon art. Munch, who enjoyed all Krohg's sympathy in his artistic manhood! Krohg does not write now to *correct* people, but to place a spanner in the works. He no doubt feels that all his academic rules are persuasive. All this seems to us to do violence to his true self. Sadly, many of us are asking: What has become of Christian Krohg?

A gritty, bloody-horned snail with a brothel on his back.

Munch potters about among his animals at Ramme in Hvitsten think-ing of Krohg. Krohg who accepted, who demanded, who beseeched, who threatened. Krohg, who had stood up triumphantly before all his wife's lovers and said: Last night I cuckolded *the lot of you*! Krohg who had implored his Oda to marry him, at Rammebråten close by, and helped Jæger to carry out his most serious suicide attempt, admittedly abandoned at the eleventh hour, because it was raining.

Krohg who perhaps had a lot to avenge.

What does it mean to devote one's life to a woman? What would have happened if fru Thaulow had not become fru Bergh? What would have happened if Tulla Larsen had become fru Munch? Or Tupsy? Or Ingse? Or Eva Mudocci?

Munch strolls about at Ramme with Fips, his wise dog. The soul of a wise old man has taken up residence in Fips. The dog walks about and keeps an eye on the poultry. On the grass Rousseau the horse stands grazing, slowly but surely eating itself to death from lack of exercise.

Krohg waited for Oda all those years. In the end, she came back.

Later Munch says to Rolf Stenersen: There is just as much difference between woman and man as there is between round lines and straight ones. A man who lives for a woman loses something of his own distinc-tive character. He becomes smooth and round. He can no longer be relied on. But a woman who lives with a man merely becomes even rounder and more womanly. After lovemaking, the man is tired. The woman wants to talk. The man becomes ashen-faced, has tired, vacant eyes. The woman has a golden-red glow.

It is when the man leaves her that the woman goes to pieces.

Then she is the one whose eyes look vacant. Her skin grey.

*

He had once said to himself: Is it possible to live a life without loving? Now he asks: It is possible to live a life without women?

Life without Omega. Omega constantly in pursuit of lovers and husbands. Leeches with vice-like muscles in their thighs, women have wings. They suck blood from their helpless victims.

*

It is summer 1912. The Olympic Games have been held in Stockholm and Lieutenant Hans F. Dons has made the first Norwegian plane flight with the monoplane *Start* from Horten to Fredrikstad in fifty-three minutes. From Hvitsten Munch was able to see the plane up in the sky, as Dons came in through heavy cloud over Jeløya and descended to a height of three hundred metres.

Is it possible to live without a woman? Just as Roald Amundsen returns home from a womanless polar expedition. Just as Britain's First Lord of the Admiralty, Winston Churchill, demands an additional budget for the British navy in response to the rearming of the German navy.

Munch has used Karen Borgen as model for *Alma Mater*. But she has a daughter, Ingeborg Kaurin, eighteen years of age. A buxom young girl. Without a doubt she reminds him of both Tupsy Jebe and Ingse Vibe. Women who do not have a bat's wings and a vampire's teeth. Women who show him the straightforward side of life.

Now she becomes Munch's model and from time to time moves in as Munch's housekeeper.

He calls her the girl from Moss or the Moss girl, who according to Hugo Perls is a seductive peasant girl: Young, slightly on the plump side and with a little too much cold red in her face, but in her simple way she is perfect.

Munch first paints her looking shy, in typical portrait style. But gradually seems to be overtaken by his own passion.

*

She waits in the poultry house. She waits in the sitting-room. She waits in this house he thinks looks like a flying machine.

It is perfectly clear she will never be his wife.

He paints her standing, arms crossed.

He paints her in a light-coloured blouse, hands behind her back.

He paints her as a study, a half-length portrait, *en face*.

Munch paints with an abundance of strong colours, with striking contrasts, bright green against rust-red, cold yellow and pale lilac, deep lush blue against yellow and vermilion. The colours are either painted in flat elongated areas, thrown carelessly onto the white priming layer, or are painted in scrolls and whirls, that is, unless he has not suddenly let the colours rain over the canvas in bright spots. An experimental technique which varies according to the type of motif concerned and whose purpose is always to accentuate the effect of the colours so they have maximum strength, brilliance and lift.

He has started an artistic affair with a woman. He caresses her with brush strokes and bathes her in colours. He loves her as he wishes to love a woman: from his own standpoint, making all the decisions. Perhaps for the first time since with Aunt Karen and his sister Inger at Grünerløkken, he is sharing his daily life with a woman who is also his model.

He wants to paint her in all the everyday situations. When bathing her feet, feeding the hens, standing in the midst of the flowers.

*

Then he suddenly becomes part of the picture. Ingeborg Kaurin and Edvard Munch. Adam and Eve in paradise.

He paints various different versions of man and woman in the garden. Munch has removed his moustache.

A naked face is revealed.

He will soon be fifty.

He paints the portrait of himself and the eighteen-year-old Moss girl. He calls the picture *The Seducer*.

* * *

He rents Grimsrød manor in Jeløya outside Moss, for larger and better working space.

He now has forty-three separate studios. They are distributed over four houses: in Kragerø, at Hvitsten, at Åsgårdstrand and at Jeløya.

It is 1913. The year all Norwegian women get the vote. The year Munch will paint *Passion*, *Fru Elsa Glaser*, *Fru Kaete Perls*. The year he will make lithographs of *The Glasers* and *Jens Thiis*.

Enquiries about possible exhibitions pour in. Stockholm, New York, Boston, Chicago, Stockholm again, Dresden, Breslau, Berlin, Hamburg, Oslo, Berlin again, and Vienna.

His international fame increases and increases, just as, in painting terms, he is working *against* the current. The trend in modern painting is characterized by free constructions of fragments of reality, in cubism or futurism, or in Kandinsky's abstract pictures which do not contain any references to the external world.

But it is external reality precisely that Munch makes into a predominant element of his art. The changing seasons from spring to summer. From autumn to winter. And he paints portraits of women.

*

He stands looking at her. He tries to draw all her lines, curves, shadows. Tries to crack the code. Unravel her mystery. Show all her characteristics.

The young Eve stands beneath the apple tree, as plump and ripe as an apple. Munch comes in from the right, as an older man, wearing hat and coat. What business has he in the garden of Eden? Is it not far too late?

*

As though he is toying with the idea. He can seduce her whenever he likes. Use her as he will. Face to face the man and the woman gaze at a mirror. As though he is thinking of Kollmann. As though he again becomes Faust. As though her youth gives him new possibilities.

She is the first since Tulla Larsen. A woman in his house.

And yet everything is different.

*

She removes her clothes. He sees her naked body. He paints *Weeping Woman*, *Nude Reclining on Her Stomach*, *Nude Reclining with Hair Tumbling down Forwards*, *Nude Reclining with Back Turned*, *Nude Reclining with Face Concealed by Her Hair*. He paints her in a red dress on a bluish-green sofa. He paints her as *Nude Resting on Her Elbow*, as a *Half-length Nude, Hands Under Her Head*, as *Nude in the Grass*, as *Half-length Nude with Arms Outstretched*, as a *Nude Reclining on Her Back*, *Reclining in a Blue Dress*, as a *Nude on the Divan*.

She is naked. She is young. And she is laid bare.

*

At Nedre Ramme in Hvitsten there is a long stretch of shore, a bay with a jetty, a south-facing boathouse, a bay further north with a sandy beach.

He places her there. She is naked. She is bathing. She laps up the sun. He paints *High Summer*, *In the Water by a Red Cliff*, *Sunbathing*, *Woman Coming out of the Water*. He paints with large luminous areas of colour and thinned-down paint. Or he paints in oils applied in short strokes taking the paint straight from the tube. He experiments with a form of double exposure technique. Tries to catch movement on the canvas.

He draws himself and the Moss girl in charcoal, just as he drew his first picture of blind, naked people, as though they were on Alpha and Omega's island.

It is as though he pours out all his passion over the pictures of her. But the letters between them are very neutral.

He has found his ideal woman.

*

Three Stages of Woman: In the first stage she was unattainable. He desired her beyond all reason. She could meet him at the agreed time of two o'clock. They could walk under the railway bridge. He could steal a kiss. She could come up to his studio. He could have buried his head in her lap.

The second stage: A red-haired, spiteful, spoilt *bit of a thing*. A back-street girl who needed a plaything, who absolutely wanted to be married. Who wanted to possess. A woman who pushed him down into the abyss at the same time crying: Save me!

The third stage. The model. He can dictate her movements, her expressions, her lines. He can command her to weep, to shake her hair over her eyes, to lie naked, to put on a red dress and to lie on a divan.

* * *

Dear Edvard: Many thanks for your letter, and thank you also for everything you've done for me and still are doing. Just imagine, again there was a lot of money in the account with Christiania Savings Bank. As much as fifteen hundred crowns. It was a vast sum in the old days. It's incredible that you've been able to put so much money in for us. And so indescribably good that you are thus able to secure Laura's future. Your devoted Karen Bjølstad.

* * *

Betzy Nilsen.

Once she was his model for *Study, Sick Girl, The Sick Child*. He allowed the tears to run down over her face. He painted her with shadows at the edges, as when a person looks at the world through tears. She was a servant girl for the military doctor and Aunt Karen. Her face would be known throughout the world.

Herr Munch. Forgive me for takking the liberty of writing to you but times is such now that its nigh imposible for someone with grownup sons to make ends meet. Wee have three grownup sons who have nothing and do nothing one of them came home from America and has had no work for the first year he has been maried. The other two have only had but one single job these past 2 year. Wee bort a lorry on the never-never and they also learnt to drive; but their are so many as drive lories so their is nothing to be found or to do so actualy they cant keep up the payments at all also our daughter was widowed with 3 little ones he went down on m/b Bob, lost 2 year ago also wee bort a house if only wee can manage it as then wee would have a house at least when you can't work any more you must think its funny me writing to you but I am appealing to your good heart wether you could help us out a bit even if it was only a few old clothes so my boys could use them theres always something for food but clothes is hard to come by hope you will forgive me for writing to you but I don't know wear else to turn. Respectfuly Betzy Nilsen Sick Girl Fossen Halden.

*

Munch goes with Fips in the morning to fetch the post from the letter-box. He is a passionate reader of the newspaper. Keeps himself abreast of what is happening in the world. And the number of letters keeps on increasing.

He has Nørregaard and Thiis and partly also Ravensberg, Jappe Nilssen and Gierløff to deal with exhibition arrangements. And in Bergen, Sigurd Høst is his private consultant.

But the mail in the letterbox is not just from galleries, museums and public institutions. He is starting to receive strange private enquiries. He collects all the letters in a case which he always has with him. Letters he has not read. Now and then he opens the case. Then he takes out a letter. Like a lottery. Opens an envelope.

It can be a letter from a total stranger.

It can be a letter from a scoundrel who is anxious about his children and needs money.

The children of the future. A new generation which needs a platform. Needs events. Needs a past. Munch observes the Moss girl's innocence. He sees a flock of children:

Look at that little girl there. She's tidying up. She's getting dangerous, seizing power from the others. Look at the pale, thin one there. She is murdering her. Stifling her self-confidence. And her there. She'll be one of those who can walk through a wall without anyone daring to raise a finger. But the fourth one, she is full of anxiety, afraid to do anything, afraid to jump, even if the other one allows her to.

Why are there those who dare and those who don't? Munch wonders.

The ones who are not afraid are those who don't know anything, aren't they? They have no inkling of the values which must not be harmed, the threads which must not be broken, the threads which will link people together, threads which will bind together each link in the chain of generations. Those who do know this become cautious, afraid of doing any harm. They're circles, aren't they? There are those who trample under foot, tear down. Those who have an inkling of eternal values, of a higher meaning, become afraid; they proceed cautiously, they are sensitive and respect the richness of existence. They seek it out.

* * *

The brother of Harald Nørregaard, a lawyer, writes an article in *Morgenbladet* of the seventh of December 1913: On Friday Edvard Munch is fifty. It is strange to think of it, my brother said when up in my brother's house at Vinderen the other day we came to talk about the fellow. Now Munch, known throughout his own country and the world, great and powerful, lives down at lovely Grimsrød on Jeløya. At the time he painted it, and he pointed to the painting we have reproduced here, there were not many people who knew him. He was rather shy and retiring. And there were not many people he was close to. In this way he has not changed much over the years. But the few people who did know him even then clearly understood what he had in him, even though they scarcely thought he would ever become a man of property and so on. This was somehow far beyond all their ideas and imaginings. Where money and property were concerned, as well as the prospect of ever acquiring such wonderful things, none of them was up to much. I met Munch for the first time in Paris in 1885. He was studying on a scholarship. I met him in the company of his friends there, Torgersen, Paulsen, Johannes Müller. Cash was scarce. But they pooled what little they had. If one of them received money from home, it went into the kitty. The purest communism. And this applied not just in Paris, but for several years after as well. I remember how furious Hans Jæger once became with Munch and what a dressing down he gave him because he had dared to go out and buy himself a pair of new boots. Actually, I didn't see very much of Munch that time in Paris. Munch took his studies very seriously. Later, in the first Bohemian days in Christiania, I spent a lot of time with Munch. He had joined our circle, he valued our company and we for our part had a clear idea of his outstanding gift and were happy that he was part of our circle. But he was never a Bohemian. Even then he went his own way in art. He could not understand why one should not paint things as one thought of them, saw them in one's imagination, in other words without a model. You can imagine what monstrous heresy this was for us then. For us it was a defection from hallowed naturalism, which itself was the subject of heated debate at the time. And ultimately it led to a break, not between him and me personally, but between him and the Bohemian movement. He began to paint his symbolist pictures, in which he sought to personify mental states and passions. Jealousy, hatred, horror and so on. He thought of it as a long frieze. He grew close to Strindberg, who came to exert a strong influence on him.

*

Harald Nørregaard discusses Munch with his brother in *Morgenbladet*. Either they are taking liberties, or their conversation has Munch's approval. The article at once mystifies and clarifies. For Munch virtually never gave interviews to the press.

Tell me something about Munch's home, the lawyer's brother asks.

His home, well, he has several, you see. For example he lives in Grimsrød. But he doesn't own the place. He just rents it. The whole house and property. But you *could* call him a property owner, if you like. You've seen his first property many times. The little yellow cottage with the garden and fruit trees in front, running right down to the sea in Åsgårdstrand. Munch lived here for several summers. He liked it there, and it was there that he painted some of his finest pictures. He had bought the little property and built a studio out in the garden. It is a long time since he has lived there and he does not come here often now. But he does not want to sell the place, even though he receives offers for it every year. He is very fond of it. His other property is at Hvitsten. This is larger. Ramme Farm. It is here he has his finest garden. Hundreds of the most magnificent roses, masses of fruit trees, apples, pears, plums, cherries and so on, which bear the most delicious fruit. But no one is allowed to touch it. He may perhaps suddenly want to paint them one day when they are bowed down with fruit. He also has a lot of animals. Turkeys and ducks and geese and cockerels, extremely beautiful cockerels, and hens. He has three beautiful dogs, a large Saint

Bernard, a Gordon terrier and a fox terrier. He also has a horse. It is very fat, as he never uses it, just paints it now and then. Munch is very fond of animals and of painting them too. Nor, incidentally, is it just animals and flowers and fruit trees he has like this but never uses. He has a little harbour too, and no less than two motorboats. But he never uses them. If he wants to go out, he *hires* a motorboat. He does not have a sailing boat. So this is Munch's property, which he really owns. But he is not content with this. He also rents another two properties. In Kragerø he has a large beautiful house with ten or twelve rooms, which he has rented for many years. He is fond of painting in this locality. Some of the finest and most important works in his entire *œuvre* date back to the year he lived here and painted in a huge burst of energy.

But at the moment Munch is actually *living* at Grimsrød in Jeløen.

*

A house with over twenty rooms and a spacious attic. Grey stone walls with deep niches. Pictures are piled up everywhere. Munch himself lives in only a couple of the rooms. Out in the garden he has built a studio. A large barn with a glass roof.

He continues to work on *The Sun*, *History* and *Alma Mater*. He has taken on Helga Rogstad as his housekeeper. Before long she will also be his model. A fine strong figure of a woman, who will soon be thirty years of age, was born into a wealthy family of tanners. Had to abandon all schooling. Earned her living at an early age as a housekeeper.

Now she accompanies Munch round all his properties. And Munch paints her *On a Bench with Dog*, *Sitting in Costume and Hat*, *Sitting on a Suitcase*. He paints her *Standing in Costume and Hat*, as *Portrait of Woman with a Lot of Hair*.

Then he takes her with him to Åsgårdstrand.

*

It all comes flooding back.

The Death of Marat. The shot in Åsgårdstrand.

Helga Rogstad as a woman staring fixedly ahead. The man lies there murdered, destroyed, on the bed behind her.

The memories of Tulla Larsen.

Helga Rogstad is the same age. Has the same build.

He paints them as man and woman in the same room, introduces a new formal element which he will come to refine in the coming years: the powerful sense of space, where the scene opens onto a room in the background, usually more strongly lit than the main room.

* * *

Workers in the Snow. *Workers Returning Home*. Grave, dour faces which will brook no obstacle. The flow of history. Munch will later say that he believes in Russia's mission. He believes they have a chance. In the French Revolution it was the bourgeoisie which fought for their civil rights, he says. In our time it is the workers.

He identifies with them. He never understood his mild and gentle father. He opted for protest.

*

Morgenposten 12 December 1913: Anyone wishing to visit Munch at his home on his fiftieth birthday will seek him in vain. During the last few days he has travelled abroad to arrange exhibitions in Berlin and Frankfurt-am-Main.

*

Munch's pictures are already hanging at the Autumn Exhibition in Berlin. As the only foreigners to be invited, he and Picasso have each been allocated one of the main rooms. The aim of this is to emphasize the overwhelming importance of Munch and Picasso for young, German art.

But as he himself says: It is France I love.

*

Back to Paris. 66 rue de Seine, then Hotel du Sénat.

The folk tale illustrator Theodor Kittelsen dies. Munch is in Paris and reads in the paper that Wagner fever is sweeping Europe and that the suffragettes in London have long since abandoned their non-violent stance in the battle for women's right to vote and equality between men and women.

Then there is suddenly an explosion of eroticism. The gospel of suffering. *Man and Woman* in woodcut, pen and ink, crayon and etchings. Munch prints a series of erotic subjects while he is in Paris. The model will later be called Celine, but the Moss girl also serves as model.

Paris is the city of eroticism. All his women have had some connection with Paris. Fru Thaulow was a chansonnette singer here, Tupsy Jebe came here, as did Tulla Larsen in order to deceive him with Gunnar Heiberg. Eva Mudocci lived here.

Munch lets Celine and the Moss girl become symbols of all stages. *Two People, Conversation, Ashes.*

But it is he who calls the tune now. He who decides. In the lithograph *The Seducer*, he portrays himself as the dangerous, the unreliable, the sinful one. Half-satyr, half-vampire, with a sly sideways glance at the Moss girl's conniving, lascivious face.

* * *

He walks into his studios at Grimsrød farm.

It is more like a castle, with tall bay windows in four-foot-thick wall recesses from floor to ceiling. He empties his pockets of papers, magazines and letters. According to Gierløff he fumbles through all his pockets with a preoccupied, anguished expression until, in the very last one, he finds his lorgnette, a crooked, rickety article, the lenses almost completely obscured by fingerprints, and which, although already a year old, is still adorned with the little green price ticket on a thread hanging from one lens.

The floor, boxes and chairs are liberally strewn with tubes and turpentine, brushes and palettes. Munch places a canvas on the easel, and squinting, peers at the model.

Yes, it's a strange business, painting, he says and takes a few steps sideways, looks for a few moments almost absent-mindedly at the woman standing in front of him. Then he squints again and with outstretched arm draws the first lines with the charcoal.

According to Gierløff one of two things can now happen: Either he will remain silent. In which case an oppressive silence will descend over the room, he will draw with increasing preoccupation, with increasing concentration, looking less and less often at the model.

After twenty minutes' sketching, he will switch restlessly to painting, a little here and a little there, increasingly engrossed. Now and then he will remove the picture from the easel, place it in another room, look at it for a second from a distance, squint, put it back on the easel, resume painting with increasing energy. Now all he will see, hear and be aware of will be the picture. The impression will be over him, in him, the silence around him will be unusual, heavy, neither the painter nor the hapless model saying a word. The only sound will be the rustling of the brush and the only movement the stretcher quivering beneath the powerful, often violent brush strokes.

Or else he will talk. And when he talks, no one else can get a word in edgeways. What to Frau Förster Nietzsche he called self-defence. A wall of words which he erects between himself and the model, so that he can paint in peace behind it. He will speak incessantly in his aphoristic way, kaleidoscopically jumping from one topic to another and with sudden shifts in his thoughts. Also in order to confuse the model, to get her to wake up, to reveal herself, to catch her off her guard, show her natural face, her undisguised ego.

Hmm, he sometimes says. This is going to be good, when it has just stood and collected itself for a while. Just wait till it's had a few showers of rain on it, till it's been scratched by a few nails and things, been lugged hither and thither in all manner of rotten leaky crates. Yes, I think this could be good in time!

*

It is the hundredth anniversary of the Norwegian constitution. A great exhibition is opened at Frogner with what the newspapers describe as impressive, stylish buildings, gardens with a mass of flowers, glinting lakes and gently rushing waterfalls, stately promenades, intriguing walks and secret paths, wonderful light effects and fine music. And restaurants as well.

The artists have been allocated their own pavilion in the Jubilee Exhibition. Fourteen highly individual artists, as they are described. They include Henrik Sørensen and Jean Heiberg. Pupils of Matisse.

*

Verdens Gang 29 April 1914: An interview with Edvard Munch. We met Edvard Munch yesterday during one of his brief 5-hour visits to Christiania and seized the opportunity to take him to task on behalf of art enthusiasts for not having seen fit to exhibit his work here this summer. You're a student aren't you, he said, well have you ever thought what it would be like to present yourself for examination by our professors over and over again and to fail? Do you think it's much fun submitting essays which get better and better and which even so are turned down? I don't think so, and I don't want to try it again when, in the faculty's view, I am not ready yet. So let's not say anything more about the assembly hall. What I can tell you though is that I am currently in negotiation with Tivoli's Director Jacobsen about exhibiting what have become known as my assembly hall pictures there.

*

Then there comes a statement from the assembly hall's two architects Holger Sinding-Larsen and F. Bødtker. They are afraid that the private committee consisting of Thiis and company may influence attitudes and foster a demand for Munch's assembly hall decorations to be the ones ultimately selected. But the architects cannot see that anything genuinely new has emerged. The architects also assert that any decoration of the assembly hall should take the form of frescoes, not paintings on canvas, for acoustic reasons among other things.

*

Munch issues the following statement which is printed in *Dagbladet* on the twenty-fourth of May 1914:

> Since the future fate of the University pictures has been discussed both privately and in the press, I feel bound to state that the purpose of exhibiting the designs this time is not to offer them to the University or to submit myself to its judgement. The purpose of showing them again is simply that I thought it might interest the Christiania public to see them collected together. I must also state that, as things are at present, even if I were offered a fair and proper chance to exhibit them honourably, I could scarcely accept. In past years I have been the victim of too much harassment for me to do so. People will also appreciate that for me the timing is not

as favourable now as it was on the previous occasion, when I was full of enthusiasm for the task in hand. In any event, I would need considerable time to think the matter over. Edvard Munch.

*

Five days later, the University accepts Munch's assembly hall pictures.

* * *

Summer 1914. Europe on the threshold of war. Archduke Franz Ferdinand is assassinated in Sarajevo. The Panama Canal is opened. Trygve Gran flies over the North Sea. The French socialist Jean Jaurès is assassinated by a right-wing extremist. The founder of the modern peace movement, Bertha von Suttner, dies. The Norwegian Government issues the following proclamation: In view of the fact that war has broken out between Austria and Serbia, we have decided to adopt a position of complete neutrality where Norway is concerned. The Bank of Norway has raised the bank rate to 6 and 6½ per cent.

Panic and the stockpiling of supplies begin to spread throughout the country. A number of places see clashes between the police and the masses. On the third of August there are riots outside a merchant's house because he has put up the price of a sack of rye flour. The shop windows are smashed. The same day sees the outbreak of the First World War.

*

By the thirty-first of July German special editions are announcing a general state of war. Kaiser Wilhelm II's speech from the throne: It is not the desire for conquest which motivates us. We are simply inspired by an unbending desire to defend the place God has given us, for ourselves and for all generations to come. I no longer recognize any parties, I recognize only Germans.

The German Government does its utmost to present the war as a war of defence and invents French acts of aggression. But it is not the French who violate Belgian neutrality. It is the Germans. For over ten years the German army leaders have been preparing for a war on two fronts.

*

Schiefler writes from Hamburg on the twentieth of August: *Lieber Freund*. It is at once a terrifying and wonderful time. The German people's unanimous uprising is a joy to behold. There was no boisterous enthusiasm, rather a quiet, reserved, almost religious mood, and then bitter anger at the fact that the Russians, the French and, yes, the British have forced our hard-working, industrious people out of work, away from the plough, from jobs in industry, from student garrets – forced us to take up arms. *Mit herzlichem Gruss Ihr Schiefler.*

*

Munch replies to Schiefler on small postcards. *Vielen herzlichen Grüsze und Viele herzliche Wünsche*. Practical information about lithographs and so forth. Later that winter he writes that he is leading a peaceful life. Remarkably peaceful. Doubly peaceful when he thinks back to a more restless time. He writes that he has problems with a very nervous and sick sister and other family matters which make him feel that all nature is surreptitiously being sucked into the war.

*

In autumn 1914 Jappe Nilssen writes to Christian Gierløff: You are quite right that Munch has not received your letter, or in any case hasn't read it. We essentially keep in touch via the telephone. And he is developing into a greater and greater eccentric. He is now convinced, to the depths of his being, that he has missed his vocation in life. Painting may well be good enough for weaklings and feckless individuals, but the art of war is for real men. He is an inspired strategist. Joffre, French, Hindenburg may as well give up now. Munch knew the lot beforehand. The invasion of Belgium, the French army's retreat to Paris, the bombing of Louvain, the occupation of Brussels and Antwerp, the Allies' advance and the Germans' retreat eastward, he knew it all before it happened, he could predict everything with mathematical precision. Didn't I say so a week ago, he says. Of course, he has never uttered a word about it. Do you remember what I said on this occasion, on that occasion? Damned if I can remember! His favourite spot is in front of *Morgenbladet*'s huge war map at Pultost. There he stands, thin and pinched, with dozens of newspapers sticking out of every pocket, in a threadbare overcoat and light blue trousers and with a top hat on his head, the nap brushed the wrong way. He looks like one of those *pauvres honteux* so numerous in large cities, but relatively rare in this country. And the war has also made him thrifty. He toys with small coins for so long that he almost wears the pattern off them yet is much less careful with large sums. I have a suspicion he may have abandoned the pricey eating places he frequented before, but as I say, we're never together now, and actually he gets his meals from the automatic food dispensers. Yet he still pays two men five crowns a day at Ramme and Grimsrød and all the animals scattered about on his various properties are eating their heads off. It's been a long, tedious autumn. I can't recollect ever having lived as quietly as in the past three months. Living it up is a concept I've all but forgotten the meaning of.

* * *

Dear Edvard: Thank you so much for your card which I received yesterday. I well understand that you must have all sorts of things on your plate as well as the many problems with your affairs in Germany which this war has caused you. And when 1914 was going to be such a wonderful Jubilee Year! Nevertheless, we're free from bombs, so we can sleep peacefully in our beds at night. The horrors of the war are an absolute nightmare just to read about. You will naturally have many acquaintances who are involved, perhaps even among the fallen. You who have seen and are so familiar with these places where war is being waged. What a beautiful month September has been, so warm and sunny, until today. I've enjoyed the sunsets, the silence on the fjord, so peaceful and quiet, such a contrast to what is going on out in the world. I'm glad you liked Inger's curtains. I wish I too could make something for you. You who have given us so much. How grateful we are. Inger came home today with a bouquet of spring flowers, wild roses. She has recently been to see Laura. Isn't it curious that I've suffered a direct loss from the war? The tourists left the country double quick without buying anything to take home, and I had sent some of my work all the way to Molde. But I'm working with a view to future sales in any case. Your devoted Karen Bjølstad.

* * *

Then his sister Laura suddenly writes to him: Dear Edvard: Thanks ever so much for last time we met and for *everything*. Aunt Karen and Inger send their greetings. I had a letter from Aunt recently. She asked me to send you their very best wishes. Inger has not been very well this autumn, *that* was why she didn't come to see me for so long. I'm expecting her in a few days, and I'm looking forward to it *so* much. Inger, Aunt and I get on *so well*. Aunt is *the apple* of my and Inger's eyes, just as you are *the apple* of Aunt's eye. I only envy Inger the *great happiness* of spending her time with Aunt. Quite different from me, who am always with strangers. At any rate, I hope to see Aunt again *this summer* and perhaps go for walks with her and Inger, to Bergen over the high mountains, for example. Aunt may well live for a while yet, but it happens *so* quickly, when you're as old as she is. It can happen quicker than one thinks, that she could die on us I mean. Apart from you, Aunt is the *only* person in the *whole world* Inger and I care about. Your devoted Laura Munch.

*

1915. A year in Munch's life. Spring and summer in Hvitsten. He continues work on the assembly hall pictures. In August he travels via Elverum to Trondheim. In September he is back at Grimsrød. In November he goes to the Autumn Exhibition in Copenhagen, where he is showing a number of designs for the assembly hall.

He paints the self-portraits *Nude with Raised Arm* and *Dance of Death*, in which he is dancing with a skeleton. But it is Kollmann who dies.

The button moulder is no more.

Peer Gynt is again alone with himself.

*

The Hermit. The Night Wanderer.

He needs yet another house to be awake in, more rooms in which to reflect on life.

He finds Ekely.

The final house.

VII

I saw all people behind their masks. (EDVARD MUNCH)

The property was previously a market garden. It stands on a knoll a few hundred metres west of Christiania. An expensive property. The main house has eight rooms. Also part of the property are a cow-shed, a greenhouse and a large garden and almost thirty acres of farmland. Munch does not want to farm. He takes the greenhouse down, sells it, neglects the garden and paints the horses. The place gradually becomes a kennel.

But he does grow some vegetables.

Ironically enough the property looks out onto the area his old enemy Gustav Vigeland will soon receive millions of crowns for making into a sculpture park. Munch is bitter at Vigeland, bitter at the authorities who make a gift of a huge area and vast sums of money to this sculptor, while Munch himself has a dogged struggle with the tax authorities, claiming they do not even accept allowances against demonstrable material expenses.

To his future friend Rolf Stenersen he will say:

Is there any sense in my contributing to the 110-metre bridge which Vigeland is making over a stream 11 metres wide? Have you seen the palace Christiania has given him? It looks like a prison, and when these sculptures of his are erected, people are going to think the prisoners have escaped. I'm glad I at least have enough money to build a fence round my house. It's going to be so high that I don't have to look at that pillar of his. Apparently it's thirteen metres high. That's quite something, my friend. A pillar thirteen metres high. But I like these wrought iron things of his.

* * *

He is taking the night train to Bergen. He has always preferred to have a compartment to himself. He does not like having to share with total strangers. He stands in the compartment waiting for someone else to turn up. Sure enough, here comes a man now. He has a limp and a pale, sallow face, is accompanied by two younger men.

Doesn't augur well, thinks Munch. A down-at-heel fellow with a very off-putting smell. Clearly ill. A smell of bath tubs and hospitals. Munch stands in the compartment noting all the details, the powerfully-shaped head which looks pale and suggests suffering. One of his companions notices Munch's inquisitive look and tells him that the stranger is just out of hospital. He has recently had an operation. Then they leave the compartment.

Munch and the sick man are alone.

The sick man speaks with the Stavanger dialect.

Two tumours, he says. Look. My skull was sawn open.

He shows Munch the scar which runs halfway round his head.

The stranger tells him about the operation. Sawn open. Two tumours. They had sawn for ages. The operation had taken four hours. They had lifted off half his skull. His brain had been exposed. A critical situation. For two minutes he had been dead. He had stopped breathing. His heart had stopped beating. But the doctors had given him massage, had called his name, had shouted him back to life.

Afterwards they had taken skin from his leg to replace the damaged skin on his head.

Here, look.

The stranger points at the seam running round his head.

Were you worried? Munch asks.

Not at all, the stranger replies. I am a firm believer. God is in me.

Munch lies in his bunk. He watches the stranger getting ready for the night, placing his hat on the table, placing a fine cloth soaked in milk around his head, around his skull, around his brain.

*

Bergen is reduced to ashes. All buildings between Muralmenningen and Møhlenpris are razed to the ground. The area burnt down was over five hundred metres long and two hundred metres wide. Altogether three hundred and ninety-three buildings have been destroyed. The cause of the fire was two workers who went into Berstad's boathouse with a lighted candle. The candle set fire to twenty bales of caulking.

Munch shows sixty paintings at the Bergen Art Association as the battle of Verdun builds up.

While he is in Bergen, he paints *Self-Portrait with Nykirken in the Background*. His face is tired and haggard, flustered and nervous.

He turns away from his past. Away from life.

* * *

Back to Ekely. Jarlsborgveien 14 at Skøyen. But he is not really happy there. His restlessness is something he has constantly reflected on. Life is a hospital in which the patients spend all their time thinking about moving beds. But he does not want to move to yet another place.

*

Ravensberg advises Munch to take on a most reliable and charming Negro, Sultan Abdul Karim, as servant, chauffeur and model. He is attached to Hagenbeck Circus.

A few days later he is taken on. According to Ravensberg Munch now has a complete menagerie out at Ekely. A Negro, a Sultan, a bear and the two pigs, Gunnar and Sivert.

He paints *Cleopatra and the Slave*. Reminiscent of fru Thaulow. A large, bold portrait with the odalisque and the naked, sensual Negro, in which the colours are taken to the extreme. A fanfare.

*

A house to move into. Collect all his belongings. Furniture from his childhood home, sad memories, the sofa on which the military doctor always used to sit. The family pictures. The wicker chair he used when he painted *Spring*. Gilt leather chairs worn out by his forebears, a table and a bed. He collects together all his books, Hans Jæger's and Przybyszewski's novels. Dagny Juel's writings. Thiis's book on Leonardo da Vinci. Crates of books. Letters and newspaper cuttings. Strindberg! Chess set and a children's card game, fretsaw and childhood book binding items. Long-case clock. Graphic works. The paintings. Rousseau, Fips and the bear. Several housekeepers. And one Negro.

* * *

He lets his sister Laura into the house, lets her visit him before Aunt Karen and Inger. But on the sixth of September, the day before his sister Sophie would have been fifty-five years old, he invites all three of them.

Dear Edvard: Thank you so much for yesterday! It was such fun and so good in every respect. The splendid drive in such a comfortable car was such a change for us. We were so lucky with the weather, I mean that we could sit outside during the afternoon after a lovely chicken lunch. Now I have a clear picture of what it is like at Ekely, the beautiful house and garden, the fields, the studio, the tenant farmer's place and then the house with all the nice rooms and everything just so. How lovely it is to think about now that I can see it so clearly before me. Your staff seem to be excellent, so considerate and obliging. Laura was busy showing us round, and in the end fruit and vegetables were pressed upon us because you had left instructions to that effect. I think that was going a bit far, but it was no good trying to argue. We set off back home at 6 o'clock. With thanks for everything from Inger and greetings from your devoted Karen Bjølstad.

* * *

The October Revolution in Russia. Rodin dies. The long, damp, sunless foggy days of autumn and winter.

Munch paints *Lady with a Blue Hat*.

Her name is Frøydis Mjølstad. She is a model Munch will use for many years. The portraits point to an independent, strong-willed woman. She becomes one of his many housekeepers.

He paints her in the wicker chair. Says that she has such interesting arms. Wants to paint her at Hvitsten in the light of the summer night.

She receives her baptism of fire. Arrives to find a stove which is more or less unusable. On it she makes hard-boiled eggs.

He paints her *At Ekely with Hat and Coat*, *In a Blue Dress*, *In the Wind*, *In a White Dress*, *Sitting on a High-backed Chair*, *Sitting with Hand against Cheek*.

He plays down the erotic element.

* * *

Munch exhibits *The Frieze of Life* once more. He began to paint these subjects twenty-eight years ago and has carried on painting them throughout his whole life. The vision from the Montagnes Russes. What he thought of as his life's mission. He has sold some of the paintings. Others he has hung on to. Now he is thinking of them in terms of embellishing an entire wall in a temple of art, these pictures together constituting a frieze. What he is thinking of is a circular hall. In Munch's view there is such a common thread running through about half the paintings that they can very easily be combined to form one single long picture. The paintings featuring the shore and the trees. The same tints crop up again and again. The summer night provides the unifying element. The trees and the sea provide vertical and horizontal lines. These are repeated throughout all of them. The shore and the waves provide the undulating tones of life. Strong colours running throughout the pictures provide harmony.

A room containing *The Frieze of Life*. A dedicated space. Perhaps the future town hall which is planned for Christiania?

But for the time being it is Blomqvist's.

The public comes. The public sees. It has seen many of the pictures before. But the public does not understand. In the newspapers it says that the pictures do not go together. In *Aftenposten* Kristian Haug writes ironically: What our artists seem to do now is strike one note, one large, decisive note, as often as possible. Exhibitions are the vehicle for it. A few years ago, an artist hit on the lucky idea of moulding his beautiful works into a whole. A slogan was born: *The city with the fountain*. Now we have another slogan: *The City with the Frieze of Life*. The more intellectually impoverished an age is, the greater the number of geniuses it has.

*

For once, Munch cannot contain himself. In October 1918, under the heading 'Criticism of *The Frieze of Life*', he writes:

> It is incomprehensible to me that a critic, who is also a painter, cannot find a common thread in the collection of pictures. No common thread, he asserts. Half the pictures have so much in common that they can very easily be assembled to make one great long picture. Admittedly, most of the pictures are notes, documents, sketches, themes. That is their strength. If there had been

the necessary encouragement at the right time, the effect would no doubt have been different and *The Frieze* would most likely have been different in size and would probably have provided a richer, stronger picture of life than these documents. I would ask the critics I am thinking of to go up there one day when there is such strong sunshine that the attendant haze blends the series of pictures into a whole. Do not focus so pedantically on varying techniques and inadequate artistry. I nevertheless believe that they would see the intention and also see a great deal of harmony in the series of pictures. I hope another critic is not flattering himself that I am taking note of him. The pathetic cross between a hopeless painter and a hopeless critic who has filled a vacant post at *Aftenposten* as driver of the muck wagon which for forty years has carried the muck from the Augean stables to the garden of art. Well, well! As I have repeatedly explained, I have purposely not given the picture a definitive form. The unrelentingly bitter and boring reviewer in the intellectual review *Intelligenssedlerne* states that he knows all the pictures from before. Of course, it is obvious that the paper which is regarded as the most boring in the country should also have a boring reviewer, but he should nevertheless consider his advancing age – he will soon be in his dotage – and he should know that a new generation has grown up since *The Frieze* was last exhibited. The same critic predicts that a patron may well find room for *The Frieze*, buy a plot and put up a building in which to house it. In this case he was right. I have now built such a building myself. And if one day he can get rid of that cross look of his, he is welcome to call and see it.

* * *

He has no time to die. He scorns others on account of their age. It is now that he paints *Death of a Bohemian*. Memories of Jæger. In a series of paintings between 1917 and 1925, Munch explores this motif. It was Jappe Nilssen who related what happened that February day in 1910. Jæger rented a room in Tostrupgården, rented it for a month, knowing that he would die long before that. The proprietor was furious and tried to throw him out. But Jæger had the tenancy agreement in his hands. A wretched, unworthy death. Henrik Lund's wife sat faithfully beside the bed. He lay there eyes closed. A woman paced furiously to and fro in the room, screaming that she knew that Jæger had six hundred crowns in a chest of drawers to which money she was legally entitled, and if she did not get it straight away, she would throw herself out of the window. She also wanted all Jæger's manuscripts and letters.

Outside in the corridor an alcoholic painter paced restlessly up and down, in the belief that the dying man had half a bottle of whisky, or at least the remains of one, in his possession. Throughout the entire death agony impatient footsteps could be heard out in the corridor. Hans Jæger must also have heard them, as when Jappe Nilssen entered the room, he opened his eyes and said, fully conscious:

Farewell, dear Jappe. Thank you for your friendship.

Just after that fru Lund said:

Hans Jæger is dead.

In the resulting confusion, the painter seized his chance to nip in and pinch the bottle of whisky.

* * *

The Armistice is signed. The First World War is over. Munch catches Spanish 'flu.

The influenza virus is a strain of swine fever. It is a world-wide pandemic. In a number of places, half the population falls ill. In Europe there are 2.6 million deaths. The global death toll is twenty million.

Fever. Hallucinations. Violent pains in the joints. Breathing difficulties. Munch is at Ekely and feels the sickness overtake him, while he continues work on pictures for *The Frieze of Life*. He has been knocked down countless times. But never has he been as ill as this.

Death is pitch black. Colours are light. To be a painter is to work with beams of light. Perhaps dying is like having one's eyes put out. In front of him is a large dark bird, with dark brown feathers, it emits bright blue light, which turns green and then . . . a yellow stripe, a circle. It moves as though he was walking through the room. Wherever it passes with its colours everything moves. Snakes are crawling round the chair leg and the table leg. Thick snakes twist and writhe round the chaise longue in the most wonderful colours. From vermilion to golden yellow. The bird flies up the wall and the whole room moves. Snakes twist round everything in gold, green, red and deep brown.

To rot away. To gently slip into another form of matter. In his youth this thought became an ecstatic vision. Now things are different. He sits in the armchair, old and weak. His mouth agape. He yawns.

During his illness he paints *Self-Portrait during Spanish 'Flu*. Later, he asks a guest:

Does it seem stuffy in here?

How do you mean?

Don't you notice the smell?

The smell?

Yes, can't you see that I'm on the point of rotting?

The bottom of the sea. With its slime. Its maggots. To surrender to it. To lie with a woman. Suddenly death and woman have the same smell.

Who is it who has sent him flowers? Why has he received flowers today? He's not ill after all. Does he look ill? Take these flowers away, please. Didn't I say I don't want any hyacinths here? Who has sent me hyacinths?

He does not know what is going to happen. Again he·has the feeling of being on a little ship without a helmsman. Why did they not like *The Frieze of Life*? Why did he have to explain something he had already explained before? He is at Ekely and is furious.

Gradually he gets better.

*

Dear Edvard: Let me thank you again for the lovely raincoat and all the money and things. Thank you for all the fruit and flowers this summer and autumn. I hope I have an opportunity *sometime at least* to do *a little something* in return for everything you've done for me and given me over the last few years and *still are* doing. We can only hope for a *happy* outcome *as soon as possible*, that the four of us who are left will be *reunited*. With greetings from your devoted Laura Munch.

*

Aunt Karen and his sister Inger live on the other side of town. From Ekely he can see right over to Ekeberg, where they live. Laura lives in Geitmyrsveien. Munch starts to drink wine again. But not like before. A bottle of wine during the night. A little champagne while working.

* * *

The model undresses. He has engaged Annie Fjeldbu, a woman of humble origins, but who is making a name for herself both as a model and as a cabaret artiste. Between tours she works as model for Munch.

He nicknames her The Cat.

He often rings her in the middle of the night. He is a night wanderer in his own house. He gets ideas at night. He paints *The Artist and His Model*. The model stands in her night-dress and is putting on her bathrobe. The artist himself stands turned away, hands in pockets, clearly in inner turmoil. Bowed. Ageing. There is huge tension in the picture. The woman has opened up to the man for a moment. Now she is turning in upon herself again. He stands turned away, powerless. Is dominated by the feeling of his own age. His body which is already becoming bowed. Decay. But not just his body. His nerves are still weak, extraordinarily sensitive to any attack, from anyone at all, from total strangers who beg for money, or from distant relations.

*

He lives in a house full of pictures. His only personal possessions are a grand piano, a bed, an upholstered bench, a wall clock, a mirror, two cupboards, nine chairs and three tables. Though meagre, the kitchen utensils are beautiful. Five cups, eight glasses and six spoons, knives and forks. The lamps have no shades. The windows have no curtains. The floors are uncarpeted.

*

To Schiefler he writes that he is very nervous. And also cannot sleep. He also complains of long-standing bronchial problems. He feels tired and has no will to work.

He practically never sees the family. His meetings with friends are a rarity. The housekeepers are silent servants who do his least bidding. He engages a permanent chauffeur, who can drive him wherever he wants to go, to Grimsrød, Ramme or Åsgårdstrand. He let Kragerø go in 1915.

He reworks the pictures he does not need a model for, the original scenes of *The Frieze of Life*, the shore or the rooms or the ridge where the actors are engraved on his mind for all time. He thinks of new monumental paintings, the call from the world, a frieze depicting workers, perhaps. What attitude should one adopt toward the unrest and famine in Germany, the general strike in Denmark, the growth of social democracy in Sweden, everything that is happening in Russia? The workers demanding their rights? Revolt? All this he can understand. But who is this Hitler proclaiming in Munich a twenty-five-point programme for the National Socialist Workers' Party? And who are these Dadaists who invite people to the *Mass*? In other words, a complete rejection of all earlier, bourgeois art. Photocollages, collages, cartoons and stuffed dolls. People who would burn everything from Rubens to Kokoschka: Art is dead. Long live Tatlin's new machine art! What about all that? Munch makes a lithograph of *Frederick Delius*, the noble soul whose physical condition is steadily deteriorating, who in a few years will be blind, paralysed, and confined to a wheelchair. He makes the lithographs *The Final Hour*, *Ghosts* and *Osvald*, a reminder that Munch's own sun is not as unambiguously good or reliable as some would have it. He feels uncertain, despondent, tired and ill. And to cap it all, he reads in the paper that Knut Hamsun, two days before his fifty-seventh birthday, receives the Nobel Prize for Literature and is acclaimed in all four corners of the globe.

* * *

At Ekely one day in 1921 there is a ring at the door.

As usual, Munch's housekeeper answers the door. A young fellow is standing on the steps. She asks if he is delivering a parcel. No one comes to Ekely uninvited unless they have something to deliver.

I should like to meet Mr Munch, says the young stockbroker Rolf Stenersen.

The woman disappears. Stenersen rings again.

Munch comes to the door.

So begins the last of Munch's friendships.

*

Herr Munch, I should so much like to buy a picture.

Have you anything to pay for it with? You're only a young chap.

It's money I've made myself. I've made it on shares.

Can anyone make money on shares? Everyone tells me they've only lost on shares.

Well, I've made money. I borrowed some shipping shares and sold them when they were high.

Stenersen. As strange in appearance as Munch himself. A sprinter, economist and writer. He will soon write with as much insight about Britain's abandoning of the gold standard, reflation propaganda, the statistical position of the rubber market and the so-called rubber dispute, as about the sex drive, three women, two dreams and the Princess of Mecklenburg-Strelitz. He is a man who has an extremely complex relationship with his own father, is an art enthusiast and an economist of world stature, a pioneer of modern Norwegian prose.

Now he enters Munch's home Ekely. He sees Munch's own copy of *Kiss*. He wants that picture. He wants it very badly. He has fourteen thousand crowns to spend on pictures. Would Munch consider selling *Kiss* for five thousand?

Won't you sit down? says Munch. Wouldn't you like a glass of wine?

No thank you. Stenersen is a teetotaller. And he does not smoke either. He is in training for a race.

I see, says Munch. So you're a sprinter, are you? When I was young, we took a dram when we wanted our pulses to beat faster.

He goes on to say that he too is a sprinter. The brief moments when he is painting. They are his life's sprint.

Stenersen asks whether he will sell *Kiss* for ten thousand crowns.

Stenersen writes that Munch glanced at him.

Twelve thousand?

Then Munch begins to talk of shares and gambling. He tells the young man that he himself never gambles.

Stenersen asks him whether he can buy *Kiss* for fourteen thousand crowns.

Munch pursues the topic of gambling. Tells Stenersen that, during the First World War, people sold like mad, but recently he himself has sold practically nothing.

He does not sell *Kiss* to Stenersen. It is part of *The Frieze of Life*. The pictures he always has with him. His most valued possession. The series of pictures which the public suddenly did not understand. As though time had ebbed from his own life.

He must paint new versions. But he does not sell.

*

Munch buys seventy-three prints from German artists to help them financially. He is asked by an art dealer whether he has any winter landscapes one metre by one metre. He replies that alas he has just sold the last one.

But he receives a commission for a frieze to embellish the dining room in the Freia chocolate factory.

A polished parquet floor, light-coloured birch panels on the walls, small tables and chairs of the same wood, a vaulted, white plaster ceiling with overhead windows. Munch is painting for the factory workers. Back to Grünerløkken. A stone's throw from the scenes of his childhood. He paraphrases *The Frieze of Life*, the shoreline from Åsgårdstrand, tall round-topped trees, idyllic white fishermen's houses, lush green foliage. Bright summer days and midsummer nights with their eerie twilight. Weekday life and Sunday life. The fisherman setting out with the little boy at his heel. He hoists the sail in the morning sun and waves to his wife who stands on the shore with their youngest in her arms. There are the children, walking hand in hand into the forest. There are the parents picking fruit from ripening trees. There is the night, dusk and the full moon which climbs up the sky and stretches its golden bridge from land to land, and the young people emerge from the houses and wander down to the shore, where the dance is in full swing between the tall straight pine trees, to the long, plaintive notes of the accordion.

* * *

What's happened to the moon, Stenersen? I was strolling here one evening recently and there was such bright moonlight.

Stenersen points to the crescent moon in the sky.

There it is, Munch.

That's not the moon, Stenersen. Don't you know that the moon is round?

*

Stenersen is a useful chap. He can get him domestic help. He becomes like a guard, able to take care of bills, find out which of Munch's pictures are actually for sale and where, and to make a bid for them, so that Munch will not have to worry about their being sold too cheaply. He can drive down with the keys when Munch has gone to Åsgårdstrand or Ramme and cannot get in. He informs journalists when Munch has something to say. He helps him with tax matters, arranges exhibitions and the sale of pictures and, not least, sits quietly and listens to Munch when there is something he wants to say.

Sometimes Munch does not ring his new young friend for many months. At others he rings him eight times a day.

The young sprinter is convinced that living conditions can be improved if the money supply increases at the same rate as the supply of goods. He is convinced that it is possible to save and become poor. He sees that society is rich when everything is in plentiful supply. He sees that the rich on the contrary are rich when they have things most people are without, dilapidated old houses which are worth a lot of money just because there is a shortage of houses. He sees the difference between money and wealth and is convinced that the State should take over the banks as soon as possible. He has seen that there are more than twelve acres of cultivable land for every living person. Only a fraction of that is fertilized and farmed. The earth could feed ten times as many people. In the earth's crust there are hundreds of kilometres of coal. A kilogram of coal provides as much energy as twenty people in one hour.

Munch: I know you mean well, Stenersen. But each of us is going to have to mind his own business. You mind your business and I'll mind mine. I don't know how you've wormed your way in here. I didn't ask you to come. You stick your nose in my affairs. Now things have reached such a pass that I find out from a newspaper that I'm having an exhibition. Yet I don't know a thing about it.

*

1923. Munch has his major retrospective at the Kunsthaus in Zürich with seventy-three paintings and three hundred and eighty-nine graphic works. The director of the museum, W. Wartmann, wants Munch to have as dominant a position as Arnold Böcklin and Ferdinand Hodler.

Back in Norway he begins work on the composition *Morning, Midday, Evening, Night*. In other words, woman at all times of the day, and more precisely The Cat, Annie Fjeldbu, who will now be wakened in the morning, or in the middle of the night. Ordered to sleep, stand or lie, to be a nude study for pictures with no erotic undertones. The model stands there naked, unashamed, on the contrary, proud of her profession, devoted in her belief in the importance of her body and her personality. Naked in her being. Naked on the bed. Naked when she gets up in the morning. Naked when at the lunch table she sits there with the light flooding in over her body. Or when, in the evening, in a softer light, she turns her head away.

*

But when she is not there, he walks silently about the house.

The night wanderer. Just as he walked about at the hotel in Taarbæk, two nights before his admission to the clinic, dragging his leg behind him.

The nervous one. Unsuited to live the life everyone else lives. Cannot pick the fruit from the trees and eat it with a clear conscience.

Cannot enjoy the sun in spring. Cannot even meet his own family. Aunt Karen who always understands and supports him.

He walks from room to room. Sees his own pictures staring at him, remote and mysterious. A housekeeper lies fast asleep in the stables. She has access to two of the rooms at Ekely. The rest are locked.

Munch's footsteps. John Gabriel Borkman's footsteps. Outside it is a starry night.

The night wanderer is ill. He has yellow hair, red ears, he walks past his grand piano, gazing at the observer. Thin. Shoddily clothed. Stooping. With an enquiring look on his face.

Behind him is the ice-cold winter sky and the distant lights from the city.

In the kennel a fierce dog howls at the moon.

*

He is sixty years old. The Germans celebrated his birthday a year early. Crammed all the newspapers and periodicals with tributes, called him painting's answer to Knut Hamsun, the founder of modern Scandinavian painting.

Munch's most recent self-portraits have been characterized by conflict. *Seated Figure with Beard. Inner Turmoil.* An ageing man with far too many thoughts in his head.

It is December 1923. His arch enemy *Aftenposten* is at the door:

> But Edvard Munch himself is the same strange, lonely person, who lives in his own world, as untouched by success and wealth as by failure and poverty. The great and much admired master is as stubborn and unapproachable as the struggling young genius. He lives alone in his rambling house out at Skøyen. Recently many journalists have beaten a path up to Ekely, but have found locked doors and have had to leave without getting the mandatory birthday interview which other people are so keen to have on their birthdays. I tried my hand after a little tuition on tactics from Munch's close friend Halfdan Nobel Roede. At five o'clock. This was reputedly the least inconvenient time. It was already dark, and all lights were blazing in the large house with no curtains. From the veranda steps I peer into a living room with the lights on, in which two Airedale terriers fly out from under a grand piano, jump up against the door, and bark. There is no bell and not a soul to be seen. But, I think, he's surely bound to come to find out what the dogs are barking at. The barks sound angrier and angrier. Finally Edvard Munch comes and opens the door, rather hesitantly. I hasten to say that Roede has sent me and refer to a sailing trip ten years earlier, the most memorable event of

which moreover was the fact that Munch sat on a packet of sandwiches filled with Italian salad all the way to Steilene and was
completely at a loss to think where his sandwiches could have got
to as the rest of us searched for them. Whether it was Roede or the
Italian sandwiches that did the trick I can't say, but I got in and
announced the reason for my visit. No, Munch said, I don't want
to be interviewed. To begin with, I'm not celebrating my sixtieth
birthday. That's surely something I must be allowed not to do. I
live completely alone. I can't tolerate the company of other people
now, I must have peace and quiet. And anyway, people were so
kind and made a great fuss of me when I was fifty. You can't go
pestering your fellow human beings by celebrating every tenth
year. Apart from that, I absolutely do not want to be interviewed
by *Aftenposten*. I don't like *Aftenposten*. But? No, it's not what you
think. I bear no grudge against your paper, it's just that I don't
want anything to do with it. *Aftenposten* no doubt has its points as
a newspaper and so on, but it has always barked up the wrong tree
in artistic matters. It always expresses the opinion of the public.
That is why I've decided I don't want anything to do with
Aftenposten. It's a principle of mine. You can write that if you like,
then you'll have your interview after all.

*

The interview is a stranger's impressions of Ekely.

Won't you have a glass of wine? Munch asks all of a sudden.

Yes thank you, says the journalist. He observes that Munch puts on
his winter overcoat, which is lying on a divan, and goes down into the
cellar.

Meanwhile, he has a look round the solitary occupant's house.

He sees the small table where he sits. On it lie books by Baudelaire
and Balzac. *Télémaque* in a seventeenth-century edition and a few
German art journals. Nude studies, friezes, older and more recent
pictures hang on the walls. A large mahogany cupboard stands by the
window in the conservatory. That, a grand piano, and two large family
portraits are the only conventional objects in this house. Two ugly and
uncomfortable brown plush chairs are the only hint of comfort. In the
dining room there is a dining table in front of the window and in front
of it an unpainted bench. The crockery is still lying on the table after
lunch and in the third room the unmade bed can be seen through an
open door. Not the least attempt anywhere to create a homely atmosphere. For the journalist the interior bespeaks the home of a person who
lives in another world, but not in his own rooms.

Munch re-emerges from the cellar with a bottle of champagne.

But he can't open it. Sits there helpless looking at the wire top.

The journalist offers to help him and is soon filling the glasses.

But he is overcome with shame. Here he is pestering this old man, the great artist, who lives in his own world and thinks that *his*, the journalist's, world is so incredibly irksome.

The journalist realizes that he has intruded upon this great lonely man all for the sake of a birthday article, which is as insignificant to Munch as anything else in the world. He is abusing Munch's kindness by taking up his time and forcing his company upon him. He therefore hastens to take his leave.

He is accompanied to the door by Munch and two brown dogs.

* * *

Dear Aunt: Thanks for the letters from yourself and Inger. It was interesting to see the Christmas decorations. I seem to remember we used to do that. I usually have a little tree in the living room, even though I don't decorate it. My gardener cuts off the top of a fir from the hedge round the house. I was recently in Grünerløkken, but I tend to get the many places we lived in a bit mixed up. What I mean is: I'm not quite sure whether it was on the left-hand side of Olaf Ryes Plass that we lived. Of course, I remember the large red living room, which was where Inger had her first pupils. There was also a little blue room where we slept. And at the time Andreas was a cadet. Or was it somewhere else? Nor can I remember whether we lived in two places on the left-hand side? The blue room was in Fossveien perhaps. In any case, I remember that that was where I had my first attack of rheumatic fever. I think it must have been in 1882. Yes, it would be nice to drive round there together sometime soon. The weather is fantastic, isn't it, it will do us all good. It's a long time since I've been so well. On the Riviera and in Italy it is below zero, which means they'll be frozen stiff down there. As I'm the first to know. I hope you're all well. Greetings to you and Inger and Happy New Year. Your devoted Edvard Munch.

* * *

There is a ring on the cowbell at the gate. Munch peeps out. A tall young woman is standing there. It is very rare that he lets people in. But he opens the door to Birgit Olsen, later Birgit Prestøe.

The Gothic maiden.

What made you come here? Did someone send you?

No, she replies, she has come of her own accord.

Munch feels reassured.

You've come at just the right moment, he says. I've just lost a highly-valued model. The Cat. She's married a count in Sweden.

Munch asks Birgit Prestøe to come the following day, wearing the same clothes.

She is wearing a russet-coloured dress with some green on it.

*

Almost in the spirit of cubism he feels free to flatten out the woman's body, as though he is more remote from the model as subject than hitherto.

She sits before him. She sits on the divan as a nude study.

Would you believe my old friends are getting themselves young girlfriends, says Munch. When I meet one of them, I can't help asking: What kind of tomfoolery do you think you're up to? The young girls hoodwink the old chaps into thinking they're in love with them. But love can't be bought like bread.

He talks to the girl on the divan, talks to his model. The nervous girl is talkative. Self-defence. It is the model's job to be his intimate work companion. She must think like him and with him. For his part the painter thinks every minute about how she looks, how she sits, stands and moves. She is transfixed by his thought. She changes mood in tune with him.

He paints her head. The long, slim neck. *Birgit with Pearl Necklace, Standing Nude with Cloth.*

You're not silly enough to get engaged, are you, he says. I've lost many of my good models because they've gone and got themselves engaged. When I've found one that suits me, I tend to stick to her. I shall make you famous.

*

He wants her to walk along the path from Ekely down through the garden to Hoffsalléen. He goes to the greenhouse and cuts some roses.

Here's a pale rose for you, frøken. It suits you so well.

*

He follows her along the path.

I don't understand women, he says to her. I've known so few women in my life. When a woman is chaste, she's respected. But when a man is, he's ridiculed for it. Male chastity has become a joke.

*

It is Christmas Eve at Ekely. Munch has brought the tree in and stood it on the floor. Then he rings Birgit Prestøe.

I'm alone. Would you like to come round?

She does so. She sees that the table is decorated with fruit. Munch invites her to help herself.

She reaches out for an apple. He stops her in mid-movement:

Keep sitting like that, just like that.

He fetches pad and pencil and draws her.

* * *

When she is about to go, he says:

Another time you should say: Can't I stay the night? But it's not worth ... They're waiting for you at home. On Christmas Eve the family should be together.

* * *

He is alone with his own sketch. The beginning of the picture *The Bohemian's Wedding*. The almost Cézanne-inspired still life created by the huge surface of the table, seen in perspective. On the table, apart from some empty bottles, there are used glasses and a couple of apples, a baroque soup terrine with a snakelike lid.

The snake and the apple. Faithlessness and the fall from grace. The City of Free Love. The woman who cannot even be faithful at the wedding banquet. Around her all is black with jealousy. A man sits beside her, broken by his own desire. On the other side, the bridegroom, already highly suspicious. In one version a gentleman with a stick is leaving the table. On the other side a roué of the Gunnar Heiberg type sits and laughs contemptuously at a man with Munch's features.

It is Tulla Larsen's marriage to Arne Kavli. Or an imagined version of Munch's own wedding which never was.

Munch continues to work on the motif, which eventually becomes *Self-Portrait at the Wedding Table*.

Birgit Prestøe relates: One day when I was sitting for Munch, he sat down beside me and started to draw himself. He could see the image in a mirror there. He did not speak for a long time, simply drew. Suddenly he said: This could be father and daughter sitting chatting together. Or we could say it is an old man who has fallen in love with a young girl. This sort of thing happens a lot in the Old Testament. All kinds of things do. It's common for an old man to fall in love with a young girl, but it practically never happens that a young girl falls in love with an old man.

* * *

On 1 January 1925 the city is no longer called Christiania. Its name is Oslo.

During the summer, Munch travels through Gudbrandsdalen to Åndalsnes and Molde, and home through Vågådalen. He sees Peer Gynt's mountain. Reminders of Hægstadtunet. The button moulder is dead. He never met Solveig. And Mother Åse is a wise old aunt.

But Anitra is there. And the lady in green.

He sees Tøfte farm. Finds it curious. Eats lunch at Lesja Works. It troubles him that they are hunting a poor bear somewhere deep in the forest.

*

He sits in the back seat of a roomy 1916 model motor car and through the window sees that the world exists. Then he returns to Ekely.

He has become a suspicious man. By his bed he keeps a gas pistol and a small axe. He has spring locks on all doors. Hildur Christensen is his housekeeper and model.

He is surrounded by a host of people. People he can ring up at any time of the day or night and ask to do errands for him. He is not a practical man. When he prepares food in the kitchen, he throws the leftovers out of the window. It begins to smell. Then he rings a cleaning agency and asks them to come and clean up. After bouts of influenza, he throws all the dirty laundry at the foot of the stairs. A substantial pile accumulates. Then he rings the laundry Vel Vask and asks them to come and fetch it.

One day he rings the taxi stand at Smestad.

How many cars are there just now?

Four, says a driver.

Come on up, all of you.

The four cars pull up in front of Ekely.

Munch stands waiting for them with four rakes.

Soon the four taxi drivers are raking leaves in the enormous garden while the taxi meters tick away.

*

Rumours start to circulate about the eccentric painter at Ekely.

People wake him up in the middle of the night because they have placed bets on who can get him to talk.

And people start to shoot at his dogs.

*

Munch writes to Nørregaard, telling him that Inger has rung him up, nervous about one thing and another and especially about a message she had received from a relation. Munch asserts that it would be a disaster for himself and his sister if an attempt were made to transfer financial responsibility for his relatives' children to himself and his sister. He knows that he is growing older and older, more and more tired. Nobody asks him if he *can* pay, they merely ask him if he *will*. He writes that just the thought of these children would be the end of him. Apart from this, his relation should bear in mind what *he* inherited from a rich grandfather and two wealthy uncles: a flat-bottomed rowing boat worth twenty crowns at most. Munch cannot recall inheriting anything at all in his hour of need after his father's death.

* * *

Faces emerge from the darkness, float past him for a second, and melt back into the darkness. He has been appointed honorary member of the Bavarian Academy of Pictorial Arts.

Then it is suddenly Christian Krohg's turn to die.

Oda sits beside the bed. Krohg lies peacefully on his deathbed. He

338

has asked his son Per to paint him after he has died.

A doctor comes into the room, feels his pulse and says:

Christian Krohg, you are dying.

Munch is at Ekely. Sitting at the window gazing down towards the path which goes up from Hoffsalléen. Perhaps a young woman he can paint may come by. It is autumn. October. The leaves are falling from the trees. He feels a tightening in the chest, as always at this time of year. He knows that he will soon have another bout of influenza. Of bronchitis. Two serious bouts in autumn 1925.

Krohg did not die because he was ill. He died because he was exhausted.

Krohg was there the whole time. Coached him at Pultosten. Defended him in the press during the difficult years. Attained enormous proportions and an equally enormous beard. Then got a brothel on his back. Then became a snail.

Then he became an enemy, a rival.

What became of all the postcards? The bombardment from Germany? What was it he had actually written to Krohg? Munch tries to remember.

Stenersen will say: Introverted types like Munch can't cope with extroverts.

Munch is at Ekely, strokes a dog, ponders what to do about the funeral.

* * *

Strong extrovert people. Dandelions which choke more delicate flowers.

Laura falls ill. Once upon a time she was teased because she allowed herself to be a child. Then she became nervous Laura, sitting in the middle of an empty room. There was a vase on the flaming red table. Laura stared with great dark lacklustre eyes. Munch sees a round form in all people. One moves, not on the earth but *in* the earth. A drawing in his diary as early as 1909. The individual with his circles and his periphery. The periphery intersects the rotating ether and the rotating earth. Man does not walk on the earth, but lives in a declivity on the earth. Like the creatures at the bottom of the sea.

*

Dear Inger: I'm afraid I may have alarmed the two of you. We must hope for the best. It's heartening to know that Laura has been happy in her little home and that she has been out to visit you so often. It must have given her a lot of pleasure. When I spoke to her last, she said she was not afraid of death. Your devoted Edvard Munch.

*

He is driving by car to his sister's deathbed. *Death in the Sickroom*. It is so long since the last one. Now it is no longer a motif.

He has painted his mother, his sister Sophie, Christ, Jæger, either dead or dying. But he will not paint Laura thus.

He visits his sister who suffers from cancer and sees that, paradoxically, cancer has made her more mentally stable. He sits with her and feels a special kind of solidarity. She is fifty-nine years old. She is in an old people's home attached to the nursing sisters' association, where she has lived the past few years. She was born on the wrong planet. Munch can still hear the screams from the mental asylum over thirty years before. At that time, she had been convinced that both she and her family were completely doomed. Impaired lungs and nervous problems. She simply wanted to die. She stuffed snow down between her breasts hoping she would catch pneumonia.

He remembers her joy in the garden at Ekely. She was overwhelmed by the fruit and flowers. He never regarded her as mentally ill.

Munch writes to Aunt Karen: She died peacefully.

* * *

Self-portraits in bright spring light. The mirror reflects his own age back at him with painful brightness. Everything clear. Contrasts and strong colours. It is now that he works on the fifth version of *The Sick Child*. *The Bohemian's Wedding*. *Death of The Bohemian*. *The Red House*.

He travels to Lübeck, Berlin and Venice. He wants to visit Dr Linde and Professor Glaser. Big plans. Writes to Schiefler that, when the weather is bad, one should go straight to Egypt, writes that he no longer sees anyone, not even his closest friends, writes that he has had three further serious bouts of bronchitis. He has begun to keep a diary again, moods and reflections on art, the jottings of thirty years. Perhaps it can be published. Again he complains that people think he is so rich, that he has over ten properties. He feels he ought to inform Schiefler of his affairs.

* * *

He comes to Paris. Café de la Régence.

Dear Jappe! Here again at last! There's no other city like it. At the moment it's grey. No sign of spring. Most resembles a day in late October. But all the same! It buzzes with life and there's something interesting everywhere. I've had a successful trip. Venice is also quite special. Unique of its kind. Beyond all expectation. I'm going to have to go abroad again this autumn and then perhaps continue as far as Rome. I think it was a good thing I had a change of scene now. The worst thing for me about a journey is my absent-mindedness. It plays many tricks on me. Your Edvard Munch.

* * *

The Mountain of Mankind. People who clamber upwards towards the light. Munch sent in his design for the picture on the rear wall in the competition for the University assembly hall. It was rejected. Munch painted *The Sun* instead.

In 1926 he is again working on the *Mountain of Mankind* motif. Zarathustra's mountain. Or Dante's. As though Munch's life becomes one long Ibsen drama. He has lived like Osvald, like Peer Gynt, he is living like Borkman. Now he is also living like Rubek. The sculptor from *When We Dead Awaken*, who uses his previous model Irene as inspiration for his masterpiece *The Day of Resurrection*.

Munch uses Birgit Prestøe as inspiration for *The Mountain of Mankind*.

Gustav Vigeland already had a contract with Oslo municipality relating to a studio for the construction of a fountain which in due course could be the main attraction in a museum. Subsequently the plans grew in scope. The idea is now a sculpture park and an almost-seventeen-metre high monolith with one hundred and twenty-one figures. *The Mountain of Mankind*.

Vigeland the plagiarist. A common pickpocket. Munch feels robbed. To his annoyance, he sees that his imitator gets the sort of contract with Oslo municipality that he himself could but dream of.

But the idea is still Munch's. It is *his* mountain of mankind. Birgit Prestøe stands before him. He is making a Study for the foreground figure in *The Mountain of Mankind*. He paints the major work *Towards the Light*.

* * *

Dear Inger, Thanks for the letter. It doesn't surprise me that you can't stand company. Myself I haven't been a dinner guest for fifteen years. I think we've been weaned of such things. Little trips to Åsgårdstrand are a good thing, I think. Walks which are not too strenuous are a good thing. You get away from everything that is on your mind at home. Now I want to try salt baths. What's the one called that *you* use? I thought I might come out tomorrow, but don't know if I can make it. It's tired me out having two exhibitions and now I have a third one to organize in Germany. I shall try and find a quiet seaside place where I can go swimming. I hope everything is all right with you. Greetings to Aunt. Your devoted Edvard.

*

It is 1926. He spends the autumn and winter abroad. The winter Monet dies at Giverny, eighty-six years old. Paris is actually best when you take it gently and don't dash about. The Louvre during the day and the Opéra in the evening. Back home from the Moulin Rouge at one o'clock in the morning. Munch is on a diet and feels younger than for many years. Grand Hotel in November. A place for the wealthy. Munch can allow himself a little luxury, at least for a few days. Then he is going on to Mannheim and thence to Rome.

After that anywhere, no matter, and with no time limit.

* * *

Dear Edvard: How strange that you should have become so strong, you who were so weak when you were little. Once, when you were about 2 years old, Aunt sat on the sofa with you sleeping on her arm. She sat quiet as a mouse for hours so as not to waken you. When you awoke, your head was bathed in sweat. Aunt was wet through and the arm of her new blue dress was bleached where your head had lain. Your devoted Inger.

*

Dear Inger: I'm sending you 5,000 crowns instead of the 2,000 crowns per year I promised you extra. Many greetings from E. Munch.

*

Berlin 1927. Munch exhibits two hundred and twenty-three paintings, twenty-one watercolours and drawings in the Crown Prince's Palace. It is the thirteenth of March. *Aftenposten* writes:

> The reality exceeds all expectations. The opening took place in the presence of almost everyone who is anyone in the Berlin art world. The authorities were also well represented, with Minister for Culture Becker to the fore. In his opening address, he called to mind Munch's first exhibition thirty-five years before, which had to close only a few days after opening. Such was the ill-will and opposition that his art awakened. Today the National Gallery has made the whole of the Crown Prince's Palace available for a comprehensive exhibition of the same artist's works. The Norwegian legation was there to a man, led by Minister Scheel. When we wander through these rooms today, we cannot comprehend that it was these same pictures that people once rioted against in the sacred name of art. Once again, said Becker, we see that yesterday's revolutionary becomes today's classic. It has been an enormous pleasure for the Prussian Art Administration to extend the hand of hospitality to the greatest son of a foreign nation. All the newspapers discuss the exhibition in long, enthusiastic reviews. All of them underline the overwhelming impression the exhibition makes. It is not just the greatest but the most important exhibition devoted to any artist since Corinth.

*

Dagbladet 26 April 1927:

An hour with Edvard Munch in the morning. He tells us about

his exhibition in Berlin and his trip to Rome, where he has become interested in frescoes. We visit him during the morning at his large property west of Hoff. The south-facing garden slopes downwards with blue carpets of scylla and violets in the sunshine, fruit trees sporting thin porcelain tags with Latin names, greenhouses and uncultivated areas, a ploughed field, almost ready to be painted. And there on the steps stands Edvard Munch himself, bronzed and wearing his lightest summer suit, just as though he were still in Italy. He nevertheless feels tired and nervous, he says.

Were you pleased with Berlin?

I was anxious about the large exhibition. In the other places there were more recent, selected works, but in this one everything was supposed to be included. It was a risk, but I'm very pleased. The Crown Prince's Palace is a far from ideal place for an exhibition. But the Germans had gone to great lengths, converted round pillars to square ones so that they would suit the pictures.

Did you help with the hanging yourself?

No, hardly at all. And when the opening drew near, I left. I don't like going to openings.

You were described as the world's greatest painter, weren't you?

I'm not sure about that. To be that, you have to exhibit your work a lot less. You have to be secretive and never let anyone see your pictures. If you did that, you might perhaps be not just the greatest contemporary painter, but the greatest painter of all time.

Didn't it cause surprise that Minister Scheel did not say a word in reply to the long address by the German Minister for Culture at the opening?

That's something I don't want to comment on in public just yet.

But didn't anyone suggest to him that he should reply?

Yes, I think so.

How was your stay in Rome?

I was constantly looking at things. There were new churches all the time in which I discovered excellent frescoes even though by less well-known masters.

Would you envisage working in fresco yourself?

I've never painted on walls at all. But the technique doesn't look difficult, and I'd like to give it a try.

But in the past, the colours they favoured were different from yours, weren't they?

Yes, I wonder whether people's actual desire for colour hasn't become different. Many of my bright colours would be hard to transfer to fresco after all, but *The Frieze of Life* for example ought to work as a mural.

In the City Hall?

That's a matter for the future.

* * *

One month later, a railway goods wagon carrying Munch's pictures trundles into Oslo. Adam's Express. The wagon is lifted from the rails by a crane. With the utmost care, the wagon is placed onto the undercarriage which is to be used to transport the load through the streets. Between twelve and one o'clock Thiis, Director of the National Gallery, stands at the gates and takes delivery of the eagerly awaited treasure, as the freight firm's practised staff carefully carry the precious packages inside.

*

Munch in the National Gallery. The rehabilitation of a genius, says the Gallery's director Thiis in his opening address. A handsome gesture by a nation, even if late in coming.

8 June 1927. The entire Langaard room is crowded with representative dignitaries. Hambro, President of Parliament, Prime Minister Lyche, as well as numerous other cabinet ministers, almost the entire *corps diplomatique*, everyone who is anyone in the city.

*

But Munch is at Ekely talking to *Stockholms Dagblad*. He discusses the importance of Gauguin. Rembrandt and Velázquez. Reminisces about how Strindberg used to burn the candle at both ends at Zum schwarzen Ferkel. Days on end without sleep.

Munch strolls through the garden with a Swedish journalist.

There are too many flowers here, says Munch. Flowers belong to youth.

* * *

It is 1928. Roald Amundsen perishes near Bjørnøya when the seaplane *Latham* crashes during an attempt to save Amundsen's Italian colleague Umberto Nobile. Eyolf Soot dies. Astrup dies. And Alexander Fleming discovers a mould, *penicillium notatum*, which, by its antibacterial effect, can prevent a number of infections, including pneumonia, from having fatal consequences.

Munch now makes frequent entries in his diary. He writes about the earth, about planets and atoms and their planets. Is the earth a passive orb which revolves round the sun? The earth, which has the same round form as all that shoots up in spring, all that provides nourishment for humans and animals. A living atom with its own will and thoughts. Which breathes. Its breath settles as clouds over it. It breathes. It has blood. Boiling lava.

He writes of Tulla Larsen, relives the nightmare: I had resolved never to marry. It was the thought of the disaster that the inheritance of

344

consumption from my mother and madness from my father could spell for my offspring.

Munch is at Ekely and recalls the fierce battle around the turn of the century. To tie oneself to another person. Or to choose solitude. He has chosen. He sits in bare rooms working. He experiences moments of strength. Almost of health. Then sudden relapses. Bronchitis, infection, mucus which must be brought up. Nerves at night. Insomnia.

He reads all his jottings going back forty years. Another age has dawned. Then it was the hour of realism. You were supposed to believe in godlessness. But that was also belief. Many who lived and died in that belief derived their security and peace from it. For belief is belief. Discoveries had been made that were practical and earthbound. Railway, steamship, hydroelectric power. But invisible forces as well. Something else. Electricity. Munch's own ideas. Planets in space. Atoms. Kollmann's mysticism. Speculation about television.

Electricity is an invisible force. It expresses itself only through its power. But it is earthbound, has to travel along wires. Now comes the wire-less transmission of electricity. Wave lines which go through solid matter. Which go through space.

Munch's thoughts in 1928. Everything he had discussed with Helge Rode and Frederic Delius. Delius who became chained to his wheel-chair. Blind and paralysed. But thought can be transmitted through space. X-rays have been discovered. Radio has been invented.

At Whitsuntide 1928 Munch is at Ekely writing about the spirit which descended in the form of a dove. The Father, the Son and the Holy Spirit. To what does Christian belief owe its power? Even though for many people it is so hard to believe in. Even if one cannot believe in God as a man with a long beard, there is still a great deal of truth in the ideas. Munch writes about God, about the power which must after all be behind everything, which directs everything, which directs the light waves, energy waves, the very source of power. He writes about Christ, the son, the power which has come down into a human being. What awesome power filled Christ. Divine power. The supreme power of genius. Divine sources of power for man's radio stations. Munch writes about sacred moments, in which the mind and thoughts are made recep-tive to wavelengths. One turns one's receptive apparatus away from the earthbound forces, which in the interior of the earth boil and burn in lava and earth blood, the earthly hell, where everything earthly is remoulded.

Then he writes about *The Sick Child*. The breakthrough. That picture contains everything he later developed. Art's subsequent trends. In this picture, if you examine it closely, you will find traces of pointillism, expressionistic line, both symbolist expression and Jugendstil. Around the face, and in a circle around it, you will find that a pointillist under-coat is used. Munch recalls that he painted with a pointed brush. Applied the colour point by point. In the mother's arched back, you will also find the curved lines of Jugendstil. While the picture itself is expressionistic in conception. And the composition is constructed and built up in a cubist manner.

* * *

Bødtker is dead. The poodle has died. How strange.

He thinks wistfully of his old enemies. At one time he had thought of them as animals. But now he has become very fond of animals. For example someone has just turned up suggesting that his white horse should be shot. To which he replies:

How can one possibly shoot a person?

Instead they murder his dog.

They shoot the Gordon setter. It stands on the kitchen steps its nose a-quiver for the scent of strangers. Then it starts barking. His beloved handsome dog. They say it is fierce. It is shot from somewhere down on the road with a shotgun. Munch comes out and finds the animal lying on the steps soaked in blood.

For eight years Munch never walks on the road again. Now he only goes by car. He asks his doctor and friend Schreiner whether he can accompany him to the Anatomical Institute and watch the professor dissect a corpse. He enters the autopsy room and sees an old man stretched out on the table. Then Professor Schreiner takes out his scalpel.

A naked old man. Munch sees the tired body, the pale, bald head, the soulless face. It reminds him of his father.

He makes a lithograph of himself on the autopsy table. He lies just as impotent and lifeless.

Professor Schreiner dissects the corpse which has Munch's features.

* * *

Gunnar Heiberg dies in February 1929.

Suddenly the whole menagerie is gone. But was Heiberg really an enemy? Munch wonders about it. Heiberg, on whom he has lavished so much attention, who has been the object of so much of his fury. Was he in fact only on the periphery of his enemies? He has other enemies now after all.

It is the tax office which has become the enemy. The enemy sits with paper and pencil and scrutinizes the painter's tax return. Oughtn't Munch to pay capital gains tax on his stock of works? His supply?

They come to Ekely to assess his pictures. They are pleasant, polite people. They enter a house which does not look very much like their own homes. They come to a house which is crammed with pictures.

What about this picture here, Munch? With the sort of prices you command, you ought to be able to get five thousand crowns for that, oughtn't you?

* * *

Not easy to decorate a castle in the air, says Munch.

He anxiously awaits the plans for the decoration of the City Hall.

*

The Frieze of Life stuck up in a tower? A room which can only be visited by lift? Impossible. But a tribute to the city's workers and builders? Yes, it might appeal to him to portray Oslo. To portray the city just as the Vika district is being razed to the ground. Hans Jæger's former stamping ground. Where Munch himself has been once. The home of misery. The docks. Poverty and prostitution.

But I cannot give an opinion on a commission I still haven't received, says Munch. Besides, it's going to be rather complicated when one cannot stand in the room oneself and assess the effect.

Do you still keep most of what you paint yourself?

Yes. Despite the fact that every morning the milk boy advises me to sell.

* * *

March 1929. Drawings and graphic works at Blomqvist's. Pastels and watercolours. In *Dagbladet*, Gunnar Larsen writes an advance notice. We go to the bookbinder's, and there we find a series of brilliant sketches in pastel and watercolours, here are the first sketches for what will certainly become the major work of his maturity: the decorations for Oslo City Hall. Some are ideas which were developed on a smaller scale for the Freia factory, others are based on designs from that time. But a great many are from the past few weeks and clearly show that Munch is devoting himself body and soul to the grandiose project. There are female workers in front of the factory, there are men coming home grimy with soot, the bright little figure of a girl waves to one of them, this is the family of workers *en masse*, walking down the street, there are magnificently coloured pictures of the docks with blue-overalled shipworkers and red-lead coloured ships in the sun, there are two people on a bench in Studenterlunden, a couple on a Sunday excursion to Bygdøy. There is Oslo under slush and in summer sun, and Munch has managed to bring out the beauty of Trinity Church, the meat markets, and uses these well-known city sights as a backdrop to the figures. And the horses, the disappearing carthorses, are given their own prominent place in the portrayal. The whole thing amounts to an apotheosis, a homage to those who build. There are scenes showing workers tearing down old hovels, others showing workers busy on building sites.

347

And in a large central area, monumental structures tower like a vision up into the air and light behind a row of working men.

* * *

In the morning at Ekely he plays with his dogs.

He feeds them himself. They are his closest friends. Setters, terriers, St Bernards. He paints *Lady with Dog*. A lady holds her hand up to her breast, as though to protect herself from the boisterousness of the dog.

He builds the winter studio. A roomy structure in brick in a place where wooden sheds have stood since 1918. A half-roof through which rain, sleet and snow have blown in. He has stood knee-deep in snow, painted pictures and coughed up mucus. Now he can paint indoors. A studio built on a design by Henrik Bull. No longer a case of four wooden walls with a lean-to roof, but a huge space with a play of light. Munch paints the studio as it is being built. Masons, joiners, builders. Here he can work away day and night.

* * *

Jappe Nilssen is at Ekely, sitting with his glass of wine before him.

The Gothic girl sits opposite him in a red dress.

Munch sees a picture.

Shall I look at the lady? asks Jappe Nilssen

No. You can sit looking down into the glass, that suits you best.

Munch places Rolf Stenersen in the middle.

The Oslo Bohemians. The old Bohemian sits alone opposite his young wife, and her friend has sat down at her corner of the table. A triangle. A three-cornered relationship. Comically obvious. From all his accumulated wisdom and experience, the old Bohemian knows and acknowledges what the lover now has no choice but to toast him on. Yet who is the stronger? The sad man or the humiliated, jealous lover?

That is a question only the woman can answer.

* * *

It is 1930. Gandhi proclaims civil disobedience. Nansen dies. Cousin Edvard Diriks dies. Jappe Nilssen is visibly ill. The Artists' House opens.

Accumulations of blood in his eye, far too much blood.

Tulla Larsen provides him with inspiration again for *The Murder of Marat*. Who actually was Charlotte Corday? She was the woman who murdered the man. Munch paints Marat in the bathtub and Marat and Charlotte Corday in several versions. Marat alias Amor alias the artist who leaves the woman as he is being betrayed by her.

He abandons her to her earthly fate. Luminous watercolours. The most innocent woman stands in Munch's garden at Ekely holding a little bouquet of flowers to her heart. Absolute innocence.

This is what a murderer looks like.

He uses Hanna Brieschke as model. Hanna Selquist as she then was. A beautiful model, very much in demand, from Silsand on Senja, who had actually thought of emigrating to the United States.

She is a friend of Birgit Prestøe. She will be Munch's sole professional model until 1942.

He calls her the Nordland Girl.

He paints her as Marat's murderer. He paints her *Standing Nude*, as *Half-length Nude in the Wicker Chair*, as *Study*, as *The Girl from Nordland*. And he paints her as *Gretchen*. Faust's duality. A dramatic tension which is spontaneously resolved without the action in the picture playing any decisive role. What is decisive is the presentation, the pure, bright colours which are applied to create strong contrasts and also the obsessive rhythmical stroke. The Faust motif is bound up with the young girl complex he developed in Åsgårdstrand. Youthful girls, with Ingse Vibe in the lead, who challenged his desire and who at the same time made him feel old. They egged him on to the fight with Ditten. Their eyes shone with admiration. Afterwards they sat in the garden singing his praises.

Hanna Brieschke. He dresses her in white, wants to use her in all his work. Suddenly she becomes the white-clad Ludvig Karsten in the streets of Åsgårdstrand.

In May 1930 a blood vessel bursts in one of Munch's eyes. He notices that he is partially blind.

The dark bird. There it is again. It flits about in front of him. A large dark bird. Dark brown feathers, emitting something bright blue. Then it becomes green and then ... yellow!

The snakes slither around the table and chair legs. Vermilion and golden yellow.

At night, when he drinks his wine, another world lights up. Fireworks of gold rise and fall and are surrounded by burning yellow clouds which open and close. An inferno of blood-red and yellow flames bursts forth. Before long there are a hundred snakes writhing about. Now and then wonderful colours. A deep blue vase. Never has he seen anything like the pure, delicate shade of it.

Just as stone and crystal have life and will, so do humans. Even if the human's body is damaged, the soul can be saved. The idea. The human will.

Munch thinks: religion is about preserving this idea. He thinks that the predominant wavy lines in his earlier pictures and etchings are linked to the rotations of the ether. The feeling of links between bodies.

Medusa's hair. The invisible rays he has always seen round people.

* * *

He tries to cure his insomnia by sleeping with his clothes on, which actually means wearing lighter night clothes.

He takes a bath. He does not go to bed until the early hours. It is not something he can explain. He does not expect anyone to understand such a cure.

He can never be in company. If he breaks this rule everything goes awry. He thinks he can explain it through psychoanalysis.

Something has happened in his life. Something which has had a decisive effect on his fate. He writes that his awareness of this has been stored in his subconscious. It seems like a warning. It rises up like ghosts from the dark cellars of the mind. Now, suddenly, he remembers 1908. When he was at the psychiatric clinic in Copenhagen. To his friend Goldstein he had said:

I feel that what's wrong is right up here.

He had pointed to a place on his chest.

Here.

*

He believes that at last he understands the mystery of sleep. The whole time he was growing up he was very ill. He often spent half the winter in bed. Right until he was a man. This is why, in his subconscious, bed has become synonymous with the sickbed.

When he lies fully clothed on a *chaise-longue*, this awareness is not as strong, since at any moment he can get up and step onto the floor.

* * *

Suddenly one day he runs into Blix on Karl Johan.

Twenty years before he gave him a dressing down in a Paris hotel room, together with Karsten, when he was describing his picture of hell, in which Gunnar Heiberg was to sit next to the devil and the others were to be arranged in a hierarchy of his own devising rising up towards heaven. On that occasion Blix had offered to sit at the bottom with Heiberg. Now Munch walks cautiously up to the cartoonist: Isn't it Blix?

Yes, it is.

I hope you've forgotten what happened last time we met.

Yes, of course I have.

Munch seizes Blix's hand and squeezes it hard.

Oh, thank you so much, says Munch. I was as mad as a hatter then, you know.

* * *

Munch views the prospect of another decade. Will he survive it? So many are already dead.

There were times when it looked as though he was forging ahead.

Now he writes that the last half of his life has been a fight just to tread water, to keep his balance. He has jumped from stone to stone. Across abysses. From mountain top to mountain top. Or on bottomless swamps. From one clump of grass to another.

*

Once again he is somewhere in the past. The drop of blood. In the grey rooms drops of blood were a common sight. Spots of blood. Bright, bright red fresh blood. Old rust-coloured blood on hand-kerchiefs. On old sheets. Finally like old relics. What had belonged to the family's now-dead members would be taken out of the cupboard. The rust-coloured spots of blood were still there.

*

He thinks of Aunt Karen and his sister Inger.

They are moving house. They want to move to Lovisenberg. He wants to find a suitable place for them, preferably with a little garden which could afford them a little enjoyment. A change.

It must be possible to buy a large house.

He thinks: arrangements must be made for the graves. Otherwise everyone may come to regret it. Cremation or burial? Hadn't Frits Thaulow returned to Norway in a bottle?

He hears that Aunt Karen is not well and writes to Inger that at the beginning of a bout of bronchitis one should not give oneself cold rub-downs.

* * *

Munch sits listening to the radio at Ekely. A talk about light waves and matter. The speaker refers to the latest findings which conclude that just as light consists of waves, so does matter.

But he had written that in his diary twenty or thirty years ago. He wrote that everything is movement, that even in a stone there is the spark of life. He wrote that there are simply different types of move-ment. Munch is passionately interested in what the speaker says. That the electrons in atoms must be considered as movement. Electrical dis-charges too. The type of movement gives the matter form.

* * *

Dagbladet January 1931. Europe a madhouse, says Edvard Munch.

In the journal *Die Dame*, the Danish writer Hans Tørsleff has written about a visit to Edvard Munch, the hermit of Ekely, in which he enthu-siastically and amusingly shares his impressions of a few hours spent with Munch. He gives a very detailed account of his visit, from his meeting with Munch's ferocious dogs, which frighten all visitors, to the solitary but hospitable man. The contrast resides in the friendliness with which the host himself receives his guest and the courtesy with which he answers the interviewer's questions. To his horror he sees that

351

the maestro's works, which people would otherwise look after with the greatest care to ensure that they came to no harm, lie thrown carelessly about.

Furious barking. Two Greenland pointers tear madly about the yard. In answer to the Danish journalist's ring, Munch appears on the hillock in front of the house. From a distance he looks gigantic, reminiscent of Hamsun and Nansen. But when the journalist gets nearer, he sees the difference. The transparent, luminous quality in his appearance. He drags one leg slightly. But there is strength in his movements.

Hurry up and come in! The dogs don't bite. It's just for show. If the guard dogs are making a fuss it's just because they're glad there's a visitor. Will you do as you're told, you rascal! Yes, it's hard work with our four-legged friends. Here you spend your time making sure that the dogs, which are supposed to guard you, don't run off. No, but I do have one that's wide awake. The old rat catcher down there by the sheds. But he's so old and stiff in the legs that he'll soon be needing crutches. He's wide awake all right, but he doesn't bite. No, a dog must not bite. Can you credit people who, to protect themselves and their money, set bloodthirsty monsters onto milk boys, delivery men and other useful people? I can't.

Munch and a journalist. He talks about the radio. Church music pours into the room. It is Sunday morning. Munch likes fiddling with the radio. He has several radios. All of a sudden Stockholm, Copenhagen and Oslo are all preaching at once signalling conflict not union between the Nordic countries. Talk about the United States of Europe! Do you remember how those who talked about that twenty years ago were ridiculed? And now so-called serious statesmen are working towards that goal. The United States of Europe is bound to come, that is, if we do not perish as decadent barbarians in an excess of mechanical culture and in moral collapse. I cannot but see that we have already been downgraded to a backwater of the cultural world. America is now doing precisely what young Rome did when it attracted the cultural forces from Greece, which was disintegrating. The best people go to the United States. But they don't improve by being there. When you look at contemporary Europe, you often have the feeling of being in a madhouse. Where are the doctors who can cure us?

* * *

Aunt Karen dies aged ninety-two.

Does he really grasp what has happened? Aunt Karen. The first person to notice when he tried to recreate the procession of blind people on the floor at home at Grünerløkken, and who continued to follow his progress when he went abroad. She was careful to keep her distance, never demanded to be with him. He has flashes of memory. The bottomless depths of empathy on the one hand. The towering peaks of ambition on the other. He might also have said: The museum on the one hand. Aunt Karen on the other.

*

Aunt Karen's death affects him deeply. He cannot even face attending the funeral but stands at a distance and watches the funeral procession.

Dear Inger: I could follow the funeral from the church to the grave. I hope you're not over-tired. You've had a lot to cope with. Why don't you stay at Nordstrand now until it gets warmer, and rest? You have company out there, I take it, so you will not be too lonely. I'll come out to see you soon. Spring is always the most anxious time for me, and it is also a time when I must be careful. Don't leave before we've spoken. Greetings. Your devoted Edvard Munch.

*

Dear Edvard: It was so nice that you followed everything so closely. It was an extremely good place for you, that path that runs around the churchyard. I could see you clearly. Your wreath was greatly admired. It was chronic bronchitis that Aunt had. Together with arteriosclerosis, that was what ended her life and it was a blessing. Senility would have been an intolerable prospect for her of all people. Greetings from Inger. PS: Shall I remember you to the vicar? He said such fine things about Aunt and has often visited her. He will receive 100 crowns. We had chocolate and sandwiches.

* * *

Jappe Nilssen dies at almost the same time. For years he has hobbled about, plagued by arthritis, smoking far too many gauloises. The face of melancholy, convinced that he will soon have reached the end of a totally empty life.

A half-finished article on Spanish art lies on the desk beside him. He lies down for a rest and dies of a heart attack.

*

Munch writes: What is the soul when a medicine can snatch me from the claws of the bird of prey and the crazed mind of fear, give me peace and change my attitude to life?

* * *

It is 1932. Munch's inherent contempt for the so-called money economy raises its ugly head again: that he, like Rembrandt, should have to struggle through the last years of his life in poverty and misery! But without, like Rembrandt, first having helped himself to life's banquet which was so lavishly laid out for him too.

Self-Portrait for Person Going Out.
Self-Portrait by the Corner Window I.

Self-Portrait by the Corner Window II.
Bare Trees in Winter.
Self-Portrait with the Dogs Truls and Tips.
Self-Portrait with Upturned Hat Brim.
Self-Portrait with Upturned Hat Brim and Charcoal Stick.

* * *

Dear Edvard: Despite nervous trouble we still got there in the end. Despite a wrong upbringing. It wasn't at all right of father to expose us to such powerful ghost stories from when we were little. But, as Laura often said, we all had such energy. And when father's nervous attacks were over, we had such a lovely time together, he always took such an interest, in card games of an evening, at half-past eleven, and reading to us. Aunt kept us all on an even keel. Now you mustn't worry about me any more. I can easily manage my household chores. And I love living frugally. Greetings from your devoted Inger.

* * *

Suddenly there he is in a shop scrutinizing the features of a little old lady. It is she whom he had played hopscotch with sixty-one years ago. He can clearly visualize the lines and patterns drawn on the ground.

Her name was Emma.

She had large dark eyes and a slightly roguish smile. Her hat always slightly at an angle. Her sister Emilie was also pretty, but not as pretty as Emma.

He thinks she looks just the same. Her eyes are strangely dark. Her smile is the same. A slightly roguish smile. Even her hat is the same, slightly at an angle. She is standing at the counter ready to pay. He stands a little way off. But he lets his gaze linger on her. Does she recognize him? What if he were to go up to her and . . .

He stands there at length following her movements.

It is like it was before. She is enveloped in a strange warmth.

Should he write to her: I loved you. I still feel the same now. Do you remember me? I stood close to you one Sunday morning in spring. Can you remember? You were my sister Sophie's friend. The sun was warm and cast long shadows.

* * *

He thinks of the man who, in his short life, did not allow his flame to be extinguished. Vincent van Gogh. His brush aglow with fire. In only a few years he burned himself out for the sake of his art. Munch knows that he has been graced with more years. More money at his disposal. He does not want the flame to be extinguished on that score. Burning paintbrush. He wants to paint until the end, as he tries to write about the life he has chosen:

The flame. The torch. It flickered and shrank until it almost went out and he glanced around fearfully in the darkness. Had he lost his way? Who was he? Had he lost the way? He ran. He fell. He struggled through the wilderness. Fought his way forward with ruined limbs. Where was the road? Dragged himself on. Look at him, people said. He is searching for gold. Gold! He believes he is hiding treasures. He looks for gold in the earth. They scorned and mocked him. The miser. The gold digger. Let us find the gold. Then he said: stop. I am seeking a lofty distant goal, he said. You fools. You think I am wearing myself to the bone for money. That's enough. I am giving up. I shall put on clean clothes, polish my shoes, put carpets on all the floors. Please come in. Let me invite you to a cup of tea. Here is a table with some cakes and biscuits. And please, here are ten crowns!

* * *

Munch has presented his sister Inger with a camera. Now she stands in the middle of the river Aker, water up to her waist, taking photographs. She is making a collection of photographic postcards.

Dear Inger: Thank you for river Aker. I must say it looks extremely beautiful. Congratulations on it and on your success. I think you'll sell a lot of copies. But the main thing is that it has turned out so successful and interesting. Surely now you can relax in your lovely apartment. Your devoted Edvard Munch.

* * *

1933. In Germany Adolf Hitler is appointed chancellor and fêted with a torchlight procession through the Brandenburg Gate. A few weeks later the anarchist Marinus van der Lubbe sets fire to the Reichstag. Jews are removed from public positions. The first concentration camps are set up. The German author Bertolt Brecht goes into exile.

To Birgit Prestøe Munch says: A new war is inevitable despite all the pacifists write about there never being another war. Humans are a degenerate species, war there has been and war there will be, and I doubt whether it will ever be any different. Considering everybody is arming it's bound to be war. America wants to skim off the cream.

Munch talks to Birgit Prestøe about Russia's mission. She knows that he has got hold of Karl Marx's *Das Kapital* and is very absorbed in it. But he is against the fact that the Russians rejected religion:

It is not religion as such which should be attacked, but the manner in which it is practised by those in power. People will always need religion.

* * *

Munch writes letters which he delivers by car.

Dear Thiis: There are various things I should like to talk to you about. To begin with, it is essential that you, who have devoted so much attention to my art, should know a thing or two about the problems I have had with the cabal which has persecuted me for 40 years. I have hinted at these things in a few letters, but have no desire to go into further detail about this in writing. These things have also influenced the development of my art and it is as well you should know about it. I refer to events at the beginning of the century and especially in 1905. I do not want a few drunken louts who at the time started a vendetta and a campaign of lies against me to somehow contrive to get themselves into history. There were also scheming women behind all this, of course. During the past few days I have again ventured onto the country road here and resumed some of my previous walks which were always how I kept fit and well. I go out at half-past four in the morning. At that time there are no youths who I risk being pestered by. Most people are away at the moment anyway. It is eight years now since I have dared to walk along the Aker road. I still wouldn't be able to walk up to your place. I'm in too poor a state for that. You must try to come out and see me and, accompanied by one of Theodor Olsen's wonderful Rhine wines, we would therefore have a lot to talk about. If you are at home and could come out to see me in the car it would be lovely. If you are at home but cannot come, tell the chauffeur when I can come and collect you. Your devoted Edvard Munch.

* * *

Dear Inger: It was lucky I came up to see you. How can you treat a fever like that? Jumping in and out of bed, and going out into the cold passage. It's remarkable that your condition didn't deteriorate still further. With a fever you have to stay in bed for several days after. No, you must look after your health a lot better than this, both your nerves and your throat. If you don't, life will be one long Calvary. Don't bother yourself now about the river Aker. What counts is that it was a success and that it will be of lasting interest. It was so lovely and peaceful at Åsgårdstrand. Neither you nor I can stand Oslo with all its cars and racket. I also think that, like me, company is not good for you. At the chemist's they said that the 'flu this autumn was very bad, with a high temperature. And oh, that nervousness. I also caused you problems that time at your house with my nervousness. I've had too much to cope with. Your E.M.

* * *

For a longish period he lives at Åsgårdstrand again. He walks along the shore and into the forest. The forest of *The Frieze of Life*. The woman's place has been taken by a dog.

In August he writes to Nørregaard, asking him to explain to his begging relative in the clearest possible terms that it is *absolutely* necessary for him now and for a long time to come to be *completely* removed from everything to do with business. Munch writes that he has explained this to her in detail through Inger and it surprises him that his relation doesn't just let the matter drop. To avoid everything to do with business as well as other interruptions he has constantly moved from place to place for nine months. He admits to Nørregaard that it is wearing, but is the only way to get a little peace. He stuffs letters unopened into a case he has with him when he travels. He thinks people should understand that times are difficult for painting too. He is not selling anything. Who can afford to pay a lot for pictures? Germany is closed. And even if he could sell, he can't stand all the trouble involved. He asks Nørregaard to give his relation his kindest regards and every good wish. He does not expect he will ever meet her. But what does that matter since all his relation talks about is money?

* * *

It is 1933, the year Munch becomes seventy, the year Pola Gauguin and Jens Thiis each publish a major biography of Munch.

In *Morgenposten* Felix writes:

> One evening in autumn I knocked at the door of the solitary artist. He is loath to be interviewed, yet on occasion does agree and this evening he came out onto the steps.
>
> I explained why I had come. An interview.
>
> Impossible.
>
> He stood up on the high steps leading from the living room down into the garden.
>
> No, I don't think I have time for interviews. First I'm going to eat my meal. Then I'm going to do some painting and then I have to go back to Oslo.
>
> But Munch always comes back. It could just as easily be an evening in February as a morning in September. If he is in the mood, he can talk to all and sundry, get them to talk about their daily lives and is a good listener. And he may well use the opportunity to hold forth about vegetarianism.
>
> Just imagine a calf, says the painter. An ordinary red calf. Have you ever looked into its eyes? Have you seen how deep they are and how innately good? And it is this creature with these eyes that we suddenly strike brutally in the forehead, slit its throat, then eat both its blood and its flesh?

*

Munch sits in a car and is driven from one place to another. He has bought oranges and bananas which he has stuffed into the wellingtons lying on the back seat. On arriving back at Ekely he sees that a ladder is propped up by the first-floor bedroom window. There he sees his foreman Ingvar Øvstedal nosing about.

Munch loses his temper and tells the man off.

But I thought you were ill! says Øvstedal crossly.

Suddenly Munch laughs. No, not ill, Øvstedal. You thought I was dead, didn't you?

* * *

Munch receives the Grand Cross of the Order of St Olav. It is decided that negotiations should start with Munch and the national authorities regarding the creation of a Munch Museum. He is regarded as Norway's greatest painter and the world's most endearing misanthrope. A tent-dwelling nomad always on the move.

A journalist asks in a telephone interview where the artist plans to spend his seventieth birthday. Munch laughs heartily, as though at a good joke.

That's something the tent-dwelling nomad doesn't know, he says. A tent requires certain conditions too. He has no idea where it will be standing on the twelfth of December, but he does live in a beautiful country.

Are you dreading the inevitable tributes on your seventieth birthday? asks the journalist.

Munch laughs again. It's not much fun when two thick books are written about you, he says. That's going to take some getting over.

What has it been like reading about your own life?

It's been most interesting actually. That's all there is to say about it. Now that I've become so fit and healthy I've also become diplomatic.

*

Thiis had wanted to fête him with pomp and ceremony. But Munch had asked:

Me? A torchlight procession? You mean I ought to stand high on a balcony and wave? In that case, it would have to be to draw it.

*

Østlandsposten Monday 11 December 1933: Edvard Munch in Larvik. Arrived Saturday lunchtime and left Sunday afternoon.

Aftenposten the following day: Munch Day in Oslo – but no Munch in Oslo. Munch was tracked from Oslo to Moss, Horten, Tønsberg and Larvik, but then vanished on the mail boat!

*

He is sitting in a roomy car.

Nobody knows where he is, apart from his chauffeur.

Telegrams arrive from all over the world. Minister for Propaganda Joseph Goebbels congratulates him as, ironically enough, do the despised Jews Max Reinhardt and Max Liebermann. Three crates of telegrams. Munch returns to Ekely the following day and has the crates containing the unread telegrams placed down in the cellar.

*

Dear Thiis: So after all there was a party with flowers, old friends and the most unusual gifts. Friends from forty or forty-five years ago came.

There are not many of them left. And would you believe I made a speech, though it was really no more than just my ordinary conversation speeded up and a bit louder. Despite the fact that you categorically decided that I was neither ill nor full of cold, I was and have been ever since I caught a bad cold on my birthday. I am now weak and feverish after five nights bathed in sweat. I must now set about the long process of curing my bronchitis. It's hard to shake off. But in any case I hardly dare show myself in public for at least a year after so many descriptions and portrayals of me. Your old friend, Edvard Munch. P.S. It's hardly surprising that I caught a bad cold after flitting up and down the coast in cold cars and fair to middling hotels. It's surprising it wasn't the death of me. Especially when I'd only just recovered from three months of bronchitis.

* * *

He lets his hair grow and paints a new self-portrait: *With Glasses and Beard*. He writes to Nørregaard:

I'm now going to withdraw completely. It's the only way I can live and perhaps paint a little again. It's been dreadfully busy with interruptions by visitors from Oslo and from abroad. There's no alternative but to keep myself completely to myself. But then, I've always been able to be alone. I'm in the process of writing my memoirs and am currently dealing with the period around 1905. Some rather personal rumours were put about concerning me. You know that I thrashed Karsten after something he said. Then I got the then manager of the Co-op to come and see me and with the benefit of surprise and the use of cunning, got him to tell a quite outrageous lie about me. He will probably not forget the occasion when he had to take it all back. I have nothing at all to reproach myself with in 1905. It was the continued persecution I was the victim of for several years that finally destroyed me. From about 1902 I was the victim of attacks every year back home at precisely the time the Germans launched a large-scale campaign to support me. Naturally this was my undoing in the end and it was also the undoing of three poor women. I shall set down everything I went through from about 1900 to the clinic in 1908. When I now relive the years 1902–1905 it is incredible that I managed as well as I did. Those were the years that broke me. What happened in 1902 I don't need to tell you, it was the great inaugural fanfare. Then with a maimed hand I had to become the habitué of well-to-do families, put a brave face on it and paint commissions.

* * *

He is driven up to Holmenkollen. Goes for walks there, just as he had done eight years earlier. Walks along the old familiar paths. Muses about life.

What if mankind had an aim, what if it asked: where am I going to, or where do I *want* to go to? What if mankind knew where it wanted to get to and constantly asked: Is this the right way? Will this path take me there?

He looks down on Oslo. Christiania. From a distance the city does not look bad.

Far away to the east, in draughty streets, he spent his childhood.

He gets lost in his memories. How is he to get at all this?

His autobiography. Borkman again. As though high up over the city he is in another room in the house at Ekeberg. When should he go out into the snow to die?

He passes the statue of Colonel Angell. A little further down he sees his friend from the old days, Gustav Lærum, sitting on a bench.

Munch pretends not to notice him until he is right in front of him. Then he suddenly jumps aside:

Oh my goodness, I thought you were a statue!

*

He writes to Nørregaard, telling him that he has spent a lot of time at Nedre Ramme and Åsgårdstrand. Now he had thought of travelling about a little in Sweden. He has been a vagabond for much of his life. Now one of his relations thinks he should take over her two children. This is unreasonable, he writes to her. To start with, he cannot take on any more purely from the health standpoint. He writes that keeping his next of kin has been hard going. A labour of love, but tricky and exhausting. Now he is too worn out, he's reached the limit. He is fully occupied with trying to sort out his financial affairs so that he will not face ruin. He feels that it is his art and the large-scale works he has embarked on which are at stake. No increase in the sales of his pictures can be expected. His property Ekely is large but not worth a great deal. A drain and roads need to be put in. It will not be possible to recoup any money from it during the first fifteen years. Whether he can help his relations later on he will not be able to say until he has sorted out his affairs enough to know how much money he has. It is difficult to sell pictures and difficult to find out who the few potential buyers are. He no longer has any cash in the bank. Then he writes that his relative has been out to see him twice. He was away on both occasions, either at Ramme or Åsgårdstrand, but feels it would be best to postpone talking to her as he is still unable to make her any promise of financial assistance. It may be that he will become strong enough through his travels to make a meeting possible.

*

He paints *Self-Portrait as Seated Nude*. A human being or a demi-god. Vulnerable, stripped naked.

He writes entries in his journal, notes down memories, sketches for a deeply personal tell-all autobiography. He has a strong desire for the record to be set straight.

*

He constantly uses Hanna Brieschke as a model and works on the same theme on several canvases at once. *Uninvited Guests*, *The Fight*, *The Splitting of Faust*.

Suddenly he feels the enemy at close quarters.

Ekely becomes a snakepit.

One of the dogs growls all night.

* * *

Dear Inger: I've thought a lot about Hvitsten and you, because if you really would feel well down there, I mean permanently well and less nervous, it would naturally be excellent. Yet care will have to be taken to ensure that our relatives don't get power over you and become successful in their schemes. Because we have seen that, despite the fact that they are good and nice as individuals, they are extremely self-centred and ruthless business people. It is clear that they have had designs on Nedre Ramme and their attempt to gain a foothold there at one time reveals how calculating they are. Their idea was originally to come and bathe there. Once they've started it will be impossible to get rid of them. Now and then you could live with me for a few days in a room on the first floor.

* * *

It is 1935. The year surrealism comes to Norway. Munch lives in each of his three properties in turn. He makes fresh versions of *Jealousy* and *The Ladies on the Jetty*, pens further entries in his journal, lives with his animals and tills the soil with increasing enthusiasm. On one occasion he asked a doctor for advice, a municipal medical officer who had built a mental asylum and an old people's home, who was also an architect and became a member of parliament and cabinet minister, sat on a score of committees and was asked for advice about everything under the sun. Munch had asked him what he should grow on his estate. Plant cabbages, had been his reply. Growing crops is the most profitable thing. Munch planted a huge field of cabbages. It was during the period of speculation. Wages were expensive, every head of cabbage costing him two crowns. Munch lost a vast amount of money. The doctor came to visit him many years later. Munch wanted to say something to him, something like: I want to move to town. But he got no further than the word I. The doctor's mind was already fast at work:

I? I is the first person. You are the second person. He is the third person . . .

But I want to move to town! said Munch.

*

The German painter Macke who fell in the war wrote to Munch: We carry you on our shields.

This immediately puts Munch in mind of his fellow countrymen:

They crush me between their shields.

*

Thorolf Holmboe dies in March. Harald Solberg dies in June. Schiefler and Signac die in August. Oda Krohg dies in October and Henrik Lund in December.

Munch feels that his blood pressure is too high.

* * *

Dear Inger: I'm surprised how lackadaisical you are about such a cold or dose of 'flu. It's surprising you didn't get worse. I also often used to be amazed that you took colds so lightly and got up out of your sickbed. When you have a cold with a temperature you absolutely must stay in bed for as long as the temperature lasts and then a few days. It is this that has impaired your hearing. Well, careful thought should be given to how you should deal with your cold and your nerves. I must admit, I didn't think you really could have had a temperature or been that poorly when you were so full of beans and jumped up out of bed. My goodness, what a careless way of carrying on. And then up too soon. There mustn't be many repeat performances of this. I hope your leg is better. Have you tried a pine needle bath? Your E.M.

* * *

Stenersen comes out to see him on the morning of Christmas Eve bringing some flowers. When he gets up to go, Munch says:

Can't you stay for a little while? I'm so lonely. Everyone seems to think I like being on my own. Nobody likes being lonely. Whom should I ring? Jappe's dead. All my friends are dead. There isn't a soul I can visit.

If you'd like to come home with me, Stenersen replies, you'd be most welcome.

No, you must be with your children. Go round the Christmas tree and things like that. I haven't even got a Christmas tree. Couldn't you come with me to buy a tree? Then I'll drive you home.

In the car down to town Munch talks about the old days. When the car stops, he has forgotten what it was they were going to buy.

A Christmas tree, says Stenersen.

A Christmas tree? What do I want with a Christmas tree? Oh yes, that's right. Is five crowns enough?

Munch sits in the car while Stenersen goes and buys the Christmas tree. Then they drive back to Ekely. Stenersen carries the tree in and places it by the door. To begin with Munch doesn't look at it. But suddenly he stops short and looks at it.

Have you bought that for me? he says crossly.

Yes, do you mean this? Stenersen looks at the tree. He sees the naked tree. A fir tree by the door. He takes it out with him. Before he has even had time to turn and say Happy Christmas he hears Munch closing the door.

* * *

1936. To remove one's self from the body. The ageing, decaying body. To be returned to the universe, to primeval life. Lie in the earth and decompose. Be devoured by wriggling worms and grubs. Maggots which burrow into the eye sockets, on into the brain, down the windpipe and out into the lungs.

Munch is working on the plans for the decoration of the city council chamber in Oslo City Hall. The history of Oslo. The old town. Håkon Håkonsen. Duke Skule. Bishop Nicolaus. The fire. Akershus. The new town. The City Hall which is built while the old Vika district is demolished. The workers' activities. The workers on Sunday. In the open air.

He does not know what to do about *The Frieze of Life*. To *Morgenbladet* he said: No, frankly, I'm not sure *The Frieze of Life* would be all that suitable in a room at the City Hall. It's old now, *The Frieze of Life*, and it's also far from finished, and anyway most of it is still only studies. And it's of a very intimate nature you know.

Not *The Frieze of Life*. The 'Workers' Frieze' instead. Several large sketches. Among other things, a large picture, five metres by eight. *Workers in the Snow*.

But the plans fizzle out. His physical ability to take on a major decorative commission is limited.

It is the year Rolf Stenersen, after building up a unique collection of modern Norwegian art, with Edvard Munch as the focal point, decides to present the entire collection to the municipality of Aker, if the authorities can provide suitable premises.

The thought of a museum begins to exercise Munch. But where and how?

He can peep down on his colleague Gustav Vigeland. The tall Monolith arrived in the city as early as 1926. Every day there are people chiselling away just a stone's throw below Ekely. The Vigeland open-air museum. Frogner Park. A whole life's work assembled. It will be many years before it is finished. But Vigeland is a worker. Munch can almost smell the sweat at Ekely.

* * *

Bestum 12/2/37. Dear Edvard Munch: I shall never again ring you at night. But it was well meant. As Kant says: The thought may be good but give rise to bad deeds. It can be bad but give rise to good deeds. But if the thought is good, it should shine like a diamond in the blue firmament, for eternity. The thing is that Sigbjørn and I were very fond of one another, and he was extremely interested in you. Would you like to paint my dog Morten? He is 5 years old now and beginning to behave quite strangely. A farm dog, with a fine head, black eyes. *Plus que je Connais* etc. Good wishes for 1937. Yours Herman Obstfelder, (address Bestum).

* * *

Fru Thaulow dies. Munch reads in the paper that she will be remembered for her warmth, an afterglow of which lingered wherever she had been. The journalist remembers her: young, slim, elegant and lithe, she once walked down Karl Johan like a reed.

My God, Milly Ihlen, Milly Thaulow, Milly Bergh. She could have been Munch. Milly Munch. He sits at Ekely reading about her love of small birds. She too was apparently an animal lover. And a picker of flowers. Munch lays the paper aside. Where would he really have been without her? Should he go down on his knees and thank her for her betrayal and all the lies? Once he had said: don't take this suffering from me. She had been the first to understand this, and had given him further cause to suffer, given him a reason to paint. *The Frieze of Life*. The vision from the Montagnes Russes. Now she is no more. At seventy-seven years of age she is to be laid in earth, among flowers and animals. The final total devotion.

* * *

Aftenposten, July 1937: Modern artists are abominable dilettantes, says Hitler. The war of purification on German art. In the name of the German people, Hitler bans art which he needs a manual to understand. Will Edvard Munch be dethroned in Germany after all?

The degenerate art is presented at an exhibition in Munich. Degenerate artists, with works exemplifying un-German culture and typical examples of decadent art. The campaign hits all German artists and sculptors of any standing who do not create works in tune with the ideology of Blut und Boden, including Paul Klee, Emil Nolde, Oskar Kokoschka, Lionel Feininger, Wassily Kandinsky and Ernst Barlac. Their works are confiscated after the exhibition and either burned or sold at auction to dealers abroad. Many thousands of modern works of art from a whole series of museums are destroyed. Hitler personally inaugurates the Haus der neuen deutschen Kunst in the home of National Socialism, Munich: These artists paint cripples and freaks, women who look repugnant, men who most resemble beasts and children who look as though they have been struck by the curse of God Almighty! And it is this that these abominable dilettantes dare to offer us as art and, to cap it all, present as the art of our time. So many of this type have I seen among the works submitted that one can only assume the creators have seen their fellow human beings as pathetic freaks, have seen fields as blue, sky as green and clouds as yellow. But in the name of the German people I must prohibit individuals labouring under such visual defects from producing such art, and I can only suggest that these pitiful unfortunates should be investigated and that their right to reproduce be examined by the Ministry of Internal Affairs. From now on, contemporary German artists should understand that they risk sterilization, as prescribed by German racial legislation for congenital mental defectives, imbeciles etc.

*

Dear Thiis: I have just received a cutting from *Deutsche Allgemeine Zeitung* Berlin. The article is headed Entartete Kunst. People are thronging to Dresden City Hall to see the degenerate creations which are exhibited under this title. In the same article, it is reported that they have removed my *Sick Child* and the large *Under the Tree* from the National Gallery of Modern Art. This is the second time I've been thrown out in Germany. In Mannheim something quite similar happened, but whether it has been sorted out now I can't say. There must be proper confirmation before any comment can be made. My pictures hang in Berlin, Hamburg and no doubt other places and I have also received exceptionally favourable reviews. But how long will it last? I must say I'm glad I was so loath to sell. Your devoted Edvard Munch.

*

Bergens Aftenblad 31 July: Hitler proclaims the greatest art war of all time. Edvard Munch's position in Germany is thought to be under threat. There was a note of strong irritation in Hitler's speech. The results of the war of purification which German art and the German galleries are now to wage must be watched with the closest interest.

*

Dagbladet 9 August: Museum directors are being sacked in droves. Munch and Gauguin a problem. Our correspondent at the exhibition of monstrosities: Our best artists on display here! New directors are being appointed everywhere. Now the new directors are at a loss what to do with such foreign artists as Cézanne, Gauguin, Picasso, Munch and so on. For the time being they have found a way out by hanging these condemned artists in special rooms and labelling them all as foreign. This guarantees that the German public will be able to distinguish between German and un-German art.

*

Dagbladet 16 August: *Dagbladet* has asked Edvard Munch what his own view is of the purification.

I haven't the faintest idea, he replies.

But have you heard the rumours?

Like everybody else. I read the papers after all. But I don't know any more than you do.

Are most of your works in Berlin?

I'm not really sure about that. I spend so little time in galleries. Berlin has not bought from me directly. There are perhaps four or five works there. *Military Band on Karl Johan* was presented to the gallery by Professor Glaser.

I suppose there are quite a few in Munich?

They have *Man with White Horse* and *Woman on Veranda*. I was supposed to receive 100,000 marks for *The White Horse*, but I've never drawn the money. Two or three days later it wasn't worth a cent, you see. It was during the inflation period. I've always been reluctant to sell to galleries, saying to myself: One fine day there'll be another direction in art, then the pictures will be hung in the basement. What could be worse than having them in the basement?

* * *

To Stenersen Munch says: Do you think you could buy some flowers and take them to my sister. It's her birthday tomorrow and I'd like to give her some flowers. We're so fond of one another, you see, Inger and I. Ask her how she is. Ask her whether she is well and in good health and whether she likes her new apartment. Give her my best wishes, will you, and say that I'm not well enough to come myself.

* * *

Dear Thiis: I have written to you explaining that a Munch Museum at Tullinløkken would not meet the requirements I have laid down for such a thing. I would have to have a large museum if anything, where there would be room for my friezes and monumental works. So it can expand over the years, the National Gallery needs to have Tullinløkken in its entirety. I've also explained how spiteful tricks and various misfortunes have deprived me of the will to work and spoiled so many things for me. I have therefore abandoned all thought of the museum and have gradually come to the view that a single museum would not be such a good idea for me. It is Stenersen who raised the subject of fire bombs. I agree with him that it is not a good idea for me to have all my art in one place. I can be reached by telephone at 10.00 a.m. I am never in town and never visit anyone. I need to lose myself in my art and need peace for work. Many greetings to yourself and your family. Your devoted Edvard Munch.

* * *

To bank manager N. Rygg Munch says: I don't understand how one can work as you must do, without stopping. I get lost in reverie all the time and can't do a thing. I sometimes go for a fortnight without working.

When things go against me, like this business with the tax office, it affects me so deeply that I just can't do a thing. I've stopped seeing friends and acquaintances. I can't cope with anything else. I must have solitude. I've been for a few walks, I have to do it surreptitiously so the Enemy doesn't get wind of it. I have to take the car. And I must say the car is useful, but in that case you have to drive it yourself. And I can't drive. I get too nervous. The shoes I'm wearing are too tight. I've only just bought them and the lady in the shop said they were the right size. Let me be the judge of that, I said. They fit you, she said. I have to keep myself to myself. If you go out the wind blows right through you. In your own sitting-room you're protected. And when you emerge, you meet people and get drawn into all kinds of irritating things. What is the explanation for people's restlessness? They expose themselves to dangers, get involved in quarrels and do mad things. Pascal says this is because they don't stay put quietly at home. People don't understand the art of being happy at home. I am not a portrait painter. Some portraits I've painted too fast and others too slow. I don't think anyone has been satisfied with the portraits I've painted. Ludvig Meyer wouldn't have the picture I painted of him, yet it was not a caricature. I wanted to bring out the essence of his social position. He could have had it for 200 crowns but didn't want it. I once painted Prime Minister Blehr full-length. He was said to be a nice chap. As I was going into Parliament to take a look at it, the porter burst out laughing, ha ha ha ha. Then I said: I'm very pleased to know this, because it would have had to be a terrible picture for you to have liked it. And when a dentist was drilling one of my teeth, drilling one of my teeth mind you, he said that he did not like the assembly hall pictures. And I said: I'm delighted to hear that, because I would have been really upset if you'd said you liked them. Have you heard such cheek? And while he was actually drilling one of my teeth! I'm not a country shopkeeper. I tell people my shop isn't open. I don't want to start painting rubbish. I feel a good bit better today. I've taken some bromide. It's an excellent medicine. I don't take it all that often. It's harmless even if used long-term. It also has a calming effect on the nerves during the daytime. I still cannot draw or paint using my right eye. If I stand in front of the Rygg portrait, a quarter of it is black. And if I am reading, I see a shadow. So long as I don't become totally blind. If one eye is in jeopardy, then both are. And then there's my bronchitis. My life is starting to resemble that of a man being led to the scaffold. Was it Danton or Robespierre who sat on a nail all the way to the guillotine and who expressed his gratitude for the relief he felt when it was removed? I've had my share of illness to put up with. I've had my neurasthenia. But I want to keep these weaknesses, because they are part of me after all. When you're as old as I am, illness seems like no more than a postponement. You have moved a step closer to the final solemn farewell. Nurses, yes. There's something great about sacrificing yourself to serve others. They sit at the deathbed and hold the patient's hand. Tell me, how is it that pressing hands is the way people communicate at that grave moment? It is an important and curious aspect of war that fear of death is pushed aside. Just imagine, it said in the paper that two women in Germany had their heads chopped off with an axe. It makes me shudder. Just imagine using an axe on a woman? It's not just fear of death that I feel. It's all that is left undone. It makes me so uneasy. I just can't manage to clear up my papers and my affairs. How on earth am I going to tidy up all my stuff? And what a lot of stuff I have! My literary works, letters which are highly personal, completely frank. And then there are all the intimate letters. I can't see how I am going to be able to go through it all. And then other people are going to pry into it. I'm against decorations. I haven't had an audience with the king to thank him. But I have been to the French legation where I received a high rank of the Légion d'Honneur. I don't know which. It was ages before I went there. I wandered up and down outside. Eventually I went in. The Minister made a very nice speech, then he kissed me on the cheek. It was a lovely occasion. As we stood there chatting afterwards, I shook the box a little carelessly while gesticulating, and the Minister exclaimed in alarm: But Monsieur, it is a valuable decoration. It's things like this that make me feel unsure of myself. I might slip up and that's why I didn't go to see the king. Then there are the appeals for assistance from various quarters, not least from distant relatives who don't mean all that much to me. It's not so much the amounts of money that bother me but the question of whether it's right to give help, that it is thus taken for granted that I, the wealthy man, should automatically shell out when they have dreamed up some scheme or other. And then there are the tax authorities. How ridiculous to waste one's time on such nit-picking. Over New Year 1938 I went down to spend New Year's Eve at Vestby, thus becoming liable for tax there too. But I tried one road after the other in the heavy snowfall and couldn't get through. Ten years down the drain. They have stolen, murdered my working time and artistic ambition. Now I've bought a ledger, in which I scrupulously note everything down, so all will be clear. Why didn't Thiis and the others help me then? But no, nobody lifted a finger. You know, there are people who hate me, who persecute me and seek to harm me in all possible ways. It was suggested by some people that I should migrate south. I had to tell them it was impossible. They have clipped my wings. The ideal solution would be a fortnight with a housekeeper and a month alone. I'm not dependent on help. I *can* manage alone. On such occasions, I usually eat out at lunchtime. I don't need to go out for anything, as everything is ordered by telephone. I feel so rotten today, but I'm scared of using brandy even though it soothes. When I had my eye problem six or seven years ago I used to drink a little now and then, which was wrong. You can well imagine how shocked my housekeeper was when I said I needed half a bottle of port before I had my coffee every morning. Yes, I must say a fair number of drops have dripped from my arm. But it just makes the pictures worth two thousand crowns more. It's features like this in paintings which can increase their value. Some of my paintings are practically dripping with drops. *The Sick Girl* is nothing but drops actually.

* * *

It is 1938. Hitler marches into Austria. More than ninety-nine per cent are in favour of the Anschluss. Kirchner dies. The Munich Agreement is signed. The German invasion of the Sudetenland. Kristallnacht. Werenskiold dies. First reports of the splitting of the atom. Munch paints *The Alchemist* and again suffers from accumulations of blood, in the left eye this time.

*

He knows he should have held a large exhibition in Paris. But he wants a public invitation and wants his exhibition to be held in the Jeu de Paume. After holding large exhibitions in Berlin, Zürich, Oslo, Stockholm and Amsterdam and having everywhere attracted great attention, he receives a letter from the French State. The exhibition will be held in the Jeu de Paume in spring 1939.

The French envoy to Oslo visits Munch at Ekely. Munch thanks him, but says that he needs some time.

The French envoy says he must have a reply in writing.

Write to the French State and say yes thank you?

An impossible task. Stenersen brings in Jens Thiis on the matter. Thiis rings Munch.

I don't know, says Munch. I'll have to think about it. It's no small thing holding an exhibition in Paris. You mustn't think that people down there give two hoots about what people in other countries think of my pictures.

Munch writes one draft after another, as always with letters. But he cannot complete one he thinks suitable to send. So the exhibition comes to nought.

* * *

When my enemies think they've got me, when they are sure they have me surrounded, I do what Napoleon did. A daring attack. In the dead of night, I break out of the fortress and strike through the enemy lines. I get on a train and leave. It sows confusion in the enemy camp. They run about in panic asking one another: Where has he got to?

* * *

Østlandsposten, October 1938: Edvard Munch on the index in Germany. Berlin is to be cleansed of the maestro. Three large paintings are to be sold, including *Snow Shovellers*, which is a personal gift from the artist to the German State. Some of our well-known collectors and wealthy figures have been sounded out, although no transaction has been made so far, highly substantial sums being demanded for the pictures.

*

Arbeiderbladet, December 1938: Munch pictures home from Germany. An expensive consignment arrived today by rail from Germany. Fourteen Munch pictures which the art dealer Harald Holst-Halvorsen has purchased from the German State, and which have hitherto been displayed at museums in Essen, Dresden, Munich, Cologne, Mannheim, Frankfurt and Hamburg. They are large well-known pictures such as *The Sick Child*, with the same motif as the picture hanging in the National Gallery. Another enormous picture is *Life*, which is four metres long by two metres high, and which is considered to be on a par with his later assembly hall decorations. Also part of the collection is a self-portrait of Munch from 1926 – his best, Munch himself considers – and an Åsgårdstrand picture of the Kiøsterud house from about 1900.

* * *

Dear Thiis: I've been in bed with a heavy cold and a temperature, unable to sleep. I've sent *Dagbladet*'s fundraising campaign for Czechoslovak refugees two contributions of 100 crowns each and would like to help them, good friends of mine that they are. It is now ten years since I lost the use of my right and only good eye. This is the eye I've painted my pictures with. A year ago I had a similar ailment in my left and poorer eye, so was on the point of losing the use of both eyes. This is a result of all the pressure I've been subject to from many quarters (not least the tax authorities) and then out-and-out persecution. And I've constantly been on the move the last few years and it has taken its toll. When I see how highly my pictures are prized now, it makes me feel embittered that I've been prevented from working to crown my life's work. Because I haven't been able to paint much. My colours, palettes and brushes have dried out. *Your* mind, chest and heart are in good shape. That can't be said of me. Your devoted Edvard Munch.

* * *

It is 1940. Munch paints *Self-portrait Between the Clock and the Bed*. He stands there in a stiff pose, just as though lining up in a queue. The clock immediately behind him on the left. A female nude study hangs over the bed to the far right. The clock ticks.

*

Munch is strolling in the garden at Ekely.

He stumbles.

He lies there for a long time before managing to get up again.

*

On the night of the ninth of April, Norway is attacked by German ground troops.

*

On the tenth of April there is out-and-out panic in Oslo. During the morning rumours are rife that Oslo will be bombed. After people emerge from the air-raid shelters following a plane alert at eleven o'clock, an announcement is received that the city must be evacuated by noon. This unleashes panic. All vehicles are used, and an attempt is made to evacuate the sick and the elderly in haste. Almost two hundred thousand flee the city and a number of people perish in the panic.

Munch remains at Ekely.

*

Dear Inger: It was so nice to be together on the day of panic after not seeing one another for a few years. It's frøken Due we can thank for that. It was a pity I was so busy when you came the second time. But as things are at present there's nothing to be done about it. Look after yourself and ring or come out if things get serious. Greetings. Your devoted Edvard Munch.

*

Munch stands at Ekely watching the planes come in.

They come from the south. And they circle the city.

He stands there watching them with his dogs. They fly in ever-decreasing circles.

Munch says to Stenersen: What did I tell you? It's my house they're circling. It's *me* they're after.

* * *

He is afraid they may come and take the pictures. They are Germans but they are not his friends. Not Kollmann, Schiefler, Rathenau and Kessler. But strangers in helmets and boots.

Why have they come here? says Munch to Stenersen. They're going to regret it. It won't be easy for them to get out again. Don't they know what befell Sinclair's warriors?

*

Munch notes that Knut Hamsun welcomes the Germans. The writer calls the President of Parliament, C. J. Hambro, the son of a former immigrant family which had been allowed to settle in Norway. Hamsun will eventually write two dozen articles over the coming five years which will form the basis of the accusation of treason levelled at him in 1945. His central idea is that the Germans have come to *protect* Norway from a British attack: Norwegians! Throw down your arms and go home. The

Germans are fighting for us all and are now breaking Britain's tyranny against all of us neutral countries.

*

But for Edvard Munch the Germans are not Germans.

They are not his old friends from Berlin, Hamburg, Weimar and Munich. They are riff-raff. They are the sort he has never really known. The sort of people he has flung out of the house. People he cannot understand.

*

Dagbladet 1 May 1940: Timeless art imperilled. Most of the sculptures from the Vigeland fountain are relatively safe in the air-raid shelter out on Frogner common. And the studio walls are protected by piles of sandbags. But what about Edvard Munch's studio at Ekely in Ullern? It is perhaps not quite so generally known. But in better informed circles it has been rumoured for many years now that our greatest painter, one of the greatest geniuses in world painting, has spent almost all his income buying *back* many of the pictures which in difficult times he had had to let go. Down the years this private collection of Munch's is said to have grown to utterly priceless dimensions. At the same time he has constantly been creating new masterpieces. And all this immortal, everlasting art, which it was once thought would form the basis of the Munch Museum, had been collected by the ageing artist under the more or less dilapidated roofs out at Ekely. This morning we tried to find out what safety arrangements are in force at Ekely. Edvard Munch himself replies to our inquiry that he is absolutely not in a position to reply. He has always been a man of few words in such matters.

* * *

There is a ring on the cowbell at Ekely.

Three dogs stand out on the grass barking.

Two Germans are sitting in a car outside the gate.

Munch is certain they have come to take the paintings.

He rings Stenersen.

Get here as quick as you can. It's the last time you're going to be able to see my paintings. They're here. The grasshoppers. You know who I mean, don't you? The men in green. They're here. The Germans, for God's sake.

But it is the property they are interested in. Its situation. The view over the fjord. The grounds. *Wunderschön.*

Munch is given a fortnight's notice to leave.

*

But they do not return.

The world at war. Munch is alone at Ekely. He is painting *Self-Portrait by the Window*. The world is out there, behind his back. It is nothing to do with him. Because it is winter. The trees are bare. The object gazes gloomily at its own reflection.

* * *

Major German offensive in the west. The invasion of France begins. Norway capitulates: the King goes to London. The evacuation of Dunkirk. Paul Klee dies in Locarno. The Luftwaffe is stopped by the British radar system. The British bomb Berlin. Trotsky assassinated while in exile in Mexico. The Three Power Alliance. Coventry destroyed.

Munch paints a self-portrait while eating a cod's head.

*

Dear Inger: I thought you were in Asker. On the radio I hear that, according to the German commandant's orders, people are not to evacuate. How are you? Do you feel safe where you are? To my surprise there have been sirens and bombing again. What does it all mean. Your devoted Edvard Munch. It is best only to send postcards now.

*

12/12/1940. Dear Edvard. It was a good job I got some potatoes at Volvat. At last I have good potatoes. My lodger who sews for various families says that she has only had good potatoes twice. I remember a funny episode with Obstfelder. You'll certainly recall it too. There was a party at the Vullums. We were living in the old building beside the country shop. I'd gone to bed at about ten o'clock. Then you came and asked Aunt whether she could find a bed for Obstfelder. Yes of course, said Aunt, came into me and said: hurry up Inger, Obstfelder's going to have your bed. I jumped up, gathered my bedclothes and slept on the floor in Aunt's room. And Obstfelder had a nice bed. Happy birthday again. Your devoted Inger.

* * *

Quisling's henchmen come to Ekely.

They want Munch to serve on a committee for art. They want to set up an honorary council on which it is intended Munch will sit together with Knut Hamsun, Christian Sinding and Gustav Vigeland. Knut Hamsun's son comes out to see Munch and asks him to serve on the council.

Father asks you to accept, if nothing else for the sake of friendship.

For the sake of friendship? Munch replies. Is your father any friend of mine?

* * *

Dear Edvard: Many thanks for the huge amount of things you sent. Two bags of apples, 8 bottles of milk, cauliflower, leeks, parsley and the large swede. How delicious the swede is, so sweet and tender. Then there were the carrots. First-rate food. Oh yes, and the lovely rhubarb! Many greetings from your devoted Inger.

Knut Hamsun writes: We shall live our lives in peaceful co-operation with all nations, work with them, exchange goods, art and intellectual ideas with them, help each other to develop, become part of a system of aid initiatives – in other words, national socialism.

* * *

Dear Inger: I'm sending an assortment of food. The fish sausage must be eaten during the first few days, otherwise it'll lose its flavour. There are some apples. Small but good. Hope you're well. I've been a little better since the good weather. Otherwise it was a hard winter. Greetings. Your Edvard Munch.

*

Self-Portrait with Both Hands in Trouser Pockets.

At about the same time, the villages of Telavåg and Lidice are liquidated. Molotov is in London. The Africa Korps is at the gates of El Alamein.

It is the year Jens Thiis dies. It is the year Tulla Larsen dies.

* * *

A woman rings at the door at Ekely. A young law student.

She asks whether she can pose as Munch's model. There is something strong and fresh about her which prompts him to give it a try.

Hilde and Master Builder Solness.

A breath of youth at Ekely. The old grove of large trees outside the old master builder's veranda is suddenly populated with young people who in each other's company enjoy sun and summer while Eros does his work.

Memories of Åsgårdstrand and young girls. Munch paints *Flirting in the Park*. He asks her to read Ibsen's *When We Dead Awaken*. She stands there, attractive, legs slightly apart, in long trousers with a thin blouse on the upper part of her body. She looks straight ahead, and has a full head of curls.

In the background the flaming Virginia creeper.

* * *

It is 1943. Munch is highly productive. He paints *Self-Portrait with Stick of Pastel*. He paints the second version of *The Man in the Cabbage Field*. In March he learns that Gustav Vigeland is dead aged seventy-three. Munch daily looks down on the almost-seventeen-metre-high Monolith which his rival started to sculpt in 1929.

Munch's own *Frieze of Life* has still not yet found a home.

There is an uprising in the Warsaw ghetto. Baalsrud is on the run. Near Katyn a mass grave containing the bodies of four thousand Polish officers is discovered. The Warsaw ghetto is razed to the ground. Bombing of Hamburg.

The war brings back a flood of memories. All that happened almost forty years before. Inferno. Did they really think he wanted to flee the country?

He writes to Gierløff: As I told you on the 'phone, it surprises me that, after my return home from the clinic in Copenhagen, I didn't speak to you in more detail about the – for me – so fateful stay in Åsgårdstrand in 1905. Yet I cannot help but think that you gained some impression of what happened in Åsgårdstrand. So I shall not say any more about it now. You must have understood that I could not remain in Åsgårdstrand in that atmosphere which malicious tongues and intriguing women had whipped up against me. I would only say that it surprises me that anyone outside the flock of my fanatical enemies could have anything to reproach me with as regards the tense situation in my country or think that I could have done any different. At the time I'm sure I also explained how I had been forced to leave Hamburg at the beginning of March and travelled to Norway. An outbreak of the nervous illness which had been smouldering away for a long time was triggered off by Haukland's assault in 1904, which eventually led, four years later, to the clinic in Copenhagen. After the assault I started to have hallucinations and at the beginning of March I had hallucinations three days running at Hotel Giebfried in Hamburg, which meant that, to avoid being admitted to a clinic, I had to leave. So long as the scheming, malicious clique of ladies and gentlemen, with actor Müller in the vanguard, existed – all of whom ate and drank at my expense in my little sitting-room – there was no remedy for me. I think Karsten was just a tool of the others. Anyway, you know what happened. I couldn't remain in Åsgårdstrand. I had lived in Germany since 1902 and all my pictures and studies were there. I had to put some order into them after seven months' absence. My friends in Germany were intimately acquainted with my comings and goings. That anyone could make malicious insinuations about this necessary journey is inexplicable. I would never have thought of it had not various things from those days suddenly come into my mind. Or had not – as they did until just recently – malicious insinuations grown up into a fortress around me. While I was totally engrossed in my art. *Wenn ich schliefe kommen die Schweine und fressen.* Dr Linde in Lübeck, *Landsgerichtsdirektor* Schiefler in Hamburg, Dr Rathenau in Berlin, Graf Kessler and Frau Förster Nietzsche, do you think people like these would have anything to do with a wretched fugitive? Do you think the city of Lübeck would have fitted out spacious premises for my art and named a street after me if I'd been a miserable fugitive? In 1905 was it right of that drunken actor Müller to go for me with a knife or of Karsten to rush at me with an empty bottle and insult me, when I have only one arm to defend myself with? If people insinuate that the assaults in Hamburg were a fiction, there are plenty of people who remember these assaults and my illness as well. Those who know what I've had to put up with over the last few years will hardly be surprised that my illness became acute directly after Haukland's bloody assault with his fists and the iron ring on his finger six months earlier, before those two, with a number of women, ensconced themselves in my living room and sponged off me. It was no sanatorium and it was quite natural that I should lose my self-control with a woman who struck me as rather lacking in self-control herself. But the idea that they could exact such contemptible revenge on me is incredible. I have registered with Vestby and deregistered with the borough of Vestre Aker. This means that I am free from much of the unpleasantness with neighbours and the tax authorities. Each week I come in to Ekely and stay there for a day or to.

*

Munch draws the self-portrait *The Pointed Nose*.

He draws *Self-Portrait with Stick of Pastel*.

German attack on Spitsbergen. So nowhere is safe! Munch is prepared to capitulate any time.

Then he is overwhelmed by the past again.

Dear Inger: About a month ago I came across a little box of letters, mainly from you and Aunt. It was all incredibly interesting and curious. I find so many things catch my eye when I am tidying up my affairs, a process which has been going on for quite some time now. Letters, documents and works of art. It is very strange for me to relive all those past experiences through this material.

Munch buries himself in thousands of old letters and drafts of old letters. He recognizes his own notes and reflections, reliving everything. In his journal for the 1880s he reads:

> Monday 12th January: Today I started school again. At Christmas I had got so used to staying in bed that this morning I slept right till six thirty-five. This afternoon we started joinery. I learnt to use the lathe.
>
> Thursday 15th: This afternoon father and I went to the prison shop and bought a pair of boots for me.
>
> Friday 16th: This afternoon I was at the skating rink. Today started taking cod-liver oil.
>
> Saturday 31st: The whole of this week I've been off school because of a cold.
>
> Tuesday 30th March: For over a month now I've had 'flu. It started at the end of last month with a cold which I caught in bad

weather. On Saturday the 21st I had to go to bed with a temperature. On Monday I got up again, was up for two days, then had a
relapse with quite a high temperature and had to go back to bed
again. The next day I brought up blood in my spit. Then had to
be very careful, and got up for the first time about two weeks ago.
I'm now on the mend, have palpitations and am sweating a bit,
but my cough has gone.

Sunday 10th December: Yesterday I sent three of my small
pieces down to a saleroom where they auction off a lot of paintings. The results were pathetic as most pictures went for hardly
anything more than the price of the frame. Of my three, I had to
buy one back myself, whereas the other two went for 11 and 15.50
crowns. So all I ended up with was 10 crowns.

Wednesday 10th May: Aubert showed me some of his own
work, a still life with some really good stuff in it, as well as some
landscapes and an interior whose colouring looks as though it's
going to be good. I well understand why he dearly wants to be a
painter.

*

He reads about himself and about people he once knew. Desperate letters from Tulla Larsen, earnest letters from Eva Mudocci, his own
despairing drafts of letters, chiding letters from the military doctor and
comforting letters from Aunt Karen. He sees all the people and he sees
through them.

One face stands out more clearly than the rest. The man who showed
him the way.

Hans Jæger's face.

Munch draws him again. In a lithograph.

* * *

A violent bang. An explosion in the neighbourhood, at Linnekogel's
factory at Skøyen near Ekely.

Munch is in a terrible state. The war is drawing closer. But work is
the only thing that provides relief. He paints what has happened, paints
himself in the garden at Ekely: he walks up and down with hat and coat,
shaken by the sounds of the war around him, shaken by the memories
within.

* * *

Dear Inger: We've had to kill some chickens because stricter regulations
have been brought in regarding poultry farming. I'm sending you a
chicken, an old girlfriend of mine. She was so lovely and white. I don't
eat any meat from my own farm. Then there's some fruit. The pears will
need to ripen. Hope you're still well.

On his eightieth birthday on the twelfth of December Munch experiments with a colour print.

Aftenposten 13 December 1943: A profusion of flowers and telegrams arrived yesterday for Edvard Munch's 80th birthday, but no guests and no deputations. Munch wants to be left in peace and his wish was respected. His home is an impregnable fortress with spikes on the gate and a large bad-tempered dog behind the fence. Since the beginning of the war he has not set foot outside the gates of his house. The walks he takes are confined to the garden. Munch copes better than most with the food problems caused by the war. He is a vegetarian for one thing. Apparently he greatly appreciated all the greetings he received, and that includes the flowers, the letters and the telegrams from public and private institutions. The fact that the great artist wishes to keep his distance from people does not mean that he is in any way a misanthrope. All understanding and sympathy gladdens his heart.

*

He also meets Gierløff that day. Gierløff writes that Munch sits there in quiet happiness, radiant, beaming, not a care in the world. Roses everywhere. There *was* a deputation after all, apparently by the painter Stenstavold on behalf of his colleagues. Munch and Gierløff get up and for a change Munch reads the congratulations. Suddenly the atmosphere becomes solemn. Soon they are on the point of embracing, moved to tears.

This will probably be the last time, says Munch to Gierløff.

Oh no, replies his friend. Don't say that. Think of your aunt. Drink cod-liver oil.

*

For his birthday they send him cod from Kragerø.

He eats it alone, writes to Gierløff:

I have been deeply engrossed in the thousands of old letters and drafts of old letters. Indeed, the past lives in the old letters and the dead leave their graves. It is fascinating, but often moving and sad.

* * *

He makes three sketches of Erik Pedersen, director of the Freia chocolate factory. Pedersen notes that Munch has aged considerably since last he saw him. The thin skin is stretched tight over his cranium. His features have taken on a refined expression. He is nervous and agitated, afraid of bombing, says to Pedersen that he thinks the war is dragging on terribly. He has a very strong sense of Hitler's demonic madness and fears the war may end in total annihilation.

How long can it last, Pedersen?

Oh, it'll be over by 1944 I think.

That's far too long for me. But don't move. Sit just like that. I'll try to draw you.

He draws Pedersen's head with red and blue crayon. Then he adds a few strong blue strokes as shadow.

Isn't it strange, Pedersen? Today I'm so ill and weak that I can hardly stand on my own two legs. When I'm like this I'm so sensitive that I can produce the finest work.

* * *

Then he receives a letter from Ravensberg in Sweden:

Dear Edvard: Things are really terrible now and I am very ill myself too, so it was impossible for me to write and wish you many happy returns on your 80th birthday. For four years now I have sat in my room here outside Stockholm in total isolation, as though in a prison cell, and never see a soul, but life, what once was, the memories right back to my childhood, family, friends, episodes, everything passes before my eyes here in my solitude. We didn't know how wonderful and peaceful it was for us then compared with now, when life is baring its carnivorous teeth and everything is chewed up and spat out in a way which smacks of the Apocalypse. It looks as though you and I are the only surviving members of our family, together with your sister. I am deeply worried when I think what life is like for my few remaining friends. There is little, no, almost nothing that I can do for them, but it is announced in the papers here that it is going to be easier to send parcels from here after the New Year to one's friends and relations in Norway. It's not much that one is allowed to send, a little sugar or sweets, two tins of sardines, some cakes and biscuits and a little pea flour. If you would like me to do this, and it is only a taste after all, drop me a line, then after the New Year I'll try and send one of these parcels. Do take care. Greetings to yourself and Inger. Yours Ludvig Ravensberg.

* * *

It is Sunday 19 December 1943, a day of slush and fog. A German ship lies at anchor in Oslo harbour unloading. When it is suddenly blown up, the explosives on the jetty also ignite and then many hundreds of tons of explosive detonate on the quay at Filipstad.

A whole series of colossal explosions. It beggars belief. Munch has never heard the like of it. A new and unknown power. Cruder and more brutal than anything he has known before.

Even the finest nerves are affected.

*

Several large buildings are destroyed and twenty-four Norwegians perish.

At Ekely a number of windows are shattered. The housekeeper thinks that the whole town is about to go up and wants Munch to go down into the cellar.

But Munch remains sitting thinly clad in the hall for several hours.

Then he starts pacing up and down in the garden.

Pedersen visits Munch again. He realizes that the explosion has had an overwhelming effect on Munch.

The enemy has come closer, Pedersen. A lot closer. Now anything can happen. Is there no one who can offer me shelter?

His bronchitis flares up.

*

But he writes to his sister: Dear Inger, thank you for your letter. It was lucky you were unharmed. I wish you a Merry Christmas and a Happy New Year. Your devoted Edvard Munch.

* * *

January 1944. Hans Heyerdahl dies. Thirty American citizens are accused of being behind a conspiracy to set up a fascist state. The Soviet Union crosses the Polish border. The British Fifth Army starts its onslaught on Monte Cassino. Air raids on Stettin. Allied landing of troops at Anzio and Nettuno in Italy.

Hope of peace.

*

Pedersen visits Munch on the fourteenth of January. He notes that the painter is still extremely shaken. Munch's housekeeper says that she has never seen him like this before. He talks about the war. The fact that Mussolini has shot his son-in-law Ciano has affected Munch deeply. It is as though he looks around him at a world he does not know or recognize.

Then he hands over the sculpture *Workers* to Pedersen, who has bought it on behalf of Freia and also the drawings which Munch has now signed.

Munch thanks him courteously for the commission, saying:

I don't like business dealings.

*

Nine days later, on Sunday the twenty-third of January, Munch gets up out of bed and walks about a little in the house at Ekely.

At about two o'clock he says to his housekeeper that he feels ill and goes to bed.

Professor Schreiner, the family doctor, pays a visit to see a version of the motif *Kiss in the Fields*. When he sees Munch lying in bed, he realizes that the painter will never get up again. He has difficulty speaking, but seems quite clear in his mind and instructs his housekeeper to give Schreiner some lunch.

Professor Schreiner sits at Munch's bedside eating. During the afternoon he leaves the patient after getting him to take a little beaten egg and sugar. He reckons that Munch will at least last the night.

The housekeeper remains sitting at his bedside.

He lies there eyes closed.

*

Down the years he had been obsessed with the thought of death, with what he called the Crystal Kingdom. It was not death which frightened him but the moment of death. The memories of his sister Sophie's death had dogged him throughout his life.

Was there really life after death? Could one possibly be transformed, become another kind of matter? And what would it feel like during the final minutes of life, during the first minutes of death?

At six o'clock that afternoon, he found out.

Afterword

Even if *The Story of Edvard Munch* can be read as a novel it is primarily a literary reconstruction of a life, based upon all available material.

The Munch Museum in Oslo has a unique collection of written material which has proved decisive for the writing of this book. The intention has been to allow Munch to speak for himself as far as possible. Otherwise I have relied exclusively on primary sources, letters or other documents from Munch's friends.

Apart from the diary from his earliest youth, Munch wrote five collections of literary jottings which are conserved in the Munch Museum. They deal with the time from his first meeting with fru Thaulow (in the original text called fru Heiberg) to the break with Tulla Larsen. They describe in detail everything that happened at Åsgårdstrand in summer 1885. There are descriptions of Christiania the following winter and a new meeting with fru Thaulow in Borre, either in summer 1886 or 1887. The jottings also contain a fragmentary description of the relationship with Meisse Dörnberger (including the episode of Munch's illness in Tønsberg) and with Åse Carlsen. The latter's wedding is described in detailed sketches of what occurred during the days before the wedding.

Munch's literary jottings also contain memories of childhood, his sister Sophie's death and memories of Emilie. Munch describes in detail his departure from Christiania in 1889 and his own reactions to the news of his father's death. He also portrays the time he spent in St Cloud and the vision at the Montagnes Russes, the St Cloud Manifesto. He writes about his subsequent hospital stay in Le Havre and his journey via Paris to Nice. Besides this he also portrays his stay in Nice the following year and his return home to the drama at Åsgårdstrand between Jappe Nilssen and the Krohgs. In the same sequence Munch also describes his later meeting with fru Thaulow, who was then fru Bergh, in Christiania. In a shorter and considerably later piece, possibly written in 1906, Munch also deals with his affair with Tulla Larsen.

Besides these five literary collections, the Munch Museum also has two thick files of literary texts, notes and sketches of an even more fragmentary nature. A longer sequence depicts the first meeting with fru Thaulow in a new version. There are also texts portraying the affair with Tulla Larsen in much greater detail. In the draft of a short story he depicts the white cat in Paris. He also portrays his stay at the *pension* in Nordstrand, the slaughtering of the bull and the train journey to

Bergen. There is a literary sketch from the period 1902 to 1908, which here and there in detail describes his arrest in Studenterlunden, his fights with Ditten, Haukland and Karsten and the neurotic years leading to his breakdown. There are also literary and philosophical reflections from Ekely in the late 1920s and early 1930s.

Munch's literary output is as exciting as a detective novel. But it consists of sketches, repetitions and fragments, with all that that implies. It is nevertheless to be hoped that the Munch Museum will one day have the resources to enable it to publish an unedited version of Munch's collected writings.

The main aim of this book has been to write a literary biography, large sections of which are based on Munch's own writings. It is therefore important to stress the fact that in all the above-mentioned sequences, it is to a great extent Munch's own voice we hear. But in order to tell a coherent story there *must* be editing. Munch often breaks off in mid-sentence and starts another one. Munch's own punctuation is extremely sparse – apart, that is, from a superabundance of dashes. I have endeavoured to keep as many as possible of Munch's own characterizations and descriptions. At the same time, I have interleaved Munch's own stories with letters and reflections on the history of art.

As regards the letters, all of them are authentic, though I have not retained the spelling and some words have been replaced by synonyms. Some letters are reproduced *in extenso*. Others are drastically abridged. I have also, occasionally, allowed two letters to stand as one, for narrative reasons.

Besides this, Munch's letters are archived as *drafts* in very many cases. He wrote as many as ten drafts of letters before sending them and in some cases did not send them at all. But especially in the cases of Tulla Larsen and Eva Mudocci, I have taken the liberty of also using drafts of letters as though they had actually been sent, because they are highly revealing of emotional realities.

Where the history of art is concerned, I have relied overwhelmingly on Chief Curator Arne Eggum's own work. Very occasionally I have used Jens Thiis (*Winter Pictures from Nordstrand*) and Jappe Nilssen (*The Freia Frieze*). I have also taken into account, and on several occasions used, critical assessments by Ingrid Langaard, Ragna Stang, Pål Hougen and Ulrik Bischoff.

Otherwise Arne Eggum's splendid book, *Edvard Munch, The Frieze of Life. From Painting to Graphic Art*. J. M. Stenersens Forlag. Oslo 2000, is the starting point for my own understanding of the autobiographical aspects of Munch's writings and the related processing of them in pictures.

During my work, a number of books and other documents have

been on my desk which have been of inestimable importance and which are frequently quoted from. The order of these works is determined by how much they have been used or quoted from:

*

Arne Eggum: Kjærlighet-Angst-Død. Stenersens forlag. Oslo 1990.

Edvard Munchs brev til Familien. Et utvalg ved Inger Munch. Johan Grundt Tanum Forlag. Oslo 1949.

Arne Eggum: Edvard Munch, Paintings Sketches and Studies. J.M. Stenersens Forlag. Oslo 1995.

Munch og Frankrike. Editions de la Réunion des Musées Nationaux, Paris, Munch-museet, Oslo, Spadem, Adagp. Paris 1991.

Edvard Munch og hans modeller 1912–1943. Munch-museet. Oslo 1988.

Arne Eggum: Munch og Fotografiet: Gyldendal. Oslo 1987.

Edvard Munch/Gustav Schiefler: Briefwechsel, vols. 1 & 2. Verlag Verein für Hamburgische Geschichte. Hamburg 1987.

Edvard Munch: Alfa & Omega. Oslo kommunes kunstsamlinger. Katalog A-25. Oslo 1981.

Rolf Stenersen: Edvard Munch. Nærbilde av et geni. Gyldendal. Oslo 1946.

Christian Gierløff: Edvard Munch selv. Gyldendal. Oslo 1953.

Marit Lande: ... for aldrig meer at skilles ... Universitets-forlaget. Oslo 1992.

Mary Kay Norseng: Dagny Juel: Kvinnen og Myten. Gyldendal. Oslo 1992.

Erna Holmboe Bang: Edvard Munchs kriseår: Gyldendal. Oslo 1963.

Jens Thiis: Munch. Gyldendal. Oslo 1933.

Edvard Munch og Jappe Nilssen: Etterlatte brev og kritikker. Utgitt ved Erna Holmboe Bang. Dreyers forlag. Oslo 1946.

Ragna Stang: Edvard Munch. Mennesket og kunstneren. Aschehoug. Oslo 1977.

Edvard Munch som vi kjente ham. Dreyer. Oslo 1946.

August Strindberg: Inferno og Ockulta dagboken. Bonnier. Stockholm 1914.

Edvard Munch in the Kunst og Kultur series. Gyldendal. Various volumes from 1946 inclusive onwards.

Edvard Munch. The Frieze of Life. The National Gallery. London 1992.

Hans Jæger: Complete Works. Published by author's own company.

Fredrik Juel Haslund: Etterord til Fra Kristiania-Bohemen. Forlaget Novus. Oslo 1976.

Pål Hougen: Edvard Munch og Henrik Ibsen. Oslo kommunes kunstsamlinger. Oslo. 1976.

John Boulton Smith: Frederic Delius & Edvard Munch. Triad Press. Hertfordshire 1983.

Ingrid Langaard: Edvard Munch. Modningsår. Gyldendal. Oslo 1960.

Erna Holmboe Bang: Aldrig skal du svike. Dreyer. Oslo 1948.

Jens Dedichen: Tulla Larsen og Edvard Munch. Dreyer. Oslo 1981.

Inger Sandberg. Edvard Munch, Skrubben og Kragerø. Årsskrift for Kragerø og Skatøy Historielag. Kragerø 1991.

C. Skredsvig: Dager og Netter blant kunstnere. Gyldendal. Oslo 1908.

Ulrich Bischoff: Edvard Munch. Bendikt Taschen Verlag GmbH. 1991.

Olof Lagercranz: August Strindberg. Wahlstrøm & Widstrand. Stockholm 1979.

Stanislaw Przybyszewski: Overbord. Copenhagen 1896.

Edvard Munch fra år til år. Aschehoug. Oslo 1961.

Herman Colditz: Kjærka. Copenhagen 1888. Reissued by Altera forlag. Oslo 1992, with an afterword by Harry Hansen.

Århundrets Krønike. Cappelen. Oslo 1988.

Oslo bys historie. Volumes 3 and 4. Cappelen. Oslo 1990.

Edvard Munchs Selvportretter. Gyldendal. 1947.

Arne Eide: Årsgårdstrand. Eides forlag. Bergen 1946.

Tore Dyrhaug: 1884. Nærbilde av et år. Grøndahl. Oslo 1984.

Øystein Sørensen: 1880-årene. Universitetsforlaget. Oslo 1984.

Per Krohg: Memoarer. Gyldendal. Oslo 1966.

Christian Krohg: Kampen for tilværelsen. Gyldendal. Oslo 1952.

Pola Gauguin: Edvard Munch. Aschehoug. Oslo 1933.

Inger Alver Gløersen: Lykkehuset. Gyldendal. Oslo 1970.

Inger Alver Gløersen: Den Munch jeg møtte. Gyldendal. Oslo 1956.

Adolf Paul: Min Strindbergbok. Norstedt. Stockholm 1930.

Anne Wichstrøm: Oda Krohg. Gyldendal. Oslo 1988.

Bjørn Linnestad: Vestby sett med kunstnerøyne. Vestby Historielag. Vestby 1987.

Bjørn Linnestad: Dörnberger. Maler og Musketér. Vestby kunstforening. Vestby 1989.

J. P. Hodin: Edvard Munch. Thames and Hudson. London 1972. Oslo 1992.

Gerd Woll: Exhibition catalogue for Munch in Lillehammer. 1993.

*

Various Munch literature and catalogues, including Ravensberg's diaries, can be found in the library of the Munch Museum.

All Munch's writings which have been used are to be found in the Munch Museum either as copies or in the original. The same applies to the letters. And, not least, the large collection of newspaper cuttings from which I have frequently quoted.

Film director Peter Watkins deserves special mention. His film on Munch provided enormous inspiration and a great many pointers for my own work.

Thanks

I should like to thank Arne Eggum, Chief Curator of the Munch Museum, for his inestimable knowledge of Edvard Munch and for his generosity in connection with the present work.

Similarly, I should like to thank Sissel Bjørnstad, librarian of the Munch Museum, whom I daily pestered during certain periods with my many queries and who always gave me helpful answers. I also thank her for all the inspiring discussions we had while the book was being written.

Special thanks should go to the Button Moulder – a latter-day reincarnation from *Peer Gynt* – who taught me about Munch and who has also been unstinting in his expert help.

I should also like to thank Alf Bøe, Director of the Munch Museum, for having inspired me, in his foreword to the Alpha and Omega catalogue, to go ahead with this book. I thank Harald Gierløff for his willingness to help and his inestimable assistance in connection with Munch's life in Kragerø and for his warm hospitality at Dønnevika on Skåtøy. I thank Inger Sandberg in Kragerø and Marit Lande at the Munch Museum for important information they provided me with. I thank Odd Aasen for his assistance and for his knowledge of the Ihlen family and of Munch's life in Åsgårdstrand. And I thank Jon N. Grasbekk at the Munch Museum for some very useful discussions.

Thanks also to Trygve Nergaard for stimulating suggestions in the closing stages of the project. Thanks to Morten Herlofsen, Senior Consultant at Gaustad Hospital and to Bjørn Bering, municipal archivist.

And a special thanks to Munch's model Hanna Brieschke.

Ketil Bjørnstad
Oslo, June 1993

Tessa de Loo

The Twins

Translated from the Dutch by Ruth Levitt

Two elderly women, one Dutch and one German, meet by chance at the famous health resort of Spa. They recognize in the other their twin sister they believed to be lost. They begin to tell each other their life stories the last chance to bridge a gulf of almost seventy years.

Born in Cologne in 1916, the twins are brusquely separated from each other after the death of their parents. Anna grows up with her grandfather, in a primitive farming and Catholic milieu on the edge of the Teutoburgerwald. Lotte ends up in the Netherlands because of her TB, living with an uncle who harbours strong socialist sympathies. Bad relationships between the families and the intervening war cause the contact between the two sisters to be broken. When their paths cross again so late in life, Lotte, who sheltered Jews in hiding during the war, is initially extremely suspicious of her newly-found twin sister. But through Anna's painful stories she is confronted with the other side of her own reality: the sufferings of ordinary Germans in wartime.

In this monumental novel, Tessa de Loo compellingly weaves the story of two twin sisters separated in childhood with that of two countries opposed in war, and depicts in simple yet harrowing prose the effects of nature and nurture on the individual.

One of the *Sunday Times* '100 Best Books of the Year 2000'

'The moving tale of twins, separated at the age of six, who meet by chance as elderly women at a Belgian health resort and share their life stories. De Loo doesn't seek to exonerate Germany but to tell the harrowing tale of war from two sides, to humanize history and add some ambiguity to the good–evil dichotomy' – *Time* magazine

'Details of time, place and atmosphere are acutely evoked, and the characters are presented with a generous sympathy that stops short of special pleading. Already a best-seller in the author's native Holland, the book deserves to become one here' – Christina Koning, *The Times*

The Queen's Tiara

OR

Azouras Lazuli Tintomara
*

A tale of events immediately before, during and after
the assassination of King Gustaf III of Sweden
*
Romaunt in twelve books
*
BY

Carl Love Jonas Almqvist
(1793–1866)

Translated from the Swedish by Paul Britten Austin

*

'Over Sweden's capital hovered the foul genius of regicide.
Above, its wings were black as a midnight in March; beneath, red
as the flames bursting out in a theatre at a masquerade.'

One of Sweden's greatest classics, this moving novel weaves the tale of
the beautiful but sexless androgyne Tintomara with whom both sexes
fall in love, around the assassination of the 'Theatre King' Gustav III on
the stage of his own opera house at a masked ball in 1792. Tintomara too
comes to a tragic end in what was to have been merely a melodramatic
entertainment for the court. But not before s/he causes all sorts of disastrous complications and confusion . . .

Carl Jonas Love Almqvist (1793–1866) was a leading radical thinker of
his day. Other works include the novella Sarah Widebeck, Sweden's
first feminist work of fiction. Accused of trying to poison his landlord
with arsenic, Almqvist fled to the United States, contracted a bigamous
marriage with a Philadelphia landlady and spent his last years playing
piano in a bar. Tintomara, Lars-Johan Werle's opera based on
Almqvist's novel, has been performed in London at Sadler's Wells.